Racing & Foo

FLAT RACING
GUIDE 2014

Statistics • Results
Previews • Training centre reports

Contributors: Richard Birch, Neil Clark, Nick Deacon, Steffan Edwards, Katherine Fidler, Dylan Hill, Tony Jakobson,Kel Mansfield, Steve Mellish, Mark Nelson, John O'Hara,Ben Osborne, Stuart Redding, Richard Williams

Designed and edited by Nick Watts and Dylan Hill

Published in 2014 by Raceform,
Compton, Newbury, Berkshire RG20 6NL

Copyright © Raceform Ltd 2014

A catalogue record for this book is available from the British Library.

ISBN 978-1-909471-29-0

Printed and bound by CPI Group (UK) Ltd, Croydon, CR0 4YY

Est. 1909
RACING & FOOTBALL OUTLOOK

Contents

Est. 1909
RACING & FOOTBALL **OUTLOOK**

Editor's introduction

WITH Frankel off to stud, it was always likely to be hard for racing to make the front pages last summer. As it turned out that wasn't the case – but unfortunately for all the wrong reasons.

The drugs scandal involving Godolphin trainer Mahmood Al Zarooni gave the sport months of desperate publicity, which continued into the new year when several of the affected stars made their returns in Dubai.

But thankfully for those who love our wonderful sport, racing is really about the equine superstars rather than the people entrusted with their care and there were certainly many glorious moments to light up a difficult year.

Champions Day at Ascot had to make do without Frankel for the first time, but the Champion Stakes lived up to its billing with a sensational finish as Farhh, Cirrus Des Aigles and Ruler Of The World went head to head up the Ascot straight.

That bore a stark contrast to the Prix de l'Arc de Triomphe, but the Longchamp showpiece was no less memorable as Treve produced one of the most magnificent bursts of speed in living memory to destroy a stellar field. The French filly stays in training and is due to travel abroad for the first time to run in the Prince of Wales's Stakes at Royal Ascot, which will make the summer showstopper even more unmissable than ever.

Treve's victory continued France's dominance of their middle-distance champion-

TREVE: brilliant Arc winner who looks set to light up Royal Ascot this year

NEW PARTNERSHIP: Richard Hannon Jnr and Richard Hughes team up

ship, in which even the Japanese have produced a more consistent challenge than Britain in recent times, and that has to be a growing worry for fans of the domestic game. But for the powerhouse of Coolmore feeding Aidan O'Brien's Ballydoyle operation, it would be a similar story for Ireland as well.

The one trainer who has been increasingly capable of mixing it with the big boys on a comparatively shoestring budget is Richard Hannon, but he handed over the keys at Herridge Racing Stables at the start of this year to his son Richard junior.

It will be fascinating to see how the younger Hannon gets on in the long term, but he could hardly have asked to be left with better ammunition by his father for his first season with a trio of Group 1 winners – Sky Lantern, Toronado and Olympic Glory – kept in training at four.

His main challenges for the trainers' title are likely to come from John Gosden and Mark Johnston as well as O'Brien if he can rack up enough big-race victories.

Championships are unlikely to be forthcoming for David O'Meara, but there won't be many who train more winners than this

rising star, who racked up 136 of them last year and gave an exclusive interview to Neil Clark on his string for the season ahead. Our other brilliant trainer profile comes from George Baker, another man who has been quick to establish himself having taken out a licence in 2008.

In addition Steffan Edwards runs the rule over all of this year's Classic hopes in his ante-post preview for the year, while Richard Williams has searched far and wide for his list of 30 horses to follow.

As well as all that, pedigree expert Katherine Fidler uncovers the best first-crop sires to follow; there are the unique views of Steve Mellish, Richard Birch and speed guru Mark Nelson; and Dylan Hill's guide to last season's leading form.

Then there are the stats, reams and reams of winner-finding numbers detailing the top trainers and jockeys also broken down course by course so you know who to follow at your local track.

Once again we have every base covered for a year packed with bumper profits, and don't forget to buy your copy of the RFO every week for the very latest news and tips.

Profiles for punters
David O'Meara

DAVID O'MEARA: has made a huge impact in just four years as a trainer

Profile by Neil Clark

T'S hard, if not impossible, to think of a Flat trainer in Britain who has made as big an impact in such a short period of time as David O'Meara. The former jumps jockey only took out a licence in June 2010, less than four years ago, but he has already trained close on 300 winners.

The figures tell their own story of O'Meara's remarkable progress. In 2010

he saddled 25 winners. In 2011 he got 48, a tally that included a first Group win courtesy of the admirable veteran Blue Bajan. In 2012 there were 69 winners, with two Group victories for Penitent and a second successive win in the Great St Wilfrid Handicap at Ripon for Pepper Lane among the highlights. Then in 2013 a real annus mirabilis as the winners total leaped to 136, with 105 of them on the turf.

"By any standards these are challenging figures and confirm O'Meara's operation as the most upwardly mobile in the country," was the verdict of Brough Scott – and few would disagree.

Among last year's many highlights were Chancery's win in the 1m4f Sky Bet Stakes handicap at York's Ebor meeting (his second course win of the season), stable flag-bearer Penitent's success in the Listed Fortune Stakes at Sandown in September and Louis The Pious's win in a conditions stakes at Haydock in July. There didn't seem to be any point during a great campaign when O'Meara's horses weren't troubling the judge.

O'Meara hails from 'Denman country' – Fermoy in Co Cork in Ireland. From an early age he was interested in horses, with his mother being the secretary of the local point-to-point. When he was at school he rode out for no less a person than Jim Bolger and, while he was at university in Limerick studying equine science, he rode in point-to-points for Michael Hourigan.

He spent his gap year in the United States riding track work at Keeneland and Churchill Downs, after which he came to England to ply his trade as a jumps jockey. He was first at Philip Hobbs' powerful yard in Somerset and he then moved north to join Peter and Tim Easterby in Yorkshire. Later he also worked for another top Yorkshire jumps yard: that of Sue and Harvey Smith.

Among the best horses he rode were the Tim Easterby-trained chaser Turgeonev, who was rated 156 at his prime, Bells Life, whom he piloted to success in the 2000 Aintree Fox Hunters, and the hugely popular Sue Smith-trained chaser Mister McGoldrick.

It might have been expected that, once he hung up his riding boots, O'Meara would make his name as a jumps trainer, but it's been the Flat which has been his main focus.

Roger Fell, a haulage businessman from Huddersfield, purchased the yard at Nawton, near Helmsley in North Yorkshire, in 2009, and six months later O'Meara joined him as the trainer. The two men haven't looked back since.

BIG-RACE HERO: O'Meara's career as a jumps jockey saw him win the Aintree Fox Hunters on Bells Life

"Although we do have runners over the jumps, we are predominantly a Flat yard and I'm very happy with the way things have developed," O'Meara tells me.

Asked what he puts his meteoric rise down to, he says: "I was lucky to work for some good trainers. It was a very good education for me. As to why last season was so successful, I think it's hard to pin down to any one particular reason. We've grown quite rapidly – last year we had 100 horses in and we have attracted some good owners. There's Middleham Park Racing, the Cheveley Park Stud, Coolmore and also Sir Alex Ferguson has a horse with us."

O'Meara is also keen to attract smaller owners and asks me to mention the Direct Racing Club (www.directracingclub.co.uk) in which, for a small outlay, members can enjoy the thrills of racehorse ownership with one of the most upwardly mobile yards in the country.

Top-class facilities, with great gallops and stabling for 100 horses, and an excellent staff have also played their part in O'Meara's flying start to his career, as has his ever-reliable stable jockey Danny Tudhope, who last year rode more than 100 winners.

After the great success of 2013, I ask David how he thinks 2014 will pan out.

"Last year was beyond what we could have expected. It will be tough to beat 136 winners and, although we don't set targets, it would be great to pass the 100-winner mark again."

One of the achievements of last season was O'Meara becoming top trainer at York, and one can sense he's keen to repeat the feat again this year.

"It was good as we had led the competition for a long way the year before but just lost the lead in the last couple of days. Last year we led from the Ebor meeting and kept the lead."

O'Meara will again have around 100 horses to go to war with this term, led once more by Penitent , a winner of three Listed races and two Group races for him. Watch out for when the specialist miler turns up at Newmarket, Doncaster or Sandown on his favourite soft ground as eight of his ten wins have come at those three tracks. But there's plenty of other talent, too.

David is married to Sarah and the couple have a baby daughter, Roisin, whom the trainer says takes up most of his time when he's not working.

As the old adage goes, nothing breeds success like success, and given the ammunition he has at his disposal it's hard not to see 2014 being another great year for the quietly-spoken Irishman who has made a big name for himself in the most competitive of professions.

CHANCERY: helping O'Meara win the prize for the year's top trainer at York

The horses

Chancery 5yo gelding
Street Cry – Follow That Dream (Darshaan)

He's just progressed and progressed. He was once beaten less than two lengths by The New One in a bumper at Cheltenham. Last year he won three times for us in a 1m4f handicap at Haydock in July off 76, a 1m2f handicap at York off a 6lb higher mark a week later and a 1m4f handicap at the Ebor meeting off 91. After that he finished fourth in a Listed race over 1m4f at Newmarket – he was travelling well but I don't think he quite got home because of the uphill finish. He's got the speed for 1m2f and the stamina for an easy 1m4f. He's rated in the high 90s now and we will hope to win a Listed race with him.

Custom Cut 5yo gelding
Notnowcato – Polished Gem (Danehill)

He joined us over the winter having been trained by George Kent in Ireland. He won four races in a row in 2012 but his only win since then came in the Gladness Stakes at the Curragh last April. He came back in training early and the same race will be his target again. He loves a bit of cut in the ground.

Mont Ras 7yo gelding
Indian Ridge – Kayrat (Polar Falcon)

He's been an absolute star for us. He won four times on the turf last year, landing handicaps at Redcar, Haydock (twice) and York, then proved his versatility by winning on the all-weather at Kempton in December and has since won in Dubai as well. All those wins came over 7f or a mile. He started last season on a mark of 85 and went up to 103, which means he's gone up to the stage where we will have to look to win conditions or Listed races – perhaps even a Group race. He loves fast ground.

MONT RAS: prolific winner

Move In Time 5yo gelding
Monsieur Bond – Tibesti (Machiavellian)

He's a really good sprinter who did very well for us last year. He won over 5f at Musselburgh and 6f at Doncaster early in the season, was third in the Group 3 Abernant Stakes at Newmarket and beaten only a head in another Group 3 at Longchamp. He goes on most ground and his target will be Listed and Group races over 5f and 6f.

Open Eagle 5yo gelding
Montjeu – Princess De Viane (Kaldoun)

Formerly trained in France, he won at Carlisle in September on his debut for me and then ran a blinder in the November Handicap when he finished third. He seems to like soft ground and his target will be the Chester Cup.

Out Do 5yo gelding
Exceed And Excel – Ludynosa (Cadeaux Genereux)

He joined us over the winter from Luca Cumani, for whom he won twice over 6f. He's a huge horse and is rated 91. He could make up into a horse for the Great

PENITENT (left): has been a tremendous flag-bearer for O'Meara

St Wilfred [which O'Meara has won twice in the last three years] or Ayr Gold Cup.

Penitent 7yo gelding
Kyllachy – Pious (Bishop Of Cashel)

He's a superstar who has been our flag-bearer and heads up the yard. He has now won three Listed races and two Group races for us. He loves soft ground and when he does get his conditions at that sort of level he's hard to beat. He's entered in the Lincoln, but I'm not sure if we'll start him off there. We will look for more Listed races over a mile for him.

Repeater 5yo gelding
Montjeu – Time Over (Mark Of Esteem)

He joined us in the summer from Cheveley Park Stud for a change of scenery having been trained by Sir Mark Prescott. He ran a blinder in the Doncaster Cup on his first run for us, travelling like the winner and finishing a close third. He has loads of ability but he does need to be held up and because of that he is better on tracks which have a long straight like Doncaster. He showed he can operate at a mile and a half when fourth in the Cumberland Lodge but has shown he can stay two and a half

miles. He will be aimed at all the top Cup races and Listed staying races.

Smoothtalkinrascal 4yo gelding
Kodiac – Cool Tarifa (One Cool Cat)

He's a hold-up horse who loves 5f and is good over 6f. He ran really well to be second in the Epsom Dash last season and won at Leicester and York. He acquitted himself well for his three-year-old season mainly against older horses, but this year, as a four-year-old, there's a better programme for him. He'll be out early, maybe in the Cammidge Trophy at Doncaster, and we'll look for conditions or Listed races with him.

Sweet Lightning 9yo gelding
Fantastic Light – Sweetness Herself (Unfuwain)

He joined us over the winter having been trained by Johnny Murtagh in Ireland and has been in Dubai. He's won two Lincolns – both the English and the Irish – and is entered in this year's Lincoln at Doncaster. He should go well as he's suited by a straight mile and after that we'll go for conditions races with him. He loves soft ground.

Profiles for punters
George Baker

GEORGE BAKER: making the most of his "world-class facilities" at Manton

Profile by John O'Hara

G EORGE BAKER has a terrific philosophy on racing – "Good fun is our mantra" – and the majority of his burgeoning band of owners are having a great time.

'Good Time' George started off working as a banker in the City, after which he became the Lambourn correspondent for the ill-fated paper The Sportsman.

In 2008 he made the decision to become a trainer and on March 1 that year Music Box Express was his first runner. Until the final yards of the race it looked like a dream start but he was eventually beaten a head.

The newest trainer to the ranks didn't wait long before getting his name on the board when the same horse prevailed at Wolverhampton, turning the tables on

Avontuur, who had denied him first time out. Baker finished his first season with 15 winners and has gone from strength to strength since then.

Baker is already training from his third yard but certainly believes he has found the right place in historic Malton.

"It's a world-class facility," he says. "If you can't send winners out from here then you couldn't from anywhere."

He started out at Moreton Morrell in Warwickshire, where he sent out a100 winners, and then moved for a short time to Whitsbury, where he added another 56 successes to his tally.

Since the latest switch Baker has maintained a constant increase in his prize-money tally, earning £291,328 last season thanks largely to the exploits of Belgian Bill, who landed the Hunt Cup at Royal Ascot last season.

He recalls: "We have had some very enjoyable days over the years at the royal meeting, but nothing can compare to having a winner as a trainer. There have been some great parties at Royal Ascot but we never had anything to celebrate like that.

"I worked him in cheekpieces six days before the race and he was like a different horse so we knew he was considerably better than the 33-1 shot the bookmakers had chalked him up at. It was a day I shall never forget. Now of course we have to build on that."

While Baker's winners total has slipped to 34 and 32 in the last two seasons from a peak of 49 in 2011, the exposure garnered by Belgian Bill has seen the string increase, with exciting new owners to boot, and he is confident of a new personal best this term.

Baker already has some high-profile owners in the yard and his latest coup is to be added to the Highclere Thoroughbreds roll of trainers. "I haven't received a horse yet, but I understand we will get one from one of the breeze-ups which is very exciting for all of us."

Among his current list of patrons is best-selling author E L James, who is known for the 'Fifty Shades' series, pop star Peter Andre, Sir Alex Ferguson and the Heineken family.

Last year Baker started off with 55 horses but 2014 sees a record 70 horses in his care and the future looks very bright. "I think 50 winners is a very realistic target this season," he says.

BELGIAN BILL: wins the Hunt Cup for Baker at Royal Ascot last season

The horses

Belgian Bill 6yo gelding
Exceed And Excel – Gay Romance
(Singspiel)

This horse will always have a very special place in my heart as he gave me my first winner at Royal Ascot when taking the Hunt Cup last year. We had fancied him in 2012 when he ran well in seventh and he got it right 12 months later. That race is his aim again, and although it will be tougher as he starts the year on a 7lb higher mark of 104 you are always hopeful with him as he just loves the hustle and bustle of a big field. The plan is to have him nice and fresh so I will give him just one run before. He seems to have really thrived for his break.

Boomshackerlacker 4yo gelding
Dark Angel – Allegrina (Barathea)

He hasn't won since taking the Listed Prix Saraca at Maisons-Laffitte in October 2012, but last season he still ran some very good races. This term the plan is to go to Doncaster for the Lincoln. He will be high up the weights, but if the ground came up very soft he would run a big race. He was beaten twice by Penitent last year and I feel that with another year on his back he could be an interesting runner in big handicaps. I would also envisage several trips around Europe with him searching for good prize-money in Group 3 and Listed races.

Eton Rambler 4yo gelding
Hard Spun – Brightbraveandgood
(Smart Strike)

He won at Brighton and Chepstow last season which was a little surprising as he was mentally immature. He should be better this season and I expect him to win two or three races. He is not short of pace and we could even run him over hurdles during the summer.

Fiftyshadesofgrey 3yo gelding
Dark Angel – Wohaida (Kheleyf)

One of his owners is E L James, who wrote the global best seller of the same name and is involved in two other 'Fiftyshades' horses in the yard. He ran very well at Royal Ascot and Glorious Goodwood and it was very important we got a win out of him, which happened at Wolverhampton in September. I am looking to the Czech 2,000 Guineas for him and he will certainly be running all over the continent this term. I am very happy with how he has done since last season.

Flutterbee 2yo filly
Equino – Dunya (Unfuwain)

She is a beautiful mover with a wonderful attitude. I love the way she covers the ground as she does it so easily. We haven't pressed any buttons yet and she won't be starting in 5f maidens, but I hope by mid-summer she may be out. She is a nice prospect.

Humidor 7yo gelding
Camacho – Miss Indigo (Indian Ridge)

He hasn't won for over two years but has run some fine races in defeat. We sent him to Dubai for the last two winters and he never really had a good break, so this winter he has had a long holiday. He looks the ideal type for the Wokingham and we will have him ready to run first time out in that race as he goes well fresh – he could get in with a nice weight and would be very interesting. He loves some cut but acts on quicker ground. We are looking forward to a better campaign this year.

I'm Fraam Govan 6yo gelding
6 ch g Fraam – Urban Dancer
(Generous)

We've had some good times training for

JACK'S REVENGE (far side): finishing a close third at last year's Shergar Cup

Sir Alex Ferguson and when this fellow won the London Middle Distance Series Final at Kempton just before Christmas it was a great day. You don't get many £60k handicaps at that time of the year so it was very competitive and he did it nicely. We will bring him back to Kempton for something like the Magnolia or the Rosebery. Although those races are on the Polytrack, he is also smart horse on turf and if all goes well he could develop into a Wolferton horse for Royal Ascot.

Jack's Revenge 6yo gelding
Footstepsinthesand – Spirit Of Age (Indian Ridge)

He started off in the Lincoln last season, finishing fifth, and continued to run some huge races without winning. He went up 4lb through the year from 91 to 95, but he has really strengthened up over the winter and if everything falls into place for the cranky old bugger he could pick up a big one. He loves big fields and the Lincoln is the starting point again for him. I love him to pieces.

Joey's Destiny 4yo gelding
Kheleyf – Maid Of Ailsa (Pivotal)

He hosed up on his juvenile debut and

we thought he looked special, but he fractured a tibia and it took us a long time for him to get his confidence back. We had to show lots of patience and he won back-to-back races at Leicester and Goodwood in the summer before running another big race when placed at Windsor. I think he could be better than his mark of 80 as he is pleasing me no end at home.

Laurelita 3yo filly
High Chaparral – Chervil (Dansili)

She won her maiden on her second outing last year before we put her away. I think the form is quite good and I would be very disappointed if she weren't better than her mark of 81. I am keen to sneak some black type with her and that could mean a few trips abroad early on.

Mendacious Harpy 3yo filly
Dark Angel – Idesia (Green Desert)

She is still a maiden but gave us plenty of encouragement in her five runs. The key is to get a win under her belt and I think we can find a little fillies' maiden early on and achieve that goal quickly as she won't mind soft ground. If we box clever we may just nick some black type with her along the way.

Nenge Mboko 4yo gelding
Compton Place – Floppie (Law Society)

He is named after a character in the film Trading Places and his owner also owned Billy Ray Valentine from the same movie. You wouldn't describe him as a flash character, in fact if you met him in a pub you would say he is a bit dull. We won two sellers with him as I never mind running mine in the basement level if it helps get some confidence. He ran a massive race at Glorious Goodwood when hitting the front a furlong out before just missing out on a place. He is a solid, sound horse and he can take his owner to many of the big summer meetings.

Orlando Rogue 2yo colt
*Bushranger – Boston Ivy
(Mark Of Esteem)*

I like him because he does everything so easily. I have not pressed any buttons yet but everything about him – his presence, his demeanour – has me excited and he has a touch of class. He won't be starting out over 5f but by late summer he could be exciting.

Yul Finegold 4yo gelding
Invincible Spirit – Mascara (Mtoto)

It is disappointing he is still a maiden after eight runs, but he has some reasonable form. I still retain faith in him and I hope to find a winnable maiden early on. We can then progress and I think he will prove my optimism to be correct.

Zubaidah 2yo filly
*Exceed And Excel – Bedouin Bride
(Chester House)*

I love Exceed And Excel as a sire and I am very pleased with this filly. She does everything so easily at home and looks as if she will be right up there with my best juveniles. We may start off over 5f but she will definitely get further.

NENGE MBOKO: should be going to many of the big summer meetings

RACING & FOOTBALL Est. 1909

OUTLOOK

Ante-post preview by Steffan Edwards

2,000 Guineas

GROUP 1-winning two-year-olds usually find themselves at the head of the ante-post market for the 2,000 Guineas, but this year the winners of the Dewhurst, the Racing Post Trophy and the National Stakes all find themselves relegated behind a pair of highly-touted Group 3 winners.

Kingman and Australia are extremely well bred, represent top connections and have both shown plenty of promise in their starts to date, but it's difficult to pick between the two at shortish prices.

Kingman couldn't have been more impressive on his debut at Newmarket and it was interesting that his trainer John Gosden sent him to the Solario Stakes afterwards, a race he won with the top-class Raven's Pass six years earlier. He won cosily, but without the panache of Newmarket, the steady early gallop no doubt preventing him from showing all he could do.

By Invincible Spirit out of a French Guineas winner, a mile on fast ground should be ideal for him this year. However, he did have minor surgery at the end of last season, and, for all that he proved himself a high-class performer later on in the year, Raven's Pass only finished fourth in his Guineas, so I still question how prepared Gosden is to rush his horses for the first Classic of the season.

Aidan O'Brien couldn't have been more effusive in his praise of **Australia** after he beat Dermot Weld's Free Eagle by six lengths at Leopardstown on Irish Champion Stakes day. While we've been here before to a certain extent, there's no doubting the regard in which he's held and O'Brien does have plenty at home to judge him against.

That said, his pedigree (by Galileo out of Oaks winner Ouija Board) is one of a Derby contender, not a Guineas winner. While Coolmore managed to win the Guineas with a similar horse quite recently in Camelot, he only just won by a neck in unusually soft ground from what in hindsight was a truly tragic bunch of rivals.

Dewhurst winner **War Command** didn't do a lot wrong at two and normally a horse with his profile would be favourite for the Guineas. He might not have quite lived up to the high expectations held for him after his runaway win in the Coventry Stakes, but it's hard to knock his form and his Dewhurst win came on unsuitably easy ground over Champagne Stakes and Breeders' Cup winner Outstrip. Granted fast ground he looks to me the more solid contender from Ballydoyle.

Racing Post Trophy winner **Kingston Hill** is a half-brother to Ramona Chase, who stayed 1m4f, so at first glance he wouldn't look a natural for the Guineas, but she was by High Chaparral and he's by the speedier Mastercraftsman, so you never know. However, there's another concern as he's completely unproven on a sound surface. Given all that I'd want a bigger price than the current 10-1.

Toormore showed great versatility at two, quickening up from behind to cheekily win the Vintage Stakes at Goodwood and then making every yard to win the National Stakes at the Curragh. He's always looked strongest at the end of his races so it might not pay to dwell too much on his pedigree, but for the record he's by Arakan out of a Danetime mare, which hardly screams miler.

Anyway, Richard Hannon Jnr is far from one-handed as he has a couple of other runners capable of going to Newmarket with a proper chance.

The first one is **NIGHT OF THUNDER**, who couldn't have been more impressive in winning both his starts last year. He didn't make his debut until October, but he won with any amount in hand that day at Goodwood and less than a fortnight later he came out and took a Listed race at Doncaster, again quickening up in style.

Both those races were over 6f on soft ground, so a mile on faster ground will pose a very different test, but there are reasons to be optimistic. First of all, he's a son of Dubawi out of a Galileo mare who won over 7f at two, so he's not bred to be a speedball. Secondly, for all that the progeny of Dubawi tend to handle some cut better than others, they actually have the same strike-rate on good to firm as they do on soft (18%). He's just a very good sire. In fact, all three sons of Dubawi to have so far contested the 2,000 Guineas made the frame, with Makfi winning in 2010 at

WAR COMMAND: looks the best of Aidan O'Brien's Guineas contenders

NIGHT OF THUNDER: taken to extend Dubawi's great Guineas record as a sire

33-1, Dubawi Gold finishing runner-up in 2011 at 33-1 and Hermival finishing third in 2012 at 16-1, so they all outran their odds by quite a bit.

As he lacks a little in experience Night Of Thunder might benefit from running in a trial, which will give him another chance to impress and for his Guineas price to contract.

The other Hannon runner in whom I'm interested is **SHIFTING POWER**, who looks the type to have progressed hugely over the winter.

He looked useful, but nothing more, when taking a weak Sandown maiden on his debut, but he found 20lb improvement on his next start in a novice race at Newmarket. He scampered clear of a decent field there despite having raced keenly early and all the time he was looking around, not really knowing what he was doing and edging right when asked to quicken. The form of that win couldn't have worked out

much better, with the runner-up, beaten six lengths, taking the Group 3 Acomb Stakes next time out and the fourth, beaten over eight lengths, easily winning a nursery off 85 on his next start, so there's plenty to suggest that Shifting Power put up a smart performance that day.

A huge colt, he was just a big, green baby last year and can't do anything but improve from two to three. He's not the most fashionably bred (by Compton Place out of an Alzao mare) and he was a relatively inexpensive purchase, but that doesn't worry me when it comes to this yard as in that respect he's not dissimilar to any number of other horses the Hannons have developed into top milers, including Canford Cliffs. He looks the type who might need a run to put him spot on and a trial would be good for him in terms of experience as well, so it would be good to see him in the Craven first time up.

Berkshire stayed on strongly to win the

Chesham at Royal Ascot, form that reads well. He wasn't nearly as impressive in the Royal Lodge at Newmarket on his final start, but I'm prepared to forgive him that. He never looked like a two-year-old really, having plenty of size, so this should be his year. He's bred to stay further than a mile, though, and I can see him improving as the season goes on, especially over a longer trip.

Outstrip, winner of the Breeders' Cup Juvenile Turf, relished the fast ground out in Santa Anita and might be able to improve if he gets his conditions at Newmarket. That said, he was comfortably beaten in the Dewhurst by War Command and that horse would have been equally unsuited by the easy ground that day.

Possibly of more interest from the Godolphin stable is **Be Ready**, who beat Barley Mow (not disgraced in the Lagardere next time) easily in a Doncaster Listed race in September. He was supplemented at a cost of £30,000 into the Dewhurst afterwards but had to miss the race because of a dirty scope. The decision to supplement showed that he's highly regarded and, as he's bred to be a miler, the Guineas is likely to be his big target. I'd rather wait and see, though, and perhaps back him on the day.

Lat Hawill, **Gamesome** and **Ertijaal** all won their maidens impressively but would have to show up well in one of the trials to get my serious attention.

The Middle Park winner **Astaire** has the potential to be more than just a sprinter this year, at least on pedigree, but it's rare these days for a Gimcrack or Middle Park winner to take the Guineas.

Noozhoh Canarias, who finished second in the Prix Jean-Luc Lagardere, is being targeted at the Guineas. He started his career off in Spain by winning over 4f, but he's out of a Singspiel mare and should, in theory, be able to get the Guineas distance. He shows a lot of speed, though, and I find it difficult seeing him winning over the stiff mile at Newmarket.

Giovanni Boldini has been nominated for the US Triple Crown races so that looks the way he'll be going, while **Great White Eagle** showed so much pace at two it's hard to believe he'll be anything but a sprinter this year. **Indian Maharaja**, on the other hand, looks more of a Derby horse.

No Nay Never would have been a fascinating runner, but apparently the Wesley Ward-trained Norfolk Stakes and Prix Morny winner will be staying in America until Royal Ascot, where his target is the St James's Palace Stakes.

2,000 Guineas

Newmarket, 4 May

	Bet365	Betfred	Boyles	Coral	Hills	Lads	PPower	SJames
Kingman	6	5	5	6	4	5	6	6
Australia	7	6	6	6	6	5	11-2	7
Toormore	8	8	8	7	8	7	8	6
War Command	7	7	8	8	8	8	8	11-2
Kingston Hill	8	10	9	8	10	8	10	8
Berkshire	12	14	14	12	12	12	12	12
Be Ready	16	16	16	16	16	16	16	20
Night Of Thunder	14	16	20	14	20	14	20	16
Outstrip	20	20	20	16	20	20	16	20
Indian Maharaja	20	16	20	25	-	-	16	25
Shifting Power	25	25	-	-	20	-	-	25
Lat Hawill	25	-	-	25	16	-	-	25
Great White Eagle	25	-	25	33	-	-	20	25
Astaire	33	-	25	33	20	-	25	33

each-way 1/4 odds, 1-2-3
Others on application, prices correct at time of going to press

MISS FRANCE (near side): looked impressive in the Oh So Sharp at Newmarket

1,000 Guineas

LAST season's leading juvenile fillies took turns to beat each other and as a result the 1,000 Guineas market, headed by Andre Fabre's Miss France, looks wide-open.

It's hard to argue with **Miss France** given that she beat the subsequent Marcel Boussac winner Indonesienne (gave 4lb) second time out and then put up a really impressive performance to win the Oh So Sharp Stakes on her final start. She travelled like a class act and quickened up well, clocking a smart time in cosily defeating Lightning Thunder.

However, at 11-2 she can be taken on. For a start the form of her Oh So Sharp win can be questioned, with one or two rivals failing to run their races and Lightning Thunder disappointing, albeit with an excuse (she was in season), in the Rockfel afterwards. It's also worth bearing in mind that Miss France is by Dansili out of a mare who stayed 1m4f and was placed in the

Group 1 Prix Vermeille, so a mile is likely to be the bare minimum for her this year.

Radiator was sent off a short-priced favourite for the Oh So Sharp but finished well beaten. A 15l winner of a Lingfield maiden on her previous start, she surely didn't give her true running at Newmarket, and she's well bred and should make a miler this year so can't be written off.

The first three from the Moyglare are all prominent in the betting, with the winner, **Rizeena**, probably the pick of the trio.

Despite being successful three times over 5f early in the year, she was far from just an early two-year-old and improved as she stepped up in distance. She looked to have a bit more size and scope than the placed horses in the Moyglare and she lost little in defeat when beaten by the ill-fated Chriselliam in a steadily-run Fillies' Mile, in which she was too keen early.

That said, on paper she has little in hand of **Tapestry**, who was a little unlucky in running at the Curragh and is bred to improve from two to three. By Galileo out of Rumplestiltskin (champion two-year-old filly and seventh in Speciosa's Guineas), she has the pedigree, but the bookmakers are giving nothing away at 7-1.

Kiyoshi put up the most impressive performance of the year when taking the Albany Stakes at Royal Ascot. She showed an electric turn of foot that day and was immediately given quotes of no bigger than 10-1 for the Guineas. Things didn't go to plan afterwards, though.

She hit the front too soon in the Moyglare and hung right, just as she had at Ascot, in the process hampering a weakening rival. She was more tractable in the Cheveley Park on her final start, but the turn of pace was missing at Newmarket and her connections were left scratching their heads.

She's by Dubawi and her dam stayed 1m4f, so dropping back to 6f was, in hindsight, probably a mistake, and she should get a mile well this year. Being by Dubawi, a drop of rain probably wouldn't go amiss either.

Ihtimal improved as the year went on and, given that the race wasn't run to suit, ran okay in the Fillies' Mile. She's since run well out in Dubai, but whether she'll translate that back to Britain is questionable as the track record of similar types isn't great.

Judged on the bare form of her Duchess of Cambridge Stakes (formerly Cherry Hinton) and Lowther wins, **Lucky Kristale** has as big a chance as any of taking the Guineas. She beat Rizeena (gave 3lb) comfortably in the former and confirmed form with Queen Catrine (subsequently placed in Marcel Boussac) in the latter on 3lb worse terms. She also finished in front of Cheveley Park runner-up Princess Noor on a couple of occasions.

The problem is her pedigree, which strongly suggests a mile will stretch her stamina. She's a half-sister to a couple of winning sprinters and I can't trust that she'll stay.

Both the Cheveley Park winner **Vorda** and the Rockfel winner **Al Thakhira** disappointed at the Breeders' Cup. They had excuses, the former being caught wide and the latter finding the ground too fast, but both are speedy types far from sure to get a mile this year.

In contrast, I expect **Joyeuse** to improve for a mile. This half-sister to Frankel created plenty of buzz when winning easily on her debut and ran creditably to finish

LUCKY KRISTALE: has strong form claims but stamina cannot be trusted

TERRIFIC: could extend the remarkable record of Galileo fillies in the Guineas

third in the Albany after a troubled passage. She was rather workmanlike in taking a Listed event at Salisbury afterwards, though, and was then well held in the Cheveley Park, albeit after refusing to settle off a dawdling early pace.

She has a bit to prove, but one thing we know about her family is that they improve from two to three, and stepping up to a mile in a well-run race is also going to be in her favour – her brother Morpheus was a mile handicapper at three.

Sandiva didn't get home in the Marcel Boussac but the ground was very testing that day and her previous form reads well. She should get a mile on pedigree and could still be a player.

My Titania's two-year-old form doesn't read as strongly as some, but she impressed with the turn of foot she showed to win her last two starts and her trainer John Oxx has always held her in high regard.

A daughter of Sea The Stars, she's going to relish stepping up to a mile – and probably further in time as well – and the Guineas is the plan. She could easily improve a good deal for the winter and, probably she gets decent ground to run on, she will be one to fear at Newmarket.

Amazing Maria wasn't seen after making all in the Prestige Stakes despite having been pencilled in for the Fillies' Mile. She's another who promises to improve from two to three and a mile on decent ground will probably be her thing this year, but I'm not sure if Ed Dunlop is the type to rush a filly out for the Guineas.

Here's a little stat for you. A daughter of Galileo has been placed in the 1,000 Guineas in five of the last six years, from just seven runners, which is a better overall record than his sons can boast in the 2,000 Guineas. In contrast to the six colts to have run during the same period, all of whom were sent off at 9-1 or shorter (one winner, Frankel, at 1-2 and two placed, including New Approach at 11-8), all but one of the six fillies to have run in the 1,000 Guineas were sent off at 9-1 or longer, suggesting they're being undervalued.

Eyecatchingly, two were placed as genuine outsiders, including Together, who was a 33-1 shot when runner-up to Blue Bunting in 2011, and this could be significant because I think her sister, **TERRIFIC**, has a fighting chance of at least emulating her and perhaps going one place better at an equally juicy price.

Terrific cost a whopping 1,300,000gns at the sales and, while that's no guarantee of success on the track, the Coolmore crew bought Was at the sales for 1,200,000gns not so long ago and she went on to win the Oaks.

Clearly on paper Tapestry is the most likely of the Galileo fillies to make the frame, but we've seen before with fillies from Ballydoyle that the pecking order at the end of the two-year-old campaign can be turned upside-down in the Guineas.

Just last year Moth, who was a maiden at two, progressed to be the stable's number one (finished third) in the Guineas and the previous year Homecoming Queen, who was just a Listed winner at two, hacked up in the Guineas, while the yard's short-priced favourite, Maybe, could only finish third.

Terrific has yet to compete in Pattern company and has a good deal to prove, but there's no doubting the promise she showed at two. She was too green to show much of anything on her debut, but Aidan O'Brien slapped some blinkers on her for her second start and she made virtually all to win her maiden over a mile at the Cur-ragh, seeing off a Johnny Murtagh-trained filly who'd run creditably against Australia on her debut in the process.

Third time out she dropped back to 7f for a fillies' race, again at the Curragh, which has produced some good winners in recent years, namely Gile Na Greine (third in the Guineas), Banimpire (fifth in Irish Guineas and second in Irish Oaks) and Snow Queen (fifth in last year's Guin-eas). Once again she made every yard, and the time was smart, 0.91sec quicker than that recorded by War Command in winning the Group 2 Futurity Stakes later on the card.

She looks the type who'll keep improv-ing with racing and appears very tough. I can see her making the Guineas a real test and being tough to pass once she gets rolling at Newmarket.

It's worth remembering that her sister Together ran eight times at two and eight times again at three. She made her reap-pearance, oddly it seemed at the time, in the Tattersalls Millions Three-Year-Old Trophy over 1m2f before dropping back in trip for the Guineas. Running in that valu-able race over a longer trip did her Guin-eas chance no harm, so perhaps Terrific, who holds an entry in the same event, will follow a similar path.

1,000 Guineas

Newmarket, 5 May

	Bet365	Betfred	Boyles	Coral	Hills	Lads	PPower	SJames
Miss France	**11-2**	5	5	4	9-2	5	5	4
Tapestry	7	7	7	7	7	5	7	**9**
Rizeena	**10**	**10**	**10**	**10**	**10**	8	9	**10**
My Titania	**12**	**12**	**12**	**12**	**12**	**12**	**12**	**12**
Ihtimal	12	**14**	12	**14**	**14**	12	12	**14**
Lucky Kristale	**16**	14	14	12	**16**	12	12	**16**
Kiyoshi	**16**	**16**	14	14	14	14	14	**16**
Al Thakhira	14	12	12	**16**	**16**	14	10	**16**
Amazing Maria	16	16	16	16	16	**20**	16	16
Vorda	16	12	12	**20**	**20**	14	14	**20**
Sandiva	**25**	16	16	20	20	20	20	**25**
Joyeuse	**33**	**33**	25	**33**	25	**33**	25	**33**
Terrific	**33**	-	-	-	-	-	-	**33**
Radiator	**40**	-	33	33	33	-	-	**40**

each-way 1/4 odds, 1-2-3
Others on application, prices correct at time of going to press

Derby

AS has become the norm in recent years, the Derby ante-post market is not only headed by an Aidan O'Brien-trained colt but his yard has loads of other credible candidates in the list as well.

Picking between them is a nightmare as they're all well bred, invariably by super sire Galileo, they've all won their maidens impressively, some winning in better company since as well, and almost all should make better three-year-olds over middle distances. It's just guesswork as to who will progress fastest.

Only last year the stable was represented by five runners in the Derby and the winner, Ruler Of The World, hadn't even raced at two and was the stable's second string on the day.

I think the prudent course is to take on Ballydoyle ante-post, then possibly back the best of them nearer the time or on the day. For all their power, it's not like they win the Derby every year. Sure, they've won it the last two years, but they went nine years without winning it before that.

The main selection with which to take them on is **BERKSHIRE**, who slid in the betting after his unimpressive success in the Royal Lodge Stakes. Not much went right for him that day because he got stirred up in the preliminaries, got no real cover in the small field and raced keenly as a result. It was only his third start and he hadn't run since Royal Ascot, so he can be forgiven still being green.

I think the bunched finish suggests the bare form is misleading as he beat Mark Johnston's Somewhat by just a neck at Newmarket having thrashed him by eight lengths at Ascot. That's the piece of form that makes him interesting as a Derby contender as he tanked through the Chesham and beat some quality rivals with ease. The runner-up, **Bunker**, with whom the Hannon team are planning to go the Dante-Derby route this year, beat the Lagardere winner Karakontie in a French Listed race

BERKSHIRE: looked a superstar in waiting when landing the Chesham Stakes

AUSTRALIA: too short for the Derby given Aidan O'Brien's strength in depth

next time out, and the third, Ihtimal, went on to prove herself one of the best fillies around, winning the Sweet Solera and May Hill.

The Chesham is run over 7f fairly early in the season and is restricted to horses whose sires won over at least 1m2f, so it's designed for horses more likely to be staying types. For all that Berkshire is being aimed at the Guineas first, I'd be more than satisfied with a solid sixth or seventh there, as I expect him to improve a lot for the extra half-mile at Epsom. In 1997 Berkshire's trainer Paul Cole sent out Central Park to win the Chesham, and that colt went on to win the Italian Derby the following year after finishing in mid-division in the 2,000 Guineas. I can imagine similar improvement from Berkshire when he goes up in trip.

My second pick is more speculative but is a price to match. **WESTERN HYMN** created quite an impression when winning on his debut at Kempton in early December. He may not have beaten much, but the way he powered past the entire field in the straight, despite the early pace having been fairly modest, strongly suggested that he's a smart colt.

By High Chaparral out of a Cape Cross mare who won over 7f as a two-year-old and is half-sister to a 1m4f Group 3 win-

ner and top two-year-old filly Fantasia, he should stay all right, but he's clearly not short of tactical speed either, which can be very useful at the top level.

Having made his debut so late in the season, the concern is whether he'll be ready to be campaigned with the Derby in mind, but John Gosden's colt has the talent to be given a shot at a trial and that's all that can be asked for at the moment.

Roger Varian doesn't think faster ground will be an issue for Racing Post Trophy winner **Kingston Hill** this year, but it will remain a question mark until he actually proves it. In addition, while his pedigree gives hope that he'll get the Derby trip, it by no means guarantees it. At the current odds we can pass.

Free Eagle won impressively on his debut but was then handed a thrashing by Australia on his next start. Dermot Weld didn't think he was at his best that day, although nothing came to light post-race, and he'll have a bit to prove when he reappears, probably in the Derrinstown Derby Trial.

If **Australia** is as good as Aidan O'Brien claims he is then he's going to take a lot of beating, but he's 4-1 on the back of defeating an arguably below-par Free Eagle in a four-runner race and that's a world away from what he'll face in the Derby.

25

TRUE STORY: looks the most likely Godolphin challenger at Epsom

Clearly he couldn't be better bred for the job, but I'm happy to wait and see as there are plenty of others from the stable who could emerge with claims just as strong, if not stronger, nearer the time.

Geoffrey Chaucer and **Indian Maharaja** may be the most likely to step up at the moment. The former is a half-brother by Montjeu to multiple Group 1 winner Shamardal, while the latter is by Galileo out of an Irish 1,000 Guineas winner. Both went 2-2 last year and are quite capable of becoming leading players by way of the trials, which in recent times Ballydoyle have dominated.

Though still a maiden, **Johann Strauss** is another to be put in the mix. He might not be the easiest of rides as it looks like he needs to be delivered as late as possible, but he travels well and there's a chance that he'll perform better in stronger races.

If lightning is to strike twice then it might not even be worth discounting **Annus Mi-rabilis**, who, like Ruler Of The World, to whom he's closely related, didn't step foot on a racetrack at two.

Another yet to race is **Hydrogen**, trained by Peter Chapple-Hyam and the subject of plenty of hype on the back of how much he cost at the sales as a yearling. A 2,500,000gns purchase, he's a half-brother by Galileo to Derby winner Authorized and it will be interesting to see how he gets on when he finally makes his debut.

Scotland got experience of the track at Epsom last year when taking a conditions race there in September. It's not out of the question that he could get himself into the conversation with a prominent effort in a trial, but he'd need supplementing as he's not entered in the Derby at the moment.

On what we've seen so far **Altruistic** has a bit to find, but he should progress from two to three, could improve for fast ground and is likely to be given every chance by his trainer/jockey Johnny Murtagh to make the grade. I can see him running an

26

excellent St Leger trial at Epsom.

Seagull Star is another who apparently needs fast ground to be seen at his best. A debut winner at Newmarket, he's by Sea The Stars out of Dash To The Top, whose career highlight was finishing second in the Yorkshire Oaks, but she was far from straightforward, eventually refusing to race. Seagull Star looked a model professional on his debut, so perhaps he's taken more after his father than his mother, and 1m4f on decent ground should suit him well.

Godolphin have one or two worth considering. **Pinzolo** was sent off 4-1 for the Racing Post Trophy on the back of two wins in lesser company, but he bombed out at Doncaster. He could easily bounce back and is bred to stay well, but he might just need ease in the ground to be seen at his best and perhaps the St Leger will be more his race.

True Story is the most interesting of the Godolphin colts. Beaten only by his speedier stablemate Outstrip (subsequent Champagne Stakes and Breeders' Cup Juvenile Turf winner) on his debut at Newmarket over 7f, he went one better next time over the same course and distance, drawing clear of a strong field of maidens with ease. The second, third, fifth, sixth

and tenth all won next time out, giving the form substance, and his pedigree suggests he has every chance of getting 1m4f this year, being by Manduro out of a Darshaan mare. The only concern is that he didn't run again after winning his maiden in July.

Kingman won't stay 1m4f if breeding is anything to go on and **Be Ready** also looks more of a Guineas horse, as does **War Command**, who'll surely go the traditional route for milers, taking in the Irish 2,000 Guineas and the St James's Palace Stakes after Newmarket.

If Andre Fabre is to bring one over then I hope it's **Gallante**, who won a maiden for unraced colts at Longchamp in September. He quickened up nicely and showed a good attitude to see off a persistent challenge from the runner-up, and the pair finished six lengths clear of the rest.

It's invariably a strong maiden as recent winners include future Group 1 scorers Tamayuz and Maxios, and Gallante's pedigree (brother to Plinth, a 1m5f winner on the level and a useful juvenile hurdler) suggests he'll be very much suited by the Derby trip. He is, however, owned by the Coolmore crew, so they might think they already have enough ammunition this side of the Channel.

Derby

Epsom, 1 June

	Bet365	Betfred	Boyles	Coral	Hills	Lads	PPower	SJames
Australia	**4**	**4**	**4**	**4**	7-2	7-2	**4**	**4**
Kingston Hill	8	6	9	8	5	**10**	**10**	8
Free Eagle	14	14	14	14	14	-	12	**16**
Geoffrey Chaucer	**16**	14	12	14	**16**	**16**	14	12
Indian Maharaja	**16**	**16**	**16**	**16**	**16**	**16**	**16**	14
Ectot	**16**	-	-	-	-	-	14	**16**
Be Ready	16	-	-	-	-	-	16	**20**
War Command	16	16	16	16	16	16	-	**25**
Berkshire	16	20	**25**	**25**	20	20	16	20
Kingman	16	-	-	12	12	14	-	**25**
Johann Strauss	20	-	**25**	-	**25**	-	25	**25**
Hydrogen	33	-	33	33	**50**	-	33	**50**
True Story	40	-	-	25	-	-	-	**50**
Western Hymn	**100**	-	-	-	-	-	-	**100**

each-way 1/4 odds, 1-2-3
Others on application, prices correct at time of going to press

Oaks

NO filly stamped herself an outstanding candidate for the Oaks last year and the betting reflects how open the race looks at the moment, with the bookmakers going 12-1 the field.

I'm going to take a chance on a couple of maiden winners who have the right pedigree, hail from prominent stables and are listed at backable prices.

First up is **CAMBRIDGE**, who made a successful debut in a backend 1m Nottingham maiden. There were plenty of big stables represented and they went a good gallop yet she travelled like the winner throughout, quickening smartly when asked to pick up Ralph Beckett's Regardez, who came into the race with far more experience and bolted up on her next start at Doncaster.

Cambridge is a half-sister to Dux Scholar, who was at his best at 1m2f (Listed winner and Group 3-placed) when trained by Sir Michael Stoute but later went on to compete successfully abroad over as short as 5f. He was by the sprinter Oasis Dream but Cambridge is by Arc winner Rail Link so the signs are that she should relish middle distances this year.

She looked to have plenty of size about her so she should train on well from two to three, and don't be surprised if her trainer, Charlie Hills, uses the Cheshire Oaks as her trial for Epsom. Not only does the yard have a great record at the track, but Cambridge's dam, Alumni, won the Cheshire Oaks and Alumni's siblings Prolix (Dee Stakes) and Bangalore (Chester Cup) also won big races at the track. Perhaps it's in the genes.

The second filly I'm interested in is **TAGHROODA**, who won her maiden on the Rowley Mile at Newmarket in September. This is a race previously won by Sir Henry Cecil's Oaks winner Light Shift and his Oaks runner-up Midday.

Taghrooda wasn't particularly fancied, being sent off at 20-1, but Dane O'Neill never had to get that serious with her as she swept through from the back of the field to win a shade cosily. The form looks strong, with the favourite, Casual Smile, who came into the race with two very good runs to her name already, taking second, and a gap back to the third, who won easily at Salisbury next time out.

Taghrooda is bred to thrive over middle distances this year, being by Sea The Stars out of a Sadler's Wells mare who won at Listed level between 1m2f and 1m6f.

John Gosden has yet to win the Oaks, but he's had a couple go quite close in recent years – The Fugue finished an unlucky third in 2012 and Izzi Top filled the same position in 2011 – and this filly might just be the one to change his luck.

Runner-up to Taghrooda, **Casual Smile** is not to be dismissed from Oaks calculations despite still being a maiden. Trained by Andrew Balding, she shaped with a deal of promise on each start, travels well and is bred to come into her own this year, being by Sea The Stars out of the stable's Oaks winner Casual Look.

As usual Aidan O'Brien has several possible contenders. **Tapestry** will no doubt be going to the Guineas first before heading to Epsom, but while she has a fair chance of getting the Oaks trip on pedigree, she did show plenty of pace to win over 6f on her debut, so there has to be some doubt over her stamina for 1m4f.

Bracelet, a sister to Rockfel winner Wading, has decent prospects of getting the trip, and although **Marvellous** is out of a fairly speedy mare in Cherry Hinton winner You'resothrilling, she is by Galileo and looked all about stamina when taking her maiden over 1m last autumn.

In contrast, **Terrific** is a sister to Together, who was placed in the Guineas and was basically a miler, and is also a half-sister to Jan Vermeer, who didn't stay in the Derby and was at his best over 1m2f, so she might struggle to get 1m4f.

Dazzling, who failed to build on a promising debut win in two subsequent starts in Listed company, is a sister to Roderic O'Connor, who was at his best over a

CAMBRIDGE (right): among several maiden winners who can step up this year

mile, while **Wonderfully**, not disgraced in Group 1 company last term and a sister to Mars (sixth in last year's Derby), is another for whom there are stamina concerns.

Dermot Weld has a couple of possibles in Balansiya and Carla Bianca.

The maiden **Balansiya** won by an eased-down seven lengths may not have been the strongest, and it was slowly-run, but she showed a smart turn of foot on ground her trainer felt was as soft as she'd like. She's by Shamardal out of a Dalakhani mare so has a decent chance of getting the Oaks trip.

Carla Bianca is still a maiden but she's only had two starts and in both she showed a great deal of ability. On her debut she chased home Derby favourite Australia and then on her next start she was pitched in to Group 1 company in the Moyglare and was far from disgraced in fourth behind some speedier types. By Dansili out of a half-sister to Profound Beauty, who

won at up to 1m6f, she should stay.

The question with both fillies is whether they'll travel to Epsom. Weld has a habit of keeping his best horses for the Irish Classics and for that reason it's not worth the risk of backing Balansiya or Carla Bianca for the Oaks at this stage.

Sinnamary is an interesting filly. Trained by Mikel Delzangles, she won impressively on her debut over 1m1f at Longchamp. She's a half-sister to last year's Irish Oaks winner Chicquita, but whereas that filly was by Montjeu, this one's by Galileo and there was no sign of her being bonkers like her older sibling. It has to be odds-on that she'll stay at home for the French Classics, but if she were to travel over she would demand respect.

Surcingle and **Lady Tyne** won their maidens impressively, but the former disappointed upped in class on soft ground on her next start, while the latter's win came in heavy ground and it's hard to know if she'll be as effective back on a sound surface. Both have potential, though.

Ihtimal looks more of a Guineas type to me, as does **Amazing Maria**, but My Titania and Miss France have good prospects of staying the trip on pedigree. Together with Aidan O'Brien's Tapestry these two look the likeliest to have leading chances at both Newmarket and Epsom.

The problem with **Miss France** is that she could easily be pointed in the direction of the Prix de Diane after the Guineas, while the invariably well-watered ground at Epsom could go against **My Titania**, who needs a good, fast surface to show her best.

Several unraced fillies have time to make an impact. O'Brien's **Ruby Tuesday** takes the eye most of all, being a half-sister to, among others, Quarter Moon, Yesterday and All My Loving, all of whom were placed in the Oaks.

Others worth keeping an eye out for are **Hadaatha**, trained by Roger Varian, who is by Sea The Stars out of a well-related Linamix mare; **Cantabella**, trained by David Wachman, who is by Galileo out of a sister to Holy Roman Emperor; and **Azama**, trained by John Oxx, who is another Sea The Stars filly and a half-sister to her connections' top-class Azamour.

Recommended bets

2,000 Guineas

Night Of Thunder 1pt 20-1
(generally)

Shifting Power 1pt 25-1
(generally)

1,000 Guineas

Terrific 1pt each-way 33-1
(bet365, Stan James)

Derby

Berkshire 2pts 25-1
(Coral)

Western Hymn 1pt 100-1
(bet365, Stan James)

Oaks

Cambridge 1pt 33-1
(Stan James)

Taghrooda 1pt 33-1
(Hills)

Oaks

Epsom, 31 May

	Bet365	Betfred	Boyles	Coral	Hills	Lads	PPower	SJames
Tapestry	10	**12**	10	8	**12**	8	11	8
My Titania	**16**	14	**16**	14	14	-	-	**16**
Ihtimal	**20**	**20**	-	16	16	-	12	14
Bracelet	16	16	16	16	-	-	**20**	**20**
Marvellous	-	16	-	**20**	-	-	-	-
Amazing Maria	20	20	-	20	**25**	20	-	**25**
Dazzling	25	-	20	-	14	-	16	**33**
Taghrooda	20	25	-	-	**33**	-	-	25
Cambridge	25	25	-	25	-	16	-	**33**
Balansiya	**33**	25	-	-	**33**	-	-	25
Joyeuse	**33**	-	20	25	-	-	20	**33**
Tarfasha	25	**33**	-	25	-	-	-	**33**
Carla Bianca	**40**	33	25	25	**40**	-	25	**40**

each-way 1/4 odds, 1-2-3
Others on application, prices correct at time of going to press

Est. 1909
RACING & FOOTBALL OUTLOOK

Richard Williams' horses to follow

BAAREZ 3 b c
Hard Spun – Sortita (Monsun)
21-

A promising second on his debut at Newmarket when he might well have won but for hanging left, Baarez made no mistake on his second start at Haydock in October when sent off at 1-2 and dispatching 11 others with ease. It was a workmanlike performance and the soft ground didn't help the visual impression. However, Roger Varian has said that he was a big two-year-old and that he is much stronger now. A half-brother to smart stablemate Mutashaded, who was third in last year's King Edward VII Stakes, he can also make his mark at Pattern level.

Roger Varian, Newmarket

BALANSIYA 3 b f
Shamardal – Baliyana (Dalakhani)
1-

The Aga Khan now has horses with Dermot Weld and this filly, by influential sire Shamardal and a first foal of a Group 3 winner, could be anything. She won her only race, a 7f Leopardstown maiden, by seven lengths with jockey Pat Smullen easing her close home. Some of her ten rivals were from top yards so the form is likely to be decent, and entries in the 1,000 Guineas and Irish Oaks suggest Weld thinks a lot of her.

Dermot Weld, The Curragh

BE READY 3 ch c
New Approach – Call Later (Gone West)
21-

Made his debut in the 7f Listed Washington Singer Stakes at Newbury in August, coming second to Somewhat, who subsequently got within a neck of the classy Berkshire in the Royal Lodge. This fellow went on to win a Listed race at the St Leger meeting by three lengths. Taking a keen hold that day, he only really got into a rhythm in the final two furlngs and powered home. He could be yet another New Approach colt to go on to big things.

Saeed Bin Suroor, Newmarket

BRETON ROCK 4 b g
Bahamian Bounty – Anna's Rock (Rock Of Gibraltar)
271312-

Breton Rock started off last season on a mark of 86 and ended up racing off 103, a case of steady rather than sharp improvement. Along the way he picked up a 7f handicap at Doncaster and an apprentice handicap at Ascot on Champions Day over the same trip before finishing second when stepped up to a mile on his final start at Nottingham. Expect him to start off in some of the better handicaps over 7f and a mile and he may well then graduate to Pattern races. Soft ground will be a big help to him.

David Simcock, Newmarket

EBASANI 3 ch c
Manduro – Ebatana (Rainbow Quest)
1-

Had his only start in a mile maiden at Navan maiden in early October, beating eight others with horses from the O'Brien, Bolger and Weld yards filling the next four places. Although the winning margin was only a length, he won with something in hand on tacky ground which wouldn't have done him any favours. This maiden has been won by Soldier Of Fortune and Kingsbarns in the past, and although Ebasani has a long way to go to match those Group 1 winners, there's no reason why he shouldn't develop into a smart three-year-old.

John Oxx, Currabeg

ENCKE 5 b h
Kingmambo – Shawanda (Sinndar)
1231/

This horse, who was banned from racing last year because his former trainer Mahmood Al Zarooni injected him with steroids, will be under an intense spotlight this season, but he should still be followed. There is no suggestion that his last victory in the St Leger – a truly-run race in which he beat Camelot fair and square – was achieved under the influence of drugs. Lightly-raced, he should have matured since winning the 1m6f Doncaster Classic, and whether he takes the staying route or returns to 1m4f, he is sure to be a factor in several top races.

Charlie Appleby, Newmarket

FLINTSHIRE 4 b c
Dansili – Dance Routine (Sadler's Wells)
121148-

Flintshire won the Grand Prix de Paris in the style of a smart colt. Longchamp's 1m4f Group 1 test for three-year-olds in July is regarded by many as the true French Derby and has been won by the likes of Arc winners Bago and Rail Link. This colt went on to defeats in the Prix Niel and the Arc, never able to show his class in either race on the soft ground. Unraced as a two-year-old, the late-maturing Flintshire is the sort for races such as the King George and Queen Elizabeth Stakes in mid-summer when the ground should be quick enough for him.

Andre Fabre, Chantilly

FLYING JIB 3 ro f
Oasis Dream – Jibboon (Mizzen Mast)
411-

This Khalid Abdullah-owned filly won a 7f maiden at Dundalk in August by four an a quarter lengths before reappearing two months later in a mile Listed race at the Curragh. She really looked the part in beating Chicago Girl (touched off by My Titania in the CL Weld Park Stakes on her previous run) by a length and a half in a time over two seconds quicker than that taken by Aidan O'Brien's smart Century to win a maiden over the same trip earlier on the card. She is in the betting for the 1,000 Guineas and wouldn't look out of place in that race.

Dermot Weld, The Curragh

FREE EAGLE 3 b c
High Chaparral – Polished Gem (Danehill)
12-

Free Eagle ran a lacklustre sort of race when beaten six lengths by Australia on his last outing in September over a mile at Leopardstown. However, it's worth remembering the impact of his debut which had led to him being made favourite for the Derby. Running over the same course and distance as his later flop, he thrashed Aidan O'Brien's Orchestra, who was a comfortable winner next time out, by five and a half lengths. His subsequent run was too bad to be true and this colt will surely bounce back and prove top-class.

Dermot Weld, The Curragh

GARSWOOD 4 b c
Dutch Art – Penchant (Kyllachy)
174163-

Two wins from six starts was a respectable haul for this sprint-bred colt. His two victories both came over 7f as he started off in April by notching Newmarket's European Free Handicap and later added Goodwood's Group 3 Lennox Stakes by a neck. But it was his third to Moonlight Cloud in the Group 1 Prix de la Foret which was his best effort as he finished a whisker behind Gordon Lord Byron with some smart sorts in behind. While 7f seems to be his trip, don't be surprised if Richard Fahey steps him up to a mile at some point.

Richard Fahey, Malton

GEOFFREY CHAUCER 3 b c
Montjeu – Helsinki (Machiavellian)
11-

This unbeaten colt could have much to offer this year having had a relatively low-key two-year-old season. There was nothing exceptional in his first win when he beat two others narrowly at Leopardstown, but there was much to like about his Beresford Stakes victory in September. That race has gone to some top-class horses including Sea The Stars and the runner-up went on to win a big sales race at Newmarket with the third filling the same spot in the Racing Post Trophy. This half-brother to Shamardal should get at least 1m2f.

Aidan O'Brien, Tipperary

INDIAN MAHARAJA 3 b c
Galileo – Again (Danehill Dancer)
11-

Unbeaten in two runs, the first of which was a six-runner mile maiden at Gowran which he won by six and a half lengths despite running green. He was then dropped to 7f for a Listed race at Tipperary when the margin of victory was three lengths. He must have been doing something special at home because he was sent off 4-5 for his debut and just 3-10 next time. By Galileo and a first foal of Again, who won the Irish 1,000 Guineas, he is bred in the purple. And although he hasn't beaten much, he could turn out to be Group class.

Aidan O'Brien, Tipperary

KINGSBARNS 4 b c
Galileo – Beltisaal (Belmez)
63-

Kingsbarns has something in common with his erstwhile stablemate St Nicholas Abbey in that they were both emphatic winners of the Racing Post Trophy but did hardly anything the following season. This colt disappointed beyond measure when coming home over a distance behind The Fugue on his first outing but ran with some merit when four lengths behind Olympic Glory in the Queen Elizabeth II Stakes with some smart sorts, including Dawn Approach, behind. A step up to 1m2f will see him at his best.

Aidan O'Brien, Tipperary

MAGICIAN 4 b c
Galileo – Absolutelyfabulous (Mozart)
1191-

It's great news that Magician stays in training because this Classic winner hasn't had enough opportunities to show the world how good he is. A four-length win in the Dee Stakes was followed by another clearcut success in the Irish 2,000 Guineas, even with such a dramatic drop in trip. He was sidelined by injury after a flop at Royal Ascot but reappeared in the Breeders' Cup Turf over 1m4f when just beating good yardstick The Fugue. All the top European 1m2f and 1m4f prizes will be considered for him and he might even return to the Breeders' Cup in November.

Aidan O'Brien, Tipperary

MARAKOUSH 3 b c
Danehill Dancer – Mouramara (Kahyasi)
2-

Made his debut on Irish Cesarewitch day at the Curragh in a mile maiden in which he was sent off 15-8 favourite. However, he couldn't quite get to Aidan O'Brien's Century, who is one of the top-notchers at Ballydoyle and was the yard's most fancied runner at 6-1 in the Racing Post Trophy next time. Marakoush looked a picture in the paddock (I am not making this up – I was there!) and should be decent this season over middle distances. Bred by the Aga Khan, he is a half-brother to Mourilyan and Mourayan.

John Oxx, Currabeg

MISS FRANCE 3 b f
Dansili – Miss Tahiti (Tirol)
911-

Having beaten subsequent Prix Marcel Boussac winner Indonesienne, this French raider followed up with a narrow win in the Oh So Sharp Stakes, a Group 3 at Newmarket over 7f, holding Lightning Thunder by a head. That didn't tell the whole story, though, because Mickael Barzalona didn't touch her with his stick as the pair made up plenty of ground from the rear and there were five lengths back to the third. Miss France is a powerful, strapping filly and, if Andre Fabre brings her back to the Rowley Mile for the 1,000 Guineas, you should take note.

Andre Fabre, Chantilly

MY TITANIA 3 b f
Sea The Stars – Fairy Of The Night (Danehill)
211-

John Oxx won the CL Weld Park Stakes five times in the 1990s, including with Breeders' Cup heroine Ridgewood Pearl, and his filly My Titania lifted this Group 3 at the Curragh in taking style, doing just enough at the end of 7f to hold off Chicago Girl by half a length. She showed a turn of foot in the last two furlongs, the sort that will be needed if she is to contest Classics. Oxx has entered her in the 1,000 Guineas and the Oaks, as well as their Irish counterparts, and she runs in the same colours as her sire Sea The Stars.

John Oxx, Currabeg

PALE MIMOSA 5 b m
Singspiel – Katch Me Katie (Danehill)
174-

Lightly-raced, with just seven races under her belt, Pale Mimosa has plenty more to offer and could make an impact in the staying division. The winner of York's Galtres Stakes in 2012, she began last season by winning a Listed race at Leopardstown in June. Well beaten next time by former stablemate Voleuse De Coeurs in the Irish St Leger, she ran much better at Ascot when a close fourth to Royal Diamond in the 2m Long Distance Cup. Coming from so far behind didn't help her cause and neither did the soft ground. She must be considered for the Ascot Gold Cup.

Dermot Weld, The Curragh

PIT STOP 3 b c
Iffraaj - Journey's End (In The Wings)
1-

Sheikh Mohammed's colt won his only start at two in the sort of unfussy manner which suggested that he had something up his sleeve. The win came at Dundalk in October over 7f and the form was quickly franked when the runner-up, Magnolia Beach, won a maiden at the same venue on his next start. Michael Halford reports that this big horse has done well over the winter and, when asked about his preferred conditions, he said: "He would like good ground and a mile will be a good trip for him." Enough said.

Michael Halford, Kildare

REMOTE 4 b c
Dansili – Zenda (Zamindar)
3111-

John Gosden's horses don't often go off at 25-1 but with William Buick on a stable-mate in the same 1m2f Newbury maiden, Remote was overlooked in the market. Khalid Abdullah's colt made a nonsense of those odds, hacking up by three lengths on the good to firm ground. He then landed a Doncaster handicap by six lengths before rounding off his season with a Royal Ascot victory in the Group 3 Tercentenary Stakes. Gosden is looking towards those juicy end-of-season prizes with this son of Dansili and won't start him off until early summer.

John Gosden, Newmarket

SAILORS SWAN 3 b c
Henrythenavigator – Society Hostess (Seeking The Gold)
4-

There was a strong 14-runner 7f maiden at the Curragh in October won by John Oxx's Ebanoran from Aidan O'Brien's Tiger Rock, both of whom are quoted for the 2,000 Guineas. But perhaps the one to take out of it was the fourth, Sailors Swan. Catching the eye in the paddock, he didn't get off to a great start and raced along at the back of the field before making inroads in the straight. Being by sire of the moment Henrythenavigator and out of a speedy mare, the colt won't want much further than a mile. Rely on Dermot Weld to place him to advantage.

Dermot Weld, The Curragh

SEUSSICAL 4 b/br c
Galileo – Danehill Music (Danehill Dancer)
1131-

At the end of last season Luca Cumani picked up Seussical from David Wachman's Irish yard and the Galileo colt seemed to appreciate the change of scenery because he scorched home to land a 1m2f handicap at York by four lengths off a mark of 103 with some good sorts, including Area Fifty One, First Mohican and Excellent Result, in behind. His owners are Australian and, with his trainer so desperate to finally win the Melbourne Cup, it doesn't take much to work out what his end-of-season target will be.

Luca Cumani, Newmarket

SHORT SQUEEZE 4 b g
Cape Cross – Sunsetter (Diesis)
52531115-

In the second half of last season Short Squeeze started to make rapid progress up the ratings. A Sandown win off 75 was followed by a York win off 82 and a Haydock victory off 94. The aggregate winning distance was just short of 12 lengths. After that the 1m1f Group 3 Darley Stakes proved beyond him, but that's not to say he won't be profitable to follow this season. Hugo Palmer may start him in the Doncaster Mile or the bet365 Mile at Sandown and the trainer already has an ambitious autumn campaign mapped out with races such as the Cox Plate on the radar.

Hugo Palmer, Newmarket

SNOW SKY 3 b c
Nayef – Winter Silence (Dansili)
3418-

Snow Sky's season was all about gradual improvement until he was beaten 12 lengths by Kingston Hill in the Racing Post Trophy. On his debut he came third to Almuheet and Red Galileo (subsequently a neck second in the Haynes, Hanson & Clark) and he won his third race by 11 lengths. It was on heavy ground, but you still don't often see a horse win by that margin, especially when there are 13 runners in the field, and the time was 1.53 seconds faster than the first race on the card over the same trip. He will be interesting over middle distances with soft ground a bonus.

Sir Michael Stoute, Newmarket

TALENT 4 ch f
New Approach – Prowess (Peintre Celebre)
11723-

It's great that we have last year's Oaks and Derby winners still in training and Talent has what it takes to enhance her reputation in 2014. There was no fluke about the way she came home in isolation in her Classic, three and three-quarter lengths in front of her stablemate Secret Gesture. She went close in the St Leger, finishing just over a length behind Leading Light. Her early-season target is the Coronation Cup and, with a bit of improvement, she can serve it up to the colts, perhaps even clashing with Ruler Of The World. A bit of ease in the ground would help.

Ralph Beckett, Andover

TELESCOPE 4 b c
Galileo – Velouette (Darshaan)
121-

Telescope ended last season with a Group 2 win, but that haul wasn't quite what had been expected initially when he was being talked about as if he was the second coming and was as low as 12-1 for the Derby. Training problems kept him off the track until July when he won a 1m2f conditions event at Leicester by 24 lengths. Then followed a second in the Rose of Lancaster Stakes followed by that win in the Great Voltigeur over 1m4f. His regular rider Kevin Bradshaw says that he is much stronger now and he is an exciting prospect for top-class middle-distance races.

Sir Michael Stoute, Newmarket

TIGER CLIFF 5 b g
Tiger Hill - Verbania (In The Wings)
1218-

Tiger Cliff was with Lady Cecil last season and won Europe's richest handicap, the Ebor, over 1m6f at York in August. He had earlier put in another great effort when second to Well Sharp in the 2m2f Ascot Stakes in June having been given plenty to do, though he failed to get home under a more prominent ride in the Cesarewitch. Henry Ponsonby sent him to Alan King at the end of the Flat season, the idea being for him to go hurdling. But connections decided to give him one more year on the Flat and he could well pick up another long-distance handicap.

Alan King, Wroughton

TREE OF GRACE 3 ch c
Gold Away – Three Times (Domynsky)
1-

Frankie Dettori will be relishing the chance to get on board the Sheikh Joann Bin Hamad Al Thani-owned colt Tree Of Grace, who won his only start at two. This took place on the all-weather at Lingfield in October in a 7f maiden and the newcomer overcame experienced opposition to score quite cosily by half a length. Richard Hannon Snr was well known for giving his two-year-olds plenty to do but he clearly didn't ask too much of this one with a view to the future, making Tree Of Grace one to follow.

Richard Hannon, East Everleigh

WRANGLER 3 b c
High Chaparral – Tipsy Me (Selkirk)
3-

Wrangler made his debut at the backend of last season in a Yarmouth maiden over a mile and it was an experience this colt will benefit from under the excellent tutorship of Kieren Fallon. The pair were beaten two and a quarter lengths in third behind Marco Botti's promising Mannaro. This year Wrangler will be a more developed sort, one who could work his way up the ratings as he goes up in distance. He has stamina on both sides of the family tree, with his dam's family tracing back to Time Charter.

William Haggas, Newmarket

ZARIB 3 b c
Azamour – Zariziyna (Dalakhani)
831-

Michael Halford took a patient approach with Zarib at two and the end result was worth waiting for. Having shown progress in his two previous maidens, the Aga Khan's colt got off the mark at the third attempt as he beat Ger Lyons' Vector Force by a length over a mile at Dundalk. The form was boosted when the runner-up won his maiden a month later and the pair pulled nicely clear. Halford reports that Zarib has strengthened into his large frame and will be suited by distances of 1m2f to 1m4f on good ground.

Michael Halford, Kildare

Top ten horses

Baarez	Magician
Flintshire	Miss France
Flying Jib	Pale Mimosa
Garswood	Remote
Geoffrey Chaucer	Seussical

Est. 1909

RACING & FOOTBALL OUTLOOK

Pedigrees for punters by Katherine Fidler

R ARELY are pedigrees so important to punters than in juvenile races when a new crop of two-year-olds begin to test out their wares on the turf for the first time. Their chances rely on a whole host of factors that cannot be found in the form book, so the more information the better.

However, when it comes to those by first-season sires, the punter's armoury is without even the past performances of each runner's paternal siblings to act as a guide. Are they likely to be precocious? Will they begin to shine when the trips go up? Or will they find a stiff five furlongs to be their forte throughout the season?

This will only be fully answered by each performance itself, but there are indicators elsewhere to be found that help in the search for winners – and those who will provide them.

Below are profiles of six of the most high-profile first-crop sires this year plus a brief round-up of others who will be having their first runners.

Alfred Nobel
Danehill Dancer – Glinting Desert (Desert Prince)

A tough and precocious juvenile, Alfred Nobel made eight starts between the April and November of his two-year-old campaign, the highlight of which was victory in the Group 1 Phoenix Stakes, before two outings at three added a Group 3 place to his tally.

It is not just his precocity on the track that makes for compelling support as to his potential. Alfred Nobel is by Danehill Dancer, not only a champion sire and reliable source of top-class two-year-olds but also the sire of Mastercraftsman, the reigning champion first-crop sire who was highlighted here last year as one to watch.

In addition, Alfred Nobel hails from the illustrious family of New Approach, the champion second-crop sire and first-crop champion before that.

With just shy of 60 juveniles on the ground this year, he isn't represented by the largest crop, but all the right ingredients are there to help the Coolmore resident rack up some winners.

Equiano
Acclamation – Entente Cordiale (Ela-Mana-Mou)

Sons of Acclamation have built a solid reputation as fast and early two-year-olds, a trend to which Equiano followed.

Originally trained in Spain by Mauricio Delcher Sanchez, Equiano finished second on his debut over four furlongs in the May of his juvenile campaign, although did display enough stamina to come third over a mile that October.

However, a return to sprint trips was clearly the way forward after he won the King's Stand at three, reclaiming that crown at five after a move to Barry Hills.

Colts by Acclamation have also proved a popular commodity at stud, Equiano's paternal siblings Harbour Watch and Lilbourne Lad joining the stallion ranks in recent years while Dark Angel enjoyed a breakthrough year in 2013 courtesy of his Group 1-winning sprinter Lethal Force.

Equiano, like Alfred Nobel, is a member of the shuttle stallion ranks, covering in Australia during the southern hemisphere season. His yearlings fetched six-figure sums in both hemispheres, and with around 90 juveniles on the ground in Britain and Ireland, there should be plenty of opportunities to see if he lives up to expectations.

Lope De Vega
Shamardal – Lady Vettori (Vettori)

A runner who didn't make his debut until the August of a three-race juvenile campaign may not appear the obvious choice for a leading first-season sire, but while the offspring of this dual Classic winner will likely thrive at three and beyond, there is evidence to suggest they could be in the mix at two.

There are many comparisons to be made between Lope De Vega and his sire Shamardal, both of whom have given their stock a similar stamp, and while most of the latter's top-rated progeny excelled at three, they also have a strong strike-rate at two, spearheaded by Racing Post Trophy hero Casamento.

In addition, many shrewd judges parted with six-figure sums to secure a Lope De

EQUIANO: dual King's Stand winner by a sire known for fast juveniles

BIG EARNER: the €360,000 Makfi half-sister to Moonlight Cloud at Arqana

Vega yearling last year, the most expensive of whom sold for 400,000gns at Book 1 of the Tattersalls October Yearling Sale, and a number already have entries for this year's sales races, including a half-sister to unbeaten juvenile and champion colt Toronado.

Makfi
Dubawi – Dhelaal (Green Desert)

If there was one yearling everyone wanted to get their hands on last year, it was a Makfi yearling. Of the 46 offered, 39 sold for an average of 61,565gns and a high of 300,000gns – more than justifying his £25,000 2011 covering fee. Most keen to snap up a Makfi yearling was Rabbah Bloodstock, who bought every lot by the sire during one session in Book 2 of the

Tattersalls October Yearling Sale.

Interestingly, though, Makfi made only one start at two – in November. Yet he won that race with ease before going on to Classic glory and taking the notable scalp of Goldikova in the Jacques le Marois, and nestled in his pedigree can not only be found Arc winner Solemia and Derby hero Authorized but also Dewhurst winner and sire Alhaarth, a half-sister to Dhelaal, the dam of Makfi.

But by far the biggest advert for Makfi is his sire, Dubawi. Makfi belonged to the first crop of Darley's flagship stallion, who is one of the hottest stallions on the planet with a fee raised this year to £100,000. His yearlings commanded hundreds of thousands at the sales last year, as did those by Makfi, whose first crop includes a half-sister to Moonlight Cloud bought for €360,000 at Arqana and a close relation to

41

his paternal sibling Poet's Voice.

Rip Van Winkle
Galileo – Looking Back (Stravinsky)

It is hard to imagine now, but in his first two-year-old crop Galileo sired just one black-type winner, the Listed scorer Innocent Air. That was soon rectified when they turned three, as shown by Irish 1,000 Guineas heroine Nightime.

These days the five-time champion sire has a plethora of top-flight scorers at all ages, while his young stallion sons have also proved themselves more than capable of producing talented offspring – highlighted by New Approach and Teofilo, both of whom sired Group 1 winners in their first crop.

Granted, the pair themselves were perhaps better at two than Rip Van Winkle, but his seventh-place finish in the Dewhurst belies the fact he was just two lengths adrift of Intense Focus, while he belongs to arguably one of the best three-year-old crops of recent years, that of Sea The Stars and Mastercraftsman, both of whom sired black-type winners in their first crops last year.

In addition, Rip Van Winkle is represented by one of the largest crops this year, a generation who as yearlings sparked many fierce bidding wars between the top players, selling for a high of 400,000gns and attracting interest not only from their sire's own patron, Coolmore, but also Peter and Ross Doyle, David Redvers and Charlie Gordon-Watson among others.

Zebedee
Invincible Spirit – Cozy Maria (Cozzene)

Those in search of speed can do far worse than look to Irish National Stud resident Invincible Spirit, who, as well as being a versatile influence, boasts the likes of Fleeting Spirit, Mayson and Moonlight Cloud among his offspring.

His son Zebedee epitomised the ultimate two-year-old – finely-built, precocious and lightning-fast, winning all but

one of his seven outings including the Flying Childers at Doncaster's St Leger meeting. But as his trainer Richard Hannon said, Zebedee was on the small side, and taking on three-year-olds may have been a tough ask.

We'll never know how he would have fared, given he retired to Tally-Ho Stud after the Flying Childers, but what we do know is that with 116 two-year-olds on the ground – of whom 36 had already been named by January – his yearlings fetching up to 220,000gns and the most early entries out of our picks, Zebedee has the right profile in every sense to provide plenty of juvenile winners.

This year's first-crop sires retired to stud in 2011, and the intake that year was one high in both numbers and quality.

Fast Company, another by Danehill Dancer, made quite an impact from just three starts at two before retiring to stud, winning twice and finishing half a length adrift of New Approach in the Dewhurst.

Approve was one of the toughest juveniles seen in 2010, winning or placing in seven of his ten starts between May and November. His sire Oasis Dream has no shortage of top-flight juveniles, while paternal sibling Aqlaam enjoyed a promising first season with his runners last year before his untimely death in October.

Another son of Oasis Dream, Prix Morny winner **Arcano**, should not be omitted from the list of top juveniles and enters the first-crop battle this year with a similar number of runners with whom to do battle as Approve – 92 to 82. Progeny by both were in demand at the sales last year, 64 of the 69 yearlings by Approve selling, while an Arcano colt, named Musharrif, was knocked down to Shadwell for 300,000gns at Tattersalls.

Showcasing, an Oasis Dream half-brother to Camacho – the sire of last year's Flying Childers winner Green Door – is another who could make his mark, and while youngsters by dual-hemisphere hero **Starspangledbanner** are few and far between owing to fertility problems, those who made the sales were well-received.

KINGSTON HILL: spreadegles his opponents in the Racing Post Trophy

Newmarket by Aborigine

ROGER VARIAN is one of Newmarket's young lions and his Racing Post Trophy hero **Kingston Hill** has an outstanding chance of giving him his first home Classic winner in the Qipco 2,000 Guineas.

Varian learned his trade under the late Michael Jarvis and he has adopted his mentor's relaxed and patient approach to training. This was evident with Kingston Hill, who was allowed plenty of time to develop, not making his winning debut until late September at Newbury before winning the Autumn Stakes next time.

The Mastercraftsman colt then underlined his potential by striding home four and a half lengths clear of Johann Strauss in the Racing Post Trophy.

The good news for his many ante-post supporters is that he looks a picture out on the heath and the plan is to go straight for the Guineas on the first Saturday in May.

Ambivalent stays in training as a five-year-old and there's no doubt she'll add to her laurels, which included Varian's first ever Group 1 success in the Pretty Polly. Varian intends to use the Middleton Stakes at York's Dante meeting, in which she was second last year, as a launching pad for another highly profitable season.

JOHN GOSDEN did not reach the dizzy heights of his 2012 trainers' championship win last year but his smart mare **The Fugue** kept this master trainer in the limelight. The good news is that she will carry on as a five-year-old.

The daughter of Dansili hit form in midsummer, cruising home by four lengths from Venus De Milo in the Yorkshire Oaks.

She showed her versatility when dropping to a mile and a quarter in the Irish Champion Stakes and accounting for Al

Kazeem. Back up to a mile and a half for the Breeders' Cup Turf at Santa Anita, she hit the front a furlong from home only to be run out of victory in the closing stages by Magician.

It was heartbreaking for William Buick and her connections, but The Fugue still has plenty in the locker before she is retired to stud.

On the Classic front Gosden is best known as the trainer of St Leger winners but in **Kingman** he has a genuine challenger for the 2,000 Guineas.

Kingman went into a lot of shrewd judges' Classic notebooks when making it two from two in the Solario Stakes at Kempton.

This son of Invincible Spirit needed a minor operation for a chip of bone in the autumn but Gosden refuted reports that all was not well with him in January. He'll be trained for the 2,000 Guineas, though I reckon his pedigree leaves some doubt about him getting the Derby trip.

LUCA CUMANI has won the Derby with Kahyasi (1988) and High-Rise (1998), and while he does not appear to have anything in that category this year he has his usual well balanced team at the Bedford House Stables.

The canny Italian is well known for his ability to get a horse well handicapped and then go onwards and upwards. This could be the case with **Ajman Bridge**.

This lightly-raced Dubawi four-year-old has won two of his four starts and, as he was beaten on his final run at Doncaster, he goes into the season off a handy rating.

Among his three-year-olds, Cumani is very enthusiastic about **Lawyer**, who improved steadily through last year. He rounded his campaign off with nursery wins at Wolverhampton and, as he has wintered a treat, he should keep up the good work.

THE FUGUE: has been a fantastic success for the John Gosden team

DANK: won at the Breeders' Cup last season and will be going for a repeat

A maiden winner at Yarmouth in September, **Mount Logan** had his sights raised in the Group 3 Autumn Stakes here on the Rowley Mile but had to settle for seventh behind Kingston Hill. Everything about him suggests that he will come into his own over longer trips.

Adding strength to the Cumani colts in this age group is **Roseburg**, who indicated that we'll be hearing more about him with his fast-finishing three-quarters-of-a-length second to Evening Attire at Doncaster.

SIR MICHAEL STOUTE boasts one of the strongest teams of older horses in the town, headed by the inveterate traveller **Dank**, who won four of her five starts last year.

A winner at Arlington Park and the Curragh, she finished on a high with a smooth win from Romantica in the Breeders' Cup Filly & Mare Turf at Santa Anita. A similar campaign beckons this season.

Among the four-year-old colts at Freemason Lodge the injury-prone **Hillstar** and **Telescope** have the ability to hit the bullseye at the highest level if they can be kept sound.

WILLIAM HAGGAS enjoyed a tremendous 2013 and, with both his main yard at Somerville Lodge and his overspill Flint Cottage Stables full, he will again hit the headlines.

His lightly-raced four-year-old **Muthmir**'s work suggests he is well ahead of the handicapper, while stablemate **Seagull Star** will make his presence felt in top three-year-old company and **Satellite**, who joined the yard from Warren Place, has been showing plenty of promise.

ED DUNLOP's globe-trotting dual Melbourne Cup runner-up **Red Cadeaux** will reappear in the Dubai World Cup, in which he was runner-up to Animal Kingdom last spring. More success awaits this genuine, evergreen eight-year-old.

Amazing Maria is the most exciting prospect in Dunlop's La Grange team. After two promising runs she won twice at Goodwood, signing off with an emphatic win in the Group 3 Prestige Stakes.

Everything she has been doing indicates that we will be hearing a great deal more about her, with the Qipco 1,000 Guineas her initial target.

The *GEORGE MARGARSON*-trained **Lucky Kristale** could be her most serious opponent having been beaten only once in five starts.

The way she stormed from last to first

under a supremely confident ride from Tom Queally in the Lowther Stakes at York marked her as a future star and it would be great to see one of racing's lesser lights hit the heights.

At a lower level the affable Margarson will be targeting the valuable Ascot handicaps through the season with **Excellent Guest** and don't rule out big things from **Rebellious Guest**, whose smart home form hasn't yet been reproduced in public.

LADY CECIL faces a daunting task on her own this year, but she saddled plenty of winners in the autumn and the lightly-raced **Retirement Plan** is clearly a likely money-spinner for her.

Unraced as a juvenile, he scored on his debut in a Doncaster maiden before beating the smart Goodwood Mirage by three lengths at Goodwood in August.

Though the Monsun colt didn't run after that, he is a fine, strong individual and figures on a good handicap mark.

The Niarchos family have also persevered with the Dansili filly **Sea Meets Sky**. Unraced as a juvenile, she was an Ascot maiden winner in the spring before being sidelined through injury. All is now well and judged on her gallops she has thrived between the ages of three and four. There is more to come from her.

TRADE STORM: a serious weapon

WILLIAM JARVIS learned his trade as assistant to Sir Henry at Warren Place and expects **Raskova** to add to her one previous success.

That was at Newbury, where Frankie Dettori brought her with a well-timed run to beat Fatima's Gift over a mile and a quarter.

It's over that distance or further that she should be supported, especially when she gets soft ground.

Jarvis also rates the prospects of the lightly-raced **Blurred Vision**. Though the Royal Applause colt has yet to win, he seems sure to find a suitable maiden early on having rounded his season off by finishing fourth to Mushir in a 6f Listed race at York. Everything he has been doing on the heath indicates that he will hold his own in good sprinting company.

JAMES EUSTACE expects **Spa's Dancer** to be his flag-bearer this season, starting off with a bid for the Lincoln, while the Royal Hunt Cup is also on the cards.

DAVID ELSWORTH trains at the historic Egerton Stables behind the July Course and believes his Middle Park fourth **Justice Day** will deliver the goods. He has also inherited **Zain Eagle** from the disqualified Gerard Butler and rates him a surefire winner.

HUGO PALMER expects **Short Squeeze** to contribute to his keep in Pattern races and *ED WALKER*, who rents a couple of yards at Warren Place, is hoping that **Indian Jack** will move through handicaps into Group races.

DAVID SIMCOCK has already struck with **Sheikhzayedroad** in Dubai and once he returns to Newmarket his devastating late burst could carry him to further triumphs. Stablemate **Trade Storm** is another serious weapon that Simcock will be firing off at the highest level.

Hot off the Heath
Kingston Hill
The Fugue
Trade Storm

Ireland
by Jerry M

A RUNAWAY win in the Irish championship, plus second place in Britain, with three Classic victories and a couple of Group 1-winning two-year-olds would have been an incredible season for most trainers, but *AIDAN O'BRIEN* must still have been left with a feeling of what might have been after last year.

Many of O'Brien's best horses were hit by injuries as he was deprived of the services of the ill-fated St Nicholas Abbey and triple Classic hero Camelot after June and top three-year-olds Magician and Kingsbarns missed much of the year.

However, the upshot is that O'Brien now has one of his strongest ever teams of older horses assembled, with **Magician** and **Kingsbarns** both given another chance to prove their brilliance.

Magician still had a superb year, winning the Irish 2,000 Guineas and the Breeders' Cup Turf, but there was also a five-month absence during the heart of the season following a bizarre incident when he was spooked by a sparrow that flew into the equine spa as he was nearing the end of a swimming session and banged a hind leg.

O'Brien admits that he shouldn't have rushed him back to run the following week in the St James's Palace Stakes when he finished well down the field, leading to his long period off the track.

However, it was a superb training feat to bring him back for the Breeders' Cup Turf, which he won with a devastating turn of foot to prove his versatility with Group 1

KINGSBARNS: *largely absent since this win in the 2012 Racing Post Trophy*

wins from a mile to a mile and a half.

He will clearly have all sorts of options this season and all ground seems to come alike, for while his Group 1 wins came on quick going he also won on heavy ground as a two-year-old and ran away with the Dee Stakes last May on good to soft.

Kingsbarns was an easy winner of the 2012 Racing Post Trophy as a two-year-old but missed last season's Classics as he developed a foot infection after tearing off a shoe during a routine exercise in the spring.

He ran no sort of race on his return in the Irish Champion Stakes but suggested all his old ability was still intact when third on desperate ground in the Queen Elizabeth II Stakes which played into the hands of more race-fit rivals.

That mile trip is probably the bare minimum for him these days so expect to see him step up to a mile and maybe even further at some point, though he has yet to prove himself on quicker ground.

The gamble of keeping a Derby winner in training didn't pay off with Camelot, but that hasn't put off "the lads" – as O'Brien calls his bosses at Coolmore – from persisting with last season's Epsom hero **Ruler Of The World**.

Unraced as a juvenile, Ruler Of The World was having only his third start when winning the Derby so he was always likely to carry on improving and he ran another terrific race when a close third in the Champion Stakes.

He got little credit for winning the Derby so still has a point to prove and may well surprise a few pundits in the top middle-distance races.

Coolmore rarely keep their fillies in training after their Classic campaign, but even after Was disappointed last year another exception has again been made for **Venus De Milo**, who only made her debut last June but progressed quickly to finish second in the Irish Oaks and Yorkshire Oaks.

Both those runs came on good to firm ground so she can be forgiven a poor run in the Prix Vermeille on soft and should be competitive in top races against her own sex over a mile and a half.

Every new season begins with a search

VENUS DE MILO: stays in training

for the next O'Brien superstar and **Australia** looks most likely to fit the bill after a six-length win in a Group 3 at Leopardstown last September that saw him propelled to the head of the Derby market.

By Galileo out of Ouija Board, both of whom won Epsom Classics, he should have a great shot at emulating them, especially as he was never the finished article last year, learning all the time. Whether or not he has the speed for the Guineas is another matter.

O'Brien's main contender for that race will probably prove to be **War Command**, who didn't really live up to expectations after running away with the Coventry Stakes by six lengths. He still got the job done in the Dewhurst, though, and is likely to prove much better on quicker ground.

Tapestry is prominent in the Guineas and Oaks betting and she could have a real chance in both races.

She needs a bit of time to hit top gear, which means the interference she suffered in the Moyglare was more costly and may well have lost her the race, but there will be no filly finishing better on the Rowley Mile. Her running style also suggests she will have no problems staying further.

JOHNNY MURTAGH: rode and trained Royal Diamond to his victory at Ascot

DERMOT WELD had several promising juveniles last season and should provide plenty of competition to the Ballydoyle team in the top domestic races.

Weld remains convinced that **Free Eagle**, one-time Derby favourite after an easy debut win, is much better than he showed when well beaten by Australia and he will probably get the chance to prove the point in the Derrinstown Stud Derby Trial.

It's harder to pinpoint the best of Weld's fillies, but **Balansiya** and **Tested** clearly have unlimited potential having won their only starts last season.

Balansiya won by seven lengths on soft ground at Leopardstown yet is expected to improve on better going by Weld, while

Tested was very green in winning at the Curragh and also has much more to offer.

JOHN OXX suffered his worst season for more than 20 years last season, but he may have a filly to put that right in **My Titania**.

Boasting a pedigree that suggests she could excel from a mile to a mile and a half, she was a smooth winner of a Group 3 at the Curragh and was doing very little in front according to her rider.

JIM BOLGER made a huge success of training Dawn Approach for Godolphin last season and he's been given another chance to train for Sheikh Mohammed's team following their purchase of **Trading Leather**.

He performed with huge credit in top middle-distance races all last year, highlighted by victory in the Irish Derby, and should again pay his way on quick ground.

However, Bolger lacked a high-class two-year-old last season, something that wasn't a problem for rising star *PAUL DEEGAN*, with **Avenue Gabriel** probably the best of his team.

She was only fifth in the Fillies' Mile but wouldn't have been suited by the slow pace given her future lies over a mile and a half.

WILLIE McCREERY is delighted to have been given another chance to win a Group 1 with **Fiesolana** even though she was sold for 960,000gns in the winter.

She disappointed when stepped up to that level in the Matron Stakes, but that's one of just two defeats in her last seven races as she stepped up from handicap company and ended up winning the Group 2 Challenge Stakes at Newmarket.

JOHNNY MURTAGH enjoyed an outstanding first season, crowned by victory for his veteran stayer **Royal Diamond** on Champions Day at Ascot, where **Belle De Crecy** also ran a fine race to finish second in the Fillies and Mares Stakes.

Murtagh's prospects for this season were boosted when Belle De Crecy failed to reach her minimum price at the sales, meaning she's back to push for victory in top middle-distance races restricted to her own sex, while Royal Diamond will continue to run well in good staying contests.

EDDIE LYNAM has few peers when it comes to training sprinters and he has several strings to his bow this year.

Stable star **Sole Power**, who won last year's King's Stand Stakes, will continue to be a threat at the top level and he will be joined in many of the top races by **Slade Power**, who showed his quality when winning the Champions Sprint at Ascot in October.

Lynam also trained the third that day, **Viztoria**, and she should benefit from sticking to that sort of trip having failed to stay a mile earlier in the campaign, although she did win the Park Stakes over 7f at Doncaster.

> # *Invincible Irish*
> ## Magician
> ## Australia
> ## Fiesolana

FIESOLANA: fetched 960,000gns following this win at Newmarket

Berkshire
by Downsman

L AST year proved a vintage one for our region, led by Al Kazeem, Lethal Force and Chriselliam, and the arguments over who achieved the most kept the pump-smiths at that legendary Lambourn hostelry and debating chamber. the Wheelright Arms, busy for the entire winter.

It is sad to think that not one of these top-class horses will be running this season. Al Kazeem and Lethal Force have retired to stud, and the death of Chriselliam from a leg infection during the winter was a hammer blow to *CHARLIE HILLS* and his staff.

Nonetheless, hopes remain high that one of a clutch of other high-class juvenile fillies from Hills's school of 2013 can fill the void left by Chriselliam and strike lucky in the 1,000 Guineas at Newmarket in May.

Favourite to make the line-up is **Kiyoshi**, who produced one of the most impressive performances at Royal Ascot to land the Albany Stakes despite losing valuable ground in the closing stages by hanging right across the course.

Although beaten on her two attempts at Group 1 level, she produced solid efforts and there were valid excuses for her on both occasions. She has wintered very well, and it will be interesting to see just how she fares.

Queen Catrine came mighty close to the highest level, finishing second in the Lowther Stakes among other fine performances. She has pleased connections with her progress and should be up to winning at Pattern level.

So too could **Qawaseem** when she tackles longer distances.

Cambridge was a less exposed two-year-old last year. A half-sister to the smart Dux Scholar, she won her only start at rewarding odds and there seems no reason why she cannot attain black type.

Love Excel and **Passing Star** are two

KIYOSHI (left): carries the hopes of Charlie Hills' team after Chriselliam's death

more fillies tipped for good things. Both were in action on the all-weather during the winter.

The colts did not achieve anything like as much as their female counterparts in 2013, but some of the better ones had their issues, including **Tanzeel** and **Greeb**.

Although both managed to win races during their first season, they had their campaigns shortened by breathing afflictions. They have been operated on and, at the time of writing, the signs of a successful outcome are encouraging.

Nathr was out of action even longer having not run after two placed efforts in May. He has been striding out well on the Faringdon Road all-weather and looks sure to make his mark at around a mile.

Best of the lot could be **Marmoom**, who looked a lovely sort on his debut at Newbury and ran a lot better behind Barley Mow than his final position, seven lengths behind the winner, suggests. He was in need of the race that day and connections then decided the one run was enough. He looks sure to do much better in his second season and is definitely one to note.

Amuhalab proved costly to follow on his only start at Newmarket but should do better in due course.

Mention should also be made of the unraced **Computer** – by Mizzen Mast out of a Seeking The Gold mare – who was weak last season but has flourished during the winter, and **Excellent Royale**, an impressive winner on the all-weather.

Just The Judge, the winner of the Irish 1,000 Guineas, takes pride of place among the older horses and she is back to try to double her Group 1 tally. A mile and a quarter could be her trip, even though she was beaten on her only run over the distance in the Nassau at Goodwood.

Englishman is also very talented but has been equally hard to train. Knee problems have troubled him since his debut win at Newbury in April 2012, but he is back in training and moving very well at the time of writing. Glenard is relatively lightly raced and should do well over longer distances in heritage handicaps.

ROGER CHARLTON enjoyed a record-

SECONDO: promising sprinter

breaking season for prize-money thanks largely to the exploits of Al Kazeem, but **Thistle Bird** also played her part and Charlton will be pleased that there has been a change of plan with Lady Rothschild's high-class mare for 2014.

She was due to be retired to stud at the end of last season, but there has been a change of mind and she will be back to spearhead another interesting team of older horses.

Thistle Bird will be again aimed at some of the top mares' races and her trainer is hoping that elusive first Group 1 success can come her way. She came close last season when beaten a neck in both the Nassau Stakes and the Prix de l'Opera, both over a mile and a quarter, which should again prover her optimum.

Given Charlton's great record with sprinters, it would be no surprise to see **Secondo** progress from last season. A winner of a maiden and a handicap last term, he looks capable of taking in some of the heritage handicaps and perhaps a Listed race as well.

53

PEARL SPECTRE (centre): well regarded by the Andrew Balding team

So Beloved hails from a very good family and he should be able to win a decent handicap off his mark. He looks open to improvement and was gelded during the winter.

Huntsmans Close was bought out of Michael Bell's yard in December and is an interesting new arrival, while Al Kazeem's half-brother **Kazak** is bred to do better with age and should do progress as a four-year-old.

Charlton has plenty of unexposed talent among the three-year-olds and one of the most talked-about is **Continental Drift**.

A daughter of Smart Strike, her dam Intercontinental won 14 races and there was much to like about her debut win at Kempton. More victories should follow this term.

Hiking is from one of Khaled Abdullah's very best families, being a half-sister to both Bated Breath and Cityscape. She won on her first two outings and was then unlucky, and she has scope.

Amber Isle is yet another blue blood from the Abdullah Juddmonte operation. A full sister to Charlton's high-class Dundonnell, she ran just once as a juvenile and returned injured after finishing fourth in a maiden at Newbury. Hopefully she will be back.

The more stoutly-bred **Magic Shoes** made just one appearance and will do well when stepped up in trip.

Fray and **Lady Tyne** managed to win as two-year-olds at Newmarket and Newbury respectively and should be able to win again.

There is a clutch of well-bred unraced fillies for the new season. **Catadupa** is closely related to classy Cubanita, **Sleep Walk** is another who hails from the family of Bated Breath and Cityscape, and **Scarlet Run** is a good-looking daughter of Pivotal out of the Nell Gwyn winner Scarlet Belle.

There were no real headline-makers among the juvenile colts last season, but there is plenty to look forward to, chiefly **Sea Defence**.

A son of Mizzen Mast, he was strongly fancied to win a maiden at Newmarket towards the end of the season and delivered in most authoritative style. Charlton rates him an exciting prospect.

Observational and **Laugharne** showed plenty of of promise in light first campaigns. Laugharne flopped in a Group 1 at Saint-Cloud on his final start, but the ground was very soft that day.

The tough conditions also went against **Dark Leopard** on his second and final start, but he still ran very well and is definitely one to note.

Hooded, a son of Empire Maker out of

the high-class stayer Yashmak, should do well when tried over longer distances, while **Stomp**, a half-brother to Charlton's smart sprinter Mince, should progress and **Old Guard**, a half-brother to Thistle Bird by Notnowcato, is a good-looking sort.

ANDREW BALDING had no superstar with whom to do battle in 2013, but he still produced a personal best and pierced the £1m mark in prize-money.His team were in cracking form in the closing weeks of the season, not only on the equine front, but also with his happy band of apprentice jockeys!

Highland Colori was the most prolific money-earner, and among others from the older generations to do well were **Dungannon**, **Chiberta King** and my favourite **Mysterious Man**.

If there was something missing, it was a large contributions from the two-year-olds, but there are a number who might put that right at three in 2014.

Scotland takes pride of place among the colts. By Monsun, he possesses plenty of stamina and is a nicely-balanced colt. Having shown promise on his debut, he won very cosily on his next start at Epsom and the second did not let the form down when third in a Group 3 on his next start. He could make his presence felt in a Classic trial, especially on soft ground.

Pearl Spectre has always been well regarded by the Balding team and he won two of his three starts. He still looked immature when winning at Lingfield but still got the job done and should progress. The Britannia at Royal Ascot could be a possible target.

Highland Acclaim, who left the money behind at Nottingham on his final start, has plenty of ability and looks another capable of working his way up the handicap in inimitable Balding style, while **End Of Line** won his only start at Doncaster and proved his ability to handle the mud.

The same applies to fillies **Field Of Fame** and **Wylye**, who are unbeaten after winning at Salisbury and Newbury respectively.

Casual Smile surprisingly did not manage a win, but she showed more than enough to suggest she should do well in her second season. By the great Sea The Stars out of the Balding-trained Oaks winner Casual Look, she just needs any win to boost her paddock value but is capable of more.

From one relatively young shaver to one of our more old and crusty sorts and one of the highlights of the Valley's year, the performances of **Berkshire** for *PAUL COLE*.

It is some time since Cole has had a top Classic contender, but the imposing Berkshire looked the part in winning the Chesham Stakes and may just have been a gallop short when following up in the Royal Lodge on his return from a long summer break. The decision to go quietly with him after the royal meeting should pay dividends this season.

Cole's **Complicit** also deserves a mention as he gears up for an outing at the new All-Weather Championships at Lingfield on Good Friday.

Complicit broke the course record at the Surrey course in booking his place at the big meeting and then followed up at Deauville. He was really wayward during his turf campaign, but the Whatcombe team have done a fine job with him.

CLIVE COX enjoyed another magnificent season in 2013, which was richly deserved for a brilliant trainer and his equally fine team. Although he has lost his champion sprinter Lethal Force and his brilliant 2012 two-year-old Reckless Abandon, he has one or two up-and-coming youngsters, most notably **Shankly**.

The Monsun colt justified plenty of stable confidence on his debut in a good conditions event at Salisbury and the ground was desperate when he failed to fire in a Group 1 at Saint-Cloud in November. He will be bigger and better this season and will be best over middle distances.

Berkshire's best

Marmoom

Continental Drift

Shankly

The North
by Borderer

NORTHERN racing is as healthy as it's been for years and the region has plenty of horses capable of mixing it with the big southern yards this summer.

Chief among them is **Top Notch Tonto** from the *BRIAN ELLISON* yard. He was one of the stories of 2013 and has earned a place in the season's top mile contests.

The four-year-old was officially rated 87 when having his first run for Ellison at Newmarket in July, but he made phenomenal progress and justified a £70,000 supplementary entry fee by grabbing second in the Queen Elizabeth II Stakes on Champions Day. He ideally needs soft ground and there is a Group 1 in him when conditions are suitable.

KEVIN RYAN had a day to remember at Newmarket in October when he landed a famous one-two with **Astaire** and **Hot Streak** in the Middle Park Stakes, in which Hot Streak battled gamely against his stablemate but couldn't quite get past the front-runner and had to settle for second.

Whether either of them can develop into Classic contenders remains to be seen as there are obvious stamina concerns, but both have the physique and natural talent to become very smart sprinters in a division that lacks an outstanding champion.

A profitable 2012 left **Trail Blaze** too high in the weights to strike last summer but he looked as good as ever on a couple of occasions, particularly at Ascot in September when he finished fourth in a valuable 7f handicap.

He starts the season only 3lb above his latest winning mark and would be particularly worth noting if heading to Haydock, a track he didn't visit last summer but one at which he was twice successful in 2012.

TOP NOTCH TONTO: capable of winning a Group 1 if he gets soft ground

PENIAPHOBIA (No 7): reels in Lilbourne Lass to land the Super Sprint

RICHARD FAHEY had one of his most lucrative seasons to date with nearly £2.5m in prize money, with **Peniaphobia** one of the biggest contributors.

The colt won three of four starts and his big payday came at Newbury in July when he won the Super Sprint. He travelled strongly and did just enough to catch Lilbourne Lass in the dying strides. That was a decent effort giving 8lb to a filly who won next time, and he can make his mark in Listed and Group sprints this summer.

Supplicant was another of Fahey's top juveniles, winning four times and ending his campaign with a midfield finish in the Middle Park Stakes. His half-brother Penient got better with age and he could easily do the same, especially when stepping up to 7f or 1m.

Brian Noble is much less exposed. Named after the coach of owner Marwan Koukash's Salford rugby league team, the young colt overcame signs of greenness to win on his debut at Haydock in September. He picked up well when the penny dropped and is one to follow when reappearing.

Of the older brigade, **Farlow** is worth noting. The gelding hasn't won since May 2012 but posted some decent efforts in defeat after joining Fahey in the early part of 2013 and showed he was down to a decent mark when fifth in the Ayr Bronze Cup. The gelding raced on the wrong side that day but came home clear of his pack.

He should find a sprint handicap or two this summer and could easily head back to Doonside as a leading contender for one of the Cups in the autumn.

Now that *MARK JOHNSTON* is so closely linked to Godolphin, it will always be hard for him to hang on to his really good ones and he lost Maputo and Statutory to the boys in blue over the winter, but the Middleham machine still produced 216 winners last season and made a flying start to the new year.

Somewhat is one who could be a Classic contender for Johnston. Soft ground was a valid excuse when the colt disappointed in the Racing Post Trophy but he had previously looked smart and was only narrowly beaten in two Group races at Newmarket. That shows he is fully effective at HQ and he could easily reward each-way support in the 2,000 Guineas.

Universal unfortunately suffered a bad injury that prematurely ended his career,

SOMEWHAT: left as the class act at Mark Johnston's yard

but he won a brace of Group 2 races last season after starting his campaign on the all-weather and **Hunting Ground** could be set to follow a similar path.

He came up short in turf handicaps last summer but was sent off an odds-on favourite when stepped up to 2m and had little trouble landing the odds. He has a beautiful pedigree and it wouldn't entirely surprise if he took part in some of the big staying races this season.

Glorious Goodwood is always a happy hunting ground for Johnston and, while it's hard to know exactly what he'll run on the Downs at this stage, anything he sends to the big summer meeting in August will be well worth considering.

Brown Panther is still bravely carrying the flag for *TOM DASCOMBE*, with a Goodwood Cup win the obvious highlight of his campaign in 2013.

He has fully recovered from some superficial injuries picked up in the Melbourne Cup and will bid for more success in the top domestic staying races. At six years old, he should be at the peak of his powers and would be a serious contender if connections target the Gold Cup, especially as one of his best ever performances came at the royal meeting back in 2011.

Crowley's Law looked a filly worth following when winning at Beverley in September. The daughter of Dubawi was sent off at odds-on after showing promise at Ascot on her previous start and her supporters didn't have a moment's concern as she travelled strongly and forged clear. A mark of 77 is very fair and she is probably capable of making an impression in Listed races further down the line.

Wall Of Sound is another unexposed filly to watch closely. She struck twice last summer and ended her campaign with a personal best at Haydock. A winter holiday should have done her good.

DAVID O'MEARA has quickly established himself among the elite northern trainers and he nearly doubled his previous best with over 130 winners last season. He will do well to beat that but has some nice types to go to war with.

Two For Two was bought from France and repaid his new connections with an early win at Ripon last April. He was unable to strike again, but he was beaten less than three lengths at York in October when suffering a troubled run and he has a decent prize in him over a mile.

TIM EASTERBY has a phenomenal record in the Redcar Two-year-old Trophy and **Ventura Mist** gave the Yorkshire trainer a fourth victory last October. She might not find things that easy in 2014, but her stablemate **See The Sun** also ran in that race and is more interesting.

He was last of the 23 runners that day but his other form was much better and he bounced back to finish runner-up to the in-form Musical Comedy at Haydock next time. His best runs came on quickish ground and he could be the sort to run well in the valuable 6f handicap at York won by his trainer with Body And Soul last June.

DAVID BARRON doesn't have many winning newcomers so **Indy**'s victory at Doncaster in November was particularly impressive. The young colt hadn't been with Barron for long but that didn't stop him producing a good performance to see off odds-on favourite Penny Drops by four lengths with the rest a long way back. There should be plenty more to come this summer.

ANN DUFFIELD was perhaps a bit optimistic with some of the assignments she set **Willie The Whipper** last season, but he wasn't disgraced in the French Derby and only just lost out in a Listed race at Ayr in September. Duffield should have little trouble finding a race for him if sights are lowered to a more realistic level.

ALAN SWINBANK is not afraid of introducing smart horses in bumpers before sending them on to the Flat. On that basis **Molly Cat**, who is certainly bred to be useful on the level and was very impressive when winning at Wetherby in January, could well bolster his summer team.

North of the border *KEITH DALGLEISH* took another step forward with 58 winners in just his second full season and there will be plenty more to come this year.

Neuf Des Couers should have little trouble getting on the scoresheet. She finished midfield in her first two maidens but improved when stepped up to 7f at Musselburgh in September, catching Porthos Du Vallon in the closing stages. The style of that victory suggests she will enjoy a bit further and a mark of 63 is a decent starting point for handicapping.

Hawkeyethenoo has been a great credit to *JIM GOLDIE* and he has unearthed another smart performer in the shape of **Jack Dexter**. Last season saw him establish his place in the top rank of sprinters, finishing second behind Slade Power on Champions Day at Ascot and ending his campaign with a game win at Doncaster in November. He deserves respect in all of the top contests this season.

Angels of the north
Brown Panther
Jack Dexter
Top Notch Tonto

JACK DEXTER: Scotland's best hope of bagging some top prizes this year

The West
by Hastings

RICHARD HANNON JNR, who took over the licence from his father at the start of the year, can get off to a dream start by plundering the 2,000 Guineas with awesome prospect **Toormore**.

Last May he revealed a glimpse of things to come when running on strongly to deny subsequent impressive winner Ertijaal, with the pair seven lengths clear of the also-rans, in a warm 6f maiden at Leicester.

With that positive experience in the locker, he raised his game in the Vintage Stakes at Glorious Goodwood when showing a good attitude to get the better of Outstrip, who franked the form by winning the Champagne Stakes at Doncaster and Breeders' Cup Juvenile Turf at Santa Anita. Toormore displayed an electric turn of foot to claim the lead close home that day and then proved his tactical versatility by making all in the Group 1 National Stakes at the Curragh.

With an International Classification rating of 122, he ended a flawless campaign as the top-rated European juvenile, an accolade that eluded even the yard's former superstar Canford Cliffs.

Toormore is just the type to continue progressing with age, and if a prep race is needed to complete his Classic preparations, it will likely be the Greenham at Newbury where he avoids a penalty.

Bunker also has the makings of a Classic contender. In May he made a good first impression when finishing strongly to land a Haydock maiden with daylight to spare.

His stamina and class then came to the fore when he chased home Berkshire in the Chesham at Royal Ascot before he edged out subsequent Group 1 winner Karakontie in a 7f Listed event at Deauville in August on his last start.

He could well emerge as a serious Ep-

TOORMORE: definite Guineas player

som Derby player if making a successful return in something like the Dante at York in May.

Big things are expected of **Anjaal**, who stepped up on a much-needed Newmarket debut eighth to win next time out over an inadequate 5f at Beverley.

The 105,000gns yearling then made a seamless transition into Group 2 company when denying Figure Of Speech in the 6 July Stakes at Newmarket.

He's bred to stay and that was evident in the Dewhurst at Newmarket on his latest start when a good fourth behind War Command. He's definitely worth another crack at the highest level once upped to a mile and beyond during his second season for Sheikh Hamdan Al Maktoum.

Hannon's **Washaar** is expected to pick up Group prizes in the same colours.

Last summer he travelled and asserted

like a class act when picking up Listed races at Ascot and Salisbury. He then didn't look out of place in the Group 2 Royal Lodge at Newmarket, finishing fourth, hot on the heels of Berkshire, an effort that further underlined his ability and stamina. His career can continue on the up this summer.

A darker horse expected to be making his mark in Pattern company as a three-year-old is Hannon's **Windshear**.

Having been given plenty of time as a juvenile, his connections' patience was rewarded by a ready maiden success over a stiff mile on soft ground on his belated debut at Sandown in September. He did well to recover from missing the break to win going away at that stiff track and will be all the wiser for the experience. He rates an exciting proposition once upped to middle distances in the months ahead.

Another expected to deliver for Hannon is **Shifting Power**, who made short work of dismissing his rivals in a maiden at Sandown and a novice stakes at Newmarket.

The strapping half-brother to three winners possesses more than enough size and scope to make a splash in much better grades as he continues to thrive and fill out this season.

It should only be a matter of time before the well-regarded **Chief Barker** picks up a Group race.

Last August he overcame greenness to take a Sandown maiden and Newmarket nursery, both over a mile. Then, in a Listed race at Haydock, he drew upon those positive experiences when once again finding plenty for pressure to get the better of the ill-fated Chriselliam, who gave the form a massive lift by plundering both the Fillies' Mile and the Breeders' Cup Juvenile Fillies Turf.

Although he handles some cut in the ground, Chief Barker was possibly undone by soft when unable to sustain his effort in sixth behind Kingston Hill in the Racing Post Trophy, an effort probably best ignored.

Another to check out as a three-year-old is **Tanqeya**, who found an extra gear once switched into the clear by jockey Dane O'Neill to catch James Fanshawe's Invasor Luck in a mile maiden on Lingfield's Polytrack in October.

His form and pedigree both point to even better to come once upped in distance and, with that in mind, he ought to bag a handicap at the very least.

The highly-regarded **Night Of Thunder** can also get results in his second season. He certainly made a big impact when

TANQEYA: should do better when upped in trip and can land a good handicap

OLYMPIC GLORY: back for more

handsomely justifying market support having shown ability at home to knock his rivals for six in a Goodwood maiden, travelling and quickening like a smart recruit.

On his only other juvenile sighting it proved a similar story when he was far too strong for the hat-trick-seeking Aeolus in a Listed event on soft ground at Doncaster, and a switch to better surfaces this summer shouldn't inconvenience him. He has yet to be pushed by a rival and, with a great deal more to offer if made to work, he could well reach the top.

Among the older, more established stars expected to continue burning brightly is **Olympic Glory**.

As a juvenile he crowned a fantastic season by plundering the Group 1 Jean-Luc Lagardere at Longchamp. Last season he only just failed to add to a Greenham success when beaten inches in the Group 1 Marois at Deauville, but the combination of deeper ground and first-time blinkers resulted in a majestic win in the Queen Elizabeth II Stakes at Ascot in October.

He's clearly best with juice in the ground and when conditions are conducive he will be very hard to beat in the mile division, likely kicking off in the Lockinge.

Another of the older brigade destined to pick up big prizes is **Toronado**.

The top-class juvenile returned with a Craven win at Newmarket and was unlucky not to catch Dawn Approach in a memorable St James's Palace at Ascot before again unleashing that trademark finishing kick to exact revenge on that rival in the Sussex Stakes at Goodwood.

He ran too badly to be true when out with the washing in the Juddmonte International at York and could well repair any lost reputation by making a successful return in something like the Queen Anne at Royal Ascot.

Sky Lantern can also add significantly to Hannon's Pattern-race haul this season having won the 1,000 Guineas and Sun Chariot at Newmarket and the Coronation Stakes at Ascot last summer.

Although she was a flop in the Hong Kong Mile when last seen, she should soon be back in business on home soil possibly starting out in the Falmouth at Newmarket in July – a race she was unlucky not to win last year having been carried across the track by Elusive Kate.

Arranger can pick up a handicap or two. Last August she quickened nicely to finish two lengths ahead of Our Duchess in a Salisbury maiden. She was far from disgraced when fifth in a warm 7f Doncaster nursery won by subsequent Listed scorer Aqlaam Vision on her final start in September. She has been dropped to a workable 75 rating and could well be back in the winner's circle again before long.

Hannon's **Potentate**, a half-brother to Group 2 scorer Firth Of Fifth, shouldn't remain a maiden for long. Last October he showed good speed to finish a close second in maidens over 6f and 7f at Kempton. The switch to grass shouldn't be an excuse.

The South
by Southerner

OLLY STEVENS made a massive impact last year when his 17 winners included Royal Ascot victor Extortionist and Green Door, who landed the Group 2 Polypipe Flying Childers Stakes at Doncaster's St Leger Festival.

Those kind of high-profile successes in your first season as a licensed trainer can be something of a double-edged sword.

While the publicity is beneficial it raises the stakes and there will be plenty of critics ready to suggest it was a false dawn if things don't go quite so well this time.

However, as the renowned bloodstock agent David Redvers is a close friend and mentor and his owners include Qatar Racing's Sheikh Fahad Al Thani, a director of British Champions Series sponsors Qipco, there's every chance Stevens' state-of-the-art stables at Robins Farm in Chiddingfold

deep in the heart of the beautiful Surrey countryside can become a long-term power in the sport.

Extortionist and **Green Door** should continue to earn their keep, although second seasons are often tricky for exposed three-year-old sprinters.

The less precocious **Lightning Thunder** has the potential to become the main flagwaver for the yard this year.

The Dutch Art filly ran out an impressive winner of a 6f Newbury maiden on her debut in August before getting the better of a good battle with the useful colt Justice Day in a 6f conditions stakes at Doncaster the following month.

She lost her unbeaten record but enhanced her reputation two weeks later when going down by a head to the Andre Fabre-trained Miss France in the 7f Group 3 Oh So Sharp Stakes at Newmarket .

LIGHTNING THUNDER (second right): just loses out to Miss France last season

BECKETT BEAUTIES: Talent (right) and Secret Gesture (centre) stay in training

Her campaign ended on a slightly downbeat note when she was only fourth to Al Thakhira in the 7f Group 2 Rockfel Stakes back at Newmarket in October but she scoped badly afterwards and showed signs of coming into season, so it's easy to forgive her that lapse.

With Miss France heading the betting over the winter for the 1,000 Guineas, Lightning Thunder will be worth her place in the fillies' Classic at Newmarket in early May if she comes to hand in time.

Stevens expects his Rock Of Gibraltar colt **Gamesome** to develop into a "proper horse" this season.

After showing promise from a bad draw when 11th of the 17 runners on his debut at Glorious Goodwood in August, he turned a 6f Nottingham maiden run on easy ground later the same month into a procession on his only other appearance last year.

That form ended up looking even better than it did at the time when the 3l runner-up, Speedfiend, went on to finish fourth to Astaire in the Group 1 Middle Park Stakes.

Stevens made a fast start last season with his two-year-olds and he has several early types among his juvenile squad this year, including **The Paco Kid**, a neat son of first-season sire Paco Boy, who should be well worth watching in the first few weeks of the new campaign.

The Oaks victory of **Talent** was the highlight of an excellent campaign last year for *RALPH BECKETT*.

That success has resulted in even more demand for Beckett's services and a new 20-box barn has been built at his Kimpton Down Stables in Hampshire.

Talent, who went on to finish second in the Ladbrokes St Leger, remains in training, as does **Secret Gesture** who chased her home at Epsom to give their trainer a rare Classic one-two.

Beckett reports that the Galileo filly has done well over the winter and the objective is to make her a Group 1 winner this year.

There are a host of promising three-year-old in the yard this season with **Lightning Spear** one of the most interesting.

This chestnut son of Pivotal won a 7f Kempton maiden in good style on his sole juvenile outing, after which his trainer said: "He is a colt who has always shone at home and has the frame to make up into a proper three-year-old."

Cape Caster made an encouraging start to his career when running on well to be third in an above-average 1m maiden at Lingfield in September and is the type to make a useful second-season performer.

The same can be said for **Secret Archive** who improved significantly from his debut tenth in a 7f Kempton maiden to land a similar event at Lingfield in November.

You have to either be foolish or very shrewd to claim a horse who has just been beaten 20 lengths in a claimer.

Well, *WILLIAM KNIGHT* is no fool and his decision to fork out £3,000 for **Beacon Lady** after she'd trailed home last in a mile claimer at Kempton as a juvenile proved to be an extremely wise investment as she's gone on to win six times for the West Sussex trainer, including four on the bounce last year, culminating with victory in the amateurs' Derby at Epsom in August.

Beacon Lady's handicap mark went up by an incredible 35lb last year and the handicapper will take a long time to forgive her, but she's still worth noting on switchback tracks and, as she goes well for an inexperienced rider, her trainer will have no qualms about using an apprentice to take a few pounds off her back.

Knight, who has been keeping things ticking over at Angmering Park during the winter by running several of his older horses on the all-weather, looks like having a particularly strong group of three-year-olds this season.

Beach Bar ran promisingly in maidens at Goodwood and Leicester and signed off with a clearcut victory in a mile maiden at Lingfield in November.

The son of Azamour had a few quirks last year and wore a hood for his final two starts, but he's been gelded since and should make up into a useful handicapper.

The Footstepsinthesand filly **Tullia** ran well on all four appearances last year when she won a Salisbury maiden on soft ground in October on her final outing. She hails from a good family who tend to get better with age and she should pay to follow in the months to come.

Percybelle showed a good deal of promise last year when staying on late to finish in the frame in mile maidens at Kempton and Lingfield and the easy-moving Sir Percy filly should pay her way, especially when moving up to middle distances.

Gavlar failed to trouble the judge in three starts last year but was by no means disgraced on any of his runs and is another who should come into his own in handicaps over longer trips this season.

Crafty Exit has plenty to live up to, being a half-brother to the top-class sprinter Sole Power and the 15-times winner Cornus. He made an encouraging start to his career when seventh in a 7f Newmarket maiden in August on his only juvenile start and it will be interesting to see how he gets on this year.

The strapping Acclamation colt **Exalted**, who was working very nicely before sustaining an injury witch prevented him running last year, is one to watch out for, as is **Soundtrack**, an Excellent Art colt who has bags of scope and was too immature to race as a juvenile.

Knight never rushes his two-year-olds, but Ashapurna, Goodwood Moonlight and Solar Flair are three youngsters to note.

Solar Flair is by the very speedy Equiano and his dam's only other offspring, Warbird, won a juvenile maiden in Ireland last year.

Ashapurna is by the useful sire Tamayuz out of a Group-placed dam, while **Goodwood Moonlight** also has a nice pedigree.

AMANDA PERRETT has some nice young horses coming through the ranks at the famous Coombelands complex in Pullborough, headed by **Torrid**.

After promising runs when placed in good maidens at Newbury and Leicester on his first two starts as a juvenile, the Khalid Abdullah-owned chestnut powered home by eight lengths in a mile maiden at Nottingham in October.

Alzanti, who is also owned by Abdullah, quickened well to land a 7f Kempton maiden in November on her debut. The Arch filly has size and scope and should make a useful three-year-old from a mile to a mile and a quarter.

Winning a 7f maiden at Kempton in October on the second of his two starts last year was a bonus for **Best Kept** as he was just a shell of a horse as a juvenile. He's one of the yard's big hopes for this term.

Pack Leader promises to stay well. The Hurricane Run gelding was running on nicely at the finish when second in a couple of maidens at Goodwood in the autumn.

Twice a winner as a two-year-old, **Jelly Fish** should pay his way in handicaps this season, and the New Approach colt **Black Shadow**, who was a close sixth in a Lingfield maiden in October on his sole juvenile outing, should build on that promise this year.

Perrett's youngsters to watch out for this year include the Myboycharlie colt **Lightning Charlie**, the Dandy Man colt **Bouncing Czech** and the Teofilo colt **Front Five**.

GARY MOORE, who oversees the biggest dual-purpose operation in Britain, has been enjoying a highly successful jumps season with the likes of Sire De Grugy and there will be no slackening of the pace at his Cisswood Stables in West Sussex during the summer months.

Dutch Masterpiece showed Moore's skills with Flat performers last season.

The speedster began the campaign with a fifth in a Newmarket handicap in April but improved so much while chalking up a hat-trick in the summer that he wound up being sent off favourite for the Group 1 Prix de l'Abbaye.

He failed to run to his best in France, trailing home 17th behind Maarek, but he was beaten less than seven lengths and, with just ten starts under his belt, the four-year-old should still have plenty more to offer.

Southern stars
Ashapurna
Lightning Thunder
Talent

DUTCH MASTERPIECE (centre): an exciting prospect for Gary Moore

Midlands
by John Bull

I T'S ten years since *ED McMAHON* started training and the Lichfield handler can look back with satisfaction at a decade of solid achievements. Among the highlights were winning two Group races within an hour at Newbury on one unforgettable afternoon in September 2010 and more recently last season's excellent run by **Winning Express** in the 1,000 Guineas.

In this column last year we advised an each-way interest in the Camacho filly if she lined up at Newmarket and, at the two-furlong pole when the 33-1 shot hit the front, it looked as if McMahon was on the brink of a famous victory.

Alas, it was not to be, and the grey was overhauled and agonisingly pipped for third on the line in a close finish in which only two lengths separated the first four.

"A couple of furlongs out I was thinking of what I was going to say in the Channel 4 interview afterwards," McMahon recalled.

"It was a great run in what proved to be a very strong Guineas. We all know what the winner Sky Lantern and the second Just The Judge went on to achieve."

After her Newmarket heroics Winning Express dropped back to 7f to comfortably land a Listed race at Warwick in June. At Glorious Goodwood, in the Group 3 Oak Tree Stakes, she was sent off 2-1 favourite but unfortunately wasn't given the best of rides and hit the front too soon. She was passed in the final furlong and could finish only second behind 14-1 shot Annecdote, who was officially rated 10lb inferior.

"That was annoying as she really should have won that day," McMahon said. "It was the one that got away."

In her final run the filly was dropped back to 6f for a Listed race at Newmarket, a race in which she finished second behind Group 3 winner Mince, and she is likely to keep to that distance this season.

WINNING EXPRESS: will win more

Winning Express looks set for another good campaign and she should gain compensation for hitting the crossbar in her last three runs of 2013.

McMahon says he is keen to avoid a clash between Winning Express and his other star performer from last term, **Artistic Jewel**.

The Excellent Art mare ran only three times last summer but recorded two wins (in 6f Listed races at Haydock and Pontefract) and an excellent second place in a 6f Group 3 at The Curragh.

"I was going to start her off in the Kilvington at Nottingham, but she had what you could call 'women's problems' so we went to the Cecil Flail at Haydock instead. One of her targets this year may be the Summer Stakes, a Group 3 race for fillies and mares at York in July."

Although she does have a two-year-old win on soft ground to her name, the five-year-old does seem to perform at her best on quicker with her record on good to firm reading three wins, two seconds and a third from six runs.

Of his three-year-olds, McMahon nominates his Araafa colt **Aelous** as a horse who should pay to follow.

"He's out of the same mare, Bright Moll, as Tartiflette, who won three times for us and has now been sold.

"He won his maiden by seven lengths going away at Chester when he didn't get the best of runs and then won a nice nursery at York.

"He finished the season by running a cracker in a Listed race at Doncaster behind Richard Hannon's Night of Thunder. He's rated 101 now. He'll be campaigned over 6f/7f and hopefully we can do well in

Listed and conditions races. I think he can improve further."

McMahon has one Classic entry this year, a Nayef colt called **Age Of Discovery** who is entered in the Derby.

"He's a nice horse and a half-brother to Mukhadram. He's never run and is no more than a speculative entry at this stage," he said.

Stable stalwart **Noble Storm**, who has been with McMahon since his two-year-old days and won nine races for the yard, remains in training at the age of eight and should pick up another conditions race when he gets his favoured good to firm going.

"I would love to have won a Group 3 with him but he's probably too old to achieve that now. He is prone to viruses, but when it's all in his favour he is still a good horse. He's been a terrific servant for the yard."

Certainly the son of Yankee Gentleman

BANCNUANAHEIRANN: likes Goodwood, so look out for him at that track

looked no back number when he recorded a pillar-to-post victory in a condition stakes at Leicester in September.

Newark trainer *MICK APPLEBY* saddled 19 turf winners on the Flat in 2012 and matched that total again last year.

The yard was in cracking form on the all-weather over the winter – recording five winners from seven runners in a red-hot spell late January and early February – and hopes are high for another good campaign.

Appleby will have around 50 horses to go to battle with over the summer, and the quality of his horses is improving all the time, making it a great stable to follow.

Bancnuanaheireann was flagged up in this section last year and he didn't let us down, winning at Goodwood in May at 9-2 before landing the Silver Cambridgeshire at Newmarket in September at 14-1.

"He'll probably be out in late March," Appleby told me. "We'll try to win a big handicap with him – he likes Goodwood so Glorious Goodwood will be on the agenda and he also has a great record at the Cambridgeshire meeting at Newmarket. He should get in the Cambridgeshire this year and if he does he'd have a good chance."

Sprinter **Demora** won twice last summer, at 4-1 at Nottingham in June and 8-1 at Haydock on her final start in September.

"This is likely to be her last season before she retires to stud and it would be good to get some black type and win a Listed race with her," Appleby said of the five-year-old.

"We'll see how we go with her but the Prix de l'Abbaye could be a target as long as the ground wasn't too soft. She could go to Dubai in the winter following that before retiring."

One positive regarding Demora's Abbaye chances is that she's won in late September/October for the past two seasons and, if she continues to improve and gets her favoured going conditions, she could be an interesting contender.

Cordite and Danzeno are two exciting three-year-olds who look set for a profitable summer campaign.

"**Cordite** had four runs as a two-year-old. He won his maiden at Leicester in October and then finished fourth in a Group 3 at Newbury. He probably wouldn't be good enough for the English Guineas but we we're thinking of targeting him at the German Guineas in May.

"**Danzeno** was quite impressive when winning his maiden at Redcar last October. I think he could be really good and he'll be aimed at Group 1s or Group 2s, with 6f/7f being his best distance."

Popular Peterborough handler *PAM SLY* had a tough time of things in 2013, with a broken femur leaving her confined to a wheelchair for three months.

But 2014 got off to a good start with her jumps horses in fine form and hopefully there'll be more to cheer about this summer on the Flat.

Ghinia, a Mastercraftsman filly, ran three times last year with her best effort being a third at Leicester in September. Watch out for her as she goes handicapping at distances around 1m as she should fare a lot better this year.

Asteroidea is a Sea The Stars filly out of Sly's 2006 Classic-winning heroine Speciosa. She had two runs last September, both over a mile at Haydock and Newmarket, but should do better when she is stepped up in trip this season.

"She was big and backward. She's big and looks like a National Hunt horse and she'll be campaigned around 1m4f."

Sly has two promising juveniles by the 2006 Derby winner Sir Percy who will be in action this summer, both unnamed at time of going to press.

One is out of Black Salix, who ran without success for Sly eight times, but the better prospect could be the other, who is out of Kaloni, a consistent mare who won twice for Sly in 2009 and finished in the first four in seven of her 11 starts.

> *Midlands magic*
> **Aelous**
> **Danzeno**
> **Winning Express**

69

Est. 1909

RACING & FOOTBALL **OUTLOOK**

Steve Mellish – the man on the telly

Amazing French filly Treve has top billing for 2014

FOR many, the 2013 Flat season will be remembered for the wrong reasons: the drugs scandals that bookended the season and resulted in lengthy bans for Mahmood Al Zarooni and Gerard Butler.

The Zarooni/Godolphin saga was one of the biggest news stories for years in racing. The BHA deserves plenty of credit for the way they dealt with the case – the testing procedures are clearly effective and they weren't scared of tackling one of the biggest stables in the world.

But justice and sentencing was meted out very quickly, too quickly in the eyes of many, and the net result is that we have to accept Al Zarooni was acting alone.

On the track two French fillies, Moonlight Cloud and Treve, were the stars.

Moonlight Cloud was retired at the end of the season having added another three Group 1s to her impressive CV, but we get to savour **Treve** for another year. She's unbeaten after five starts and was one of the most brilliant winners of the Arc I can remember.

She's the headline act for 2014 and it's not hard to predict big things for her again. It's not so easy, though, to see where the next stars are coming from though.

There wasn't a Dawn Approach among the two-year-olds last season – a horse whose level of form was good enough to take an average 2,000 Guineas. The way is clear for some lightly-raced type to make abnormal improvement and jump to the top of the pile.

Richard Hannon has retired and won't be around to defend his trainers' title. His son, Richard junior, has taken over the license, but he's been sharing the training duties for years and I doubt things down Wiltshire way will change very much. Roger Varian and William Haggas both had an excellent 2013 and they look sure to be very strong again this year.

Of the jockeys, Tom Queally could have a good year. He'll be riding as a freelance, after several years attached to the Cecil yard, and is sure to be popular. He hasn't ridden 100 winners in a season since 2011 but that could become a target if he rides winners early and builds some momentum.

Here are five horses that might be worth keeping a close eye on in 2014.

Angus Glens 4yo gelding
53454- (David Dennis)

This son of Dalakhani cost 100,000gns as a yearling, but he's yet to score. A backward type, he didn't run at two, and in fact he never made it to the track until the July of his three-year-old season. He then had five runs crammed into a three-month period, showing a degree of promise each time. He begins the season off a mark of 75, which is fair on what he's shown, but he's bred to improve with age and could turn out a fair bit better in time. Distances of a mile and a half or more should suit him this year.

Casual Smile 3yo filly
232- (Andrew Balding)

By the brilliant Sea The Stars out of the Oaks winner Casual Look, this filly is bred to come into her own over middle distances at three. It's therefore very encouraging that she's already shown a good level of ability. She's been given a mark of 89 after placed efforts in two maidens and a conditions race. The furthest she's tried is a mile and her running style, backed up by that pedigree, screams improvement when upped to ten furlongs and more. A maiden should be a formality and it would be no surprise if she developed into a Pattern-class filly.

Mighty Yar 4yo colt
1/1- (Lady Cecil)

This is a very exciting colt. A big, scopey grey, he's only made it to the track twice in two seasons, winning each time. He got up late to take a mile maiden on the Polytrack at two and wasn't seen again until July last season when running in a 1m2f handicap at Sandown off 76. Again, he was strong at the finish, leading inside the final furlong and quickly drawing clear. Longer trips

MIGHTY YAR: a very exciting prospect for Lady Cecil this season

were certain to bring about considerable improvement and connections were entitled to have races like the Melrose or even the Leger in mind. Sadly he wasn't seen again, but let's hope he stays fit and well this term as he's got enormous potential. Put up to a mark of 88 after Sandown, he could make a mockery of that when moving up to a mile and a half and more.

Postponed 3yo colt
512- *(Luca Cumani)*

One win from three starts as a juvenile is Postponed's record. That success came in a Yarmouth maiden, but it's his next start when runner-up in a valuable sales race at Newmarket that marks him down as a horse to follow. All his races have been at 7f but that distance looked very much on the sharp side as he stormed up the hill to grab second behind the useful Oklahoma City. A really good-looking colt,

with a trainer who isn't hard on his horses at two, he'll definitely be suited by longer trips at three and it's possible he'll take after his dam and stay a mile and a half. He could be a Derby horse if he does.

Sbraase 3yo colt
441- *(James Tate)*

Stamina helped this colt get off the mark at the third attempt as a juvenile when he kept on gamely in a Wolverhampton maiden over an extended 1m1f. A quick look at his breeding confirms the impression that stamina is his forte. By the Derby winner Sir Percy and from a family that includes winners of the Prix du Cadran and St Leger, Sbraase is very stoutly-bred and distances of a mile and a half and further will be required this season. His mark of 78 is not too bad at all and he's an interesting horse for handicaps when getting a trip.

SBRAASE (inside rail): fourth on his debut behind Downturn at Sandown

Est. 1909
RACING & FOOTBALL **OUTLOOK**

Richard Birch

Read Richard every week in the RFO

Not a shock if Russian Realm won Group race

ANYBODY who reads my weekly RFO column regularly will know I am a massive fan of **Russian Realm**, and it will come as no surprise that Sir Michael Stoute's four-year-old tops my list of horses to follow for the 2014 Flat season.

The son of Dansili caught the eye when third in a hotly-contested Newbury maiden on Lockinge day last May, the form of which couldn't have worked out any better with the winner, Remote, going on to land the Group 3 Tercentenary Stakes at Royal Ascot.

An opening handicap mark of 77 looked generous when Russian Realm lined up over a mile at Salisbury in August and the colt made no mistake, quickening smartly under Ryan Moore to beat Beedee by three-quarters of a length.

Russian Realm starts the season on 85 and I will be amazed if this lightly-raced colt doesn't boast a triple-figure rating by mid-summer.

He will improve further when stepped up to 1m2f, has Royal Ascot winner written all over him, and should then develop into a Group 3 performer at the very least.

Mubaraza progressed nicely during a short campaign in 2013, finishing fourth in the Ascot Stakes and third in the Northumberland Plate, after which he was gelded with a Cesarewitch bid in mind. However, Ed Dunlop's five-year-old missed the Newmarket marathon and wasn't seen out again.

He rates a leading contender for all the major staying handicaps this year and would be particularly interesting if connections can find a suitable race at his local track ahead of the Cesarewitch. Both of his career wins to date have been recorded at HQ.

Talking of staying races, nothing makes more appeal for the Cup events than **Statutory**, who improved significantly throughout his first campaign with Mark Johnston, rounding off with a 14-length thrashing of Mutual Regard in the Phil Bull Trophy at Pontefract.

Now with Saeed Bin Suroor, the Godolphin-owned four-year-old could well develop into a leading contender for the Ascot Gold Cup, with the Henry II Stakes at Sandown a likely early target.

David Nicholls has seen his stable strength fall markedly in recent years, but there is no doubt he remains a master with sprinters and I can't wait for the reappearance of 57-rated **Manatee Bay**.

A big shell of a horse last year, Manatee Bay won on his second start in handicap

73

company, showing a nice turn of foot under Joe Fanning to score at Hamilton in September.

Given just one more run a week later, Manatee Bay still exhibited clear signs of inexperience in finishing third and was sensibly put away for the year immediately afterwards.

I will be amazed if Nicholls cannot do some serious damage with Manatee Bay's mark in the first part of the season and the gelding looks just the type who could improve 20lb before July.

Telegraph was desperately unlucky not to land a 6f Chester handicap for Andrew Balding in September, but the consolation for his followers is that he will start his three-year-old career rated just 68.

Balding has made no secret of the regard in which he holds this gelding and the high cruising speed he possesses rubber-stamps him as a definite horse to follow off such an attractive mark.

Alluring Star is bred to get better with age, being by Gentleman's Deal, and the way in which she began last season as a five-year-old suggested she was going to win multiple handicaps in the north.

However, after paralysing her rivals in a Beverley handicap over a mile, she failed to add to her tally in 12 further races despite performing creditably on several occasions.

As a result she starts this turf season rated just 3lb higher than when successful last year and I have a feeling she will return stronger this time and hold her form much better.

Look out for her in fillies' handicaps early in the season, particularly if returned to Beverley, which lends itself perfectly to Alluring Star's powerful front-running style.

Discovery Bay, trained by the brilliant Brian Ellison, is rated 128 over hurdles at

MANATEE BAY: should benefit from David Nicholls' great touch with sprinters

ALLURING STAR (left): by Gentleman's Deal so bred to get better with age

the time of writing yet starts the Flat season with a mark of just 71.

If Ellison cannot exploit that rating in the first part of the campaign I will give the game up, and it would come as no surprise if he is already eyeing the 1m4f handicap at York's Dante meeting in which the gelding was so desperately unlucky last May.

Tanking at the top of the straight under Silvestre De Sousa, Discovery Bay found himself trapped in a pocket for two furlongs and, when the gap finally came, his winning chance had evaporated.

He looks a definite money-spinner for 2014, as does his 76-rated stablemate **Bishop's Castle**.

Third of 19 in a York handicap in September, the son of Distorted Humor is very much one to keep on side for big-field mile or 1m2f handicaps this year.

His high cruising speed will always prove a powerful weapon in those types of events and, with the likelihood of him being even stronger this year as a five-year-old, it is a fair bet the best from him is very much yet to come.

Keith Dalgleish is a trainer going places, and the one I like from his stable for 2014 is the sprinter **Salvatore Fury**.

A winner three times last summer – all on good or faster ground – he remains very feasibly handicapped on a mark of 68, and is sure to add to his tally in 6f handicaps.

Salvatore Fury will kick off in Class 5 or Class 4 handicaps, but I have no doubt he can progress into a Class 3 performer given his optimum conditions.

75

Est. 1909

RACING & FOOTBALL | **OUTLOOK**

Time Test with Mark Nelson

French stars could have big say in Classics

ALTHOUGH there's not one horse significantly ahead of any other judged on last year's juvenile speed figures, the numbers make interesting reading when looking ahead at the ante-post markets for the first Classics of the season, especially in relation to the fillies.

Two share top honours, and while **Rizeena** was a decent benchmark throughout the season, the best Time Test figure posted by a juvenile filly beyond sprint distances was recorded by **Indonesienne** when winning the Prix Marcel Boussac at Longchamp last October.

The French-trained filly ultimately won two of her three starts last term, her only defeat coming at the hands of **Miss France**, who subsequently came to New-

market to win the Oh So Sharp Stakes.

While Miss France was made favourite for the Guineas on the back of that effort, it should not be forgotten that Andre Fabre's filly was receiving 4lb from Indonesienne at Chantilly. The clock also shows that Indonesienne has improved since, clocking her best figure of the season in the Prix Marcel Boussac, which eclipsed anything that Miss France has achieved on the stopwatch.

At the very least there doesn't look to be too much between the pair, so the disparity in price between them in the Guineas market doesn't look justified. Perhaps the likelihood of participation is skewing the prices, but should Christophe Ferland send Indonesienne to Headquarters, then she's the one clockwatchers should be siding with.

For those not familiar with the yard, the French handler is probably best remembered for his association with Dabirsim and it's worth noting that he scored with his sole runner on these shores last season.

Tapestry has form with Rizeena, and although she could only manage second behind Clive Brittain's filly in the Moyglare, she might prove to be the best of the pair in the long term.

The Moyglare was another race that wasn't run at a particularly strong clip and it was a combination of experience and speed that saw Rizeena prevail, with Tapestry taking much longer to engage top

INDONESIENNE (near side): would be a leading 1,000 Guineas contender

gear than the winner.

Tapestry had returned a smart figure the time before and was unbeaten in two starts prior to that defeat, so although she's just outside the top three juvenile fillies on the clock, there's reason to believe she might be better than her current figure suggests. She remains a serious prospect.

Moving on to the colts, it was very tight at the top of last year's juvenile ratings, with just three points separating the top five.

While **Sudirman** tops the table, his best figures all came at six furlongs and there didn't appear to be any excuses when he was held by **Toormore** in the National Stakes when stepping up to seven for the first time.

Indeed, it's Toormore who posted the best figure of any juvenile at distances beyond six furlongs and he looks to have serious claims of landing the Guineas for Richard Hannon Jnr in his first season with a licence.

While the youngster has plenty of speed in his pedigree, he finished strongly when taking the Vintage Stakes at Goodwood before confirming that good impression by nailing Sudirman at the Curragh. On that evidence he should be able to get a mile as a three-year-old and, having posted improved Time Test figures on every visit to the recourse so far, it's impossible to say where that progress may end.

War Command is next best on the colts' figures for performances beyond six furlongs and, while he didn't impress on every occasion last season, his overall record is hard to knock.

His short-priced defeat in the Phoenix Stakes simply has to be overlooked as a blip. He clocked a belter when winning the Coventry Stakes at Royal Ascot, won as he should when dropped in grade for the Futurity Stakes, and there was nothing wrong with his speed figure when rounding off his season with a win in the Dewhurst.

So, although his figures aren't on a sharp upward curve like that of Toormore, they remain of a very decent standard and he's another with obvious Guineas claims.

Aidan O'Brien is also responsible for a couple more lightly-raced youngsters destined to show improvement at three.

I'm pretty sure **Great White Eagle** failed to handle the ground in the Middle Park stakes, but as he returned solid figures in two starts in Ireland, there should be better to come this year.

Australia heads the ante-post market for the Derby and, although he was adrift of the very best juveniles on Time Test figures, he returned improved numbers on each of his starts last year and, after just three outings, is open to any amount of improvement.

Looking at the best juvenile figures that were produced at a mile and beyond, it's the French-trained **Ectot** who stands out.

Trained by Elie Lellouche, this son of

Hurricane Run took the Criterium International at Saint-Cloud in a good time and is now unbeaten in four starts since finishing second on his debut. Longer trips beckon this term and he could prove to be a Derby candidate if his progress continues at three.

There were plenty of positives on the clock among the older horses last year, with decent numbers being returned among all divisions.

Despite winning on only two of his five outings last year, the leading sprinter on the clock was Lethal Force and only ground conditions dented his dominance. He was unbeaten on good ground or better and returned a belting time when winning the July Cup.

However, he's now been retired to stud so the door is open for a new sprinting champion in 2014.

The top three-year-old and best overall miler on last year's figures was the Richard

GREAT WHITE EAGLE (second left): clocked two solid figures in Ireland

MAGICIAN: could take high rank on the strength of his Irish Guineas win

Hannon-trained **Toronado**.

Something was amiss when he tried a mile and a quarter for the first time in the Juddmonte International, but he'd previously posted a top-class figure when finally mastering the now-retired Dawn Approach in the Sussex Stakes. It's tremendous news that he stays in training.

Another four-year-old bidding for top honours will be **Magician**, whose 2013 campaign was badly affected by injury.

He clocked a proper figure when winning the Irish Guineas and, while a subsequent setback meant we didn't see

the best of him in the St James's Palace Stakes, he returned in scintillating form at the Breeders' Cup. His return is much anticipated.

The best middle-distance number of 2013 came courtesy of Novellist, who handed out a proper drubbing to his rivals in the King George at Ascot despite the ground being a shade faster than ideal. He covered the mile and a half in 2min 24.60sec which shaved over two seconds off the previous course record.

Unfortunately a raised temperature meant he was unable to contest the Arc and he was subsequently retired.

His absence at Longchamp paved the way for **Treve** to triumph and in all likelihood the result may not have been any different as the French filly put in a tremendous performance.

Criquette Head-Maarek made no secret of the regard in which she held the filly and she duly delivered on the day, despite an unhelpful draw and a wide passage, in a race which produced the best figure of the season by any filly.

The 2014 season will be all the richer for the fact she remains in training and the British public may get to witness the French heroine at Royal Ascot this June when she will bid for a crack at the Prince of Wales's Stakes.

Top two-year-old colts of 2013

	Horse	Speed rating	Distance in furlongs	Going	Track	Date achieved
1	**No Nay Never**	**62**	**5**	**GF**	**Ascot**	**Jun 20**
2	Sudirman	62	6	GD	Curragh	Aug 11
3	Toormore	61	7	GD	Curragh	Sep 15
4	Big Time	60	6	GD	Curragh	Aug 11
4	War Command	60	7	GS	Newmarket	Oct 12
6	Extortionist	59	5	GD	Ascot	Jun 18
7	Anticipated	58	5	GD	Ascot	Jun 18
7	Coach House	58	5	GF	Ascot	Jun 20
7	Supplicant	58	5	GD	Ascot	Jun 18
10	Astaire	57	6	GS	Newmarket	Oct 12
11	Hot Streak	57	5	GS	Ascot	Oct 5

Top two-year-old fillies of 2013

	Horse	Speed rating	Distance in furlongs	Going	Track	Date achieved
1	**Indonesienne**	**59**	**8**	**SF**	**Longchamp**	**Oct 6**
1	**Rizeena**	**59**	**5**	**GF**	**Ascot**	**Jun 19**
3	Lesstalk In Paris	56	8	SF	Longchamp	Oct 6
4	Tapestry	55	7	GD	Curragh	Aug 11
4	Wind Fire	55	5	GF	Ascot	Jun 20
6	Amazing Maria	53	7	GD	Goodwood	Aug 24
6	Lucky Kristale	53	6	GF	Newmarket	Jul 12
8	Sandiva	52	7	GD,	Deauville	Aug 17
8	Sweet Emma Rose	52	5	GF	Ascot	Jun 19
10	Cape Factor	51	6	SF	Newmarket	Nov 1
10	Flying Jib	51	8	GD	Curragh	Oct 13
10	My Titania	51	7	GF	Curragh	Sep 29
10	Queen Catrine	51	8	SF	Longchamp	Oct 6
10	Royalmania	51	8	SF	Longchamp	Oct 6

Est. 1909

RACING & FOOTBALL OUTLOOK

Group 1 review by Dylan Hill

1 Qipco 2,000 Guineas Stakes (1m)
Newmarket May 4 (Good To Firm)
1 **Dawn Approach** 3-9-0   Kevin Manning
2 **Glory Awaits** 3-9-0   Jamie Spencer
3 **Van Der Neer** 3-9-0   William Buick
11/8F, 150/1, 20/1. 5l, 2¼l. 13 ran. 1m
35.84s
(J S Bolger).

Unbeaten in six starts as a juvenile, **Dawn Approach** still reigned supreme as he destroyed a modest field, racing prominently throughout and powering clear in the final furlong. The other leading players were below their best, most notably **Toronado**, who was found to be suffering from a soft palate problem after fading into fourth, while **Mars** was also yet to reach his peak on only his second start. That meant there wasn't much competition for the places (only one of the first eight to come out of the race even got placed next time when beaten at 8-13 in a maiden) and **Glory Awaits** was a clear second at 150-1, leaving his previous form behind in first-time blinkers, though he benefited from racing alone in the centre as **Van Der Neer**, drawn widest of all on that side, also stayed on into third.

2 Qipco 1,000 Guineas Stakes (Fillies) (1m)
Newmarket May 5 (Good To Firm)
1 **Sky Lantern** 3-9-0   Richard Hughes
2 **Just The Judge** 3-9-0   Jamie Spencer
3 **Moth** 3-9-0   Joseph O'Brien
9/1, 7/1, 9/1. ½l, 1½l. 15 ran. 1m 36.38s
(Richard Hannon).

Several fillies were slow to come to hand after the incredibly cold winter and early spring, among them **Sky Lantern**, who had yet to come in her coat, but she still proved good enough to land a cosy victory without any of the fireworks she would produce later. Sky Lantern was produced late to cut down **Just The Judge**, while **Moth** stayed on well from the rear in contrast to **Winning Express**, who just failed to last the mile having looked like doing better than her eventual fourth. Favourite **Hot Snap**, who had beaten the winner in the Nell Gwyn, was only eighth and would prove better when stepped up in trip.

3 JLT Lockinge Stakes (1m)
Newbury May 18 (Good To Firm)
1 **Farhh** 5-9-0   Silvestre De Sousa
2 **Sovereign Debt** 4-9-0   Adam Kirby
3 **Aljamaaheer** 4-9-0   Paul Hanagan
100/30, 80/1, 16/1. 4l, nk. 12 ran. 1m 35.43s
(Saeed bin Suroor).

A long-overdue Group 1 win for **Farhh**, who took advantage of the yawning chasm left in the division by the retirements of Frankel and Excelebration. The Godolphin star was hugely impressive as he romped clear of **Sovereign Debt** and **Aljamaaheer**, pointing to the improvement he would show later in the Champion Stakes, though the bare form was modest with the runner-up beaten much further on his three subsequent runs in Group company. Aljamaaheer, still finding his feet at the top level, was never seriously put into the race from the rear, while **Declaration Of War** was a bitterly disappointing fifth having reportedly hit his head in the stalls.

JUST THE JUDGE: quickens away from a poor field in the Irish 1,000 Guineas

4 Tattersalls Irish 2,000 Guineas (1m)
Curragh (IRE) May 25 (Good To Firm)
1 **Magician** 3-9-0   Joseph O'Brien
2 **Gale Force Ten** 3-9-0   Seamie Heffernan
3 **Trading Leather** 3-9-0   Kevin Manning
100/30, 7/1, 6/1. 3½l, 1½l. 10 ran. 1m 36.81s
(A P O'Brien).

A very strong contest won in comprehensive fashion by **Magician**, who confirmed his class later in the season when stepped well up in trip to win the Breeders' Cup Turf. Off a strong gallop that seemed to suit horses capable of staying further, Magician stormed clear of the subsequent Jersey Stakes victor **Gale Force Ten** with a couple of future Group 1 winners, **Trading Leather** and **Havana Gold**, finishing next. **First Cornerstone** was fifth as only that quintet finished within 11l, with **Van Der Neer** among the also-rans.

5 Tattersalls Gold Cup (1m2f110y)
Curragh (IRE) May 26 (Good To Firm)
1 **Al Kazeem** 5-9-3   James Doyle
2 **Camelot** 4-9-3   Joseph O'Brien
3 **Windsor Palace** 8-9-3   Seamie Heffernan
9/4, 4/11F, 33/1. 1½l, 9½l. 4 ran. 2m 14.48s
(Roger Charlton).

A breakthrough win for **Al Kazeem**, who had landed his previous two starts in terrific fashion split by a year-long absence and won on his first step up into Group 1 company to kick off his memorable season. In doing so Al Kazeem delivered a telling blow to **Camelot**,

who still had plenty to prove despite winning three Classics having dominated what proved to be a poor generation and was comfortably outgunned in the closing stages.

6 Etihad Airways Irish 1,000 Guineas (Fillies) (1m)
Curragh (IRE) May 26 (Good To Firm)
1 **Just The Judge** 3-9-0   Jamie Spencer
2 **Rehn's Nest** 3-9-0   Ronan Whelan
3 **Just Pretending** 3-9-0   Seamie Heffernan
2/1F, 40/1, 14/1. 1½l, hd. 15 ran. 1m 39.37s
(Charles Hills).

Just The Judge took advantage of the absence of Sky Lantern as she landed a soft Classic win. With **Maureen**, the only other top-six finisher at Newmarket to run, below her best in filling the same position, Just The Judge needed only to run to form to see off **Rehn's Nest** and **Just Pretending**, who would prove best over much further.

7 Investec Oaks (Fillies) (1m4f10y)
Epsom May 31 (Good To Soft)
1 **Talent** 3-9-0   Richard Hughes
2 **Secret Gesture** 3-9-0   Jim Crowley
3 **The Lark** 3-9-0   Jamie Spencer
20/1, 3/1, 16/1. 3¾l, ¾l. 11 ran. 2m 42.00s
(Ralph Beckett).

A one-two for trainer Ralph Beckett, who won with his least fancied filly as **Talent** stormed home from **Secret Gesture**. Talent got the run of the race, coming fast and late whereas Secret Gesture was the only horse ridden prominently to seriously figure, but she still won with real authority, coming well clear in the final furlong with a devastating turn of foot. Secret Gesture did well to hold on for second ahead of **The Lark** and **Moth**, with nearly 4l back to **Liber Nauticus**, who was the only other filly to finish within 12l as the principals proved vastly superior to the rest of a field desperately lacking depth, which led to the overall form being unfairly maligned prior to Talent's two good placed efforts at the top level and The Lark's Group 2 win at Doncaster later in the campaign.

8 Investec Derby (1m4f10y)
Epsom June 1 (Good)
1 **Ruler Of The World** 3-9-0   Ryan Moore
2 **Libertarian** 3-9-0   William Buick
3 **Galileo Rock** 3-9-0   Wayne Lordan
7/1, 14/1, 25/1. 1½l, shd. 12 ran. 2m 39.06s
(A P O'Brien).

A tactical masterpiece by the Ballydoyle team as they laid a trap for red-hot favourite **Dawn Approach** and propelled **Ruler Of The World** to victory. The pace was slowed up to such a degree that Dawn Approach fought for his head throughout, eventually being forced to move into the lead at halfway before fading out of contention soon after, and that left Ruler Of The World in pole position as he soon quickened into a decisive lead and held on comfortably. The fast-finishing **Libertarian** led the blanket finish for second by a pair of short-heads from **Galileo Rock** and **Battle Of Marengo**, with French raider **Ocovango** just behind them before a small gap to **Mars** and German hope **Chopin**. The early crawl led to less than 4l covering that septet and made the form easy to criticise, especially after the first two flopped on much quicker ground in the Irish Derby, but Ruler Of The World at least proved the knockers partly wrong later in the year when going close in the Prix Niel and the Champion Stakes, with several others also doing well enough to suggest this was a much better Derby than originally felt.

9 Investec Coronation Cup (1m4f10y)
Epsom June 1 (Good)
1 **St Nicholas Abbey** 6-9-0   Joseph O'Brien
2 **Dunaden** 7-9-0   Jamie Spencer
3 **Joshua Tree** 6-9-0   Ryan Moore
30/100F, 4/1, 10/1. 3¾l, 7l. 5 ran. 2m 37.76s
(A P O'Brien).

A straightforward duel between the two highest money-earners in Europe as **St Nicholas Abbey** saw off fellow veteran **Dunaden** in the absence of any younger talent on what would sadly prove to be his swansong. St Nicholas Abbey, completing a hat-trick in the

race to follow up a tremendous win in the Sheema Classic, looked better than ever as he stormed clear, making it even more of a pity that he was denied the chance to prove himself again.

10 Queen Anne Stakes (1m)
Ascot June 18 (Good)
1 **Declaration Of War** 4-9-0 Joseph O'Brien
2 **Aljamaaheer** 4-9-0   Paul Hanagan
3 **Gregorian** 4-9-0   Tom Queally
15/2, 8/1, 16/1. ¾l, ½l. 13 ran. 1m 38.48s
(A P O'Brien).

Not a vintage renewal with Farhh absent through injury and the only previous Group 1 winners **Elusive Kate** and **Animal Kingdom** below their best, particularly the American raider, but the form still proved fairly solid and **Declaration Of War** was better than the bare result. Leaving behind the form of his return in the Lockinge, Declaration Of War had to be switched left at the furlong pole having been blocked in his run, but he flew home when in the clear to nail subsequent Summer Mile winner **Aljamaaheer** with more in hand than the winning margin. **Gregorian** was third ahead of Elusive Kate, who just needed the run after an eight-month absence, while **Trade Storm**, **Libranno**, **Chil The Kite** and **Penitent** also finished within 5l of the winner.

11 King's Stand Stakes 5f)
Ascot June 18 (Good)
1 **Sole Power** 6-9-4   Johnny Murtagh
2 **Shea Shea** 6-9-4   Christophe Soumillon
3 **Pearl Secret** 4-9-4   Jamie Spencer
8/1, 11/4F, 10/1. nk, 1¼l. 19 ran. 58.88s
(Edward Lynam).

Placed three times at the top level since his breakthrough win in the 2010 Nunthorpe, **Sole Power** finally had things fall his way again in a thrilling finish. Held up well in rear, Sole Power produced a powerful late burst to just pip the South African champion **Shea Shea**, who didn't quite live up to expectations during his stint in Britain as he failed to exploit the continuing lack of major domestic talent over the minimum trip. The form behind was solid, led by the potentially top-class **Pearl Secret**, who missed the rest of the season through injury, followed by subsequent Group 3 winners **Jack Dexter** and **Heeraat**, who were split by **Reckless Abandon**.

12 St James's Palace Stakes (1m)
Ascot June 18 (Good)
1 **Dawn Approach** 3-9-0   Kevin Manning
2 **Toronado** 3-9-0   Richard Hughes
3 **Mars** 3-9-0   Ryan Moore

ESTIMATE: with her happy owner

5/4F, 5/1, 10/1. shd, 2¾l. 9 ran. 1m 39.23s (J S Bolger).

A remarkable achievement for **Dawn Approach** to bounce back to his best less than three weeks after his Derby nightmare as he held off **Toronado** in a magnificent battle, though Toronado's subsequent Sussex Stakes win suggests he may have been an unlucky loser. Toronado seemed to come off worse in scrimmaging early in the straight as both were making a forward move, after which he could never quite get past Dawn Approach during a protracted duel. It was 2¾l back to the staying-on **Mars** with a decent field well strung out behind, including **Magician**, who had been the subject of an injury scare leading up to the race and eased home in last having been affected by the trouble in running.

13 **Prince of Wales's Stakes (1m2f)**
Ascot June 19 (Good To Firm)
1 **Al Kazeem** 5-9-0   James Doyle
2 **Mukhadram** 4-9-0   Paul Hanagan
3 **The Fugue** 4-8-11   William Buick
11/4, 14/1, 13/2. nk, 3¼l. 11 ran. 2m 3.06s (Roger Charlton).

Not much strength in depth with **The Fugue** needing the run and **Camelot** unsuited by the fast ground on what would prove his final start, but **Al Kazeem** and **Mukhadram** were vastly superior with the winner producing a top-class performance. Mukhadram came desperately close to making all the running and at one point held a seemingly decisive advantage in the straight, but Al Kazeem quickened up well to peg him back and was pushed to the best Time Test figure of Royal Ascot beyond sprint trips. That also confirmed that, far from being allowed a soft lead, Mukhadram was a genuine Group 1 performer, as he would prove at Sandown, with the pair pulling 4l clear of The Fugue.

14 **Gold Cup (2m4f)**
Ascot June 20 (Good To Firm)
1 **Estimate** 4-8-11   Ryan Moore
2 **Simenon** 6-9-2   Johnny Murtagh
3 **Top Trip** 4-9-0   Mickael Barzalona
7/2F, 5/1, 7/1. nk, 1l. 14 ran. 4m 20.51s (Sir Michael Stoute).

The staying division lacks a real star and **Estimate** filled the void on this occasion to land a historic victory for the Queen, though the form proved to be modest and she was well beaten in the Long Distance Cup on Champions Day, albeit when reportedly unsuited by much softer ground. The extra half-mile probably helped her as she saw out the trip too strongly for **Simenon** and **Top Trip**, while defending champion **Colour Vision** ran his best race since his 2012 win in fourth. The subsequent Prix du Cadran winner **Altano** was probably the best horse in the race, but he was given far too much to do before finishing strongly in fifth.

15 **Coronation Stakes (Fillies) (1m)**
Ascot June 21 (Good To Firm)
1 **Sky Lantern** 3-9-0   Richard Hughes
2 **Kenhope** 3-9-0   Thierry Jarnet
3 **Just The Judge** 3-9-0   Jamie Spencer
9/2J, 33/1, 5/1. 4l, nk. 17 ran. 1m 39.75s (Richard Hannon).

A devastating performance from **Sky Lantern**, who stepped up hugely on her 1,000 Guineas win by coming from last to first with a stunning turn of foot. Still well in rear turning for home, Sky Lantern stormed down the outside and drew clear of old rival **Just The Judge**, who ended up being pipped for second by **Kenhope**. The French filly franked the form with a good third to Elusive Kate in the Prix Rothschild, in which the fourth, **Maureen**, also finished closer, while Park Stakes winner **Viztoria** was only sixth, finding the mile beyond her.

16 Diamond Jubilee Stakes (6f)
Ascot June 22 (Good To Firm)

1 **Lethal Force** 4-9-4   Adam Kirby
2 **Society Rock** 6-9-4   Kieren Fallon
3 **Krypton Factor** 5-9-4   Luke Morris
11/1, 4/1F, 25/1. 2l, 1¾l. 18 ran. 1m 13.36s
(Clive Cox).

A clearcut win for the progressive **Lethal Force**, who had his superiority questioned having not won over 6f since his maiden but would prove to be the rising star of sprinting. The draw certainly helped Lethal Force on a day when it paid to race on the stands' side as the winner and the third, **Krypton Factor**, came from two of the highest four stalls, whereas **Society Rock** was left with plenty of ground to make up once switched to the rail from a middle draw, but it was subsequently shown to have made only a marginal difference as Lethal Force made virtually all the running, showing great speed to open up a decisive lead and staying on strongly. **Gordon Lord Byron** was a little more unfortunate as he found the ground too loose on the far side with the only three drawn outside him finishing among the last five, while **Slade Power** missed the break in seventh.

17 Dubai Duty Free Irish Derby (1m4f)
Curragh (IRE) June 29 (Good To Firm)

1 **Trading Leather** 3-9-0   Kevin Manning
2 **Galileo Rock** 3-9-0   Wayne Lordan
3 **Festive Cheer** 3-9-0   Seamie Heffernan
6/1, 9/1, 33/1. 1¾l, 1¾l. 9 ran. 2m 27.17s
J S Bolger).

A good win for **Trading Leather**, who took advantage of woeful performances from **Ruler Of The World** and **Libertarian** as the Derby third **Galileo Rock** instead proved his main threat. A stronger gallop was expected to suit that horse better than at Epsom, but Trading Leather still managed to stay on more strongly having raced handily throughout, relishing the quick conditions far more than most of the field. Ruler Of The World and Libertarian were particularly uneasy on the ground as only outsiders **Festive Cheer** and **Cap O'Rushes**, the subsequent Gordon Stakes winner, finished within 10l of the winner in a slightly disappointing contest.

18 Oxigen Environmental Pretty Polly Stakes (Fillies & Mares) (1m2f)
Curragh (IRE) June 30 (Good To Firm)

1 **Ambivalent** 4-9-10   Johnny Murtagh
2 **Was** 4-9-10   Joseph O'Brien

3 **Shirocco Star** 4-9-10   Kieren Fallon
10/1, 5/2F, 11/2. ½l, nk. 9 ran. 2m 4.83s
(Roger Varian).

The 2012 Oaks form had been shown up over the rest of that year and the Epsom one-two **Was** and **Shirocco Star** were again beaten by a surprise winner in **Ambivalent**. Setting out to make all the running, Ambivalent fought off a string of challengers as just 1½l covered the first five, with three-year-olds **Harasiya** and **Say** also going close in a very weak Group 1.

19 Coral-Eclipse (1m2f7y)
Sandown July 6 (Good To Firm)

1 **Al Kazeem** 5-9-7   James Doyle
2 **Declaration Of War** 4-9-7 Joseph O'Brien
3 **Mukhadram** 4-9-7   Paul Hanagan
15/8F, 4/1, 15/2. 2l, 1¼l. 7 ran. 2m 4.35s
(Roger Charlton).

A terrific race with five horses who won or placed across three different races at Royal Ascot and the Prince of Wales's Stakes form held sway as **Al Kazeem**'s season peaked early with a career-best performance to complete a Group 1 hat-trick. Once more **Mukhadram** provided Al Kazeem's main challenge, setting a more sedate pace and kicking for home early in the straight, but Al Kazeem gave him little leeway and was the only horse to go with him, steadily getting on top before drifting across his rival and forcing him to be snatched up. Mukhadram would otherwise have finished a fine second again but was instead passed by **Declaration Of War**, who stayed on well on this step up in distance but was let down by an overly conservative ride as he was never close enough to land a blow. **Mars** was one-paced in fourth as that quartet came clear of 66-1 shot **Miblish**, who had the disappointing pair **Pastorius** and **The Fugue**, the subject of a dirty post-race scope, behind him.

20 Etihad Airways Falmouth Stakes (Fillies & Mares) (1m)
Newmarket (July) July 12 (Good To Firm)

1 **Elusive Kate** 4-9-5   William Buick
2 **Sky Lantern** 3-8-10   Richard Hughes
3 **Giofra** 5-9-5   Christophe Soumillon
3/1, 4/7F, 5/1. nk, 2l. 4 ran. 1m 40.54s
(John Gosden).

A controversial finish saw **Elusive Kate** survive a lengthy stewards' inquiry despite carrying the desperately unlucky **Sky Lantern** all the way across the track. Elusive Kate had dictated a moderate gallop and quickened up well despite hanging, but Sky Lantern, already inconvenienced by the slow tempo, was left with little chance of passing her and was surely the best filly in the race judging by her victories in the Coronation and Sun Chariot Stakes, both times beating fillies who had pushed Elusive Kate closer.

21 Darley July Cup (6f) Newmarket (July) July 13 (Good To Firm)

1 **Lethal Force** 4-9-5   Adam Kirby
2 **Society Rock** 6-9-5   Kieren Fallon
3 **Slade Power** 4-9-5   Wayne Lordan
9/2, 11/2, 16/1. 1½l, ¾l. 11 ran. 1m 9.11s
(Clive Cox).

Another tremendous victory for **Lethal Force**, who confirmed himself a true champion by making all the running in a course-record time. Lethal Force showed such blistering speed that he had all his rivals in trouble from an early stage and reasserted again in the final furlong to win well from **Society Rock**, who got slightly closer than at Royal Ascot but had no excuses this time in second, with the improving **Slade Power** also beaten fair and square in third. King's Stand one-two **Shea Shea** and **Sole Power** ran better than the bare form suggests, with Shea Shea the only horse to briefly look a threat before failing to see out the trip well enough and Sole Power staying on well having been drawn on the wrong side. It was 2l back to **Gale Force Ten** as he struggled on his drop in trip.

22 Darley Irish Oaks (Fillies) (1m4f) Curragh (IRE) July 20 (Good To Firm)

1 **Chicquita** 3-9-0   Johnny Murtagh
2 **Venus De Milo** 3-9-0   Seamie Heffernan
3 **Just Pretending** 3-9-0   Joseph O'Brien
9/2, 6/1, 8/1. ½l, nk. 7 ran. 2m 35.01s
(A De Royer-Dupre).

Chicquita was sent to the Curragh to escape the shadow of the magnificent Treve, who had beaten her into second by 4l in the Prix de Diane, and she backed up her old rival's brilliance by winning with far more in hand than the narrow margin of victory suggests. Chicquita did herself no favours by hanging left throughout and then veering dramatically that way in the last half-furlong, but she overcame her wayward tendencies to overhaul **Just Pretending** and **Riposte**. That pair had also been given far too much rope in front off a slow gallop, whereas **Venus De Milo** and **Scintillula** did well to make up ground late and force a bunch finish in which just 1½l covered the first five.

23 King George VI and Queen Elizabeth Stakes (1m4f)
Ascot July 27 (Good To Firm)
1 **Novellist** 4-9-7   Johnny Murtagh
2 **Trading Leather** 3-8-9   Kevin Manning
3 **Hillstar** 3-8-9   Ryan Moore
13/2, 9/2, 5/1. 5l, ¾l. 8 ran. 2m 24.60s
(A Wohler).

A hugely impressive win from German raider **Novellist**, who tore the field apart in a course-record time and may well have had more big days to come but for injury. Ridden close to a furious pace, Novellist kicked clear early in the straight and stormed home from **Trading Leather**, who ran another rock-solid race in second to uphold the Classic form fairly well. The King Edward VII winner **Hillstar** was next, staying on well and enjoying the longer trip far more than when beaten more comfortably by the runner-up over 1m2f, as that pair pulled 3l clear of the disappointing **Cirrus Des Aigles**, who was below his best at the time and unsuited by the quick ground, and the Princess of Wales's Stakes winner **Universal**.

24 Qipco Sussex Stakes (1m)
Goodwood July 31 (Good To Soft)
1 **Toronado** 3-8-13   Richard Hughes
2 **Dawn Approach** 3-8-13   Kevin Manning
3 **Declaration Of War** 4-9-7 Joseph O'Brien
11/4, 10/11F, 7/2. ½l, 2½l. 7 ran. 1m 36.29s
(Richard Hannon).

Another sensational duel between **Dawn Approach** and **Toronado**, with the latter turning the tables this time, as the pair confirmed their brilliance by putting a strong older challenge firmly in its place for the first time. Dawn Approach seemed to run up to his best, committing for home early and staying on strongly to the line, but Toronado was able to make his move far more smoothly than had been the case at Ascot and quickened up well to edge past close home. **Declaration Of War** couldn't live with the first two, yet he still travelled strongly and was beaten just 3l, pulling well clear of **Trade Storm** and **Gregorian** as he extended his superiority over that pair from the Queen Anne. The Irish raider was a closer fourth to Moonlight Cloud next time in the Prix Jacques le Marois to confirm the quality of the first two and the fact that Dawn Approach, disappointing in that French race and the QEII, was over the top by then.

25 Markel Insurance Nassau Stakes (Fillies & Mares) (1m1f192y)
Goodwood August 3 (Good)
1 **Winsili** 3-8-11   William Buick

2014 RFO Flat Guide

NOVELLIST: enjoys a brilliant swansong in the King George at Ascot

2 **Thistle Bird** 5-9-6   James Doyle
3 **Hot Snap** 3-8-11   Tom Queally
20/1, 33/1, 5/1. nk, 2l. 14 ran. 2m 6.19s
(John Gosden).

With few top-class older fillies around and the two best – The Fugue and Dank – absent, this looked at the mercy of the Classic generation, though **Thistle Bird** would prove highly progressive when going on to finish a close third in the Prix de l'Opera and at least pushed **Winsili** to a smart performance in victory. A non-stayer when stepped up to 1m4f in the Ribblesdale, Winsili still had too much stamina close home for Thistle Bird and **Sajjhaa**, while **Hot Snap** stayed on well to split that pair. **Sky Lantern** was twice blocked in her run to prevent the chance to judge whether she really got 1m2f, though **Integral** would clearly benefit from dropping to a mile after finishing seventh, while **Ambivalent** failed to act on the track and **Just The Judge** ripped off a shoe.

26 Juddmonte International Stakes (1m2f88y)
York August 21 (Good To Firm)
1 **Declaration Of War** 4-9-5   Joseph O'Brien
2 **Trading Leather** 3-8-11   Kevin Manning
3 **Al Kazeem** 5-9-5   James Doyle
7/1, 5/1, 11/8F. 1¼l, 1½l. 6 ran. 2m 5.74s
(A P O'Brien).

Declaration Of War seemed to have had his limitations exposed after three defeats since his Queen Anne win, but connections finally found the key to him as a more forceful ride over this longer trip saw him land a brilliant win. Ridden too conservatively in the Eclipse, Declaration Of War benefited from a more aggressive ride as he stuck close to **Al Kazeem** throughout and responded immediately when that one kicked for home early in the straight, quickening past him and staying on strongly. Al Kazeem was clearly below his best as he also allowed the front-running **Trading Leather** to battle back past him, as was **Toronado** as he trailed home last of six having suffered more breathing problems, but Declaration Of War would prove every bit as good as that outstanding pair when just touched off in more stamina-sapping conditions on dirt in the Breeders' Cup Classic.

27 Darley Yorkshire Oaks (Fillies & Mares) (1m4f)
York August 22 (Good To Firm)
1 **The Fugue** 4-9-7   William Buick
2 **Venus De Milo** 3-8-11   Ryan Moore
3 **Secret Gesture** 3-8-11   Jamie Spencer
2/1F, 9/4, 6/1. 4l, 3¼l. 7 ran. 2m 28.29s
(John Gosden).

An outstanding win for **The Fugue**, who had been unlucky not to win more than one Group 1 previously and underlined her class in tremendous fashion. The Fugue was always going well behind a strong gallop and eased alongside **Venus De Milo** before quickening clear of the Irish Oaks runner-up, who proved much the best of the three-year-olds in second. **Secret Gesture** was next, again looking capable of better as she was briefly short of room and not given a hard race thereafter. She still pulled clear of **Scintillula**, who was starting to lose her form after a busy schedule on her fourth run since the Irish Oaks, and the below-par **Riposte**.

28 Coolmore Nunthorpe Stakes (5f) York August 23 (Good To Soft)

1 **Jwala** 4-9-8   Steve Drowne
2 **Shea Shea** 6-9-11   Frankie Dettori
3 **Sole Power** 6-9-11   Johnny Murtagh
40/1, 3/1F, 4/1. ½l, nse. 17 ran. 57.34s
(Robert Cowell).

Yet another strange result in a race renowned for shocks as **Jwala** held off the late challenges of **Shea Shea** and **Sole Power**. The placed horses set the standard on their King's Stand form and weren't as inconvenienced by the ground as many felt, with it still being quick enough for Jwala to beat standard time, but they weren't helped by being drawn on the far side – no others from the bottom seven stalls finished in the first ten – which left them with too much ground to make up. In contrast Jwala, a previous course-and-distance winner, was always prominent in the centre of the track along with another York specialist, **Hamish McGonagall**, whose presence in fourth, beaten little over 1l, holds down the form. **Kingsgate Native** and **Tick-**

led **Pink** were next from good draws with **Rosdhu Queen** and **Swiss Spirit** next best of those from low berths.

29 Betfred Sprint Cup (6f) Haydock September 7 (Good To Soft)

1 **Gordon Lord Byron** 5-9-3   J Murtagh
2 **Slade Power** 4-9-3   Wayne Lordan
3 **Hoof It** 6-9-3   Graham Gibbons
7/2, 9/1, 33/1. 3l, ¾l. 13 ran. 1m 12.25s
(T Hogan).

Soft ground helped **Gordon Lord Byron**, but there was much more to his victory than favourable conditions as he absolutely demolished an admittedly moderate bunch of rivals. Second in 2012 on much faster ground and more adaptable than most to some cut, Gordon Lord Byron showed his class as he kicked clear into a huge lead before the furlong pole and was able to coast to a comprehensive victory, though it was put into context by his subsequent thrashing at the hands of a real superstar in Moonlight Cloud. **Slade Power** was the best of the rest despite not running to his best, holding off the veteran **Hoof It**, while among the disappointments were **Lethal Force**, who was never going well, and **Garswood**, a 7f specialist who was badly outpaced even on soft ground before staying on into sixth.

GORDON LORD BYRON: coped best with soft ground in the Sprint Cup

30 Red Mills Irish Champion Stakes (1m2f)

Leopardstown (IRE) September 7 (Good)
1 **The Fugue** 4-9-4   William Buick
2 **Al Kazeem** 5-9-7   James Doyle
3 **Trading Leather** 3-9-0   Kevin Manning
4/1, 9/10F, 5/1. 1¼l, 2l. 6 ran. 2m 5.22s
(John Gosden).

A landmark win for **The Fugue**, who gained her first Group 1 against colts – and her third in total – with a fine performance to beat **Al Kazeem**, admittedly helped by the favourite's late-season dip in form. Held up early, The Fugue showed by far the greater turn of foot when asked to quicken in the straight, comfortably easing clear of Al Kazeem, who stuck on at one pace without the spark of his earlier Group 1 hat-trick. **Trading Leather** was slightly below his best on the slowest ground he had encountered since beaten in the Dante but still pulled clear of **Parish Hall**.

31 Coolmore Fusaichi Pegasus Matron Stakes (Fillies & Mares) (1m)

Leopardstown (IRE) September 7 (Good)
1 **La Collina** 4-9-5   Chris Hayes
2 **Lily's Angel** 4-9-5   Gary Carroll
3 **Say** 3-9-0   Seamie Heffernan
25/1, 14/1, 8/1. ½l, shd. 12 ran. 1m 39.00s
(Kevin Prendergast).

A desperately weak Group 1 with none of the field having won above Group 3 level in the previous two years nor any proving particularly progressive as **La Collina**, who had struggled to build on her Group 1 win as a two-year-old in 2011 and was well beaten next time in the Sun Chariot, came out on top. She stayed on well to pip **Lily's Angel** and **Say** as the trio pulled 3½l clear of the pack, led by **Kenhope**, who should have won on her best form but was given far too much to do. The progressive **Fiesolana** was another disappointment in fifth and stepped up massively on this form when winning the Challenge Stakes next time.

32 Ladbrokes St Leger Stakes (1m6f132y)

Doncaster September 14 (Good To Soft)
1 **Leading Light** 3-9-0   Joseph O'Brien
2 **Talent** 3-8-11   Jim Crowley
3 **Galileo Rock** 3-9-0   Wayne Lordan
7/2F, 9/1, 6/1. 1¼l, ¾l. 11 ran. 3m 9.20s
(A P O'Brien).

Leading Light produced a gutsy victory as he held off a trio of Epsom principals, all of whom seemed to stay the trip well enough to give the form a solid look. The most proven stayer in the field having won the Queen's Vase at Royal Ascot over 2m – and perhaps unsuited by dropping in trip for the Arc – Leading Light was ridden handily and hit the front early before staying on too strongly for Oaks winner **Talent**, who bounced back to form in second and just pipped the admirably consistent **Galileo Rock**. **Libertarian** also showed his true colours again in fourth, while **Foundry** and subsequent Cumberland Lodge winner **Secret Number** were also beaten less than 4l, running exactly to the form of their placed efforts behind the absent Telescope in the Great Voltigeur. Just 3¾l covered that sextet, but the rest were well strung out.

33 GAIN Irish St. Leger (1m6f)

Curragh (IRE) September 15 (Good)
1 **Voleuse De Coeurs** 4-9-8   Chris Hayes
2 **Ahzeemah** 4-9-11   Silvestre De Sousa
3 **Saddler's Rock** 5-9-11 Declan McDonogh
9/1, 7/2F, 16/1. 6l, hd. 10 ran. 3m 0.08s
(D K Weld).

Voleuse De Coeurs produced a demolition job that certainly turned many heads as she was subsequently sold to Australia. The fast-improving filly took up the running early in the straight and spreadeagled the field, storming clear of rock-solid favourite **Ahzeemah** and **Saddler's Rock**, who bounced back to the form of his 2012 Ascot Gold Cup third. That pair were in turn nearly 5l clear of **Red Cadeaux** and the 2012 winner **Royal Diamond**, who went on to win the Long Distance Cup under much more patient tactics, though a line through Saddler's Rock shows he would have had no chance with the winner anyway.

34 Kingdom of Bahrain Sun Chariot Stakes (Fillies & Mares) (1m)

Newmarket September 28 (Good To Firm)
1 **Sky Lantern** 3-8-13   Richard Hughes
2 **Integral** 3-8-13   Ryan Moore
3 **Duntle** 4-9-3   Wayne Lordan
7/4F, 8/1, 8/1. 1l, 2l. 7 ran. 1m 38.02s
(Richard Hannon).

Sky Lantern bounced back to her best with another magnificent victory as she saw off another potential star in **Integral**. Having tracked the ailing **Elusive Kate**, Sky Lantern was forced to dig deep as Integral made what looked a race-winning move on the opposite side of the field, but Sky Lantern picked up well to win going away. Integral still ran a huge race to finish a clear second ahead of **Duntle**, who enjoyed the fast ground far more than when second to Elusive Kate in the Prix Rothschild, whereas that filly found conditions too quick in fourth, although she would have been highly unlikely to beat Sky Lantern anyway. **La Collina** was fifth.

35 Qatar Prix de l'Arc de Triomphe (1m4f)
Longchamp (FR) October 6 (Soft)
1 **Treve** 3-8-8   Thierry Jarnet
2 **Orfevre** 5-9-5   Christophe Soumillon
3 **Intello** 3-8-11   Olivier Peslier
9/2, 2/1F, 9/1. 5l, nk. 17 ran. 2m 32.04s
(Mme C Head-Maarek).

A magnificent performance from **Treve**, who stormed clear of an outstanding international field. France's superstar filly, who had already won the Prix de Diane and the Prix Vermeille, pulled in the early stages behind a slow pace, but that suited her later in the contest as she had far too much speed for her rivals, committing early with a sensational turn of foot and drawing further clear as other class acts gave chase to spreadeagle the field. **Orfevre**, desperately unlucky when second in 2012, was thumped fair and square this time to show the strength of the form, finishing ahead of two top-class three-year-olds in **Intello** and Prix Niel winner **Kizuna**, with Godolphin-bound **Penglai Pavilion** in fifth. It was 11½l back from Treve to **Al Kazeem** in sixth, though the leading British finisher wasn't helped by a stumble around halfway and **Ruler Of The World** stayed on really well in seventh having badly lost his position turning for home. **Leading Light** lacked the pace to get involved on this drop in trip and consequently struggled to get a clear run.

36 Qipco British Champions Fillies & Mares Stakes (1m4f)
Ascot October 19 (Soft)
1 **Seal Of Approval** 4-9-3   George Baker
2 **Belle De Crecy** 4-9-3   Johnny Murtagh
3 **Talent** 3-8-10   Jim Crowley
16/1, 10/1, 7/2C. 4l, nk. 8 ran. 2m 39.09s
(James Fanshawe).

A hugely impressive victory for the progressive **Seal Of Approval**, who put several smart fillies firmly in their place in this newly upgraded Group 1. Unbeaten since her debut when completing – she had suffered a nasty fall when still just in contention in a Group 2 won by The Lark on her previous start – Seal Of Approval showed terrific reserves of stamina to grind down her rivals and win going away. The form was solid as Oaks winner **Talent** was just pipped for second by **Belle De Crecy**, who confirmed the

form of a Group 2 win over **Hot Snap** with that filly finishing a solid fifth behind the Prix de l'Opera winner **Dalkala**.

37 Queen Elizabeth II Stakes (1m)
Ascot October 19 (Soft)
1 **Olympic Glory** 3-9-0   Richard Hughes
2 **Top Notch Tonto** 3-9-0   Dale Swift
3 **Kingsbarns** 3-9-0   Joseph O'Brien
11/2, 14/1, 14/1. 3¼l, ¾l. 12 ran. 1m 44.18s
(Richard Hannon).

Olympic Glory's brilliance had gone under the radar for much of the season, but he had his day on the biggest stage with a comfortable victory. Just beaten by Moonlight Cloud in the Prix Jacques le Marois, Olympic Glory quickened up well in first-time blinkers to come clear in the final furlong. **Dawn Approach** had looked the better horse on a line through Declaration Of War after the Marois and that may well be the case, but he scoped badly after running in France and was again below his best, signing off with a disappointing fourth as several horses failed to give their running with a fierce gallop on soft ground making the race a war of attrition. That said, **Top Notch Tonto**, previously untried above Group 3 level, and **Kingsbarns**, on only his second run since the 2012 Racing Post Trophy, did brilliantly to fill the places.

38 Qipco Champion Stakes (1m2f)
Ascot October 19 (Soft)
1 **Farhh** 5-9-3   Silvestre De Sousa
2 **Cirrus Des Aigles** 7-9-3   C Soumillon
3 **Ruler Of The World** 3-8-12 Ryan Moore
11/4, 6/4F, 13/2. nk, ½l. 10 ran. 2m 12.02s
(Saeed bin Suroor).

A thrilling finish worthy of the massive prize fund, making up for the slightly questionable field, as **Farhh** saw off **Cirrus Des Aigles** and **Ruler Of The World**. The race lacked any of the season's previous 12 Group 1 winners at the trip in Europe, but Farhh, sidelined by injury since his Lockinge victory, may well have added his name to that list before this race on the strength of a fine win. Farhh was always handy behind stablemate **Hunter's Light** and kicked clear early in the straight, bravely holding off persistent challenges from Cirrus Des Aigles, who had yet to show his best form all year but at least went down fighting, and Ruler Of The World, who just lacked the speed to get to the front on this drop in trip. The trio pulled 6l clear of Hunter's Light as he just held on to fourth from **Mukhadram**, who was unsuited by a switch to hold-up tactics, and **Hillstar**.

Group 1 index

All horses placed or commented on in our Group 1 review section, with race numbers

DECLARATION OF WAR: a regular competitor in the best races last season

WINSILI (left): winning the Nassau Stakes on her first run at the top level

Est. 1909

RACING & FOOTBALL OUTLOOK

Two-year-old review by Dylan Hill

1 Alfred Nobel Rochestown Stakes (Listed) (6f)
Naas (IRE) June 3 (Good To Firm)
1 **Stubbs** 2-9-3   Joseph O'Brien
2 **Sacha Park** 2-9-3   Pat Dobbs
3 **Club Wexford** 2-9-3   Kevin Manning
8/13F, 11/4, 4/1. 1¾l, 2l. 4 ran. 1m 11.90s
(A P O'Brien).

A smart performance from **Stubbs**, better than he would manage to show when a disappointing sixth in the Coventry Stakes, as he comfortably saw off British raider **Sacha Park**, who got much closer when sixth in the Windsor Castle at Royal Ascot. The third, **Club Wexford**, had finished second to Norfolk Stakes second Coach House in another Listed race at the track earlier.

2 Coolmore Stud European Breeders Fund Fillies' Sprint Stakes (Listed) (6f)
Naas (IRE) June 3 (Good To Firm)
1 **Sandiva** 2-9-0   Pat Smullen
2 **Heart Focus** 2-9-0   Kevin Manning
3 **Fig Roll** 2-9-0   Pat Dobbs
7/4F, 8/1, 9/2. 2l, 4½l. 10 ran. 1m 10.26s
(Richard Fahey).

A strong race featuring three top-four finishers from Royal Ascot in the places and an impressive early marker from British raider **Sandiva**, who drew clear with **Heart Focus** as the pair left **Fig Roll** trailing in their wake.

3 Coventry Stakes (Group 2) (6f)
Ascot June 18 (Good)
1 **War Command** 2-9-1   Seamie Heffernan
2 **Parbold** 2-9-1   Tony Hamilton
3 **Sir John Hawkins** 2-9-1   Ryan Moore

20/1, 16/1, 6/1. 6l, ¾l. 15 ran. 1m 12.86s
(A P O'Brien).

A much weaker contest than recent runnings of what has become one of the premier two-year-old races in the calendar, but **War Command** marmalised his rivals to suggest that he was still an excellent winner. War Command wasn't well away, but he made smooth headway and stormed clear of his rivals once hitting the front. The form of those behind was only average for the grade with **Parbold** leading a distant pack ahead of **Sir John Hawkins**, **Thunder Strike** and **Jallota**, while favourite **Stubbs** was below par in sixth.

4 Windsor Castle Stakes (Listed) (5f)
Ascot June 18 (Good)
1 **Extortionist** 2-9-3   Johnny Murtagh
2 **Supplicant** 2-9-3   Tony Hamilton
3 **Anticipated** 2-9-3   Richard Hughes
16/1, 20/1, 4/1F. nk, shd. 24 ran. 59.82s
(Olly Stevens).

This race probably had more strength in depth than either of the Group 2 contests over the trip at Royal Ascot and **Extortionist** was a fine winner, doing better than he would on softer ground later in the season. **Anticipated** and **Supplicant** were next and may well have finished first and second in the Molecomb next time with more luck in running, while **My Catch** and **Wilshire Boulevard** were both future Pattern winners among those further back.

5 Queen Mary Stakes (Group 2) (Fillies) (5f)
Ascot June 19 (Good To Firm)
1 **Rizeena** 2-8-12   James Doyle

NO NAY NEVER: the brilliant American powerhouse lights up Royal Ascot

2 **Sweet Emma Rose** 2-8-12   J Rosario
3 **One Chance** 2-8-12   Andrea Atzeni
6/1, 16/1, 66/1. 2l, 1l. 23 ran. 59.29s
(Clive Brittain).

Despite soon needing much further to produce her best, **Rizeena** was still much too good for a moderate field as she ran out an impressive winner. Rizeena was understandably doing all her best work at the death, finishing well on top having taken until the final 100 yards to wear down American raider **Sweet Emma Rose**. However, the presence of 66-1 shot **One Chance** and Naas third **Fig Roll** in the next two places hinted at the weakness of the bare form and so it proved, even though Fig Roll landed a very soft Listed race at Newmarket next time.

**6 Norfolk Stakes (Group 2) (5f)
Ascot June 20 (Good To Firm)**
1 **No Nay Never** 2-9-1   J Rosario
2 **Coach House** 2-9-1   Joseph O'Brien
3 **Wind Fire** 2-8-12   Jamie Spencer
4/1, 9/4F, 16/1. 1l, hd. 14 ran. 58.80s
(Wesley A Ward).

A successful raid for American flyer **No Nay Never**, who met a fairly average bunch of juveniles and was much too good for them. Heavily restrained having been keen early, No Nay Never was always holding **Coach House** and **Wind Fire**, while there was a small gap back to **Ambiance**, with the latter pair at least good enough to win at Listed level. Flying Childers winner **Green Door** was seventh but he struggled before that Doncaster success, while Richmond winner **Saayerr** found the trip too sharp in eighth.

**7 Albany Stakes (Group 3) (Fillies) (6f)
Ascot June 21 (Good To Firm)**
1 **Kiyoshi** 2-8-12   Jamie Spencer
2 **Sandiva** 2-8-12   Frankie Dettori
3 **Joyeuse** 2-8-12   Tom Queally
8/1, 7/4F, 6/1. 3¼l, nk. 19 ran. 1m 13.82s
(Charles Hills).

A remarkable victory for **Kiyoshi**, who was good enough to thrash a strong field despite hanging all the way across the track in the closing stages. Although she was left with something to prove after two slightly disappointing efforts at Group 1 level, previous Listed winner **Sandiva** went on to frank the form, winning a strong Group 3 at Deauville and running well for a long way in the Prix Marcel Boussac, and so too did several of those behind, with **Lucky Kristale** (undercooked according to her trainer after finishing sixth) and **Wonderfully** (better over further) the most significant improvers. The exception was **Heart Focus**, who seemed over-raced after finishing fourth.

8 Chesham Stakes (Listed) (7f)
Ascot June 22 (Good To Firm)

1 **Berkshire** 2-9-3   Jim Crowley
2 **Bunker** 2-9-3   Richard Hughes
3 **Ihtimal** 2-8-12   Silvestre De Sousa
16/1, 11/4F, 7/1. 2½l, 1½l. 19 ran. 1m 28.46s
(Paul Cole).

A terrific renewal featuring a string of future Pattern winners, with **Berkshire** leading the way as he showed a terrific turn of foot to come clear of **Bunker**. Nonetheless, the bare form may just have been exaggerated subsequently with too much read into the improvement made by **Ihtimal** and **Somewhat**, who also challenged on the opposite side of the track to Berkshire in finishing third and fourth – as did Bunker – so had the worst of a strong draw bias shown throughout the day.

9 Dubai Duty Free Full Of Surprises Railway Stakes (Group 2) (6f)
Curragh (IRE) June 29 (Good)

1 **Sudirman** 2-9-3   Wayne Lordan
2 **Big Time** 2-9-3   Shane Foley
3 **Coach House** 2-9-3   Joseph O'Brien
5/1, 9/2, 8/15F. ½l, 4¼l. 5 ran. 1m 11.73s
(David Wachman).

The first of two terrific battles between the leading pair saw **Sudirman** give an early indication of his narrow superiority over **Big Time**, showing typical determination as he just got on top in the final 100 yards. The pair pulled clear of Norfolk runner-up **Coach House**, who missed the rest of the season after such a disappointing effort.

10 Grangecon Stud Stakes (Group 3) (Fillies) (6f)
Curragh (IRE) June 30 (Good To Firm)

1 **Bye Bye Birdie** 2-9-0   Joseph O'Brien
2 **Heart Focus** 2-9-0   Kevin Manning
3 **Clenor** 2-9-0   Wayne Lordan
9/2, 5/4F, 7/2. 3l, 2½l. 7 ran. 1m 10.94s
(A P O'Brien).

A clearcut win for **Bye Bye Birdie**, who improved for the extra furlong having found the Queen Mary too sharp, though she was flattered by the bare form as **Heart Focus** fell well below the level of her Albany fourth on her sixth run in less than two months.

11 Portland Place Properties July Stakes (Group 2) (6f)
Newmarket (July) July 11 (Good To Firm)

1 **Anjaal** 2-8-12   Paul Hanagan
2 **Figure Of Speech** 2-8-12   M Barzalona
3 **Jallota** 2-8-12   Martin Harley
14/1, 7/2, 20/1. nk, hd. 11 ran. 1m 11.21s

(Richard Hannon).

A moderate contest in which less than 1l covered the first four, with **Anjaal**, seen only once more when fourth in the Dewhurst, pouncing late to deny **Figure Of Speech** and possibly flattered even by the bare form as the next three all suffered misfortune in running. Figure Of Speech showed a terrific turn of foot to cut through the field in penultimate furlong but paid for that effort when folding close home, while **Sir John Hawkins** and **Jallota** raced too close to a furious early gallop that even saw subsequent Middle Park winner **Astaire** weaken badly into sixth having led at the furlong pole. **Brown Sugar** was another future Pattern winner to flop as he raced far too keenly.

12 Duchess of Cambridge Stakes (Group 2) (Fillies) (6f)
Newmarket (July) July 12 (Good To Firm)

1 **Lucky Kristale** 2-8-12   Tom Queally
2 **Rizeena** 2-9-1   James Doyle
3 **Queen Catrine** 2-8-12   James McDonald
20/1, 11/10F, 7/1. 2¼l, ¾l. 8 ran. 1m 10.76s
(George Margarson).

A commanding performance from rising star **Lucky Kristale**, who had finished only sixth in the Albany but left that form well behind under a far more patient ride, producing a devastating turn of foot. **Rizeena** was below her best, getting bumped off her stride over a furlong out and proceeding to hang left, but **Queen Catrine** would prove a rock-solid yardstick in third to show the strength of the form through her second to subsequent Cheveley Park runner-up **Princess Noor** in the Princess Margaret, although that filly was nowhere near that form this time in fifth.

13 32Red.com Superlative Stakes (Group 2) (7f)
Newmarket (July) July 13 (Good To Firm)

1 **Good Old Boy Lukey** 2-9-0   Ryan Moore
2 **Somewhat** 2-9-0   Johnny Murtagh
3 **Washaar** 2-9-0   Dane O'Neill
7/2, 11/4F, 7/2. hd, 2l. 8 ran. 1m 24.58s
(Richard Fahey).

A modest race for the grade with **Somewhat** sent off favourite despite being beaten by 8l in the Chesham and yet to reach his level later in the campaign, with Mark Johnston confirming he was still weak, though he still ran a fine race in losing out narrowly to **Good Old Boy Lukey**. The pair forced the pace throughout and had the field well strung out, with only **Washaar** finishing within 4½l, as Good Old Boy Lukey just proved strongest.

14 Silver Flash Stakes (Group 3) (7f)
Leopardstown (IRE) July 18 (Good To Firm)
1 **Wonderfully** 2-9-0   Joseph O'Brien
2 **Perhaps** 2-9-0   Seamie Heffernan
3 **Avenue Gabriel** 2-9-0   Chris Hayes
13/8F, 11/2, 9/2. 1l, ½l. 6 ran. 1m 26.65s
(A P O'Brien).

Having stayed on well into seventh in the Albany, **Wonderfully** proved well suited to an extra furlong and ran out a comfortable winner over stablemate **Perhaps** and **Avenue Gabriel**, with the placed horses both doing well subsequently to mark this out as a really smart performance.

15 Jebel Ali Racecourse & Stables Anglesey Stakes (Group 3) (6f63y)
Curragh (IRE) July 20 (Good To Firm)
1 **Wilshire Boulevard** 2-9-3   S Heffernan
2 **Oklahoma City** 2-9-3   Joseph O'Brien
3 **Mansion House** 2-9-3   W J Lee
7/1, EvensF, 12/1. ¾l, ½l. 7 ran. 1m 15.78s
(A P O'Brien).

Aidan O'Brien won this race with the wrong horse as his second string **Wilshire Boulevard** turned over his more talented stablemate **Oklahoma City**, who would prove better over further. The favourite also wasn't helped by missing the break as he had to be rousted to the front and could never shake off Wilshire Boulevard, who led at the furlong pole and stayed on well. **Jallota** was beaten just over 2l in fourth.

16 Korean Racing Authority Tyros Stakes (Group 3) (7f)
Leopardstown (IRE) July 25 (Good)
1 **Exogenesis** 2-9-3   Gary Carroll
2 **Home School** 2-9-3   Kevin Manning
3 **Sir John Hawkins** 2-9-3   Joseph O'Brien
11/8, 8/1, 11/10F. ½l, 1¼l. 5 ran. 1m 30.50s
(G M Lyons).

A good performance from **Exogenesis**, who saw off the much improved **Home School**. The runner-up relished a switch to front-running tactics having been held up without much success in the Anglesey, doing well enough to earn a move to the United States, but Exogenesis stayed on well to come out on top with **Sir John Hawkins** only third and **Simple Love** beaten further than when fifth to Wonderfully on her previous start.

17 Princess Margaret Juddmonte Stakes (Group 3) (Fillies) (6f)
Ascot July 27 (Good To Firm)
1 **Princess Noor** 2-8-12   Andrea Atzeni
2 **Queen Catrine** 2-8-12   Olivier Peslier
3 **Along Again** 2-8-12   Ryan Moore
25/1, 5/1, 9/1. 2l, ¾l. 10 ran. 1m 12.74s
(Roger Varian).

Princess Noor had been well beaten in the Albany and the Duchess of Cambridge, but she was much improved by first-time blinkers and would prove her victory was no fluke with a fine second in the Cheveley Park. Princess Noor comprehensively turned around previous form with **Queen Catrine**, who ran another solid race in second, while **Wind Fire** was below her best in fifth as she would finish much closer to the runner-up in the Lowther.

18 bet365 Molecomb Stakes (Group 3) (5f)
Goodwood July 30 (Good To Soft)
1 **Brown Sugar** 2-9-0   Pat Dobbs
2 **Anticipated** 2-9-0   Richard Hughes
3 **Ambiance** 2-9-0   Martin Harley
8/1, 7/2, 8/1. nk, 1¼l. 8 ran. 59.30s
(Richard Hannon).

A good sprint with **Brown Sugar**, a big improver having settled much better than in the July Stakes, just pipping his more fancied stablemate **Anticipated**. Brown Sugar would prove good enough to defy a penalty in the same grade on his next run, but he was fortunate to come out on top this time with the fast-finishing Anticipated denied a clear run in time and favourite **Supplicant** also badly affected in fifth in a tightly-bunched contest before making amends later in the campaign. **Ambiance**, a Listed winner at Sandown since his Norfolk fourth, ran up to form in third ahead of **Sleeper King**.

19 Veuve Clicquot Vintage Stakes (Group 2) (7f)
Goodwood July 31 (Good To Soft)
1 **Toormore** 2-9-0   Richard Hughes
2 **Outstrip** 2-9-0   Mickael Barzalona
3 **Parbold** 2-9-0   Paul Hanagan
5/4F, 5/1, 11/4. nk, 1½l. 7 ran. 1m 27.57s
(Richard Hannon).

A terrific field with **Toormore** and **Outstrip** going on to success at the top level, and the runner-up was in fact unlucky not to have won this race to boot as he paid the price for racing too close to a strong pace. Outstrip quickened clear when his fellow prominent racers dropped out quickly, but he was powerless to prevent Toormore sweeping past close home as the winner and **Parbold** in third finished strongly from the rear, seemingly benefiting from more patient tactics.

20 Audi Richmond Stakes (Group 2) (6f)

Goodwood August 1 (Good)
1 **Saayerr** 2-9-0   Ryan Moore
2 **Cable Bay** 2-9-0   Jamie Spencer
3 **Thunder Strike** 2-9-0   Richard Hughes
5/1, 20/1, 7/1. nk, 2¼l. 10 ran. 1m 10.14s
(William Haggas).

A fair contest with several runners proven at a similar level and leading pair **Saayerr** and **Cable Bay** did well to pull clear after most of the field had been in contention at the furlong pole. Disappointing at Royal Ascot, Saayerr relished an extra furlong as he just outfought Cable Bay, who was having only his second start and would go on to progress past the winner. **Thunder Strike** was third as he confirmed his Coventry form with **Jallota**, while **Figure Of Speech** split that pair and **Miracle Of Medinah** was only ninth.

21 Coolmore Canford Cliffs Stakes (Listed) (7f100y)

Tipperary (IRE) August 9 (Good)
1 **Indian Maharaja** 2-9-3   Joseph O'Brien
2 **Ceisteach** 2-8-12   Kevin Manning
3 **Fly To The Moon** 2-8-12   Wayne Lordan
30/100F, 14/1, 20/1. 3l, 1¾l. 6 ran. 1m 33.96s
(A P O'Brien).

An easy win for **Indian Maharaja**, though the form was desperately moderate and did nothing to back up his sky-high home reputation. Indian Maharaja was ridden clear to win very comfortably, but his five opponents lost all ten subsequent starts between them with

two beaten favourites next time.

22 German-Thoroughbred.com Sweet Solera Stakes (Group 3) (Fillies) (7f)

Newmarket (July) August 10 (Good To Firm)
1 **Ihtimal** 2-8-12   William Buick
2 **Midnite Angel** 2-8-12   Frankie Dettori
3 **Wedding Ring** 2-8-12   Jamie Spencer
11/4F, 3/1, 7/2. 2¾l, ½l. 8 ran. 1m 24.07s
(Saeed bin Suroor).

A comfortable win for **Ihtimal** as she took a stepping stone on the way to bigger targets ahead. Building on the huge promise she had shown in the Chesham as she extended her Ascot superiority over the fifth, **Tinga**, by nearly 3l, Ihtimal was far too good for **Midnite Angel**, with **Wedding Ring** next.

23 Keeneland Phoenix Stakes (Group 1) (6f)

Curragh (IRE) August 11 (Good)
1 **Sudirman** 2-9-3   Wayne Lordan
2 **Big Time** 2-9-3   Pat Smullen
3 **War Command** 2-9-3   Joseph O'Brien
4/1, 7/1, 2/5F. ½l, ½l. 5 ran. 1m 9.35s
(David Wachman).

War Command was below his best as he finished a one-paced third behind **Sudirman** and **Big Time**, who admittedly provided much stiffer opposition than at Royal Ascot. Sudirman and Big Time ran exactly to the form of their Railway Stakes clash, with the gutsy winner always just on top, and he may still be better than he showed over an extra

SUDIRMAN (second right): confirms his narrow superiority over Big Time

furlong in the National Stakes and on softer ground in the Middle Park. The trio pulled 3½l clear of **Ambiance** in fourth.

24 Friarstown Stud Debutante Stakes (Fillies) (Group 2) (7f)
Curragh (IRE) August 11 (Good)
1 **Tapestry** 2-9-0   Joseph O'Brien
2 **Perhaps** 2-9-0   Seamie Heffernan
3 **Avenue Gabriel** 2-9-0   Chris Hayes
4/5F, 11/4, 8/1. 1¾l, ½l. 6 ran. 1m 22.89s
(A P O'Brien).

A smooth win for **Tapestry**, who had made a big impression on her debut and stayed on strongly from off the pace to master **Perhaps** and **Avenue Gabriel**. The placed horses ran exactly to the form of their Silver Flash battle behind **Wonderfully** and pulled well clear of the remainder, who included a Listed winner in **Sacred Aspect** and another with fair form at that level in **Glassatura**.

25 Denford Stud Stakes (registered as the Washington Singer Stakes) (Listed) (7f)
Newbury August 17 (Good)
1 **Somewhat** 2-9-0   Gerald Mosse
2 **Be Ready** 2-8-11   Kieren Fallon
3 **Speedy Approach** 2-9-0 Johnny Murtagh
11/8F, 5/2, 11/2. 4½l, 3¼l. 7 ran. 1m 25.57s
(Mark Johnston).

A fine performance by **Somewhat** as he took a significant step forward on his midsummer form, making all and quickening away from a very smart rival in **Be Ready**. The Godolphin colt would also leave this form behind, unsurprisingly as he was making his debut, yet he still pulled clear of several useful rivals as **Somewhat** left the field well strung out.

26 Darley Prix Morny (Group 1) (6f) Deauville (FR) August 18 (Good To Soft)
1 **No Nay Never** 2-9-0   D Flores
2 **Vorda** 2-8-10   Gregory Benoist
3 **Rizeena** 2-8-10   Ryan Moore
7/4, 13/8F, 6/1. 1l, ¾l. 10 ran. 1m 9.82s
(Wesley A Ward).

Another big win for American raider **No Nay Never**, who faced a far stronger field than at Royal Ascot but produced an outstanding performance to win with just as much authority over an extra furlong. No Nay Never gradually wound up the pace and had the race won by the furlong pole, comfortably holding off top-class fillies **Vorda** and **Rizeena**, both of whom would also win Group 1 races on their next starts. The presence of **Jallota** in fourth could be used to knock the form, but

he seemed to run by far a career-best to finish ahead of **Brown Sugar**, who also gained a notable win next time, with that quintet pulling 3l clear of **Muharaaj**. **Figure Of Speech** and **Anticipated** were among the also-rans.

27 Pinsent Masons LLP Acomb Stakes (Group 3) (7f)
York August 21 (Good To Firm)
1 **Treaty Of Paris** 2-9-0   James Doyle
2 **The Grey Gatsby** 2-9-0   Graham Lee
3 **Il Paparazzi** 2-9-0   Neil Callan
11/1, 5/4F, 7/1. nk, 1l. 6 ran. 1m 23.02s
(Henry Candy).

A soft win for **Treaty Of Paris**, whose only success in five other outings came in a maiden. Treaty Of Paris was allowed to dictate a modest gallop that saw just over 4l cover the six runners and was allowed too much rope by **The Grey Gatsby**, who was the best of a poor bunch but took just too long to find top gear when the tempo quickened.

28 DBS Premier Yearling Stakes (6f) York August 22 (Good To Firm)
1 **Haikbidiac** 2-8-11   Liam Jones
2 **Thunder Strike** 2-9-2   Richard Hughes
3 **Nezar** 2-8-11   Johnny Murtagh
9/1, 7/1, 8/1. 2l, hd. 19 ran. 1m 10.55s
(William Haggas).

A good win for **Haikbidiac**, who had fallen short in similar company over 5f but relished an extra furlong. Haikbidiac was receiving 5lb from class pair **Thunder Strike** and **Sleeper King**, who had both run well at Royal Ascot and Glorious Goodwood, but he beat them comfortably enough to place his performance up there with strong Listed-winning form despite two subsequent disappointments on softer ground. Flying Childers winner **Green Door** was unable to maintain a searing pace having led a furlong out.

29 Connolly's Red Mills Lowther Stakes (Group 2) (Fillies) (6f)
York August 22 (Good To Firm)
1 **Lucky Kristale** 2-9-1   Tom Queally
2 **Queen Catrine** 2-8-12   Johnny Murtagh
3 **Wind Fire** 2-8-12   Jamie Spencer
5/2J, 6/1, 9/2. 1½l, hd. 9 ran. 1m 10.58s
(George Margarson).

A repeat of the Duchess of Cambridge form as **Lucky Kristale** proved far too good for **Queen Catrine**. Carrying a 3lb penalty, Lucky Kristale was unsurprisingly not quite as far in front of her old rival, but she won going away having quickened up well from the rear. Queen Catrine just pipped **Wind Fire** for second as that filly showed that she could last 6f, while there was a bunch finish behind with several fillies flattered to finish so close.

30 Irish Thoroughbred Marketing Gimcrack Stakes (Group 2) (6f)
York August 24 (Soft)
1 **Astaire** 2-8-12   Neil Callan
2 **Wilshire Boulevard** 2-8-12   Ryan Moore
3 **Parbold** 2-8-12   Tony Hamilton
5/1, 4/1, 11/4F. nk, nk. 7 ran. 1m 13.72s
(Kevin Ryan).

A competitive affair in which **Astaire** showed great speed to burn off a solid chasing pack. Having blasted into an early lead and quickened again at halfway, Astaire had enough in hand to prevail despite his stamina appearing to be stretched in the final furlong, which would improve by the time he went on to the Middle Park Stakes as a much stronger performer. **Wilshire Boulevard** stuck on well to claim second ahead of **Parbold** and **Cable Bay**, while there was a 2l gap back to **Justice Day** and the disappointing **Saayerr**.

31 Whiteley Clinic Prestige Stakes (Group 3) (Fillies) (7f)
Goodwood August 24 (Good)
1 **Amazing Maria** 2-9-0   Gerald Mosse
2 **Qawaasem** 2-9-0   Paul Hanagan
3 **Halljoy** 2-9-0   James Doyle
6/4F, 4/1, 25/1. 2½l, 3¼l. 7 ran. 1m 26.13s
(Ed Dunlop).

A commanding win for **Amazing Maria**, who didn't run again but would have been an interesting contender for Group 1 honours on this evidence. Having shown her liking for the track with a 6l maiden win there on her previous start, Amazing Maria was soon clear and kept up a fierce gallop to win in a quick time, with only **Qawaasem**, who had got much closer to Majeyda in a decent Listed race at Sandown, mounting any sort of challenge. **Midnite Angel**, who gradually lost her form over the season, was a poor fourth.

32 Galileo European Breeders Fund Futurity Stakes (Group 2) (7f)
Curragh (IRE) August 24 (Good)
1 **War Command** 2-9-6   Joseph O'Brien
2 **Mustajeeb** 2-9-3   Pat Smullen
3 **Exogenesis** 2-9-3   Gary Carroll
8/11F, 7/2, 11/2. 3l, hd. 5 ran. 1m 23.94s
(A P O'Brien).

War Command got back to winning ways with another excellent performance as he put a couple of useful rivals to the sword. War Command was given plenty to do off a moderate gallop (the time was worse than standard even though four of the other five

COME TO HEEL: progressive filly

races on the card up to 7f bettered it), but he quickened up well to reel in clear leader **Friendship**, who was hugely flattered to finish a close fourth, and showed far more speed than **Mustajeeb** and **Exogenesis**.

33 Irish Field Curragh Stakes (Listed) (5f)
Curragh (IRE) August 24 (Good)
1 **Come To Heel** 2-8-12   Wayne Lordan
2 **Hurryupharriet** 2-8-12   Pat Smullen
3 **Boom The Groom** 2-9-3   Fergal Lynch
6/4F, 9/1, 12/1. ½l, 1¾l. 10 ran. 58.87s
(David Wachman).

A cosy win for **Come To Heel**, who won with much more than the half-length margin in hand and would show her true capabilities when fourth in the Cheveley Park next time. There was little quality behind, with **Hurryupharriet**'s subsequent Listed win at Ayr coming in a very poor race for the grade.

34 Weatherbys Bank Stonehenge Stakes (Listed) (1m)
Salisbury August 30 (Good To Firm)
1 **Washaar** 2-9-2   Paul Hanagan
2 **Cool Bahamian** 2-8-13   John Fahy
3 **Dancealot** 2-8-8   Frederik Tylicki
2/5F, 10/1, 5/1. ½l, 1½l. 4 ran. 1m 43.62s
(Richard Hannon).

A second Listed win for **Washaar** since his Superlative Stakes third as he defied a 3lb penalty. Washaar was pushed close by **Cool**

Bahamian, who had his limitations exposed in other races at this level, but the winner was better than the bare form – albeit perhaps flattered by his close fourth in the Royal Lodge – as he hit the front too soon having raced close to a very strong pace and then did well to fight back when headed by **Dancealot**, just holding the more patiently-ridden runner-up.

35 Betfred Mobile Solario Stakes (Group 3) (7f16y)
Sandown August 31 (Good To Firm)
1 **Kingman** 2-9-0   James Doyle
2 **Emirates Flyer** 2-9-0   Silvestre De Sousa
3 **Music Theory** 2-9-0   Mickael Barzalona
2/7F, 10/1, 9/2. 2l, hd. 4 ran. 1m 28.38s
(John Gosden).

Made favourite for the 2,000 Guineas after his maiden win, **Kingman** scared off most serious opposition and wasn't required to show the anticipated fireworks as he came home a comfortable winner. Kingman took command in the final furlong despite showing signs of greenness and was much too good for the smart **Emirates Flyer**, who was improving all the time and finished in front of the better-fancied Godolphin runner **Music Theory**.

36 Moyglare Stud Stakes (Group 1) (Fillies) (7f)
Curragh (IRE) September 1 (Good To Firm)
1 **Rizeena** 2-9-0   James Doyle
3 **Kiyoshi** 2-9-0   Jamie Spencer
2 **Tapestry** 2-9-1   Joseph O'Brien
9/2, 13/8F, 2/1. ¾l, hd. 7 ran. 1m 22.91s
(Clive Brittain).

An extremely messy race due to the inability of **Kiyoshi** to keep to a straight line, with **Rizeena** fortunate to avoid the carnage. Rizeena was still a smart winner, appearing to relish the extra furlong as she briefly hit a flat spot when Kiyoshi quickened to the front yet found her stride and powered home in the closing stages. Kiyoshi's speed was perhaps used too soon as she failed to sustain her challenge, not helped by hanging sharply right across **Wonderfully**, which resulted in her being placed third behind **Tapestry**, who was in turn chopped up and did really well to quicken again and finish within 1l, suggesting she may prove to be the best filly in the race. Wonderfully was brought to a virtual standstill when running a fine race, dropping to sixth behind **Carla Bianca** and **Perhaps**, who was

RIZEENA (second right): sees off Kiyoshi and the impeded Tapestry (hidden)

sacrificed as a pacemaker.

37 Go And Go Round Tower Stakes (Group 3) (6f)
Curragh (IRE) September 1 (Good To Firm)
1 **Great White Eagle** 2-9-3 Joseph O'Brien
2 **Remember You** 2-9-0 Wayne Lordan
3 **Expedition** 2-9-3 Ryan Moore
1/3F, 16/1, 8/1. 2l, ½l. 9 ran. 1m 10.59s
(A P O'Brien).

A very moderate race for the grade with the exception of **Great White Eagle**, who justified his odds of 1-3 with a hugely comfortable victory. Waited with on the unfavoured middle of the track, Great White Eagle swept past the field impressively, though doubts remain over the extent of his ability after a flop in the Middle Park as the form lacked depth, with **Remember When** only fifth in a desperately poor Group 3 at Ayr and **Expedition** beaten at 2-11 on their next runs.

38 EBF Stallions & Country Gentlemen's Association Dick Poole Fillies' Stakes (Listed) (6f)
Salisbury September 5 (Good To Firm)
1 **Joyeuse** 2-8-12 Tom Queally
2 **Dorothy B** 2-8-12 William Buick
3 **Wedding Ring** 2-8-12 Mickael Barzalona
8/11F, 10/1, 4/1. nk, 2¾l. 6 ran. 1m 14.75s
(Lady Cecil).

Joyeuse set a fair standard on the strength of her Albany third and won comfortably enough despite **Dorothy B** ultimately getting close. The runner-up would also reverse the form in the Cheveley Park, but Joyeuse was off colour that day and proved herself a much better filly on this occasion. Off the track for 11 weeks since Royal Ascot, she seemed to tire in the final furlong yet had already put the race to bed with a smart turn of foot as the first two pulled clear of **Wedding Ring** and **Alutiq**, who was unlucky not to finish third having been blocked at the furlong pole.

39 Betfred TV Stakes (registered as the Ascendant Stakes) (Listed) (1m)
Haydock September 7 (Good To Soft)
1 **Chief Barker** 2-9-0 Richard Hughes
2 **Chriselliam** 2-8-9 Gerald Mosse
3 **Lily Rules** 2-8-9 Barry McHugh
5/4F, 11/2, 8/1. nk, 1½l. 5 ran. 1m 45.69s
(Richard Hannon).

Subsequent Fillies' Mile and Breeders' Cup winner **Chriselliam** was undone by an ill-judged ride as she lost out to **Chief Barker**, who was certainly flattered by the victory and could manage only sixth in the Racing Post

Trophy. Chriselliam's turn of foot was utilised far too early as she quickened through to lead in the penultimate furlong before finding little in front and allowing Chief Barker to come back past her close home.

40 totepool.com Sirenia Stakes (Group 3) (6f)
Kempton (AW) September 7 (Standard)
1 **Brown Sugar** 2-9-3 Pat Dobbs
2 **Figure Of Speech** 2-9-0 M Barzalona
3 **Simple Magic** 2-8-11 Robert Havlin
11/2, 9/2, 7/1. shd, 4l. 7 ran. 1m 11.78s
(Richard Hannon).

A virtual match between **Brown Sugar** and **Figure Of Speech** with their chief rivals well below their best, and Brown Sugar did well to defy a penalty in a desperately tight finish. The pair pulled 4l clear of maiden winner **Simple Magic**, with the Cornwallis winner **Hot Streak** unsuited by the Polytrack and favourite **Brave Boy** running no race having got upset in the stalls.

41 ICON Breeders' Cup Juvenile Turf Trial Stakes (Group 3) (1m)
Leopardstown (IRE) September 7 (Good)
1 **Australia** 2-9-3 Joseph O'Brien
2 **Free Eagle** 2-9-3 Pat Smullen
3 **Kingfisher** 2-9-3 Seamie Heffernan
5/2, 2/5F, 8/1. 6l, 3½l. 4 ran. 1m 40.30s
(A P O'Brien).

This race was expected to see **Free Eagle**, made Derby favourite on the strength of his maiden win, cement that status, but instead **Australia** emerged as a new star as he put the 2-5 shot firmly in his place. Held up well off a strong pace set by **Kingfisher**, Australia quickened up superbly turning for home, sweeping past Free Eagle and extending his advantage all the way to the line, though there was little opposition to him with connections of Free Eagle remaining convinced that he can do much better.

42 Polypipe Flying Childers Stakes (Group 2) (5f)
Doncaster September 13 (Good To Soft)
1 **Green Door** 2-9-0 Jim Crowley
2 **Wind Fire** 2-8-11 Jamie Spencer
3 **Extortionist** 2-9-0 Mickael Barzalona
18/1, 4/1, 7/1. 1¼l, ½l. 7 ran. 59.94s
(Olly Stevens).

This fell short of its usual billing as the juvenile 5f championship with none of the field having previously finished better than third at Pattern level, helping **Green Door** to land a surprise win. Much better being ridden with more restraint, Green Door used his speed to cut down **Wind Fire** in the final furlong and win going away, with Wind Fire holding off the Windsor Castle winner **Extortionist** and her fellow filly **Fast** for second. However, the latter pair were both very well beaten in similar conditions in the Cornwallis Stakes to place questions over the form and the remaining trio **Thunder Strike**, **Sleeper King** and **Ambiance** were all well below par.

43 **Barrett Steel May Hill Stakes (Group 2) (Fillies) (1m)**
Doncaster September 13 (Good To Soft)
1 **Ihtimal** 2-8-12   Silvestre De Sousa
2 **Majeyda** 2-8-12   Mickael Barzalona
3 **Lady Lara** 2-8-12   Jim Crowley
11/10F, 9/2, 12/1. 2l, 2l. 7 ran. 1m 43.30s
(Saeed bin Suroor).

A pedestrian gallop turned this race into a quarter-mile sprint, but that was more than far enough for **Ihtimal** to exert her clear superiority as she ran out a comfortable winner. Already setting the form standard, Ihtimal picked up instantly when in the clear and quickened away from fellow Godolphin runner **Majeyda**, who had won a decent Listed prize on her previous start and didn't need to improve on that to take second.

44 **One Call Insurance Flying Scotsman Stakes (Listed) (7f)**
Doncaster September 13 (Good To Soft)
1 **Be Ready** 2-9-0   Silvestre De Sousa
2 **Barley Mow** 2-9-0   Richard Hughes
3 **Voice Of A Leader** 2-9-0   Jamie Spencer
13/8F, 2/1, 100/30. 3l, 2¾l. 5 ran. 1m 28.76s
(Saeed bin Suroor).

A hugely impressive win for **Be Ready**, worthy of a much higher grade, as he built on the promise of his debut second to Somewhat by thumping a good field. Be Ready stormed clear of the subsequent Lagardere fifth **Barley Mow**, while **Brazos**, a much closer fourth in the Somerville Tattersall Stakes on his next start, and Listed second **Cool Bahamian** were among those left well strung out.

45 **At The Races Champagne Stakes (Group 2) (7f)**
Doncaster September 14 (Good To Soft)
1 **Outstrip** 2-8-12   Mickael Barzalona
2 **The Grey Gatsby** 2-8-12   Graham Lee
3 **Cable Bay** 2-8-12   Jamie Spencer
13/8J, 13/8J, 5/1. 3l, hd. 4 ran. 1m 26.90s
(Charlie Appleby).

A terrific performance from **Outstrip**, who was briefly outpaced when the tempo quickened but ended up storming clear. The subsequent Breeders' Cup hero easily shook

off **The Grey Gatsby** and **Cable Bay**, who showed his suitability for this extra furlong when going on to finish second in the Dewhurst without looking an obvious improver after four previous defeats at Pattern level.

46 **Goffs Vincent O'Brien National Stakes (Group 1) (7f)**
Curragh (IRE) September 15 (Good)
1 **Toormore** 2-9-3   Richard Hughes
2 **Sudirman** 2-9-3   Wayne Lordan
3 **Giovanni Boldini** 2-9-3   Joseph O'Brien
EvensF, 15/8, 4/1. 2¾l, 1¼l. 5 ran. 1m 22.67s
(Richard Hannon).

Toormore produced the most impressive Group 1 win by a juvenile colt all season, with the possible exception of Kingston Hill, though whether there was substance to match the style is open to question. Ridden from the front in a change of tactics to his Vintage Stakes success, Toormore responded superbly, gradually winding up the tempo and winning comfortably. However, **Sudirman** raced keenly on his first run at the trip and subsequently returned to 6f when only fifth in Middle Park, while **Giovanni Boldini** still looked green on only his second run and didn't seem to be anywhere near the level he showed subsequently.

47 **Flame Of Tara European Breeders' Fund Stakes (Listed) (Fillies) (1m)**
Curragh (IRE) September 15 (Good)
1 **Avenue Gabriel** 2-9-0   Chris Hayes
2 **Ballybacka Queen** 2-9-0   Pat Smullen
3 **Minorette** 2-9-0   Michael Hussey
4/1, 16/1, 20/1. nk, ½l. 9 ran. 1m 37.03s
(P D Deegan).

A deserved win for the Debutante Stakes third **Avenue Gabriel**, whose form was rock-solid and entitled her to be much shorter but for odds-on shot **Dazzling** being overhyped. Avenue Gabriel recovered from a nightmare passage in the straight, meaning her form can be significantly upgraded, as she showed when beating **Ballybacka Queen** far more comfortably in fifth in the Fillies' Mile.

48 **Dubai Duty Free Mill Reef Stakes (Group 2) (6f8y)**
Newbury September 21 (Soft)
1 **Supplicant** 2-9-1   Tony Hamilton
2 **Rufford** 2-9-1   Adam Kirby
3 **Hot Streak** 2-9-1   Declan McDonogh
7/2J, 20/1, 8/1. ¾l, ½l. 7 ran. 1m 13.59s
(Richard Fahey).

An average race for the grade with the outstanding performer in the field, subsequent

Middle Park runner-up **Hot Streak**, failing to see out the trip in third having raced too keenly. In contrast **Supplicant**, who had twice won over 5f since his unlucky fifth in the Molecomb, stayed on strongly over the extra furlong, seeing off **Rufford** and Hot Streak having struggled to match that pair's early speed. Rufford left the rest of his form behind, relishing the soft ground, while **Figure Of Speech** was a close fourth as just less than 3l covered the septet, including the disappointing **Shamshon** and **Anticipated**.

49 William Hill - In The App Store Firth of Clyde Stakes Class 1 (Group 3) (Fillies) (6f)
Ayr September 21 (Good To Soft)
1 **Coral Mist** 2-8-12   Tom Queally
2 **Hoku** 2-8-12   Harry Bentley
3 **Ventura Mist** 2-8-12   Duran Fentiman
11/2, 16/1, 20/1. nse, nk. 12 ran. 1m 14.24s (Charles Hills).

A desperately moderate contest with most of the principals exposed even at a lower level and just 2l covering the first eight, but **Coral Mist** was by far the best filly in the field and much better than the bare form. Held up in rear in a race that favoured those ridden prominently, Coral Mist had to switch around the entire field to get up on the line, pipping **Hoku** and **Ventura Mist**, who exploited favourable weight conditions when just landing the Two-Year-Old Trophy next time.

50 Somerville Tattersall Stakes (Group 3) (7f)
Newmarket September 26 (Good)
1 **Miracle Of Medinah** 2-8-12   Liam Keniry
2 **Cable Bay** 2-8-12   Frankie Dettori
3 **Nezar** 2-8-12   William Buick
25/1, 11/4F, 5/1. 1¼l, 2l. 8 ran. 1m 25.92s (Mark Usher).

A surprise win for **Miracle Of Medinah**, who had been written off too quickly after a couple below-par efforts as he bounced back to the form of a 33-1 Listed win at Newbury earlier in the campaign. Having made all that day, Miracle Of Medinah again relished racing prominently in a small field as he comfortably held off **Cable Bay**, whose subsequent Dewhurst second and three previous close efforts at a higher level warn against underestimating the winner. There was a decent gap back to the smart **Nezar**, who just held off **Brazos** for third, while **God Willing** challenged widest of all and would prove better than this effort.

51 Shadwell Fillies' Mile (Group 1) (1m)
Newmarket September 27 (Good To Firm)
1 **Chriselliam** 2-8-12   Richard Hughes
2 **Rizeena** 2-8-12   James Doyle
3 **Ihtimal** 2-8-12   Silvestre De Sousa
28/1, 7/4F, 5/2. 1l, 2l. 8 ran. 1m 40.00s (Charles Hills).

A shock result as **Chriselliam** produced a stunning turn of foot to cut down **Rizeena** and there was little fluke about it with several quality fillies well beaten, as she would prove when following up at the Breeders' Cup. Chriselliam stormed through to lead in the final 75 yards after Rizeena, another seemingly suited by a slow gallop on her first attempt at the trip, had quickened up well. The fact that she pulled 3l clear of Moyglare rival

CORAL MIST (far right): much better than her narrow winning margn suggests

Wonderfully and **Avenue Gabriel**, who had previously finished close behind old rival Tapestry, suggests she ran up to her Moyglare form, with **Ihtimal** also comfortably seen off as she finished in front of the Irish pair in third. Wonderfully again showed great promise, looking a middle-distance filly as she was ridden along to stay in touch before keeping on well.

52 Aqlaam Oh So Sharp Stakes (Group 3) (Fillies) (7f)
Newmarket September 27 (Good To Firm)
1 **Miss France** 2-8-12   Mickael Barzalona
2 **Lightning Thunder** 2-8-12   Harry Bentley
3 **Sweet Acclaim** 2-8-12   Pat Cosgrave
7/2, 15/2, 20/1. hd, 5l. 9 ran. 1m 24.98s
(A Fabre).

Miss France had beaten Marcel Boussac winner Indonesienne on her previous start and took this more modest next target comfortably in her stride, although her immediate promotion to 1,000 Guineas favouritism was a huge overreaction on the bare form. Miss France came through from the rear and was a cosy winner over **Lightning Thunder**, who had excuses for her subsequent flop in the Rockfel, with a 5l gap back to **Sweet Acclaim** in third. However, with hot favourite **Radiator** failing to live up to the promise of a 15l debut win and **Midnite Angel** well below her best, the opposition wasn't up to much.

53 Red Mills Cheveley Park Stakes (Group 1) (Fillies) (6f)
Newmarket September 28 (Good To Firm)
1 **Vorda** 2-8-12   Olivier Peslier
2 **Princess Noor** 2-8-12   Johnny Murtagh
3 **Kiyoshi** 2-8-12   Jamie Spencer
11/8F, 11/1, 9/4. ¾l, 1¼l. 7 ran. 1m 13.34s
(P Sogorb).

This race was severely weakened by the absence of Lucky Kristale, who was shown to be Britain's leading 6f performer by the disappointing effort of **Kiyoshi**, but French filly **Vorda** still looked a very smart winner. Full of speed, Vorda was always close up and won comfortably, though a subsequent flop in the Breeders' Cup exacerbated doubts about her staying further. **Princess Noor** dictated a moderate gallop and kept on well enough to show that she deserved more credit for her Princess Margaret win, holding off Kiyoshi, who wasn't suited by the early crawl and was reported to have found the ground too quick. **Come To Heel** and **Dorothy B** were next, the latter reversing previous form with **Joyeuse**, who raced far too keenly.

104

54 Juddmonte Royal Lodge Stakes (Group 2) (1m)
Newmarket September 28 (Good To Firm)
1 **Berkshire** 2-8-12   Jim Crowley
2 **Somewhat** 2-8-12   Gerald Mosse
3 **Sir Jack Layden** 2-8-12   Richard Hughes
11/8J, 11/8J, 40/1. nk, nk. 5 ran. 1m 39.97s
(Paul Cole).

A battling victory for **Berkshire**, who deserves huge credit for holding off **Somewhat** despite falling short of the unrealistic anticipation caused by a literal reading of his Chesham victory. The market certainly knew what to expect from joint-favourite Somewhat, who had improved hugely since Royal Ascot and produced a typically bold display from the front, but Berkshire knuckled down well to get up close home in a tight finish. Both the first two looked slightly ill at ease on the quick ground, allowing **Sir Jack Layden** and **Washaar** to finish within 1l, though they still pulled clear of **Kingfisher**.

55 Juddmonte Beresford Stakes (Group 2) (1m)
Curragh (IRE) September 29 (Good)
1 **Geoffrey Chaucer** 2-9-3   Joseph O'Brien
2 **Oklahoma City** 2-9-3   Seamie Heffernan
3 **Altruistic** 2-9-3   Johnny Murtagh
4/7F, 5/1, 3/1. 1¼l, ¾l. 5 ran. 1m 42.70s
(A P O'Brien).

It said much for **Geoffrey Chaucer** that he was backed to the exclusion of stablemate **Oklahoma City**, who had shown good form over an inadequate trip and would land the Tattersalls Millions at Newmarket the following week, and the 4-7 favourite duly won with great authority. Geoffrey Chaucer quickened up well and won readily from Oklahoma City, while **Altruistic** also franked the form when third in the Racing Post Trophy.

56 C.L. Weld Park Stakes (Group 3) (Fillies) (7f)
Curragh (IRE) September 29 (Good)
1 **My Titania** 2-9-0   Declan McDonogh
2 **Chicago Girl** 2-9-0   Johnny Murtagh
3 **Tarfasha** 2-9-0   Pat Smullen
11/10F, 14/1, 2/1. ½l, 5½l. 8 ran. 1m 24.20s
(John M Oxx).

There was little depth to this race with two maiden winners the only fillies given any chance in the market, but **My Titania** at least put up a good performance in victory. Always going well, My Titania quickened into the lead and didn't seem to do a lot in front as she comfortably held off **Chicago Girl**, who was again a decent second in a Listed race next time, with the pair pulling well clear of the slightly disappointing **Tarfasha**.

57 Anglesey Lodge Equine Hospital Blenheim Stakes (Listed) (6f)
Curragh (IRE) September 29 (Good)
1 **Shining Emerald** 2-9-3   Chris Hayes
2 **Guerre** 2-9-3   Joseph O'Brien
3 **Monsieur Power** 2-9-3 Declan McDonogh
7/2, 8/11F, 12/1. 3l, 3¼l. 8 ran. 1m 12.41s
(P D Deegan).

A solid race for the grade won in commanding fashion by **Shining Emerald**, who may well be a smart colt despite his subsequent defeat in the Killavullan Stakes. Shining Emerald quickened well clear of odds-on favourite **Guerre**, who seemed to do little wrong as he beat the rest comfortably with **Boom The Groom** and **Pleasant Bay** beaten much further than in previous races at this level.

58 BMW Cornwallis Stakes (Group 3) (5f)
Ascot October 5 (Good To Soft)
1 **Hot Streak** 2-9-0   Jamie Spencer
2 **Outer Space** 2-9-0   Ryan Moore
3 **Kickboxer** 2-9-0   Sam Hitchcott
9/2, 3/1F, 50/1. 5l, ½l. 12 ran. 1m 0.24s
(Kevin Ryan).

Finally a juvenile stamped some authority on the 5f division as **Hot Streak** demolished his rivals. Hot Streak settled better than previously and powered clear of a decent field, who were led by **Outer Space** and big improver **Kickboxer** with another 4l gap back to **Extortionist**. His Flying Childers rival **Fast** was only seventh, while the trail-blazing **Excel's Beauty**, who had shown fair form on good ground, had no chance of lasting home in softer conditions.

59 £500,000 Tattersalls Millions 2YO Trophy (7f)
Newmarket October 5 (Good To Firm)
1 **Oklahoma City** 2-9-3   Joseph O'Brien
2 **Postponed** 2-9-3   Andrea Atzeni
3 **Bon Voyage** 2-9-3   Dane O'Neill
3/1, 16/1, 25/1. 1½l, nk. 17 ran. 1m 23.66s
(A P O'Brien).

Oklahoma City brought strong Pattern form into this sales race and he proved much too good, making most of the running to run out a comfortable winner. **Postponed** and **Bon Voyage** finished strongly to grab the places from **Hunters Creek** and **Jallota** as that quintet were covered by just 2¼l.

60 £300,000 Tattersalls Millions 2YO Fillies' Trophy (7f)
Newmarket October 5 (Good To Firm)

1 **Wedding Ring** 2-9-0   Martin Lane
2 **Manderley** 2-9-0   Sean Levey
3 **Fashion Fund** 2-9-0   Kevin Manning
11/4J, 33/1, 10/1. ¾l, 1½l. 13 ran. 1m 25.19s
(Charlie Appleby).

A big sales double for **Wedding Ring** as she followed up victory in a similar race at Newmarket by landing this even bigger prize over an extra furlong. Wedding Ring had the beating of her rivals – nine of whom ran in both races – on the strength of several good runs in a higher grade, but she was arguably pushed to a higher level as the form worked out well, with **Aqlaam Vision** stepping up on her sixth in this race to win a fair Listed race at Newbury from **Oxsana**, who was second and fourth in the two races.

61 totepool Two-Year-Old Trophy (Listed) (6f)
Redcar October 5 (Good To Firm)
1 **Ventura Mist** 2-8-7   David Allan
2 **Emirates Flyer** 2-9-2   Ahmed Ajtebi
3 **Morning Post** 2-9-2   F M Berry
10/1, 5/1F, 20/1. nk, nk. 23 ran. 1m 12.19s
(Tim Easterby).

Race conditions meant **Ventura Mist** received 9lb from horses at the top of the weights and she took full advantage, grinding out a narrow victory over two of those lumbered with the maximum burden. **Emirates Flyer** ran a fine race in second ahead of **Morning Post**, who stepped up on the form he had shown when winning a weaker sales race at York, though this was also a modest contest for the money.

62 Total Prix Marcel Boussac (Group 1) (1m)
Longchamp (FR) October 6 (Soft)
1 **Indonesienne** 2-8-11   Flavien Prat
2 **Lesstalk In Paris** 2-8-11 Ioritz Mendizabal
3 **Queen Catrine** 2-8-11   Jamie Spencer
16/1, 3/1F, 16/1. ¾l, 1¾l. 12 ran. 1m 38.74s
(C Ferland).

A dramatic finish saw **Indonesienne** relentlessly make up ground to collar long-time leader **Lesstalk In Paris**, who looked an unlucky loser and did enough to suggest she was France's best juvenile filly. Favourite on the strength of a Group 3 win at Chantilly, Lesstalk In Paris quickly swept to the front from a wide draw and went on to race far too keenly, doing well to hang on until the final 50 yards when Indonesienne wore her down. The winner rates closely to Miss France, having been second to that filly when conceding 4lb at Chantilly, and Lucky Kristale, on a line

ASTAIRE (near side): leads a Kevin Ryan one-two in the Middle Park Stakes

through **Queen Catrine**, who led the British and Irish challenge by winning a blanket finish for third, which also included the busy **Wonderfully**. **Sandiva** looked sure to be placed until her stamina ebbed away in the final furlong.

63 Qatar Prix Jean-Luc Lagardere (Grand Criterium) (Group 1) (7f)
Longchamp (FR) October 6 (Soft)
1 **Karakontie** 2-9-0 Stephane Pasquier
2 **Noozhoh Canarias** 2-9-0 C Soumillon
3 **Charm Spirit** 2-9-0 Olivier Peslier
11/4F, 7/2, 7/1. ¾l, 1¼l. 8 ran. 1m 22.97s
(J E Pease).

This didn't look a very strong Group 1 with a seemingly modest British and Irish challenge comprising just **Wilshire Boulevard** and **Barley Mow** unlucky not to go close, particularly the latter. Horses ridden prominently enjoyed a distinct advantage over those coming from behind, with **Karakontie** and **Noozhoh Canarias** dominating throughout, while **Charm Spirit** did best of those held up ahead of Wilshire Boulevard. Barley Mow was blocked in his run and found room when too late, eventually finishing fifth.

64 Irish Stallion Farms European Breeders Fund Star Appeal Stakes (Listed) (7f)

Dundalk (AW) (IRE) October 11 (Standard)
1 **Giovanni Boldini** 2-9-3 Seamie Heffernan
2 **Mandatario** 2-9-3 Kevin Manning
3 **Miss Mousey** 2-8-12 Colin Keane
1/2F, 7/2, 20/1. 4¾l, 2¾l. 6 ran. 1m 25.12s
(A P O'Brien).

A straightforward task for **Giovanni Boldini**, who was dropped significantly in class after coming up short in the National Stakes but looked a far more streetwise performer as he tore apart a moderate field. Giovanni Boldini lengthened superbly when asked to quicken and stormed clear of **Mandatario**, with only the placed horses finishing within 10l.

65 Vision.ae Middle Park Stakes (Group 1) (6f)
Newmarket October 12 (Good To Soft)
1 **Astaire** 2-9-0 Neil Callan
2 **Hot Streak** 2-9-0 Jamie Spencer
3 **Justice Day** 2-9-0 William Buick
8/1, 5/1, 22/1. ½l, 1½l. 10 ran. 1m 12.33s
(Kevin Ryan).

This had plenty of depth with seven previous Group winners in the field, even if few of them looked strong for that grade, and the Kevin Ryan pair **Astaire** and **Hot Streak** proved comfortably the best of them. Astaire soon blasted into the lead and looked likely to be swallowed up when nearly joined in the penultimate furlong, but he found unexpected reserves to hold off Hot Streak, who again settled better and confirmed the progress he had shown in the Cornwallis. **Justice Day** and **Speedfiend** were next, suggesting limitations to the form given they had won just three of 12 previous races between them and just one above Class 4 level, though they both ran career-bests and there were lots of fair yardsticks behind. **Sudirman** was next, seemingly not quite coping with easy ground, followed by **Supplicant** and **Jallota**, while **Great White Eagle** was disappointing.

66 Dubai Dewhurst Stakes (Group 1) (7f)

Newmarket October 12 (Good To Soft)

1 **War Command** 2-9-1		Joseph O'Brien
2 **Cable Bay** 2-9-1		Jamie Spencer
3 **Outstrip** 2-9-1		Mickael Barzalona

10/11F, 20/1, 15/8. 1¼l, 1½l. 6 ran. 1m 25.06s (A P O'Brien).

A disappointing turnout with just four serious contenders joining a couple of pacemakers and several connections must have been left regretting not taking the plunge after a somewhat underwhelming victory from **War Command**. The Coventry winner couldn't quicken up in the same manner on ground felt by connections to be softer than ideal, but he still knuckled down well to see off **Cable Bay**, whose proximity in second after four previous defeats at Pattern level shows the level of the bare form. **Outstrip** was well below his best as he struggled to cope with the undulations, failing to confirm Doncaster form with Cable Bay and only just holding off the outclassed Anjaal for third, while **Stormardal** and **Friendship** dropped out after disputing the early lead.

67 Vision.ae Rockfel Stakes (Group 2) (7f)

Newmarket October 12 (Good To Soft)

1 **Al Thakhira** 2-8-12		Martin Harley
2 **Blockade** 2-8-12		Neil Callan
3 **Valonia** 2-8-12		Jamie Spencer

5/1, 33/1, 7/1. 3¼l, ¾l. 8 ran. 1m 25.54s (Marco Botti).

This was a weak renewal with **Lightning Thunder**, who scoped dirty after a tame fourth, the only one of six fillies carrying official entries to be rated higher than 98 and **Al Thakhira** the only one of the other two to have won last time out (making just two in total). Al Thakhira at least looked sharply progressive as she ran out a comfortable winner, though a subsequent flop at the Breeders' Cup, albeit on much quicker ground, leaves

her with something to prove. Four of the field had clashed previously at Ayr behind Coral Mist and that form was turned on its head as 33-1 shot **Blockade** finished ahead of **Valonia**, **Hoku** and **Ventura Mist**.

68 Autumn Stakes (Group 3) (1m)

Newmarket October 12 (Good To Soft)

1 **Kingston Hill** 2-9-0		Andrea Atzeni
2 **Oklahoma City** 2-9-0		Joseph O'Brien
3 **Truth Or Dare** 2-9-0		Ryan Moore

15/2, 6/5F, 16/1. 2l, 1l. 8 ran. 1m 39.07s (Roger Varian).

An excellent performance from subsequent Racing Post Trophy winner **Kingston Hill**, who claimed arguably his most notable scalp of the whole season in **Oklahoma City**. The runner-up set out to make all the running and stayed on well, but Kingston Hill was always going well and quickened past him to run out a decisive winner. **Truth Or Dare** and **God Willing** were next, with that quartet pulling 4½l clear of **Safety Check** to suggest the form was good.

69 coral.co.uk Rockingham Stakes (Listed) (6f)

York October 12 (Good)

1 **Mushir** 2-9-0		Dane O'Neill
2 **No Leaf Clover** 2-9-0		Robert Winston
3 **Brave Boy** 2-9-0		Kieren Fallon

11/2, 20/1, 7/1. hd, 4½l. 10 ran. 1m 12.92s (Roger Varian).

A strange race as several horses proven at a higher level seemed to run well below form, but time may tell that **Mushir** was a very smart winner. Mushir didn't get a clear run and had to switch around the entire field, but he showed a terrific turn of foot to reel in **No Leaf Clover**, who improved hugely on a nursery debut when back on a sound surface. The pair pulled clear of **Brave Boy**, with **Rufford**, **Haikbidiac**, **Figure Of Speech** and **Outer Space** among those well beaten.

70 Staffordstown Stud Stakes (Listed) (Fillies) (1m)

Curragh (IRE) October 13 (Good)

1 **Flying Jib** 2-9-0		Pat Smullen
2 **Chicago Girl** 2-9-0		Johnny Murtagh
3 **Dazzling** 2-9-1		Joseph O'Brien

5/1, 13/8, 11/10F. 1½l, 2¼l. 6 ran. 1m 40.08s (D K Weld).

A good win for **Flying Jib**, who showed a fine attitude when outbattling Group 3 runner-up **Chicago Girl**. The pair pulled away from the front-running **Dazzling**, who was a beaten favourite for the second time at this level and beaten slightly further under 1lb overweight.

71 Racing Post Trophy (Group 1) (1m)

Doncaster October 26 (Soft)

1 **Kingston Hill** 2-9-0   Andrea Atzeni
2 **Johann Strauss** 2-9-0   Ryan Moore
3 **Altruistic** 2-9-0   Johnny Murtagh
7/2F, 9/1, 14/1. 4½l, 2½l. 11 ran. 1m 44.83s
(Roger Varian).

A desperately weak renewal with **Kingston Hill** not required to beat a single Group winner, though the way in which he won still marked him out as a potential champion. A strong gallop on soft ground decimated the field, but Kingston Hill travelled best of all and quickened up in superb fashion before drawing clear of the staying-on **Johann Strauss**. However, the runner-up was still a maiden, as was the fourth, **Dolce N Karama**, after three runs between them in that grade, while they were split by Beresford third **Altruistic**. The front-running **Buonarroti** stuck on for fifth and was the only other one to finish within 11l as several disappointed behind, with only the non-staying **The Grey Gatsby** ever threatening to land a blow. **Chief Barker** and **Somewhat** were among the also-rans, as were promising trio **Century**, **Pinzolo** and **Snow Sky**.

72 Scott Dobson Memorial Doncaster Stakes (Listed) (6f)

Doncaster October 26 (Soft)

1 **Night Of Thunder** 2-9-1 Richard Hughes
2 **Aeolus** 2-9-1   Graham Gibbons
3 **Stubbs** 2-9-4   Joseph O'Brien
6/4F, 100/30, 9/2. 3l, hd. 5 ran. 1m 16.91s
(Richard Hannon).

A really strong Listed race in which **Night Of Thunder**, a 6l maiden winner less than two weeks earlier, made rapid strides to thrash some good rivals. Night Of Thunder was ridden close to the pace and quickened clear in the final furlong as **Aeolus** stayed on from the rear to pip **Stubbs**, who was back from a break following his disappointing Coventry sixth and improved on that form under a penalty. There was a 3l gap back to **Rufford**, racing on soft ground for the only time other than his Mill Reef second, as he faded at the death having made the running.

73 Worthington's Whizz Kids Stakes (registered as the Horris Hill Stakes) (Group 3) (7f)

Newbury October 26 (Heavy)

1 **Piping Rock** 2-8-12   Pat Dobbs
2 **Galiway** 2-8-12   Olivier Peslier

108

3 **Day Of Conquest** 2-8-12   Jimmy Fortune
3/1, 5/2F, 25/1. 2¾l, ¾l. 11 ran. 1m 30.84s
(Richard Hannon).

Piping Rock and **Galiway** both came into the race with big reputations and their class came to the fore, with Piping Rock much the best of them. The form is questionable, with little proven quality and form horse **Trading Profit**, beaten less than 3l in the Mill Reef, failing to stay an extra furlong having hit the front 2f out, but Piping Rock may well have had a big future but for losing his life to colic. Galiway stayed on for a distant second.

74 JRA Killavullan Stakes (Group 3) (7f)

Leopardstown (IRE) October 26 (Soft)

1 **Craftsman** 2-9-3   Michael Hussey
2 **Michaelmas** 2-9-3   Seamie Heffernan
3 **Shining Emerald** 2-9-3   Chris Hayes
7/1, 3/1, 4/5F. 1l, shd. 7 ran. 1m 33.18s
(A P O'Brien).

A surprise result as Blenheim winner **Shining Emerald** was only third at odds-on, though he may have run into a couple of smart prospects in Ballydoyle pair **Craftsman** and **Michaelmas**. Craftsman ensured the race was a stiff test in very soft ground and seemed to relish those conditions as he made virtually all, holding off the yard's first string Michaelmas and Shining Emerald in a tight finish as they pulled well clear of the rest.

75 Criterium International (Group 1) (1m)

Saint-Cloud (FR) November 1 (Very Soft)

1 **Ectot** 2-9-0   Gregory Benoist
2 **Earnshaw** 2-9-0   Maxime Guyon
3 **Prestige Vendome** 2-9-0   Thierry Thulliez
7/10F, 23/10, 53/10. ¾l, snk. 4 ran. 1m 50.93s
(E Lellouche).

A disappointing turnout for this Group 1, with no horses from Britain and Ireland, but all four runners had good form behind them, particularly **Ectot**, who made it four wins in a row. Allowed to make the running having been keen early, Ectot stayed on well and won a shade cosily from main market rival **Earnshaw** with **Prestige Vendome** a fair third.

76 Breeders' Cup Juvenile Turf (Grade 1) (1m)

Santa Anita (USA) November 1 (Firm)

1 **Outstrip** 2-8-10   M E Smith
2 **Giovanni Boldini** 2-8-10   Ryan Moore
3 **Bobby's Kitten** 2-8-10   J J Castellano
6/1, 3/1, 9/4F. ½l, 1¼l. 13 ran. 1m 33.20s
(Charlie Appleby).

A European one-two as **Outstrip** proved his

Dewhurst running all wrong to beat **Giovanni Boldini**. Successful on good to soft at Doncaster, Outstrip quickened superbly on much faster ground to run down Giovanni Boldini, who also deserves huge credit having perhaps sat too close to the furious gallop set by **Bobby's Kitten**. **Wilshire Boulevard** couldn't handle the tight turns.

77 EBF Stallions/Lanwades Montrose Fillies' Stakes (Listed) (1m)
Newmarket November 2 (Soft)

1 **Majeyda** 2-9-1   Silvestre De Sousa
2 **Adhwaa** 2-8-12   Paul Hanagan
3 **Island Remede** 2-8-12   Graham Lee
7/2F, 12/1, 13/2. 2½l, ¾l. 14 ran. 1m 42.30s (Charlie Appleby).

Majeyda had seen her limitations exposed at a higher level, but she showed her ability in this grade when defying a penalty for her second Listed win of the season. There wasn't much strength among the opposition, particularly with the highly regarded **Surcingle** well below her best, but Majeyda ran out a comfortable winner and the first three pulled 7l clear of the rest.

78 Eyrefield Stakes (Listed) (1m1f)
Leopardstown (IRE) November 3 (Soft)

1 **Mekong River** 2-9-3   Seamie Heffernan
2 **Achnaha** 2-8-12   Wayne Lordan
3 **Mandatario** 2-9-3   Kevin Manning
4/6F, 20/1, 5/2. 6½l, 5½l. 5 ran. 1m 54.43s

(A P O'Brien).

A devastating performance from **Mekong River**, who gained his fourth successive win and proved himself much better than he would show next time at Saint-Cloud. Mekong River was soon in front and galloped a fair set of rivals into submission, with **Mandatario**, second at this level to Giovanni Boldini, beaten 12l in third and **Ubiquitous Mantle**, a fair nursery winner off 80 on his previous start at the course, more than 15l adrift in fourth.

79 Criterium de Saint-Cloud (Group 1) (1m2f)
Saint-Cloud (FR) November 9 (Heavy)

1 **Prince Gibraltar** 2-9-0   C Soumillon
2 **Bereni Ka** 2-8-10   Tony Piccone
3 **Hartnell** 2-9-0   Joe Fanning
33/10, 21/1, 73/10. 5l, 1¾l. 12 ran. 2m 26.25s (J-C Rouget).

A runaway victory for **Prince Gibraltar**, though the form seems highly dubious as he came from last to first when ploughing a lone furrow on the stands' side in a race that saw distances greatly exaggerated anyway. With the stamina test of the longest two-year-old Group race in Europe exacerbated by heavy ground, **Mekong River** went too fast in front and could only plug on for fourth, setting the race up for Prince Gibraltar and **Bereni Ka** to come through from the rear, with progressive British raider **Hartnell** earning great credit as he was third having raced prominently.

MEKONG RIVER: gallops his rivals into submission in the Eyrefield Stakes

Two-year-old index

All horses placed or commented on in our two-year-old review section, with race numbers

CABLE BAY: finished in the first four at Group level on five occasions

Trainer Statistics

Richard Hannon

Handing over the reins to son Richard in January meant that Hannon Snr's best ever season was also his last. He had smashed the all-time record for winners in a calendar year by October, finishing with 235.

By month – 2013

	Overall			Two-year-olds			Three-year-olds			Older horses		
	W-R	%	£1	W-R	%	£1	W-R	%	£1	W-R	%	£1
January	0-5	-	-5.00	0-0	-	+0.00	0-3	-	-3.00	0-2	-	-2.00
February	3-9	33	+35.25	0-0	-	+0.00	2-5	40	+24.25	1-4	25	+11.00
March	7-29	24	+3.29	0-0	-	+0.00	7-21	33	+11.29	0-8	-	-8.00
April	24-111	22	-34.42	2-13	15	-9.90	19-72	26	-9.52	3-26	12	-15.00
May	38-200	19	-53.77	23-71	32	+4.66	12-104	12	-54.68	3-25	12	-3.75
June	37-221	17	-81.39	23-93	25	-2.90	12-102	12	-60.74	2-26	8	-17.75
July	38-186	20	-18.93	21-94	22	-4.53	13-69	19	-19.65	4-23	17	+5.25
August	30-226	13	-48.55	20-137	15	-46.63	7-70	10	-25.42	3-19	16	+23.50
September	29-188	15	-23.68	21-129	16	-33.43	6-44	14	+9.75	2-15	13	+0.00
October	23-163	14	-48.13	20-112	18	-16.13	2-35	6	-24.00	1-16	6	-8.00
November	3-49	6	-25.00	2-35	6	-15.50	1-10	10	-5.50	0-4	-	-4.00
December	3-25	12	-6.00	3-17	18	+2.00	0-7	-	-7.00	0-1	-	-1.00

By month – 2012

	Overall			Two-year-olds			Three-year-olds			Older horses		
	W-R	%	£1	W-R	%	£1	W-R	%	£1	W-R	%	£1
January	1-10	10	-8.17	0-0	-	+0.00	1-9	11	-7.17	0-1	-	-1.00
February	2-10	20	+0.00	0-0	-	+0.00	1-6	17	+2.00	1-4	25	-2.00
March	3-21	14	-12.50	0-1	-	-1.00	3-15	20	-6.50	0-5	-	-5.00
April	12-75	16	+22.33	2-11	18	-5.93	8-57	14	+25.75	2-7	29	+2.50
May	32-174	18	+27.62	12-46	26	+11.05	17-107	16	+21.58	3-21	14	-5.00
June	31-202	15	-55.51	19-90	21	-21.09	10-97	10	-31.75	2-15	13	-2.67
July	31-179	17	-2.35	22-92	24	+16.02	9-70	13	-1.38	0-17	-	-17.00
August	36-256	14	-54.75	26-148	18	+3.09	10-96	10	-45.84	0-12	-	-12.00
September	37-209	18	-27.19	27-134	20	-20.52	9-64	14	-12.67	1-11	9	+6.00
October	24-164	15	-27.25	14-107	13	-36.25	7-47	15	-7.00	3-10	30	+16.00
November	5-47	11	-23.88	5-34	15	-10.88	0-13	-	-13.00	0-0	-	+0.00
December	4-20	20	-4.25	2-14	14	-5.75	2-6	33	+1.50	0-0	-	+0.00

By month – 2011

	Overall			Two-year-olds			Three-year-olds			Older horses		
	W-R	%	£1	W-R	%	£1	W-R	%	£1	W-R	%	£1
January	5-20	25	-0.79	0-0	-	+0.00	4-18	22	-0.13	1-2	50	-0.67
February	7-21	33	+15.90	0-0	-	+0.00	5-16	31	+5.90	2-5	40	+10.00
March	9-24	38	+6.24	0-0	-	+0.00	8-18	44	+10.40	1-6	17	-4.17
April	16-104	15	-9.91	4-15	27	-4.09	11-63	17	+18.56	1-26	4	-24.39
May	21-169	12	-49.25	11-62	18	+2.99	6-83	7	-45.17	4-24	17	-7.08
June	26-204	13	-18.80	15-93	16	-3.68	7-88	8	-18.50	4-23	17	+3.38
July	27-245	11	-87.16	21-137	15	-12.47	5-82	6	-51.69	1-26	4	-23.00
August	29-193	15	+9.97	17-129	13	-5.03	10-50	20	+10.50	2-14	14	+4.50
September	39-202	19	+93.53	28-133	21	+95.37	8-55	15	-1.59	3-14	21	-0.25
October	27-145	19	+12.65	22-112	20	+15.48	4-27	15	+1.38	1-6	17	-4.20
November	9-53	17	-7.99	6-34	18	-3.79	3-17	18	-2.20	0-2	-	-2.00
December	3-28	11	-10.50	2-21	10	-8.50	1-7	14	-2.00	0-0	-	+0.00

By race type – 2013

	Overall			Two-year-olds			Three-year-olds			Older horses		
	W-R	%	£1	W-R	%	£1	W-R	%	£1	W-R	%	£1
Handicap	72-606	12	-168.24	20-142	14	-45.58	42-341	12	-107.54	10-123	8	-15.13
Group 1,2,3	16-102	16	-19.21	5-46	11	-9.25	9-38	24	+0.29	2-18	11	-10.25
Maiden	98-489	20	-63.37	83-409	20	-36.99	14-79	18	-32.37	1-1	100	+6.00

By race type – 2012

	Overall			Two-year-olds			Three-year-olds			Older horses		
	W-R	%	£1	W-R	%	£1	W-R	%	£1	W-R	%	£1
Handicap	80-574	14	+8.19	22-132	17	+9.60	50-371	13	+18.08	8-71	11	-19.50
Group 1,2,3	13-91	14	-4.88	7-44	16	-21.72	4-27	15	+15.50	2-20	10	+1.33
Maiden	88-503	17	-97.38	72-391	18	-38.08	15-111	14	-60.29	1-1	100	+1.00

By race type – 2011

	Overall			Two-year-olds			Three-year-olds			Older horses		
	W-R	%	£1	W-R	%	£1	W-R	%	£1	W-R	%	£1
Handicap	70-566	12	-81.76	27-144	19	+40.59	35-327	11	-83.81	8-95	8	-38.54
Group 1,2,3	19-95	20	+19.42	8-41	20	+23.00	7-40	18	+1.63	4-14	29	-5.21
Maiden	78-491	16	+11.23	64-417	15	+21.51	14-73	19	-9.28	0-1	-	-1.00

By jockey – 2013

	Overall			Two-year-olds			Three-year-olds			Older horses		
	W-R	%	£1	W-R	%	£1	W-R	%	£1	W-R	%	£1
R Hughes	127-530	24	-63.68	67-251	27	-29.92	47-204	23	-32.50	13-75	17	-1.25
Pat Dobbs	30-198	15	-61.41	19-118	16	-37.04	11-65	17	-9.36	0-15	-	-15.00
Sean Levey	23-191	12	-40.44	13-95	14	-14.67	8-74	11	-20.27	2-22	9	-5.50
Ryan Moore	16-89	18	-21.79	10-45	22	-8.83	6-35	17	-3.96	0-9	-	-9.00
Dane O'Neill	9-50	18	+9.13	6-29	21	+14.00	3-21	14	-4.88	0-0	-	+0.00
W Twist-Davies	8-85	9	-13.00	2-19	11	-10.75	3-44	7	-31.25	3-22	14	+29.00
Paul Hanagan	5-35	14	-10.07	5-21	24	+3.93	0-14	-	-14.00	0-0	-	+0.00
Kieran O'Neill	5-72	7	-30.75	3-37	8	-23.75	2-30	7	-2.00	0-5	-	-5.00
Jim Crowley	3-9	33	+22.73	3-7	43	+24.73	0-1	-	-1.00	0-1	-	-1.00
Frankie Dettori	2-14	14	-3.27	2-12	17	-1.27	0-2	-	-2.00	0-0	-	+0.00
Gary Stevens	1-1	100	+8.00	0-0	-	+0.00	1-1	100	+8.00	0-0	-	+0.00
Seb Sanders	1-1	100	+4.00	1-1	100	+4.00	0-0	-	+0.00	0-0	-	+0.00

By jockey – 2012

	Overall			Two-year-olds			Three-year-olds			Older horses		
	W-R	%	£1	W-R	%	£1	W-R	%	£1	W-R	%	£1
R Hughes	103-485	21	-40.02	62-237	26	-26.30	37-205	18	+4.45	4-43	9	-18.17
Pat Dobbs	32-234	14	+16.41	18-117	15	+0.08	13-102	13	+25.33	1-15	7	-9.00
Ryan Moore	21-123	17	-5.64	10-64	16	-6.43	9-49	18	-1.72	2-10	20	+2.50
Sean Levey	20-152	13	-29.63	9-71	13	-39.88	7-68	10	+0.75	4-13	31	+9.50
Kieran O'Neill	8-116	7	-83.38	2-45	4	-36.75	6-63	10	-38.63	0-8	-	-8.00
Dane O'Neill	7-37	19	+0.56	6-22	27	+13.73	1-14	7	-12.17	0-1	-	-1.00
Paul Hanagan	5-22	23	-0.67	5-20	25	+1.33	0-2	-	-2.00	0-0	-	+0.00
W Twist-Davies	5-46	11	-5.00	2-19	11	-2.50	3-23	13	+1.50	0-4	-	-4.00
Tadhg O'Shea	3-7	43	-2.04	3-7	43	-2.04	0-0	-	+0.00	0-0	-	+0.00

By jockey – 2011

	Overall			Two-year-olds			Three-year-olds			Older horses		
	W-R	%	£1	W-R	%	£1	W-R	%	£1	W-R	%	£1
R Hughes	89-439	20	+24.52	49-217	23	+27.78	30-172	17	+13.28	10-50	20	-16.54
Pat Dobbs	36-205	18	+14.16	24-107	22	+29.58	9-75	12	-15.42	3-23	13	+0.00
Kieran O'Neill	24-174	14	-7.91	17-82	21	+28.22	7-73	10	-17.13	0-19	-	-19.00
Dane O'Neill	15-111	14	-36.45	7-65	11	-28.55	6-31	19	-5.23	2-15	13	-2.67
Ryan Moore	12-114	11	-71.54	5-50	10	-35.77	6-54	11	-27.60	1-10	10	-8.17
Jimmy Fortune	6-70	9	-10.63	4-35	11	+12.63	2-24	8	-12.25	0-11	-	-11.00
Jimmy Quinn	4-12	33	+12.25	0-3	-	-3.00	4-7	57	+17.25	0-2	-	-2.00
Sean Levey	4-56	7	-17.50	4-39	10	-0.50	0-16	-	-16.00	0-1	-	-1.00
Steve Drowne	3-16	19	+1.00	1-8	13	-2.50	1-6	17	-1.50	1-2	50	+5.00

By course – 2010-2013

	Overall			Two-year-olds			Three-year-olds			Older horses		
	W-R	%	£1	W-R	%	£1	W-R	%	£1	W-R	%	£1
Ascot	29-309	9	-100.75	15-132	11	-8.62	10-121	8	-57.50	4-56	7	-34.63
Bath	31-132	23	+24.42	19-79	24	+8.72	10-49	20	+3.20	2-4	50	+12.50
Beverley	3-8	38	-0.50	2-6	33	-1.75	1-2	50	+1.25	0-0	-	+0.00
Brighton	16-90	18	-14.98	11-50	22	-14.85	2-31	6	-14.25	3-9	33	+14.13
Carlisle	0-1	-	-1.00	0-0	-	+0.00	0-1	-	-1.00	0-0	-	+0.00
Catterick	1-2	50	+7.00	1-2	50	+7.00	0-0	-	+0.00	0-0	-	+0.00
Chepstow	17-101	17	-31.60	11-47	23	-6.60	6-50	12	-21.00	0-4	-	-4.00
Chester	6-31	19	-10.20	6-17	35	+3.80	0-10	-	-10.00	0-4	-	-4.00
Doncaster	27-154	18	-3.62	20-96	21	+7.76	6-43	14	-13.38	1-15	7	+2.00
Epsom	24-121	20	-28.47	16-49	33	+18.40	6-49	12	-29.13	2-23	9	-17.75
Ffos Las	5-24	21	-3.89	2-11	18	-1.00	2-9	22	-3.89	1-4	25	+1.00
Folkestone	13-48	27	+5.86	4-22	18	-1.88	7-21	33	+4.48	2-5	40	+3.25
Goodwood	71-417	17	+33.63	36-195	18	-33.62	23-163	14	+9.75	12-59	20	+57.50
Hamilton	0-1	-	-1.00	0-0	-	+0.00	0-1	-	-1.00	0-0	-	+0.00
Haydock	15-122	12	-60.68	12-65	18	-11.50	3-47	6	-39.18	0-10	-	-10.00
Kempton (AW)	113-707	16	-50.56	58-356	16	-63.97	46-265	17	+39.49	9-86	10	-26.08
Leicester	29-148	20	-18.80	19-80	24	+17.19	9-54	17	-25.75	1-14	7	-10.25
Lingfield	13-87	15	-33.70	11-48	23	+1.64	2-35	6	-31.33	0-4	-	-4.00
Lingfield (AW)	58-324	18	-88.67	18-117	15	-34.91	34-162	21	-43.60	6-45	13	-10.17
Musselburgh	0-4	-	-4.00	0-1	-	-1.00	0-1	-	-1.00	0-2	-	-2.00
Newbury	63-519	12	-130.36	45-292	15	-37.22	16-177	9	-46.67	2-50	4	-46.47
Newmarket	40-325	12	+7.49	20-168	12	-27.64	18-141	13	+21.89	2-16	13	+13.25
Newmarket (J)	48-338	14	-16.31	30-174	17	+36.73	14-130	11	-37.52	4-34	12	-15.52
Nottingham	18-101	18	+21.32	10-56	18	+2.82	8-37	22	+26.50	0-8	-	-8.00
Pontefract	1-17	6	-12.00	1-11	9	-6.00	0-3	-	-3.00	0-3	-	-3.00
Redcar	0-4	-	-4.00	0-3	-	-3.00	0-1	-	-1.00	0-0	-	+0.00
Ripon	2-12	17	-5.13	2-10	20	-3.13	0-2	-	-2.00	0-0	-	+0.00
Salisbury	72-361	20	-42.59	45-190	24	-18.83	21-137	15	-37.76	6-34	18	+14.00
Sandown	44-301	15	-14.59	25-113	22	+8.09	15-149	10	-0.40	4-39	10	-22.29
Southwell (AW)	0-3	-	-3.00	0-3	-	-3.00	0-0	-	+0.00	0-0	-	+0.00
Thirsk	0-2	-	-2.00	0-1	-	-1.00	0-1	-	-1.00	0-0	-	+0.00
Warwick	9-70	13	-38.17	3-33	9	-16.67	6-33	18	-17.50	0-4	-	-4.00
Windsor	73-423	17	-103.55	43-187	23	-44.16	24-170	14	-25.89	6-66	9	-33.50
Wolves (AW)	25-109	23	+17.19	13-62	21	+8.98	7-35	20	-0.63	5-12	42	+8.83
Yarmouth	4-18	22	+18.00	4-11	36	+25.00	0-7	-	-7.00	0-0	-	+0.00
York	11-94	12	-32.75	8-55	15	-10.25	2-26	8	-18.00	1-13	8	-4.50

Ten-year summary

	Wins	Runs	%	Win prize-money	Total prize-money	£1
2013	235	1412	17	£3,137,720.00	£4,532,464.69	-306.32
2012	218	1367	16	£1,767,369.39	£2,821,469.49	-165.90
2011	218	1408	15	£2,283,589.58	£3,726,396.80	-46.12
2010	210	1341	16	£2,054,058.90	£3,218,574.92	-203.61
2009	188	1371	14	£1,751,642.04	£2,814,384.49	-193.61
2008	189	1406	13	£1,884,767.33	£2,982,090.39	-283.60
2007	148	1075	14	£1,192,346.67	£2,083,975.15	-178.24
2006	127	1067	12	£1,043,024.26	£1,753,310.04	-261.41
2005	145	1261	11	£1,209,719.79	£2,030,928.02	-282.57
2004	113	1201	9	£795,942.69	£1,464,125.73	-235.21

CHAMPIONS: Richard Hannon (right) has been succeeded by son Richard jnr

Mark Johnston

Johnston deserves more credit for his remarkable ability to churn out huge tallies of winners, the latest of 216 matching his 2009 peak. However, he has had just nine Group winners in three years.

By month – 2013

	Overall			Two-year-olds			Three-year-olds			Older horses		
	W-R	%	£1	W-R	%	£1	W-R	%	£1	W-R	%	£1
January	4-35	11	-5.25	0-0	-	+0.00	3-25	12	-2.25	1-10	10	-3.00
February	7-36	19	-0.14	0-0	-	+0.00	3-28	11	-7.67	4-8	50	+7.53
March	10-59	17	-20.95	0-2	-	-2.00	10-43	23	-4.95	0-14	-	-14.00
April	22-111	20	-7.72	5-12	42	+0.80	13-72	18	-13.27	4-27	15	+4.75
May	23-172	13	-74.82	4-32	13	-16.75	16-99	16	-29.82	3-41	7	-28.25
June	28-207	14	-49.61	5-52	10	-31.42	17-103	17	-6.02	6-52	12	-12.17
July	41-231	18	-10.22	6-52	12	-15.65	24-125	19	-39.45	11-54	20	+44.88
August	32-226	14	-69.38	6-68	9	-50.14	19-117	16	-15.34	7-41	17	-3.90
September	25-204	12	-66.67	12-75	16	-0.88	10-102	10	-56.62	3-27	11	-9.17
October	10-182	5	-68.71	3-84	4	-64.86	6-77	8	-49.86	1-21	5	+46.00
November	4-55	7	-34.58	2-26	8	-22.08	2-22	9	-5.50	0-7	-	-7.00
December	10-39	26	+11.83	2-12	17	-5.75	5-21	24	+6.08	3-6	50	+11.50

By month – 2012

	Overall			Two-year-olds			Three-year-olds			Older horses		
	W-R	%	£1	W-R	%	£1	W-R	%	£1	W-R	%	£1
January	14-45	31	+19.16	0-0	-	+0.00	9-25	36	+12.88	5-20	25	+6.29
February	14-49	29	-6.04	0-0	-	+0.00	8-29	28	-10.04	6-20	30	+4.00
March	19-71	27	+1.03	0-1	-	-1.00	14-42	33	+10.33	5-28	18	-8.31
April	20-91	22	-11.70	4-5	80	+13.76	12-63	19	-17.19	4-23	17	-8.27
May	18-163	11	-17.63	4-26	15	-6.38	9-104	9	-6.88	5-33	15	-4.38
June	17-178	10	-58.69	3-31	10	-19.00	11-108	10	-24.30	3-39	8	-15.39
July	19-160	12	-29.51	3-32	9	-19.63	14-106	13	-17.88	2-22	9	+8.00
August	42-193	22	+23.93	10-51	20	-4.84	28-121	23	+28.10	4-21	19	+0.68
September	33-189	17	+3.57	8-54	15	-5.22	23-110	21	+20.28	2-25	8	-11.50
October	15-153	10	-45.50	6-70	9	-47.38	7-70	10	-21.13	2-13	15	+23.00
November	2-35	6	-23.50	1-17	6	-11.00	0-11	-	-11.00	1-7	14	-1.50
December	2-17	12	-4.00	2-12	17	+1.00	0-1	-	-1.00	0-4	-	-4.00

By month – 2011

	Overall			Two-year-olds			Three-year-olds			Older horses		
	W-R	%	£1	W-R	%	£1	W-R	%	£1	W-R	%	£1
January	16-32	50	+8.82	0-0	-	+0.00	14-22	64	+13.19	2-10	20	-4.38
February	7-42	17	-14.42	0-0	-	+0.00	4-31	13	-16.17	3-11	27	+1.75
March	9-42	21	-8.56	0-0	-	+0.00	9-33	27	+0.44	0-9	-	-9.00
April	10-129	8	-84.00	0-8	-	-8.00	9-83	11	-42.00	1-38	3	-34.00
May	27-165	16	+21.02	8-35	23	+5.02	14-72	19	+9.75	5-58	9	+6.25
June	19-193	10	-57.61	5-40	13	-21.38	10-99	10	-19.23	4-54	7	-17.00
July	26-197	13	-67.04	6-50	12	-34.58	16-87	18	+5.67	4-60	7	-38.13
August	13-155	8	-48.95	4-47	9	-29.25	5-63	8	-11.70	4-45	9	-8.00
September	22-169	13	-16.72	2-54	4	-46.00	12-76	16	+8.75	8-39	21	+20.53
October	25-140	18	+31.53	9-72	13	-10.00	12-47	26	+33.70	4-21	19	+7.83
November	3-31	10	-24.14	3-19	16	-12.14	0-12	-	-12.00	0-0	-	+0.00
December	2-16	13	-10.89	0-6	-	-6.00	2-9	22	-3.89	0-1	-	-1.00

By race type – 2013

	Overall			Two-year-olds			Three-year-olds			Older horses		
	W-R	%	£1	W-R	%	£1	W-R	%	£1	W-R	%	£1
Handicap	129-1023	13	-275.05	8-118	7	-85.26	84-624	13	-215.70	37-281	13	+25.92
Group 1,2,3	3-28	11	-8.25	0-8	-	-8.00	0-11	-	-11.00	3-9	33	+10.75
Maiden	66-409	16	-92.97	31-238	13	-95.64	34-165	21	+0.67	1-6	17	+2.00

By race type – 2012

	Overall			Two-year-olds			Three-year-olds			Older horses		
	W-R	%	£1	W-R	%	£1	W-R	%	£1	W-R	%	£1
Handicap	139-921	15	-79.02	11-85	13	-28.63	97-606	16	-35.36	31-230	13	-15.04
Group 1,2,3	3-28	11	-5.75	2-15	13	-1.25	1-11	9	-2.50	0-2	-	-2.00
Maiden	55-315	17	-93.57	21-172	12	-61.60	30-131	23	-33.96	4-12	33	+2.00

By race type – 2011

	Overall			Two-year-olds			Three-year-olds			Older horses		
	W-R	%	£1	W-R	%	£1	W-R	%	£1	W-R	%	£1
Handicap	104-834	12	-152.93	6-86	7	-53.00	68-430	16	-32.93	30-318	9	-67.00
Group 1,2,3	3-30	10	-6.50	0-11	-	-11.00	3-15	20	+8.50	0-4	-	-4.00
Maiden	59-355	17	-68.28	25-191	13	-80.11	34-162	21	+13.82	0-2	-	-2.00

By jockey – 2013

	Overall			Two-year-olds			Three-year-olds			Older horses		
	W-R	%	£1	W-R	%	£1	W-R	%	£1	W-R	%	£1
Joe Fanning	93-639	15	-161.29	20-162	12	-45.66	55-343	16	-103.16	18-134	13	-12.48
Franny Norton	40-244	16	-53.36	6-47	13	-28.45	24-142	17	-30.89	10-55	18	+5.98
S De Sousa	27-156	17	+25.65	7-44	16	-22.48	15-92	16	-32.87	5-20	25	+81.00
Adam Kirby	11-34	32	+25.00	2-12	17	-3.00	4-12	33	+6.50	5-10	50	+21.50
Liam Jones	10-80	13	-13.26	1-25	4	-22.50	8-44	18	+15.91	1-11	9	-6.67
Neil Callan	7-42	17	-10.88	4-15	27	-7.38	3-22	14	+1.50	0-5	-	-5.00
Adrian Nicholls	7-51	14	-12.42	2-20	10	-7.50	4-26	15	-4.25	1-5	20	-0.67
Paul Hanagan	3-27	11	-7.63	1-13	8	+0.00	2-12	17	-5.63	0-2	-	-2.00
Gerald Mosse	2-5	40	+5.38	1-2	50	+0.38	1-1	100	+7.00	0-2	-	-2.00
William Buick	2-8	25	+2.10	0-1	-	-1.00	2-5	40	+5.10	0-2	-	-2.00
J-P Guillambert	2-13	15	-1.75	0-2	-	-2.00	2-8	25	+3.25	0-3	-	-3.00
M J M Murphy	2-27	7	-18.63	0-3	-	-3.00	2-21	10	-12.63	0-3	-	-3.00

By jockey – 2012

	Overall			Two-year-olds			Three-year-olds			Older horses		
	W-R	%	£1	W-R	%	£1	W-R	%	£1	W-R	%	£1
Joe Fanning	103-579	18	-44.99	17-132	13	-42.31	61-322	19	-30.47	25-125	20	+27.79
S De Sousa	41-238	17	-27.87	10-60	17	-19.11	28-145	19	+12.64	3-33	9	-21.40
Franny Norton	20-120	17	+23.32	4-31	13	-5.00	14-70	20	+23.82	2-19	11	+4.50
Kieren Fallon	11-60	18	-5.63	5-19	26	-1.38	5-29	17	-3.25	1-12	8	-1.00
Mirco Demuro	8-50	16	-4.38	3-8	38	-0.38	5-32	16	+6.00	0-10	-	-10.00
Neil Callan	6-34	18	-2.00	0-5	-	-5.00	6-21	29	+11.00	0-8	-	-8.00
Frederik Tylicki	3-14	21	+1.50	0-1	-	-1.00	2-9	22	+3.50	1-4	25	-1.00
Martin Lane	3-18	17	+21.00	0-3	-	-3.00	3-14	21	+25.00	0-1	-	-1.00
M J M Murphy	3-18	17	-11.33	0-1	-	-1.00	1-14	7	-11.00	2-3	67	+0.68

By jockey – 2011

	Overall			Two-year-olds			Three-year-olds			Older horses		
	W-R	%	£1	W-R	%	£1	W-R	%	£1	W-R	%	£1
S De Sousa	70-370	19	-10.58	22-124	18	-39.49	36-167	22	+25.38	12-79	15	+3.53
Joe Fanning	43-273	16	-26.31	7-73	10	-35.93	25-134	19	-27.83	11-66	17	+37.46
Greg Fairley	16-79	20	-26.44	0-7	-	-7.00	14-47	30	-1.44	2-25	8	-18.00
Franny Norton	9-59	15	+30.98	2-15	13	+3.73	3-31	10	+3.25	4-13	31	+24.00
Neil Callan	8-56	14	-2.58	1-11	9	-8.75	5-25	20	+11.67	2-20	10	-5.50
Kieren Fallon	5-49	10	-17.83	0-8	-	-8.00	4-29	14	-6.83	1-12	8	-3.00
Frankie Dettori	4-22	18	-4.75	0-3	-	-3.00	4-12	33	+5.25	0-7	-	-7.00
Daryl Byrne	4-43	9	-19.67	0-7	-	-7.00	2-20	10	-11.17	2-16	13	-1.50
Tadhg O'Shea	3-21	14	-2.25	0-3	-	-3.00	3-18	17	+0.75	0-0	-	+0.00

By course – 2010-2013

	Overall			Two-year-olds			Three-year-olds			Older horses		
	W-R	%	£1	W-R	%	£1	W-R	%	£1	W-R	%	£1
Ascot	23-249	9	-56.09	2-33	6	-24.75	16-134	12	-25.34	5-82	6	-6.00
Ayr	9-136	7	-100.75	2-52	4	-48.25	7-60	12	-28.50	0-24	-	-24.00
Bath	11-47	23	+19.83	2-12	17	-2.75	8-32	25	+22.58	1-3	33	+0.00
Beverley	56-212	26	+43.11	12-50	24	-7.63	34-122	28	+45.10	10-40	25	+5.65
Brighton	11-56	20	-3.48	3-16	19	-5.11	7-33	21	+2.63	1-7	14	-1.00
Carlisle	10-69	14	-0.75	3-21	14	+8.00	6-33	18	+1.25	1-15	7	-10.00
Catterick	20-118	17	-21.36	5-39	13	-23.75	12-57	21	+10.65	3-22	14	-8.25
Chepstow	9-37	24	+5.88	0-7	-	-7.00	7-26	27	+10.88	2-4	50	+2.00
Chester	33-201	16	+68.24	6-35	17	-11.76	15-108	14	+32.50	12-58	21	+47.50
Doncaster	16-198	8	-104.40	2-53	4	-45.00	11-95	12	-21.00	3-50	6	-38.40
Epsom	16-131	12	-51.05	4-26	15	-2.75	9-65	14	-27.80	3-40	8	-20.50
Ffos Las	8-42	19	-7.38	2-8	25	-1.88	1-19	5	-16.13	5-15	33	+10.63
Folkestone	5-17	29	-1.22	0-0	-	+0.00	4-15	27	-1.59	1-2	50	+0.38
Goodwood	24-194	12	-1.88	8-45	18	-2.26	9-87	10	-21.00	7-62	11	+21.38
Hamilton	46-203	23	+15.24	6-42	14	+1.13	33-125	26	+11.74	7-36	19	+2.38
Haydock	22-227	10	-78.01	2-47	4	-40.13	16-122	13	-3.22	4-58	7	-34.67
Kempton (AW)	48-378	13	-118.13	8-86	9	-55.25	28-210	13	-51.70	12-82	15	-11.18
Leicester	17-121	14	-18.30	9-47	19	+24.50	6-55	11	-34.17	2-19	11	-8.63
Lingfield	4-29	14	-5.77	1-6	17	-4.27	2-19	11	-4.50	1-4	25	+3.00
Lingfield (AW)	59-335	18	-102.01	4-39	10	-9.50	43-225	19	-69.27	12-71	17	-23.24
Musselburgh	33-192	17	-28.11	8-45	18	-2.10	20-106	19	-20.39	5-41	12	-5.63
Newbury	10-75	13	-22.00	5-22	23	-0.13	1-36	3	-28.50	4-17	24	+6.63
Newcastle	17-126	13	-37.17	6-37	16	-4.75	9-61	15	-10.17	2-28	7	-22.25
Newmarket	29-221	13	+34.33	5-55	9	-39.93	16-111	14	-15.12	8-55	15	+89.38
Newmarket (J)	26-178	15	+8.38	1-33	3	-31.60	18-112	16	+20.98	7-33	21	+19.00
Nottingham	7-119	6	-82.63	3-47	6	-25.63	3-60	5	-48.25	1-12	8	-8.75
Pontefract	26-174	15	-32.60	2-36	6	-28.50	20-105	19	+4.30	4-33	12	-8.40
Redcar	11-87	13	-38.06	3-33	9	-25.21	8-41	20	+0.16	0-13	-	-13.00
Ripon	18-150	12	-65.65	1-26	4	-17.50	15-94	16	-24.21	2-30	7	-23.94
Salisbury	1-22	5	-17.50	0-4	-	-4.00	1-14	7	-9.50	0-4	-	-4.00
Sandown	8-108	7	-65.25	1-19	5	-15.00	7-68	10	-29.25	0-21	-	-21.00
Southwell (AW)	60-253	24	-14.77	9-54	17	-32.92	41-137	30	+30.95	10-62	16	-12.81
Thirsk	12-110	11	-23.79	3-23	13	+3.25	7-64	11	-12.04	2-23	9	-15.00
Warwick	8-47	17	-17.50	3-13	23	-2.29	2-27	7	-19.38	3-7	43	+4.17
Windsor	6-44	14	+3.50	1-9	11	+0.00	4-28	14	+2.50	1-7	14	+1.00
Wolves (AW)	81-458	18	-96.52	8-97	8	-68.13	57-282	20	-44.75	16-79	20	+16.35
Yarmouth	12-102	12	-34.46	5-33	15	+1.98	3-50	6	-41.27	4-19	21	+4.83
York	9-204	4	-145.00	3-55	5	-36.50	3-77	4	-59.50	3-72	4	-49.00

Ten-year summary

	Wins	Runs	%	Win prize-money	Total prize-money	£1
2013	216	1557	14	£1,826,629.78	£2,743,581.49	-396.21
2012	215	1344	16	£1,545,130.29	£2,284,275.76	-148.88
2011	179	1311	14	£927,711.46	£1,550,631.62	-270.93
2010	211	1458	14	£1,657,512.68	£2,419,718.15	-377.04
2009	216	1227	18	£1,747,013.96	£2,843,943.25	-139.14
2008	164	1145	14	£1,345,669.48	£2,070,937.14	-200.11
2007	161	998	16	£1,188,791.46	£1,651,628.48	-122.33
2006	158	1005	16	£1,245,722.50	£1,868,197.71	-87.83
2005	141	885	16	£1,118,373.15	£1,864,674.04	-80.25
2004	119	799	15	£1,726,950.89	£2,437,676.95	-156.74

MAPUTO: won five out of six last season before moving to Charlie Appleby

Richard Fahey

After taking a backward step following his best total of 181 four years ago, Fahey headed back in the right direction last season. He is coping better with an expanded team, shown by an improved 13% strike-rate.

By month – 2013

	Overall			Two-year-olds			Three-year-olds			Older horses		
	W-R	%	£1	W-R	%	£1	W-R	%	£1	W-R	%	£1
January	5-26	19	-1.80	0-0	-	+0.00	2-5	40	+2.86	3-21	14	-4.67
February	3-19	16	-12.00	0-0	-	+0.00	2-9	22	-6.00	1-10	10	-6.00
March	9-51	18	-1.96	0-3	-	-3.00	2-14	14	-8.71	7-34	21	+9.75
April	20-118	17	+14.02	1-12	8	-8.25	11-50	22	+13.88	8-56	14	+8.40
May	22-169	13	-33.64	10-36	28	-1.00	6-61	10	-29.75	6-72	8	-2.89
June	15-183	8	-87.43	8-53	15	-22.93	1-58	2	-48.00	6-72	8	-16.50
July	22-168	13	-36.68	12-62	19	+12.19	5-41	12	-15.63	5-65	8	-33.25
August	31-175	18	-17.56	11-64	17	-31.43	8-47	17	+21.00	12-64	19	-7.13
September	16-170	9	-13.25	6-60	10	+3.25	4-52	8	-29.50	6-58	10	+13.00
October	18-123	15	+19.21	7-41	17	-17.29	8-38	21	+59.50	3-44	7	-23.00
November	3-45	7	-25.80	1-11	9	-8.90	1-11	9	-8.90	1-23	4	-8.00
December	0-40	-	-40.00	0-13	-	-13.00	0-9	-	-9.00	0-18	-	-18.00

By month – 2012

	Overall			Two-year-olds			Three-year-olds			Older horses		
	W-R	%	£1	W-R	%	£1	W-R	%	£1	W-R	%	£1
January	6-40	15	+8.00	0-0	-	+0.00	1-12	8	-6.00	5-28	18	+14.00
February	1-31	3	-24.00	0-0	-	+0.00	0-11	-	-11.00	1-20	5	-13.00
March	4-28	14	+13.00	1-1	100	+5.00	1-7	14	-3.00	2-20	10	+11.00
April	9-87	10	-14.83	1-5	20	+7.00	3-32	9	-10.33	5-50	10	-11.50
May	18-168	11	-75.22	4-25	16	-10.47	9-61	15	-14.75	5-82	6	-50.00
June	15-175	9	-26.88	5-34	15	+32.13	5-52	10	-4.50	5-89	6	-54.50
July	29-177	16	-25.27	12-55	22	+9.80	9-51	18	-12.13	8-71	11	-22.94
August	26-187	14	+48.67	10-70	14	+43.04	10-54	19	-3.13	6-63	10	+8.75
September	15-182	8	-93.00	8-69	12	-26.25	3-52	6	-29.00	4-61	7	-37.75
October	12-127	9	-55.13	6-49	12	-19.63	2-30	7	-17.00	4-48	8	-18.50
November	4-49	8	-28.00	0-10	-	-10.00	3-14	21	-3.00	1-25	4	-15.00
December	3-43	7	-22.00	1-13	8	-6.00	0-18	-	-18.00	2-12	17	+2.00

By month – 2011

	Overall			Two-year-olds			Three-year-olds			Older horses		
	W-R	%	£1	W-R	%	£1	W-R	%	£1	W-R	%	£1
January	10-45	22	+15.78	0-0	-	+0.00	1-13	8	-9.25	9-32	28	+25.03
February	3-29	10	-0.80	0-0	-	+0.00	0-6	-	-6.00	3-23	13	+5.20
March	2-19	11	-11.63	1-1	100	+1.38	0-4	-	-4.00	1-14	7	-9.00
April	25-113	22	+59.08	6-16	38	+10.58	7-32	22	+15.50	12-65	18	+33.00
May	27-147	18	-23.04	9-32	28	+0.28	8-39	21	+1.10	10-76	13	-24.42
June	14-156	9	-48.09	3-37	8	-4.50	4-52	8	-29.09	7-67	10	-14.50
July	15-200	8	-98.67	5-59	8	-31.50	6-64	9	-22.50	4-77	5	-44.67
August	20-154	13	-37.80	7-54	13	-3.14	2-37	5	-27.00	11-63	17	-7.67
September	14-157	9	-64.75	4-47	9	-29.75	4-41	10	-4.50	6-69	9	-30.50
October	11-106	10	-26.30	4-40	10	-12.88	0-23	-	-23.00	7-43	16	+9.57
November	4-52	8	-19.50	2-21	10	-11.00	1-9	11	+10.00	1-22	5	-18.50
December	6-46	13	-5.17	4-16	25	+6.33	1-12	8	+1.00	1-18	6	-12.50

By race type – 2013

	Overall			Two-year-olds			Three-year-olds			Older horses		
	W-R	%	£1	W-R	%	£1	W-R	%	£1	W-R	%	£1
Handicap	97-860	11	-100.73	15-81	19	+38.63	36-319	11	-40.38	46-460	10	-98.98
Group 1,2,3	5-38	13	+4.25	2-12	17	-3.00	1-7	14	-3.75	2-19	11	+11.00
Maiden	44-264	17	-90.87	30-211	14	-100.86	11-46	24	-3.63	3-7	43	+13.62

By race type – 2012

	Overall			Two-year-olds			Three-year-olds			Older horses		
	W-R	%	£1	W-R	%	£1	W-R	%	£1	W-R	%	£1
Handicap	76-855	9	-256.29	9-93	10	-1.38	32-294	11	-94.92	35-468	7	-160.00
Group 1,2,3	3-42	7	-7.50	0-8	-	-8.00	1-9	11	+0.00	2-25	8	+0.50
Maiden	37-249	15	+14.69	29-181	16	+41.10	8-63	13	-21.42	0-5	-	-5.00

By race type – 2011

	Overall			Two-year-olds			Three-year-olds			Older horses		
	W-R	%	£1	W-R	%	£1	W-R	%	£1	W-R	%	£1
Handicap	93-825	11	-168.39	7-60	12	-22.38	27-264	10	-70.25	59-501	12	-75.77
Group 1,2,3	2-27	7	-9.00	0-9	-	-9.00	2-12	17	+6.00	0-6	-	-6.00
Maiden	27-237	11	-64.94	25-203	12	-38.54	2-31	6	-23.40	0-3	-	-3.00

By jockey – 2013

	Overall			Two-year-olds			Three-year-olds			Older horses		
	W-R	%	£1	W-R	%	£1	W-R	%	£1	W-R	%	£1
Tony Hamilton	49-408	12	-154.94	25-149	17	-64.14	11-132	8	-65.86	13-127	10	-24.94
Paul Hanagan	20-164	12	-26.00	6-35	17	-15.50	7-47	15	-15.50	7-82	9	-5.25
G Chaloner	18-132	14	-5.84	3-12	25	+7.91	4-37	11	-11.25	11-83	13	-2.50
Lee Topliss	17-109	16	-41.98	8-37	22	-9.59	5-33	15	-2.75	4-39	10	-29.64
Samantha Bell	9-70	13	-2.17	2-12	17	-0.67	4-22	18	+13.00	3-36	8	-14.50
Ryan Moore	8-21	38	+25.50	3-10	30	+0.25	4-8	50	+21.25	1-3	33	+4.00
Barry McHugh	8-92	9	-21.17	0-24	-	-24.00	4-27	15	+15.00	4-41	10	-12.17
Jamie Spencer	7-27	26	+20.25	0-1	-	-1.00	4-10	40	+10.50	3-16	19	+10.75
Frederik Tylicki	4-26	15	+3.50	0-5	-	-5.00	3-10	30	+15.00	1-11	9	-6.50
Tom Eaves	4-26	15	-8.76	1-4	25	-1.13	3-17	18	-2.64	0-5	-	-5.00
Patrick Mathers	4-63	6	+16.00	3-24	13	+38.00	1-20	5	-3.00	0-19	-	-19.00
Franny Norton	3-3	100	+15.50	1-1	100	+4.00	0-0	-	+0.00	2-2	100	+11.50

By jockey – 2012

	Overall			Two-year-olds			Three-year-olds			Older horses		
	W-R	%	£1	W-R	%	£1	W-R	%	£1	W-R	%	£1
Tony Hamilton	47-383	12	-85.71	24-142	17	-2.96	13-93	14	-24.58	10-148	7	-58.17
Paul Hanagan	31-209	15	-3.38	11-41	27	+8.25	5-59	8	-24.63	15-109	14	+13.00
Frederik Tylicki	17-94	18	-1.95	3-22	14	-12.42	9-32	28	+17.13	5-40	13	-6.65
Laura Barry	9-52	17	+19.25	1-3	33	+31.00	5-20	25	+1.75	3-29	10	-13.50
Lee Topliss	8-100	8	-56.75	3-22	14	-8.25	5-27	19	+2.50	0-51	-	-51.00
Barry McHugh	6-79	8	-23.50	2-18	11	-6.00	3-38	8	-15.50	1-23	4	-2.00
David Nolan	4-52	8	+16.00	1-18	6	+33.00	2-13	15	-2.00	1-21	5	-15.00
Patrick Mathers	4-60	7	-30.50	1-22	5	-10.00	1-26	4	-21.50	2-12	17	+1.00
Shane B Kelly	4-82	5	-61.50	0-9	-	-9.00	0-23	-	-23.00	4-50	8	-29.50

By jockey – 2011

	Overall			Two-year-olds			Three-year-olds			Older horses		
	W-R	%	£1	W-R	%	£1	W-R	%	£1	W-R	%	£1
Paul Hanagan	77-478	16	-106.49	29-146	20	-38.28	19-142	13	-38.24	29-190	15	-29.97
Lee Topliss	18-147	12	-24.67	0-19	-	-19.00	3-34	9	-16.00	15-94	16	+10.33
Tony Hamilton	17-201	8	-47.21	11-83	13	+19.08	3-49	6	-9.00	3-69	4	-57.29
Barry McHugh	16-86	19	+13.23	2-23	9	-15.50	2-25	8	-18.00	12-38	32	+46.73
Frederik Tylicki	7-62	11	+10.25	1-12	8	+9.00	3-15	20	+12.50	3-35	9	-11.25
G Chaloner	4-52	8	-3.50	0-5	-	-5.00	0-10	-	-10.00	4-37	11	+11.50
Jack Mitchell	2-10	20	+14.50	0-0	-	+0.00	1-4	25	+5.50	1-6	17	+9.00
Laura Barry	2-39	5	-26.00	0-0	-	+0.00	1-9	11	-1.00	1-30	3	-25.00
Neil Farley	1-2	50	+11.00	0-0	-	+0.00	1-1	100	+12.00	0-1	-	-1.00

By course – 2010-2013

	Overall			Two-year-olds			Three-year-olds			Older horses		
	W-R	%	£1	W-R	%	£1	W-R	%	£1	W-R	%	£1
Ascot	4-110	4	-73.50	2-25	8	-13.50	1-24	4	-14.00	1-61	2	-46.00
Ayr	43-304	14	-12.59	19-79	24	+49.41	10-78	13	-8.00	14-147	10	-54.00
Bath	0-3	-	-3.00	0-0	-	+0.00	0-0	-	+0.00	0-3	-	-3.00
Beverley	25-234	11	-102.72	13-84	15	-11.05	4-82	5	-63.92	8-68	12	-27.75
Carlisle	18-144	13	-28.13	8-49	16	+14.00	3-40	8	-27.00	7-55	13	-15.13
Catterick	20-118	17	-17.92	12-49	24	+2.38	4-34	12	-7.00	4-35	11	-13.29
Chepstow	0-4	-	-4.00	0-2	-	-2.00	0-2	-	-2.00	0-0	-	+0.00
Chester	32-252	13	-54.38	10-50	20	+9.41	9-92	10	-40.92	13-110	12	-22.88
Doncaster	36-339	11	-69.77	11-84	13	-25.85	2-80	3	-61.50	23-175	13	+17.58
Epsom	8-58	14	+10.50	2-6	33	+3.00	2-12	17	-0.50	4-40	10	+8.00
Goodwood	5-114	4	-57.25	1-27	4	-10.00	2-27	7	-15.75	2-60	3	-31.50
Hamilton	27-171	16	-64.38	6-42	14	-21.74	9-60	15	-23.72	12-69	17	-18.92
Haydock	26-265	10	-76.75	7-65	11	-16.00	12-91	13	+1.00	7-109	6	-61.75
Kempton (AW)	9-137	7	-73.75	1-22	5	-16.00	2-42	5	-37.75	6-73	8	-20.00
Leicester	11-61	18	+93.00	2-18	11	+48.00	5-26	19	+12.00	4-17	24	+33.00
Lingfield (AW)	16-144	11	-31.86	6-22	27	+13.88	1-39	3	-37.64	9-83	11	-8.10
Musselburgh	44-185	24	+50.56	10-46	22	-12.05	19-63	30	+56.52	15-76	20	+6.08
Newbury	5-63	8	-30.00	2-20	10	-9.50	1-13	8	-5.00	2-30	7	-15.50
Newcastle	28-208	13	-67.32	15-58	26	-13.86	6-54	11	-16.40	7-96	7	-37.07
Newmarket	9-104	9	-29.50	1-19	5	-2.00	5-39	13	-1.00	3-46	7	-26.50
Newmarket (J)	12-91	13	-5.63	4-26	15	-7.75	3-31	10	-16.38	5-34	15	+18.50
Nottingham	9-71	13	+3.38	3-12	25	+0.13	3-32	9	-2.75	3-27	11	+6.00
Pontefract	31-181	17	+2.83	10-45	22	+17.96	8-64	13	-25.38	13-72	18	+10.25
Redcar	23-153	15	-45.36	12-66	18	-8.14	6-44	14	-15.50	5-43	12	-21.72
Ripon	29-202	14	-39.45	12-57	21	+8.20	9-61	15	-11.67	8-84	10	-35.98
Salisbury	0-2	-	-2.00	0-1	-	-1.00	0-0	-	+0.00	0-1	-	-1.00
Sandown	2-26	8	-19.25	0-8	-	-8.00	0-6	-	-6.00	2-12	17	-5.25
Southwell (AW)	32-199	16	-26.05	9-45	20	+2.73	7-44	16	-9.86	16-110	15	-18.93
Thirsk	21-161	13	-33.59	11-52	21	-4.84	4-53	8	-20.50	6-56	11	-8.25
Warwick	3-28	11	-11.33	3-12	25	+4.67	0-5	-	-5.00	0-11	-	-11.00
Windsor	6-15	40	+23.50	0-2	-	-2.00	2-5	40	+11.50	4-8	50	+14.00
Wolves (AW)	53-456	12	-114.78	14-106	13	-34.32	11-124	9	-45.65	28-226	12	-34.81
Yarmouth	9-29	31	+22.71	1-4	25	+0.33	5-16	31	+14.13	3-9	33	+8.25
York	42-529	8	-178.20	17-142	12	-25.86	8-100	8	-41.00	17-287	6	-111.33

Ten-year summary

	Wins	Runs	%	Win prize-money	Total prize-money	£1
2013	164	1287	13	£1,588,826.54	£2,455,584.17	-236.90
2012	142	1294	11	£1,213,826.13	£1,982,267.62	-294.66
2011	151	1224	12	£980,328.63	£1,650,127.14	-260.88
2010	181	1356	13	£1,325,389.94	£2,075,925.44	-273.54
2009	165	1106	15	£1,123,057.39	£1,657,128.68	+25.22
2008	113	971	12	£753,492.30	£1,247,043.13	-285.77
2007	85	926	9	£643,994.08	£1,132,827.97	-327.77
2006	87	734	12	£677,880.08	£1,098,407.35	-98.05
2005	79	768	10	£487,562.61	£802,151.94	-131.29
2004	77	649	12	£504,814.42	£740,641.01	-53.26

HEAVEN'S GUEST: progressive sprinter who proved a real money-spinner

David O'Meara

O'Meara's sudden impact is astonishing given he sent out his first runner in June 2010. Last year's total of 136 was nearly double his previous best and he is certainly a major new force in the training ranks.

By month – 2013

	Overall			Two-year-olds			Three-year-olds			Older horses		
	W-R	%	£1	W-R	%	£1	W-R	%	£1	W-R	%	£1
January	11-24	46	+6.50	0-0	-	+0.00	3-5	60	+1.80	8-19	42	+4.70
February	2-16	13	-10.50	0-0	-	+0.00	1-4	25	-1.25	1-12	8	-9.25
March	6-27	22	-11.42	0-0	-	+0.00	1-8	13	-6.00	5-19	26	-5.42
April	11-62	18	-9.85	0-0	-	+0.00	1-16	6	-8.00	10-46	22	-1.85
May	20-118	17	-8.57	2-9	22	+14.00	7-32	22	+0.56	11-77	14	-23.13
June	19-127	15	-28.15	0-12	-	-12.00	7-27	26	+1.07	12-88	14	-17.22
July	20-125	16	-45.40	3-20	15	-8.50	6-31	19	-11.90	11-74	15	-25.00
August	21-126	17	+46.19	3-16	19	+2.75	6-32	19	-4.02	12-78	15	+47.46
September	12-114	11	-16.25	1-19	5	-13.50	2-24	8	-9.00	9-71	13	+6.25
October	4-75	5	-44.09	2-12	17	+11.00	0-15	-	-15.00	2-48	4	-40.09
November	6-46	13	+7.00	0-3	-	-3.00	3-21	14	+6.50	3-22	14	+3.50
December	4-45	9	-6.75	1-8	13	+9.00	1-19	5	-16.25	2-18	11	+0.50

By month – 2012

	Overall			Two-year-olds			Three-year-olds			Older horses		
	W-R	%	£1	W-R	%	£1	W-R	%	£1	W-R	%	£1
January	2-10	20	+4.13	0-0	-	+0.00	0-0	-	+0.00	2-10	20	+4.13
February	1-8	13	-6.33	0-0	-	+0.00	0-0	-	+0.00	1-8	13	-6.33
March	2-8	25	+1.57	0-0	-	+0.00	0-0	-	+0.00	2-8	25	+1.57
April	5-41	12	+1.00	0-0	-	+0.00	0-9	-	-9.00	5-32	16	+10.00
May	7-64	11	-28.75	1-8	13	-5.13	2-10	20	-4.13	4-46	9	-19.50
June	13-94	14	-23.67	0-13	-	-13.00	4-16	25	+5.33	9-65	14	-16.00
July	12-76	16	+21.93	1-11	9	-2.50	1-15	7	-11.25	10-50	20	+35.68
August	14-93	15	+18.25	1-12	8	-5.00	7-23	30	+16.75	6-58	10	+6.50
September	7-68	10	+17.38	1-8	13	+18.00	2-13	15	+4.88	4-47	9	-5.50
October	2-43	5	-30.50	0-5	-	-5.00	1-7	14	-1.50	1-31	3	-24.00
November	1-21	5	-19.43	1-2	50	-0.43	0-6	-	-6.00	0-13	-	-13.00
December	3-16	19	+10.00	1-3	33	-1.75	2-6	33	+18.75	0-7	-	-7.00

By month – 2011

	Overall			Two-year-olds			Three-year-olds			Older horses		
	W-R	%	£1	W-R	%	£1	W-R	%	£1	W-R	%	£1
January	3-10	30	-2.97	0-0	-	+0.00	0-0	-	+0.00	3-10	30	-2.97
February	0-3	-	-3.00	0-0	-	+0.00	0-0	-	+0.00	0-3	-	-3.00
March	2-7	29	+7.00	0-0	-	+0.00	0-1	-	-1.00	2-6	33	+8.00
April	6-34	18	+10.75	0-1	-	-1.00	1-4	25	+4.00	5-29	17	+7.75
May	8-54	15	-10.13	0-8	-	-8.00	0-16	-	-16.00	8-30	27	+13.88
June	8-56	14	-14.96	1-11	9	-8.00	2-12	17	-5.29	5-33	15	-1.67
July	7-79	9	-39.00	0-14	-	-14.00	3-24	13	-9.75	4-41	10	-15.25
August	7-68	10	-24.50	2-11	18	-1.88	2-20	10	-8.75	3-37	8	-13.88
September	4-45	9	-19.50	0-4	-	-4.00	0-12	-	-12.00	4-29	14	-3.50
October	1-46	2	-38.00	0-12	-	-12.00	0-7	-	-7.00	1-27	4	-19.00
November	0-8	-	-8.00	0-1	-	-1.00	0-1	-	-1.00	0-6	-	-6.00
December	2-13	15	-6.75	0-1	-	-1.00	1-4	25	-1.25	1-8	13	-4.50

By race type – 2013

	Overall			Two-year-olds			Three-year-olds			Older horses		
	W-R	%	£1	W-R	%	£1	W-R	%	£1	W-R	%	£1
Handicap	100-664	15	-46.93	5-29	17	+12.00	26-162	16	-36.66	69-473	15	-22.26
Group 1,2,3	0-22	-	-22.00	0-2	-	-2.00	0-3	-	-3.00	0-17	-	-17.00
Maiden	10-106	9	-42.94	7-51	14	+6.75	1-46	2	-44.43	2-9	22	-5.26

By race type – 2012

	Overall			Two-year-olds			Three-year-olds			Older horses		
	W-R	%	£1	W-R	%	£1	W-R	%	£1	W-R	%	£1
Handicap	49-422	12	-64.94	1-9	11	-2.00	15-85	18	-8.04	33-328	10	-54.90
Group 1,2,3	2-8	25	+9.00	0-0	-	+0.00	0-0	-	+0.00	2-8	25	+9.00
Maiden	7-65	11	+0.50	4-41	10	-2.38	3-17	18	+9.88	0-7	-	-7.00

By race type – 2011

	Overall			Two-year-olds			Three-year-olds			Older horses		
	W-R	%	£1	W-R	%	£1	W-R	%	£1	W-R	%	£1
Handicap	40-323	12	-84.18	0-17	-	-17.00	9-87	10	-44.04	31-219	14	-23.14
Group 1,2,3	1-7	14	-2.00	0-1	-	-1.00	0-0	-	+0.00	1-6	17	-1.00
Maiden	5-60	8	-41.50	3-36	8	-23.88	0-10	-	-10.00	2-14	14	-7.63

By jockey – 2013

	Overall			Two-year-olds			Three-year-olds			Older horses		
	W-R	%	£1	W-R	%	£1	W-R	%	£1	W-R	%	£1
Daniel Tudhope	74-404	18	-41.58	7-39	18	+7.25	20-99	20	-14.50	47-266	18	-34.34
David Nolan	18-110	16	+24.06	2-15	13	+13.00	4-32	13	-17.02	12-63	19	+28.08
David Bergin	12-109	11	-29.62	0-7	-	-7.00	6-29	21	-6.70	6-73	8	-15.92
G Gibbons	11-52	21	-0.36	0-5	-	-5.00	1-15	7	-12.38	10-32	31	+17.02
Julie Burke	4-40	10	+1.50	3-18	17	+6.50	1-14	7	+3.00	0-8	-	-8.00
M O'Connell	3-7	43	+6.00	0-0	-	+0.00	1-1	100	+2.75	2-6	33	+3.25
S De Sousa	3-7	43	+9.50	0-0	-	+0.00	2-2	100	+11.50	1-5	20	-2.00
Graham Lee	2-12	17	-4.40	0-1	-	-1.00	1-2	50	+0.10	1-9	11	-3.50
S H James	2-13	15	+2.75	0-3	-	-3.00	1-4	25	-1.25	1-6	17	+7.00
Kieren Fallon	2-26	8	-13.00	0-2	-	-2.00	0-5	-	-5.00	2-19	11	-6.00
Richard Hughes	1-2	50	+6.00	0-1	-	-1.00	0-0	-	+0.00	1-1	100	+7.00
P J McDonald	1-3	33	+23.00	0-0	-	+0.00	0-1	-	-1.00	1-2	50	+24.00

By jockey – 2012

	Overall			Two-year-olds			Three-year-olds			Older horses		
	W-R	%	£1	W-R	%	£1	W-R	%	£1	W-R	%	£1
Daniel Tudhope	45-258	17	+85.82	3-28	11	+9.38	9-38	24	+2.75	33-192	17	+73.70
David Bergin	9-72	13	-11.82	0-6	-	-6.00	6-22	27	+20.58	3-44	7	-26.40
Kieren Fallon	3-13	23	+3.17	0-2	-	-2.00	0-2	-	-2.00	3-9	33	+7.17
Tom Eaves	3-21	14	-7.92	1-2	50	-0.75	1-5	20	+2.50	1-14	7	-9.67
G Gibbons	2-23	9	-12.25	1-4	25	+3.00	1-2	50	+1.75	0-17	-	-17.00
Ryan Powell	1-1	100	+10.00	0-0	-	+0.00	0-0	-	+0.00	1-1	100	+10.00
Paul Mulrennan	1-3	33	+0.75	0-0	-	+0.00	0-1	-	-1.00	1-2	50	+1.75
Robert Winston	1-6	17	-2.75	0-0	-	+0.00	1-5	20	-1.75	0-1	-	-1.00
David Nolan	1-10	10	+5.00	0-1	-	-1.00	0-2	-	-2.00	1-7	14	+8.00

By jockey – 2011

	Overall			Two-year-olds			Three-year-olds			Older horses		
	W-R	%	£1	W-R	%	£1	W-R	%	£1	W-R	%	£1
S De Sousa	20-113	18	-1.50	1-14	7	-11.00	5-35	14	-18.38	14-64	22	+27.88
Daniel Tudhope	18-161	11	-51.08	1-26	4	-23.38	3-33	9	-12.67	14-102	14	-15.04
Joe Fanning	3-7	43	+0.02	0-0	-	+0.00	0-0	-	+0.00	3-7	43	+0.02
Robert Winston	3-9	33	+14.00	0-2	-	-2.00	0-1	-	-1.00	3-6	50	+17.00
Shane B Kelly	1-5	20	+0.00	0-0	-	+0.00	0-3	-	-3.00	1-2	50	+3.00
Tom Eaves	1-5	20	+0.00	0-0	-	+0.00	0-1	-	-1.00	1-4	25	+1.00
Declan Cannon	1-8	13	-1.50	1-2	50	+4.50	0-4	-	-4.00	0-2	-	-2.00
Sean Levey	1-18	6	-12.00	0-3	-	-3.00	1-4	25	+2.00	0-11	-	-11.00
A Heffernan	0-1	-	-1.00	0-0	-	+0.00	0-1	-	-1.00	0-0	-	+0.00

By course – 2010-2013

	Overall			Two-year-olds			Three-year-olds			Older horses		
	W-R	%	£1	W-R	%	£1	W-R	%	£1	W-R	%	£1
Ascot	2-41	5	-27.50	0-3	-	-3.00	0-2	-	-2.00	2-36	6	-22.50
Ayr	10-49	20	+14.63	1-4	25	+13.00	3-8	38	+3.63	6-37	16	-2.00
Beverley	19-106	18	-7.38	0-21	-	-21.00	8-32	25	+14.68	11-53	21	-1.07
Carlisle	9-53	17	-2.13	2-9	22	-2.88	2-12	17	+1.50	5-32	16	-0.75
Catterick	24-150	16	-28.70	3-23	13	-9.10	6-33	18	-7.80	15-94	16	-11.79
Chester	2-30	7	-11.00	0-4	-	-4.00	0-4	-	-4.00	2-22	9	-3.00
Doncaster	11-141	8	-29.00	0-11	-	-11.00	1-17	6	-4.00	10-113	9	-14.00
Epsom	1-7	14	-3.25	0-0	-	+0.00	0-3	-	-3.00	1-4	25	-0.25
Goodwood	0-16	-	-16.00	0-1	-	-1.00	0-3	-	-3.00	0-12	-	-12.00
Hamilton	6-39	15	-2.25	1-8	13	+3.00	2-13	15	-5.50	3-18	17	+0.25
Haydock	12-82	15	-21.88	0-7	-	-7.00	1-14	7	-10.50	11-61	18	-4.38
Kempton (AW)	1-15	7	-9.50	0-0	-	+0.00	0-5	-	-5.00	1-10	10	-4.50
Leicester	4-14	29	+5.75	0-1	-	-1.00	2-5	40	+6.25	2-8	25	+0.50
Lingfield	1-2	50	+6.00	0-0	-	+0.00	0-1	-	-1.00	1-1	100	+7.00
Lingfield (AW)	2-6	33	-0.70	0-1	-	-1.00	2-4	50	+1.30	0-1	-	-1.00
Musselburgh	13-75	17	-7.92	0-14	-	-14.00	5-20	25	-1.38	8-41	20	+7.46
Newbury	0-6	-	-6.00	0-0	-	+0.00	0-1	-	-1.00	0-5	-	-5.00
Newcastle	12-107	11	-26.44	4-15	27	+4.50	4-30	13	-12.94	4-62	6	-18.00
Newmarket	2-28	7	-9.50	0-0	-	+0.00	0-2	-	-2.00	2-26	8	-7.50
Newmarket (J)	0-9	-	-9.00	0-2	-	-2.00	0-2	-	-2.00	0-5	-	-5.00
Nottingham	1-26	4	-18.00	0-1	-	-1.00	1-8	13	+0.00	0-17	-	-17.00
Pontefract	8-79	10	-23.75	0-9	-	-9.00	0-15	-	-15.00	8-55	15	+0.25
Redcar	25-154	16	+3.04	5-32	16	+2.50	6-44	14	-1.92	14-78	18	+2.46
Ripon	26-142	18	+26.58	4-25	16	-8.50	7-31	23	-5.75	15-86	17	+40.83
Salisbury	0-1	-	-1.00	0-0	-	+0.00	0-0	-	+0.00	0-1	-	-1.00
Sandown	3-13	23	+1.25	0-0	-	+0.00	0-5	-	-5.00	3-8	38	+6.25
Southwell (AW)	22-159	14	-51.44	2-20	10	-1.43	6-38	16	-18.15	14-101	14	-31.86
Thirsk	17-129	13	-12.30	2-16	13	+13.75	2-32	6	-21.88	13-81	16	-4.18
Warwick	0-3	-	-3.00	0-0	-	+0.00	0-2	-	-2.00	0-1	-	-1.00
Wolves (AW)	25-163	15	-38.00	1-22	5	-20.75	6-58	10	-9.25	18-83	22	-8.00
Yarmouth	0-1	-	-1.00	0-0	-	+0.00	0-0	-	+0.00	0-1	-	-1.00
York	20-177	11	-25.00	1-18	6	-14.00	7-30	23	+4.75	12-129	9	-15.75

David O'Meara speaks to Neil Clark, pages 6-10

Four-year summary

	Wins	Runs	%	Win prize-money	Total prize-money	£1
2013	136	905	15	£777,659.87	£1,159,386.21	-121.29
2012	69	542	13	£517,175.66	£709,691.68	-34.43
2011	48	423	11	£297,865.68	£479,370.95	-149.06
2010*	25	153	16	£87,754.32	£122,742.04	-29.60

*Sent out first runner in June 2010

CLASSIC COLORI (left): won four times for O'Meara last season

David Evans

The king of the all-weather managed his second century and a new personal best with 116 winners, 80 of which came on the sand. It came with his best strike-rate since he hit double figures for the first time way back in 1993.

By month – 2013

	Overall			Two-year-olds			Three-year-olds			Older horses		
	W-R	%	£1	W-R	%	£1	W-R	%	£1	W-R	%	£1
January	20-90	22	+7.38	0-0	-	+0.00	6-16	38	+7.21	14-74	19	+0.17
February	13-75	17	-8.19	0-0	-	+0.00	1-11	9	-6.67	12-64	19	-1.52
March	8-66	12	-34.72	0-7	-	-7.00	0-8	-	-8.00	8-51	16	-19.72
April	17-84	20	-12.47	6-23	26	-6.84	1-14	7	-10.50	10-47	21	+4.87
May	5-84	6	-44.25	0-28	-	-28.00	0-12	-	-12.00	5-44	11	-4.25
June	11-81	14	+46.50	5-27	19	+70.25	2-9	22	+0.00	4-45	9	-23.75
July	6-64	9	-28.25	0-20	-	-20.00	1-9	11	-6.75	5-35	14	-1.50
August	8-83	10	-6.25	2-29	7	+1.00	1-7	14	-3.25	5-47	11	-4.00
September	4-71	6	-50.00	1-27	4	-23.00	0-8	-	-8.00	3-36	8	-19.00
October	6-63	10	+11.25	3-22	14	+17.75	1-11	9	-4.50	2-30	7	-2.00
November	11-54	20	+6.75	2-16	13	-4.50	0-8	-	-8.00	9-30	30	+19.25
December	7-65	11	-25.50	3-19	16	+1.25	2-11	18	-3.75	2-35	6	-23.00

By month – 2012

	Overall			Two-year-olds			Three-year-olds			Older horses		
	W-R	%	£1	W-R	%	£1	W-R	%	£1	W-R	%	£1
January	9-60	15	+31.06	0-0	-	+0.00	5-28	18	+4.06	4-32	13	+27.00
February	5-61	8	-0.52	0-0	-	+0.00	2-22	9	+20.73	3-39	8	-21.25
March	8-45	18	+5.20	0-2	-	-2.00	4-21	19	+8.57	4-22	18	-1.38
April	7-78	9	-29.00	2-10	20	-3.75	1-29	3	-22.00	4-39	10	-3.25
May	3-66	5	-37.67	1-4	25	+0.33	1-27	4	-18.00	1-35	3	-20.00
June	8-88	9	+38.50	2-11	18	+61.00	3-41	7	-22.00	3-36	8	-0.50
July	8-71	11	-22.42	0-7	-	-7.00	3-23	13	-8.75	5-41	12	-6.67
August	10-90	11	+10.38	0-10	-	-10.00	7-37	19	+32.88	3-43	7	-12.50
September	9-84	11	-9.50	1-11	9	-3.00	3-32	9	+10.50	5-41	12	-17.00
October	2-45	4	-34.38	0-10	-	-10.00	1-9	11	-1.00	1-26	4	-23.38
November	4-31	13	-3.00	2-7	29	+4.00	0-9	-	-9.00	2-15	13	+2.00
December	9-65	14	-23.70	0-13	-	-13.00	3-18	17	-9.45	6-34	18	-1.25

By month – 2011

	Overall			Two-year-olds			Three-year-olds			Older horses		
	W-R	%	£1	W-R	%	£1	W-R	%	£1	W-R	%	£1
January	9-83	11	-43.03	0-0	-	+0.00	6-34	18	-6.03	3-49	6	-37.00
February	4-44	9	-2.63	0-0	-	+0.00	0-15	-	-15.00	4-29	14	+12.38
March	5-46	11	-28.56	2-7	29	+1.75	1-17	6	-13.50	2-22	9	-16.81
April	8-79	10	-14.75	5-40	13	+3.25	0-15	-	-15.00	3-24	13	-3.00
May	15-101	15	-4.81	3-40	8	-34.72	1-24	4	-7.00	11-37	30	+36.91
June	5-64	8	-28.00	1-20	5	-16.00	2-19	11	-5.00	2-25	8	-7.00
July	4-98	4	-85.23	2-43	5	-35.43	2-28	7	-22.80	0-27	-	-27.00
August	4-86	5	-64.25	2-32	6	-22.00	1-26	4	-17.00	1-28	4	-25.25
September	9-90	10	+27.83	5-39	13	+22.83	4-27	15	+29.00	0-24	-	-24.00
October	7-79	9	-22.50	2-35	6	-26.25	3-22	14	+11.50	2-22	9	-7.75
November	3-45	7	-27.90	1-21	5	-18.90	0-8	-	-8.00	2-16	13	-1.00
December	4-34	12	-4.10	2-14	14	+4.40	0-4	-	-4.00	2-16	13	-4.50

By race type – 2013

	Overall			Two-year-olds			Three-year-olds			Older horses		
	W-R	%	£1	W-R	%	£1	W-R	%	£1	W-R	%	£1
Handicap	84-616	14	-97.80	7-72	10	+8.75	11-103	11	-59.33	66-441	15	-47.22
Group 1,2,3	0-2	-	-2.00	0-2	-	-2.00	0-0	-	+0.00	0-0	-	+0.00
Maiden	9-95	9	+12.65	7-76	9	+23.55	1-5	20	+1.00	1-14	7	-11.90

By race type – 2012

	Overall			Two-year-olds			Three-year-olds			Older horses		
	W-R	%	£1	W-R	%	£1	W-R	%	£1	W-R	%	£1
Handicap	52-567	9	-61.82	1-21	5	-13.00	23-219	11	+19.23	28-327	9	-68.04
Group 1,2,3	0-0	-	+0.00	0-0	-	+0.00	0-0	-	+0.00	0-0	-	+0.00
Maiden	6-72	8	-4.73	2-33	6	+21.25	3-29	10	-18.98	1-10	10	-7.00

By race type – 2011

	Overall			Two-year-olds			Three-year-olds			Older horses		
	W-R	%	£1	W-R	%	£1	W-R	%	£1	W-R	%	£1
Handicap	32-472	7	-204.15	3-73	4	-45.50	11-160	7	-68.40	18-239	8	-90.25
Group 1,2,3	0-1	-	-1.00	0-1	-	-1.00	0-0	-	+0.00	0-0	-	+0.00
Maiden	8-148	5	-103.43	8-118	7	-73.43	0-21	-	-21.00	0-9	-	-9.00

By jockey – 2013

	Overall			Two-year-olds			Three-year-olds			Older horses		
	W-R	%	£1	W-R	%	£1	W-R	%	£1	W-R	%	£1
Adam Kirby	30-140	21	+5.13	2-22	9	-14.25	3-21	14	-5.75	25-97	26	+25.13
Eoin Walsh	13-93	14	-21.50	2-7	29	+0.00	1-6	17	-3.75	10-80	13	-17.75
Declan Bates	12-152	8	-51.50	2-39	5	-7.00	0-19	-	-19.00	10-94	11	-25.50
Martin Harley	7-28	25	+11.75	0-3	-	-3.00	2-5	40	+3.50	5-20	25	+11.25
Tom Queally	6-42	14	+15.75	5-28	18	+26.25	1-8	13	-4.50	0-6	-	-6.00
Luke Morris	6-45	13	-17.79	1-10	10	-1.00	2-11	18	-4.04	3-24	13	-12.75
Cathy Gannon	6-49	12	-7.09	2-23	9	-19.59	1-5	20	+1.50	3-21	14	+11.00
G Gibbons	5-25	20	+10.50	1-4	25	+4.00	2-5	40	+2.75	2-16	13	+3.75
Rob Fitzpatrick	4-14	29	+3.99	0-0	-	+0.00	0-0	-	+0.00	4-14	29	+3.99
Thomas Brown	4-17	24	+7.75	0-0	-	+0.00	0-3	-	-3.00	4-14	29	+10.75
Noel Garbutt	4-31	13	+11.00	3-16	19	+22.00	1-5	20	-1.00	0-10	-	-10.00
William Carson	4-36	11	+17.33	1-10	10	+31.00	1-11	9	-9.67	2-15	13	-4.00

By jockey – 2012

	Overall			Two-year-olds			Three-year-olds			Older horses		
	W-R	%	£1	W-R	%	£1	W-R	%	£1	W-R	%	£1
M Cosham	15-137	11	+5.57	0-8	-	-8.00	5-43	12	+22.07	10-86	12	-8.50
Cathy Gannon	13-99	13	+27.63	1-12	8	-8.75	11-52	21	+54.38	1-35	3	-18.00
Adam Kirby	11-34	32	+12.13	0-4	-	-4.00	2-8	25	-1.25	9-22	41	+17.38
Luke Morris	6-58	10	-33.25	0-7	-	-7.00	6-35	17	-10.25	0-16	-	-16.00
Richard Hughes	4-15	27	+10.38	0-0	-	+0.00	2-8	25	+9.00	2-7	29	+1.38
Martin Lane	4-26	15	+17.71	0-0	-	+0.00	1-9	11	-7.17	3-17	18	+24.88
Andrea Atzeni	4-27	15	+18.00	0-2	-	-2.00	0-8	-	-8.00	4-17	24	+28.00
James Doyle	3-11	27	+47.75	1-2	50	+49.00	1-3	33	-0.75	1-6	17	-0.50
Eoin Walsh	3-20	15	+7.00	1-2	50	+6.00	0-5	-	-5.00	2-13	15	+6.00

By jockey – 2011

	Overall			Two-year-olds			Three-year-olds			Older horses		
	W-R	%	£1	W-R	%	£1	W-R	%	£1	W-R	%	£1
Cathy Gannon	18-211	9	-77.79	8-82	10	-49.79	1-62	2	-45.00	9-67	13	+17.00
M Cosham	17-122	14	-7.79	2-22	9	+0.57	6-42	14	-3.53	9-58	16	-4.84
Kieren Fallon	6-31	19	+4.77	3-14	21	-3.43	3-11	27	+14.20	0-6	-	-6.00
R P Walsh	5-29	17	-7.50	0-1	-	-1.00	3-14	21	-2.50	2-14	14	-4.00
Luke Morris	3-15	20	+9.40	2-11	18	+7.40	0-1	-	-1.00	1-3	33	+3.00
Pat Cosgrave	3-21	14	+13.00	0-6	-	-6.00	1-6	17	+2.00	2-9	22	+17.00
Neil Callan	3-24	13	-14.68	1-10	10	-5.00	0-5	-	-5.00	2-9	22	-4.68
S De Sousa	3-31	10	-12.00	1-11	9	-8.25	1-7	14	+6.00	1-13	8	-9.75
Richard Evans	3-59	5	-42.50	0-5	-	-5.00	0-15	-	-15.00	3-39	8	-22.50

By course – 2010-2013

	Overall			Two-year-olds			Three-year-olds			Older horses		
	W-R	%	£1	W-R	%	£1	W-R	%	£1	W-R	%	£1
Ascot	0-24	-	-24.00	0-11	-	-11.00	0-4	-	-4.00	0-9	-	-9.00
Ayr	0-10	-	-10.00	0-1	-	-1.00	0-2	-	-2.00	0-7	-	-7.00
Bath	11-132	8	-67.37	3-32	9	-21.37	3-44	7	-20.00	5-56	9	-26.00
Beverley	0-3	-	-3.00	0-3	-	-3.00	0-0	-	+0.00	0-0	-	+0.00
Brighton	17-136	13	-4.13	2-10	20	+4.50	2-38	5	-14.13	13-88	15	+5.50
Catterick	2-28	7	-10.50	2-17	12	+0.50	0-5	-	-5.00	0-6	-	-6.00
Chepstow	8-131	6	-73.50	1-31	3	-19.00	3-37	8	-26.00	4-63	6	-28.50
Chester	8-158	5	-96.50	2-58	3	-45.50	2-33	6	-20.50	4-67	6	-30.50
Doncaster	1-68	1	-63.50	1-16	6	-11.50	0-23	-	-23.00	0-29	-	-29.00
Epsom	1-31	3	-24.50	0-7	-	-7.00	1-7	14	-0.50	0-17	-	-17.00
Ffos Las	16-105	15	+5.82	4-28	14	+6.12	4-30	13	-4.88	8-47	17	+4.58
Folkestone	3-41	7	-11.00	0-11	-	-11.00	0-8	-	-8.00	3-22	14	+8.00
Goodwood	0-23	-	-23.00	0-11	-	-11.00	0-4	-	-4.00	0-8	-	-8.00
Hamilton	0-11	-	-11.00	0-1	-	-1.00	0-5	-	-5.00	0-5	-	-5.00
Haydock	3-52	6	-24.00	2-18	11	+4.50	1-19	5	-13.50	0-15	-	-15.00
Kempton (AW)	34-314	11	-124.59	7-69	10	-22.00	7-94	7	-57.38	20-151	13	-45.22
Leicester	8-111	7	-45.43	3-46	7	-32.93	4-38	11	+9.00	1-27	4	-21.50
Lingfield	6-50	12	-12.00	0-7	-	-7.00	1-11	9	-1.00	5-32	16	-4.00
Lingfield (AW)	65-493	13	-142.49	2-35	6	-30.75	14-124	11	-64.16	49-334	15	-47.57
Musselburgh	1-13	8	-10.00	1-4	25	-1.00	0-5	-	-5.00	0-4	-	-4.00
Newbury	2-42	5	+33.00	2-16	13	+59.00	0-11	-	-11.00	0-15	-	-15.00
Newcastle	0-5	-	-5.00	0-2	-	-2.00	0-1	-	-1.00	0-2	-	-2.00
Newmarket	3-16	19	+6.25	2-5	40	+0.25	1-6	17	+11.00	0-5	-	-5.00
Newmarket (J)	0-20	-	-20.00	0-7	-	-7.00	0-8	-	-8.00	0-5	-	-5.00
Nottingham	12-81	15	+56.33	6-34	18	+72.50	3-26	12	-5.80	3-21	14	-10.38
Pontefract	0-10	-	-10.00	0-4	-	-4.00	0-1	-	-1.00	0-5	-	-5.00
Redcar	0-25	-	-25.00	0-13	-	-13.00	0-5	-	-5.00	0-7	-	-7.00
Ripon	3-29	10	+1.50	2-13	15	+12.50	1-13	8	-3.00	0-3	-	-3.00
Salisbury	17-106	16	+116.66	5-36	14	+70.91	4-25	16	+28.00	8-45	18	+17.75
Sandown	0-11	-	-11.00	0-5	-	-5.00	0-3	-	-3.00	0-3	-	-3.00
Southwell (AW)	18-108	17	-30.96	2-27	7	-17.75	8-27	30	+7.93	8-54	15	-21.14
Thirsk	2-30	7	-17.00	2-17	12	-4.00	0-2	-	-2.00	0-11	-	-11.00
Warwick	8-61	13	-29.06	3-17	18	-8.31	3-18	17	-2.00	2-26	8	-18.75
Windsor	15-166	9	-40.25	4-51	8	-33.25	4-50	8	-14.50	7-65	11	+7.50
Wolves (AW)	93-794	12	-159.14	21-157	13	+11.88	21-183	11	-26.64	51-454	11	-144.38
Yarmouth	6-62	10	-3.50	2-28	7	-1.00	3-11	27	+17.00	1-23	4	-19.50
York	0-32	-	-32.00	0-17	-	-17.00	0-7	-	-7.00	0-8	-	-8.00

Ten-year summary

	Wins	Runs	%	Win prize-money	Total prize-money	£1
2013	116	880	13	£371,616.59	£562,496.08	-137.75
2012	82	784	10	£237,871.64	£346,748.11	-75.06
2011	77	849	9	£207,644.41	£373,908.98	-297.91
2010	88	1019	9	£277,361.35	£488,961.34	-433.14
2009	114	955	12	£441,761.95	£674,962.77	-43.14
2008	82	819	10	£279,109.78	£427,300.22	-135.38
2007	53	587	9	£171,771.61	£320,454.87	-105.18
2006	45	465	10	£162,754.00	£285,542.23	-166.34
2005	38	542	7	£180,714.37	£291,886.61	-281.30
2004	62	694	9	£259,826.72	£412,921.05	-146.57

FOREST EDGE: one of three horses with whom Evans won at least six times

John Gosden

A third century in four years for Gosden, and while he fell short of his 2012 mark of 119, last year's 108 came at an improved strike-rate of 21%. Look out particularly for Gosden's runners in maidens.

By month – 2013

	Overall			Two-year-olds			Three-year-olds			Older horses		
	W-R	%	£1	W-R	%	£1	W-R	%	£1	W-R	%	£1
January	4-15	27	-4.91	0-0	-	+0.00	3-10	30	-2.53	1-5	20	-2.38
February	2-4	50	-0.45	0-0	-	+0.00	2-4	50	-0.45	0-0	-	+0.00
March	2-14	14	-9.63	0-0	-	+0.00	2-11	18	-6.63	0-3	-	-3.00
April	5-31	16	-11.75	0-0	-	+0.00	5-29	17	-9.75	0-2	-	-2.00
May	12-65	18	+7.92	0-3	-	-3.00	8-40	20	+16.25	4-22	18	-5.33
June	12-62	19	-6.30	2-9	22	-3.64	8-36	22	+6.08	2-17	12	-8.75
July	14-63	22	-14.87	1-17	6	-10.00	9-30	30	+1.08	4-16	25	-5.95
August	22-73	30	+28.92	8-20	40	+10.80	11-37	30	+24.24	3-16	19	-6.13
September	10-66	15	-3.30	3-25	12	+4.88	4-29	14	-12.05	3-12	25	+3.88
October	12-68	18	-0.25	4-35	11	-8.75	6-25	24	+4.75	2-8	25	+3.75
November	3-40	8	-34.69	1-25	4	-23.60	1-8	13	-6.00	1-7	14	-5.09
December	10-24	42	+24.48	9-18	50	+24.48	0-4	-	-4.00	1-2	50	+4.00

By month – 2012

	Overall			Two-year-olds			Three-year-olds			Older horses		
	W-R	%	£1	W-R	%	£1	W-R	%	£1	W-R	%	£1
January	5-13	38	+11.81	0-0	-	+0.00	4-8	50	+13.69	1-5	20	-1.88
February	4-8	50	+6.75	0-0	-	+0.00	2-6	33	+3.50	2-2	100	+3.25
March	5-23	22	-9.78	0-0	-	+0.00	1-16	6	-11.00	4-7	57	+1.22
April	11-65	17	-14.96	0-0	-	+0.00	6-45	13	-25.63	5-20	25	+10.67
May	15-92	16	-50.64	0-0	-	+0.00	10-62	16	-40.91	5-30	17	-9.73
June	22-108	20	+25.05	3-16	19	+0.63	10-59	17	-23.08	9-33	27	+47.50
July	8-58	14	-24.50	2-10	20	+2.50	3-34	9	-23.50	3-14	21	-3.50
August	10-76	13	-27.13	4-25	16	-7.13	6-37	16	-6.00	0-14	-	-14.00
September	14-66	21	+1.85	6-23	26	+7.22	5-30	17	-14.20	3-13	23	+8.83
October	17-84	20	+18.82	6-31	19	+2.49	9-40	23	+1.33	2-13	15	+15.00
November	5-19	26	+11.00	1-9	11	-5.50	4-7	57	+19.50	0-3	-	-3.00
December	3-17	18	-8.92	2-13	15	-6.75	1-4	25	-2.17	0-0	-	+0.00

By month – 2011

	Overall			Two-year-olds			Three-year-olds			Older horses		
	W-R	%	£1	W-R	%	£1	W-R	%	£1	W-R	%	£1
January	2-4	50	+14.25	0-0	-	+0.00	2-4	50	+14.25	0-0	-	+0.00
February	2-2	100	+2.48	0-0	-	+0.00	2-2	100	+2.48	0-0	-	+0.00
March	1-6	17	-3.38	0-0	-	+0.00	1-6	17	-3.38	0-0	-	+0.00
April	13-68	19	-7.26	0-4	-	-4.00	11-53	21	-13.76	2-11	18	+10.50
May	12-64	19	-14.68	0-4	-	-4.00	9-48	19	-7.55	3-12	25	-3.13
June	18-92	20	+4.98	6-19	32	+29.16	10-56	18	-23.68	2-17	12	-0.50
July	14-66	21	+14.32	3-15	20	-6.25	8-37	22	-8.93	3-14	21	+29.50
August	9-72	13	-16.75	2-29	7	-22.75	5-30	17	+0.50	2-13	15	+5.50
September	15-82	18	-0.48	7-36	19	-10.82	6-35	17	-1.17	2-11	18	+11.50
October	7-60	12	-2.63	6-33	18	+22.38	1-23	4	-21.00	0-4	-	-4.00
November	4-28	14	-9.50	1-15	7	-13.50	2-12	17	-4.00	1-1	100	+8.00
December	2-9	22	+4.33	1-6	17	+3.00	1-3	33	+1.33	0-0	-	+0.00

By race type – 2013

	Overall			Two-year-olds			Three-year-olds			Older horses		
	W-R	%	£1	W-R	%	£1	W-R	%	£1	W-R	%	£1
Handicap	37-159	23	-16.89	1-8	13	-1.50	25-105	24	-13.48	11-46	24	-1.91
Group 1,2,3	9-58	16	-8.46	1-5	20	-3.71	3-18	17	+10.25	5-35	14	-15.00
Maiden	52-241	22	+27.11	26-131	20	+4.38	26-107	24	+25.73	0-3	-	-3.00

By race type – 2012

	Overall			Two-year-olds			Three-year-olds			Older horses		
	W-R	%	£1	W-R	%	£1	W-R	%	£1	W-R	%	£1
Handicap	33-202	16	-48.59	1-9	11	-5.25	14-111	13	-44.00	18-82	22	+0.66
Group 1,2,3	13-85	15	-5.29	1-7	14	-4.25	6-39	15	-2.38	6-39	15	+1.33
Maiden	54-268	20	-55.55	19-101	19	+5.41	31-159	19	-62.19	4-8	50	+1.23

By race type – 2011

	Overall			Two-year-olds			Three-year-olds			Older horses		
	W-R	%	£1	W-R	%	£1	W-R	%	£1	W-R	%	£1
Handicap	30-188	16	+28.21	3-19	16	-2.00	16-116	14	-39.92	11-53	21	+70.13
Group 1,2,3	7-52	13	-15.00	0-9	-	-9.00	5-28	18	-0.25	2-15	13	-5.75
Maiden	56-246	23	+11.29	22-128	17	+6.97	34-117	29	+5.32	0-1	-	-1.00

By jockey – 2013

	Overall			Two-year-olds			Three-year-olds			Older horses		
	W-R	%	£1	W-R	%	£1	W-R	%	£1	W-R	%	£1
William Buick	54-265	20	-28.70	9-65	14	-24.44	33-139	24	+14.57	12-61	20	-18.83
Robert Havlin	35-134	26	+1.69	14-54	26	-1.43	16-58	28	+0.22	5-22	23	+2.91
Nicky Mackay	4-52	8	-16.70	1-17	6	-2.00	2-27	7	-7.75	1-8	13	-6.95
Ryan Moore	3-7	43	+1.83	1-1	100	+2.75	1-3	33	-1.17	1-3	33	+0.25
Paul Hanagan	3-27	11	-6.75	1-6	17	+3.00	1-17	6	-14.75	1-4	25	+5.00
Martin Dwyer	2-2	100	+28.33	0-0	-	+0.00	2-2	100	+28.33	0-0	-	+0.00
Dane O'Neill	2-9	22	+13.50	1-2	50	+19.00	1-4	25	-2.50	0-3	-	-3.00
Franny Norton	1-1	100	+0.80	0-0	-	+0.00	1-1	100	+0.80	0-0	-	+0.00
Joe Fanning	1-1	100	+1.63	0-0	-	+0.00	0-0	-	+0.00	1-1	100	+1.63
Jimmy Fortune	1-2	50	+1.75	0-0	-	+0.00	1-1	100	+2.75	0-1	-	-1.00
James Doyle	1-5	20	-3.71	1-2	50	-0.71	0-3	-	-3.00	0-0	-	+0.00
Richard Hughes	1-8	13	-6.50	0-0	-	+0.00	1-4	25	-2.50	0-4	-	-4.00

By jockey – 2012

	Overall			Two-year-olds			Three-year-olds			Older horses		
	W-R	%	£1	W-R	%	£1	W-R	%	£1	W-R	%	£1
William Buick	68-309	22	+12.44	13-60	22	+1.01	33-155	21	-41.84	22-94	23	+53.27
Nicky Mackay	16-86	19	-20.80	1-13	8	-9.50	12-60	20	-5.55	3-13	23	-5.75
Robert Havlin	14-111	13	-47.00	5-24	21	+3.42	7-73	10	-49.42	2-14	14	-1.00
Paul Hanagan	11-43	26	-0.70	4-10	40	+1.53	3-20	15	-3.93	4-13	31	+1.70
Ryan Moore	2-6	33	-3.40	0-0	-	+0.00	1-3	33	-1.80	1-3	33	-1.60
Dane O'Neill	1-1	100	+16.00	1-1	100	+16.00	0-0	-	+0.00	0-0	-	+0.00
Jim Crowley	1-1	100	+2.75	0-0	-	+0.00	0-0	-	+0.00	1-1	100	+2.75
Martin Dwyer	1-1	100	+5.00	0-0	-	+0.00	1-1	100	+5.00	0-0	-	+0.00
Luke Morris	1-2	50	-0.56	0-0	-	+0.00	1-1	100	+0.44	0-1	-	-1.00

By jockey – 2011

	Overall			Two-year-olds			Three-year-olds			Older horses		
	W-R	%	£1	W-R	%	£1	W-R	%	£1	W-R	%	£1
William Buick	53-279	19	-21.49	17-84	20	+3.26	30-159	19	-33.12	6-36	17	+8.38
Robert Havlin	17-88	19	+4.54	6-32	19	+2.71	8-46	17	-10.17	3-10	30	+12.00
Nicky Mackay	12-76	16	+8.49	3-26	12	+6.25	7-41	17	-10.26	2-9	22	+12.50
Richard Hills	6-44	14	-6.02	0-8	-	-8.00	5-22	23	-5.02	1-14	7	+7.00
Martin Dwyer	2-4	50	+14.00	0-1	-	-1.00	1-2	50	+7.50	1-1	100	+7.50
Tadhg O'Shea	2-12	17	+11.00	0-0	-	+0.00	0-7	-	-7.00	2-5	40	+18.00
Darryll Holland	1-1	100	+0.33	0-0	-	+0.00	1-1	100	+0.33	0-0	-	+0.00
Dane O'Neill	1-2	50	+7.00	0-0	-	+0.00	1-2	50	+7.00	0-0	-	+0.00
Jimmy Fortune	1-3	33	+0.00	0-0	-	+0.00	1-2	50	+1.00	0-1	-	-1.00

By course – 2010-2013

	Overall			Two-year-olds			Three-year-olds			Older horses		
	W-R	%	£1	W-R	%	£1	W-R	%	£1	W-R	%	£1
Ascot	20-139	14	+14.65	3-12	25	+9.00	7-73	10	-30.63	10-54	19	+36.28
Ayr	0-1	-	-1.00	0-1	-	-1.00	0-0	-	+0.00	0-0	-	+0.00
Bath	2-14	14	-5.50	0-4	-	-4.00	2-9	22	-0.50	0-1	-	-1.00
Beverley	1-3	33	-1.20	1-2	50	-0.20	0-1	-	-1.00	0-0	-	+0.00
Brighton	1-6	17	-4.83	1-2	50	-0.83	0-4	-	-4.00	0-0	-	+0.00
Carlisle	0-2	-	-2.00	0-1	-	-1.00	0-0	-	+0.00	0-1	-	-1.00
Catterick	1-3	33	-0.25	1-1	100	+1.75	0-2	-	-2.00	0-0	-	+0.00
Chepstow	2-7	29	-3.70	1-1	100	+0.80	1-6	17	-4.50	0-0	-	+0.00
Chester	11-41	27	+8.71	1-4	25	-1.13	9-28	32	+6.83	1-9	11	+3.00
Doncaster	28-127	22	+25.31	5-32	16	-16.70	17-70	24	+23.51	6-25	24	+18.50
Epsom	5-43	12	-23.33	1-4	25	+0.33	1-22	5	-18.25	3-17	18	-5.42
Ffos Las	2-6	33	+3.25	0-3	-	-3.00	2-3	67	+6.25	0-0	-	+0.00
Folkestone	1-3	33	-1.00	1-1	100	+1.00	0-2	-	-2.00	0-0	-	+0.00
Goodwood	15-102	15	-5.96	3-28	11	-12.92	9-46	20	+7.95	3-28	11	-1.00
Hamilton	2-2	100	+1.64	0-0	-	+0.00	2-2	100	+1.64	0-0	-	+0.00
Haydock	19-70	27	+9.44	3-15	20	-8.60	11-35	31	+6.37	5-20	25	+11.67
Kempton (AW)	53-282	19	-52.40	16-96	17	+1.38	31-152	20	-42.51	6-34	18	-11.27
Leicester	9-37	24	+3.70	3-18	17	+2.25	6-18	33	+2.45	0-1	-	-1.00
Lingfield	5-14	36	+11.00	2-5	40	+1.50	3-8	38	+10.50	0-1	-	-1.00
Lingfield (AW)	42-181	23	+23.69	9-49	18	-1.80	28-114	25	+13.88	5-18	28	+11.62
Musselburgh	1-3	33	-1.17	0-0	-	+0.00	1-3	33	-1.17	0-0	-	+0.00
Newbury	25-128	20	+24.71	6-30	20	-1.25	14-77	18	+17.13	5-21	24	+8.83
Newcastle	6-27	22	-1.97	2-6	33	+6.00	4-15	27	-1.97	0-6	-	-6.00
Newmarket	25-199	13	-8.93	9-66	14	+31.75	8-100	8	-69.79	8-33	24	+29.12
Newmarket (J)	34-180	19	+24.24	10-65	15	+12.25	19-92	21	-12.13	5-23	22	+24.13
Nottingham	7-61	11	-15.89	2-19	11	-9.00	5-37	14	-1.89	0-5	-	-5.00
Pontefract	3-19	16	-9.75	0-1	-	-1.00	3-11	27	-1.75	0-7	-	-7.00
Redcar	1-5	20	-3.50	1-2	50	-0.50	0-2	-	-2.00	0-1	-	-1.00
Ripon	1-5	20	-2.50	0-0	-	+0.00	0-4	-	-4.00	1-1	100	+1.50
Salisbury	5-47	11	-28.81	2-14	14	-3.50	1-27	4	-25.56	2-6	33	+0.25
Sandown	25-134	19	-28.39	6-31	19	-11.86	11-75	15	-25.74	8-28	29	+9.21
Southwell (AW)	9-22	41	+1.89	3-7	43	+2.44	5-13	38	-1.68	1-2	50	+1.13
Thirsk	1-6	17	-3.63	1-1	100	+1.38	0-5	-	-5.00	0-0	-	+0.00
Warwick	1-8	13	-6.56	0-1	-	-1.00	1-5	20	-3.56	0-2	-	-2.00
Windsor	11-58	19	-11.35	1-10	10	-7.75	9-37	24	+3.90	1-11	9	-7.50
Wolves (AW)	31-103	30	-17.27	6-31	19	-10.77	22-62	35	-3.26	3-10	30	-3.25
Yarmouth	16-78	21	-36.97	7-33	21	-15.54	5-35	14	-20.68	4-10	40	-0.75
York	10-59	17	-2.88	0-4	-	-4.00	5-26	19	+2.38	5-29	17	-1.25

Ten-year summary

	Wins	Runs	%	Win prize-money	Total prize-money	£1
2013	108	525	21	£1,263,914.58	£2,033,077.64	-24.83
2012	119	629	19	£2,150,284.26	£3,739,407.23	-60.64
2011	99	553	18	£1,828,265.33	£2,529,369.21	-14.31
2010	105	518	20	£1,101,277.72	£1,714,237.43	-28.71
2009	88	516	17	£1,447,841.46	£2,308,709.36	-97.55
2008	95	498	19	£1,843,697.13	£2,596,896.00	+19.30
2007	68	401	17	£1,055,409.41	£1,644,331.67	-75.22
2006	56	299	19	£605,236.89	£848,468.86	-21.24
2005	91	486	19	£1,064,566.17	£1,487,571.10	+95.30
2004	66	458	14	£741,368.45	£1,273,377.98	-88.20

REMOTE: a Royal Ascot winner for Gosden in the Tercentenary Stakes

William Haggas

It's 18 years since Haggas announced himself with Derby winner Shaamit, but his operation is now a much bigger one than it was back then and he continued to move forward last season with a first ever century.

By month – 2013

	Overall			Two-year-olds			Three-year-olds			Older horses		
	W-R	%	£1	W-R	%	£1	W-R	%	£1	W-R	%	£1
January	2-6	33	+1.50	0-0	-	+0.00	0-4	-	-4.00	2-2	100	+5.50
February	2-7	29	+1.50	0-0	-	+0.00	1-5	20	+1.00	1-2	50	+0.50
March	0-3	-	-3.00	0-0	-	+0.00	0-1	-	-1.00	0-2	-	-2.00
April	10-26	38	+16.38	1-1	100	+2.75	6-20	30	+7.13	3-5	60	+6.50
May	7-58	12	-31.12	1-8	13	+0.00	3-29	10	-21.99	3-21	14	-9.13
June	16-80	20	-34.31	3-14	21	-9.45	12-47	26	-9.36	1-19	5	-15.50
July	19-81	23	-7.13	5-19	26	-4.27	9-43	21	-19.30	5-19	26	+16.44
August	18-77	23	+0.34	4-22	18	-2.13	9-40	23	-17.03	5-15	33	+19.50
September	11-68	16	+1.50	7-31	23	+19.50	3-24	13	-15.00	1-13	8	-3.00
October	10-58	17	+24.46	5-36	14	+25.50	2-13	15	-4.00	3-9	33	+2.96
November	10-22	45	+27.36	2-9	22	+1.36	6-8	75	+19.25	2-5	40	+6.75
December	2-17	12	-9.75	2-12	17	-4.75	0-3	-	-3.00	0-2	-	-2.00

By month – 2012

	Overall			Two-year-olds			Three-year-olds			Older horses		
	W-R	%	£1	W-R	%	£1	W-R	%	£1	W-R	%	£1
January	0-0	-	+0.00	0-0	-	+0.00	0-0	-	+0.00	0-0	-	+0.00
February	0-0	-	+0.00	0-0	-	+0.00	0-0	-	+0.00	0-0	-	+0.00
March	1-4	25	-2.33	0-0	-	+0.00	0-0	-	+0.00	1-4	25	-2.33
April	5-23	22	+3.50	0-0	-	+0.00	4-20	20	+4.00	1-3	33	-0.50
May	18-58	31	+20.85	1-2	50	+1.75	13-45	29	+17.69	4-11	36	+1.41
June	13-70	19	-11.77	2-8	25	+0.25	10-54	19	-10.02	1-8	13	-2.00
July	8-51	16	-23.79	1-8	13	-3.50	7-36	19	-13.29	0-7	-	-7.00
August	12-71	17	-21.08	4-27	15	-12.00	7-34	21	-1.95	1-10	10	-7.13
September	10-72	14	-20.44	3-26	12	-6.50	4-32	13	-17.63	3-14	21	+3.70
October	12-70	17	-0.93	10-38	26	+23.19	2-24	8	-16.13	0-8	-	-8.00
November	3-21	14	-9.37	0-7	-	-7.00	2-11	18	-5.37	1-3	33	+3.00
December	1-8	13	+0.00	0-5	-	-5.00	1-3	33	+5.00	0-0	-	+0.00

By month – 2011

	Overall			Two-year-olds			Three-year-olds			Older horses		
	W-R	%	£1	W-R	%	£1	W-R	%	£1	W-R	%	£1
January	0-1	-	-1.00	0-0	-	+0.00	0-1	-	-1.00	0-0	-	+0.00
February	1-2	50	+0.88	0-0	-	+0.00	1-2	50	+0.88	0-0	-	+0.00
March	0-2	-	-2.00	0-0	-	+0.00	0-2	-	-2.00	0-0	-	+0.00
April	5-23	22	+11.13	0-0	-	+0.00	3-16	19	-2.38	2-7	29	+13.50
May	5-47	11	-38.32	0-4	-	-4.00	5-29	17	-20.32	0-14	-	-14.00
June	8-62	13	-20.95	0-6	-	-6.00	7-43	16	-4.70	1-13	8	-10.25
July	23-81	28	+19.57	6-17	35	+22.00	12-43	28	-13.93	5-21	24	+11.50
August	15-66	23	-9.36	3-23	13	-7.47	11-33	33	+4.36	1-10	10	-6.25
September	11-69	16	-31.93	3-23	13	-9.70	6-33	18	-14.75	2-13	15	-7.38
October	6-59	10	-19.30	3-36	8	-10.00	3-16	19	-2.30	0-7	-	-7.00
November	1-9	11	-7.17	0-2	-	-2.00	1-7	14	-5.17	0-0	-	+0.00
December	1-2	50	+2.00	0-1	-	-1.00	1-1	100	+3.00	0-0	-	+0.00

By race type – 2013

	Overall			Two-year-olds			Three-year-olds			Older horses		
	W-R	%	£1	W-R	%	£1	W-R	%	£1	W-R	%	£1
Handicap	47-204	23	+22.06	3-19	16	-3.39	25-108	23	-16.01	19-77	25	+41.46
Group 1,2,3	4-32	13	-16.56	1-8	13	-2.00	0-7	-	-7.00	3-17	18	-7.56
Maiden	48-200	24	+23.53	22-101	22	+42.78	24-96	25	-23.25	2-3	67	+4.00

By race type – 2012

	Overall			Two-year-olds			Three-year-olds			Older horses		
	W-R	%	£1	W-R	%	£1	W-R	%	£1	W-R	%	£1
Handicap	31-174	18	-8.87	2-18	11	+9.00	18-112	16	-20.53	11-44	25	+2.65
Group 1,2,3	3-33	9	-20.00	2-9	22	+1.50	0-13	-	-13.00	1-11	9	-8.50
Maiden	45-192	23	+2.79	16-84	19	-11.41	29-108	27	+14.20	0-0	-	+0.00

By race type – 2011

	Overall			Two-year-olds			Three-year-olds			Older horses		
	W-R	%	£1	W-R	%	£1	W-R	%	£1	W-R	%	£1
Handicap	27-160	17	-49.33	1-12	8	-7.00	21-105	20	-35.08	5-43	12	-7.25
Group 1,2,3	6-32	19	+11.75	1-5	20	-0.50	3-5	60	+27.50	2-22	9	-15.25
Maiden	33-179	18	-48.37	12-84	14	-5.17	21-95	22	-43.21	0-0	-	+0.00

By jockey – 2013

	Overall			Two-year-olds			Three-year-olds			Older horses		
	W-R	%	£1	W-R	%	£1	W-R	%	£1	W-R	%	£1
Liam Jones	15-70	21	-4.13	6-33	18	-3.50	9-32	28	+4.38	0-5	-	-5.00
Paul Hanagan	14-57	25	-16.36	3-12	25	-5.63	7-28	25	-6.68	4-17	24	-4.06
Ryan Moore	10-47	21	-5.82	3-18	17	-0.50	6-21	29	-1.65	1-8	13	-3.67
Seb Sanders	9-19	47	+28.63	2-10	20	+5.50	2-3	67	+3.38	5-6	83	+19.75
Richard Hughes	6-23	26	-6.46	1-2	50	+1.50	3-12	25	-5.33	2-9	22	-2.63
Graham Lee	5-31	16	-12.09	2-9	22	-5.59	3-15	20	+0.50	0-7	-	-7.00
S De Sousa	4-10	40	+19.83	1-2	50	+19.00	3-8	38	+0.83	0-0	-	+0.00
Frankie Dettori	4-12	33	+0.87	1-1	100	+0.62	2-6	33	+1.75	1-5	20	-1.50
Joe Fanning	4-15	27	+15.74	2-9	22	+15.36	2-5	40	+1.38	0-1	-	-1.00
A Beschizza	4-22	18	-5.00	0-0	-	+0.00	2-16	13	-6.50	2-6	33	+1.50
George Baker	3-8	38	+11.36	0-1	-	-1.00	1-3	33	-1.64	2-4	50	+14.00
William Buick	3-11	27	+1.88	1-4	25	+3.00	1-4	25	-0.75	1-3	33	-0.38

By jockey – 2012

	Overall			Two-year-olds			Three-year-olds			Older horses		
	W-R	%	£1	W-R	%	£1	W-R	%	£1	W-R	%	£1
Liam Jones	15-85	18	-20.80	3-27	11	-7.25	11-50	22	-8.05	1-8	13	-5.50
Paul Hanagan	14-59	24	-8.75	1-8	13	-6.60	8-36	22	-5.63	5-15	33	+3.48
A Beschizza	13-65	20	+8.24	4-23	17	+8.20	7-33	21	-2.63	2-9	22	+2.67
Ryan Moore	11-36	31	+8.90	4-7	57	+7.85	4-20	20	-0.45	3-9	33	+1.50
Johnny Murtagh	5-16	31	+7.30	1-1	100	+4.00	4-11	36	+7.30	0-4	-	-4.00
Phillip Makin	4-9	44	+9.66	2-5	40	+1.41	2-4	50	+8.25	0-0	-	+0.00
Richard Hughes	3-17	18	-6.63	1-2	50	+3.50	2-11	18	-6.13	0-4	-	-4.00
Joseph O'Brien	2-4	50	+13.50	0-0	-	+0.00	2-4	50	+13.50	0-0	-	+0.00
William Buick	2-6	33	+6.50	1-2	50	+8.00	1-4	25	-1.50	0-0	-	+0.00

By jockey – 2011

	Overall			Two-year-olds			Three-year-olds			Older horses		
	W-R	%	£1	W-R	%	£1	W-R	%	£1	W-R	%	£1
Liam Jones	13-77	17	-2.29	4-22	18	+16.00	8-47	17	-23.29	1-8	13	+5.00
Paul Hanagan	10-32	31	-4.14	1-12	8	-5.50	8-18	44	+0.74	1-2	50	+0.63
Ryan Moore	8-31	26	-12.38	0-4	-	-4.00	6-14	43	-1.63	2-13	15	-6.75
A Beschizza	5-26	19	+7.50	1-7	14	-2.00	3-14	21	+7.50	1-5	20	+2.00
Eddie Ahern	5-29	17	-7.36	1-8	13	-5.50	3-14	21	-7.86	1-7	14	+6.00
Kieren Fallon	5-32	16	-14.75	0-9	-	-9.00	3-16	19	-5.50	2-7	29	-0.25
Johnny Murtagh	4-14	29	+27.00	1-5	20	+3.50	3-7	43	+25.50	0-2	-	-2.00
Richard Hills	4-27	15	-18.42	2-10	20	-3.97	2-11	18	-8.45	0-6	-	-6.00
Tadhg O'Shea	3-14	21	+6.55	2-3	67	+13.80	1-10	10	-6.25	0-1	-	-1.00

By course – 2010-2013

	Overall			Two-year-olds			Three-year-olds			Older horses		
	W-R	%	£1	W-R	%	£1	W-R	%	£1	W-R	%	£1
Ascot	7-109	6	-61.50	1-14	7	+3.00	4-47	9	-25.50	2-48	4	-39.00
Ayr	0-10	-	-10.00	0-4	-	-4.00	0-2	-	-2.00	0-4	-	-4.00
Bath	6-20	30	-2.64	1-4	25	-1.75	4-15	27	-4.39	1-1	100	+3.50
Beverley	5-21	24	-5.63	2-5	40	+3.00	3-15	20	-7.63	0-1	-	-1.00
Brighton	5-17	29	+8.08	2-9	22	+3.00	3-8	38	+5.08	0-0	-	+0.00
Carlisle	1-3	33	-1.64	0-1	-	-1.00	1-2	50	-0.64	0-0	-	+0.00
Catterick	1-7	14	-4.63	0-4	-	-4.00	1-3	33	-0.63	0-0	-	+0.00
Chepstow	5-13	38	+8.65	0-1	-	-1.00	5-12	42	+9.65	0-0	-	+0.00
Chester	8-35	23	-9.39	5-9	56	+4.92	2-19	11	-12.30	1-7	14	-2.00
Doncaster	11-75	15	-28.13	1-21	5	-17.25	6-32	19	-15.38	4-22	18	+4.50
Epsom	2-28	7	-1.50	0-6	-	-6.00	1-15	7	+6.00	1-7	14	-1.50
Ffos Las	3-13	23	-0.25	1-2	50	+4.00	2-8	25	-1.25	0-3	-	-3.00
Folkestone	1-10	10	-6.00	0-2	-	-2.00	1-8	13	-4.00	0-0	-	+0.00
Goodwood	9-50	18	+3.88	2-11	18	+0.50	3-20	15	-11.63	4-19	21	+15.00
Hamilton	3-10	30	-4.65	0-0	-	+0.00	2-8	25	-5.27	1-2	50	+0.63
Haydock	18-57	32	+34.85	5-11	45	+14.88	9-26	35	+19.23	4-20	20	+0.75
Kempton (AW)	16-127	13	-28.02	5-42	12	-5.00	6-66	9	-34.31	5-19	26	+11.28
Leicester	8-28	29	+18.70	3-9	33	+21.50	5-18	28	-1.80	0-1	-	-1.00
Lingfield	6-26	23	-6.03	2-9	22	-1.20	4-14	29	-1.83	0-3	-	-3.00
Lingfield (AW)	19-100	19	-30.56	3-37	8	-24.25	11-47	23	-7.97	5-16	31	+1.67
Musselburgh	4-9	44	+3.52	2-2	100	+1.52	2-6	33	+3.00	0-1	-	-1.00
Newbury	18-88	20	+7.93	3-34	9	-8.02	10-36	28	+18.75	5-18	28	-2.80
Newcastle	10-29	34	-0.89	1-5	20	-3.80	8-19	42	+5.03	1-5	20	-2.13
Newmarket	15-139	11	-35.56	8-63	13	+13.00	6-53	11	-33.06	1-23	4	-15.50
Newmarket (J)	10-102	10	-58.15	2-29	7	-18.50	8-60	13	-26.65	0-13	-	-13.00
Nottingham	3-46	7	-39.05	0-17	-	-17.00	2-27	7	-22.80	1-2	50	+0.75
Pontefract	10-34	29	-12.13	3-7	43	+1.03	7-23	30	-9.17	0-4	-	-4.00
Redcar	5-21	24	-3.36	1-7	14	-2.50	2-9	22	-2.59	2-5	40	+1.73
Ripon	8-28	29	-6.23	2-7	29	-1.10	6-21	29	-5.13	0-0	-	+0.00
Salisbury	4-25	16	-8.83	2-8	25	+1.67	1-14	7	-12.50	1-3	33	+2.00
Sandown	11-52	21	-1.88	0-9	-	-9.00	7-29	24	+5.25	4-14	29	+1.88
Southwell (AW)	9-22	41	+4.59	1-1	100	+0.36	8-18	44	+7.23	0-3	-	-3.00
Thirsk	5-25	20	+14.92	1-5	20	+6.00	4-17	24	+11.92	0-3	-	-3.00
Warwick	6-27	22	+12.67	3-14	21	+19.25	2-12	17	-7.83	1-1	100	+1.25
Windsor	12-47	26	+0.39	2-11	18	-2.50	6-28	21	-0.73	4-8	50	+3.63
Wolves (AW)	13-97	13	-58.45	3-35	9	-27.63	10-59	17	-27.82	0-3	-	-3.00
Yarmouth	26-97	27	+8.91	10-42	24	+7.67	14-47	30	-6.63	2-8	25	+7.88
York	22-88	25	+32.85	5-20	25	+10.57	9-34	26	+15.25	8-34	24	+7.03

Ten-year summary

	Wins	Runs	%	Win prize-money	Total prize-money	£1
2013	107	503	21	£1,133,364.77	£1,896,067.18	-12.27
2012	83	448	19	£748,501.35	£1,257,840.26	-65.35
2011	76	423	18	£848,955.18	£1,228,089.25	-96.35
2010	59	361	16	£942,548.43	£1,181,417.91	-91.16
2009	69	346	20	£793,312.00	£1,320,567.05	-53.39
2008	86	425	20	£793,358.07	£1,056,524.73	+93.92
2007	66	376	18	£546,929.84	£763,916.97	+34.50
2006	59	334	18	£531,546.78	£771,050.59	+2.90
2005	53	355	15	£313,641.55	£543,899.79	-77.88
2004	46	306	15	£322,153.27	£605,726.42	+30.18

HARRIS TWEED (right): coaxed back to his best last year at the age of six

Saeed bin Suroor

Last year was clearly a desperate one for Godolphin, but Bin Suroor kept things on track with his best season since 2009 with 106 winners at an improved 20% strike-rate.

By month – 2013

	Overall			Two-year-olds			Three-year-olds			Older horses		
	W-R	%	£1	W-R	%	£1	W-R	%	£1	W-R	%	£1
January	0-0	-	+0.00	0-0	-	+0.00	0-0	-	+0.00	0-0	-	+0.00
February	0-0	-	+0.00	0-0	-	+0.00	0-0	-	+0.00	0-0	-	+0.00
March	0-0	-	+0.00	0-0	-	+0.00	0-0	-	+0.00	0-0	-	+0.00
April	0-9	-	-9.00	0-0	-	+0.00	0-7	-	-7.00	0-2	-	-2.00
May	9-28	32	+8.98	1-3	33	-0.75	1-9	11	-4.50	7-16	44	+14.23
June	23-117	20	-6.13	7-37	19	-4.42	10-48	21	-17.72	6-32	19	+16.00
July	32-122	26	+5.14	13-34	38	+14.04	16-54	30	+17.92	3-34	9	-26.82
August	16-85	19	-23.33	6-19	32	+2.28	4-33	12	-21.67	6-33	18	-3.95
September	12-72	17	+5.10	2-13	15	-8.28	7-34	21	+22.88	3-25	12	-9.50
October	9-72	13	-35.08	2-20	10	-13.50	4-32	13	-15.33	3-20	15	-6.25
November	5-18	28	+0.14	3-10	30	+4.50	2-8	25	-4.36	0-0	-	+0.00
December	0-0	-	+0.00	0-0	-	+0.00	0-0	-	+0.00	0-0	-	+0.00

By month – 2012

	Overall			Two-year-olds			Three-year-olds			Older horses		
	W-R	%	£1	W-R	%	£1	W-R	%	£1	W-R	%	£1
January	0-0	-	+0.00	0-0	-	+0.00	0-0	-	+0.00	0-0	-	+0.00
February	0-0	-	+0.00	0-0	-	+0.00	0-0	-	+0.00	0-0	-	+0.00
March	0-2	-	-2.00	0-0	-	+0.00	0-0	-	+0.00	0-2	-	-2.00
April	2-13	15	-4.17	0-0	-	+0.00	1-10	10	-5.67	1-3	33	+1.50
May	10-51	20	-14.03	0-3	-	-3.00	5-22	23	-1.67	5-26	19	-9.37
June	7-54	13	-10.25	3-5	60	+15.00	3-26	12	-9.25	1-23	4	-16.00
July	15-46	33	+5.44	1-3	33	+0.00	10-23	43	+9.57	4-20	20	-4.13
August	10-77	13	-31.13	1-12	8	-6.00	7-41	17	-18.13	2-24	8	-7.00
September	15-85	18	+20.28	6-21	29	+18.03	4-35	11	+1.75	5-29	17	+0.50
October	17-63	27	-2.02	9-27	33	-0.84	7-20	35	+11.33	1-16	6	-12.50
November	9-45	20	-5.13	4-14	29	+7.50	4-16	25	-4.13	1-15	7	-8.50
December	0-0	-	+0.00	0-0	-	+0.00	0-0	-	+0.00	0-0	-	+0.00

By month – 2011

	Overall			Two-year-olds			Three-year-olds			Older horses		
	W-R	%	£1	W-R	%	£1	W-R	%	£1	W-R	%	£1
January	0-0	-	+0.00	0-0	-	+0.00	0-0	-	+0.00	0-0	-	+0.00
February	0-0	-	+0.00	0-0	-	+0.00	0-0	-	+0.00	0-0	-	+0.00
March	0-0	-	+0.00	0-0	-	+0.00	0-0	-	+0.00	0-0	-	+0.00
April	0-7	-	-7.00	0-0	-	+0.00	0-5	-	-5.00	0-2	-	-2.00
May	4-29	14	-4.00	0-3	-	-3.00	2-10	20	+1.50	2-16	13	-2.50
June	6-45	13	-23.93	1-4	25	-2.56	2-17	12	-10.25	3-24	13	-11.13
July	10-54	19	-26.42	4-6	67	+7.63	2-14	14	-9.50	4-34	12	-24.54
August	11-66	17	-9.72	4-18	22	-5.60	3-24	13	-15.37	4-24	17	+11.25
September	9-87	10	-32.09	5-30	17	-3.84	2-26	8	-11.25	2-31	6	-17.00
October	11-69	16	-2.63	6-33	18	-0.50	4-22	18	+6.38	1-14	7	-8.50
November	7-18	39	+5.55	5-10	50	+4.82	1-3	33	-1.27	1-5	20	+2.00
December	0-0	-	+0.00	0-0	-	+0.00	0-0	-	+0.00	0-0	-	+0.00

By race type – 2013

	Overall			Two-year-olds			Three-year-olds			Older horses		
	W-R	%	£1	W-R	%	£1	W-R	%	£1	W-R	%	£1
Handicap	30-189	16	-19.63	1-4	25	-1.38	18-100	18	-1.16	11-85	13	-17.10
Group 1,2,3	9-68	13	-22.07	2-12	17	-6.15	1-15	7	-10.00	6-41	15	-5.92
Maiden	48-197	24	-20.98	26-104	25	+5.52	22-93	24	-26.51	0-0	-	+0.00

By race type – 2012

	Overall			Two-year-olds			Three-year-olds			Older horses		
	W-R	%	£1	W-R	%	£1	W-R	%	£1	W-R	%	£1
Handicap	35-207	17	-29.58	5-10	50	+9.63	24-131	18	-13.46	6-66	9	-25.75
Group 1,2,3	5-46	11	-20.00	1-4	25	+1.50	0-0	-	+0.00	4-42	10	-21.50
Maiden	34-124	27	+20.34	17-65	26	+20.07	17-59	29	+0.27	0-0	-	+0.00

By race type – 2011

	Overall			Two-year-olds			Three-year-olds			Older horses		
	W-R	%	£1	W-R	%	£1	W-R	%	£1	W-R	%	£1
Handicap	11-108	10	-39.25	2-14	14	-6.00	5-42	12	-8.75	4-52	8	-24.50
Group 1,2,3	3-48	6	-24.63	0-2	-	-2.00	0-9	-	-9.00	3-37	8	-13.63
Maiden	28-129	22	-16.44	21-78	27	+10.80	7-51	14	-27.24	0-0	-	+0.00

By jockey – 2013

	Overall			Two-year-olds			Three-year-olds			Older horses		
	W-R	%	£1	W-R	%	£1	W-R	%	£1	W-R	%	£1
S De Sousa	45-224	20	-43.57	15-56	27	+0.66	15-92	16	-45.24	15-76	20	+1.02
M Barzalona	25-110	23	-24.17	12-35	34	+8.10	11-52	21	-16.57	2-23	9	-15.70
Harry Bentley	6-21	29	+13.75	1-4	25	+5.00	4-11	36	+6.75	1-6	17	+2.00
Dane O'Neill	4-15	27	+6.75	2-3	67	+2.75	1-10	10	-3.00	1-2	50	+7.00
Paul Hanagan	4-16	25	-4.61	0-2	-	-2.00	2-7	29	-2.71	2-7	29	+0.10
Adam Kirby	3-5	60	+7.00	1-2	50	+4.00	1-1	100	+2.50	1-2	50	+0.50
William Buick	3-10	30	-0.38	2-6	33	+0.38	1-3	33	+0.25	0-1	-	-1.00
Ahmed Ajtebi	3-13	23	+32.00	0-1	-	-1.00	3-8	38	+37.00	0-4	-	-4.00
Kieren Fallon	3-26	12	-5.25	0-7	-	-7.00	0-6	-	-6.00	3-13	23	+7.75
Frederik Tylicki	2-10	20	-3.88	0-0	-	+0.00	1-6	17	-3.13	1-4	25	-0.75
Robert Havlin	2-11	18	-2.00	1-4	25	-1.00	1-4	25	+2.00	0-3	-	-3.00
Jim Crowley	1-2	50	+1.75	0-0	-	+0.00	1-2	50	+1.75	0-0	-	+0.00

By jockey – 2012

	Overall			Two-year-olds			Three-year-olds			Older horses		
	W-R	%	£1	W-R	%	£1	W-R	%	£1	W-R	%	£1
Frankie Dettori	29-148	20	-27.59	5-28	18	-12.72	12-54	22	-11.76	12-66	18	-3.12
S De Sousa	28-130	22	-19.90	9-25	36	+2.03	16-63	25	+9.69	3-42	7	-31.63
M Barzalona	12-72	17	+16.00	4-13	31	+28.00	5-36	14	-7.00	3-23	13	-5.00
Harry Bentley	3-9	33	+8.25	0-1	-	-1.00	3-6	50	+11.25	0-2	-	-2.00
Ted Durcan	3-18	17	-7.00	1-3	33	+2.50	2-10	20	-4.50	0-5	-	-5.00
Frederik Tylicki	2-4	50	+5.88	1-2	50	+5.00	1-2	50	+0.88	0-0	-	+0.00
William Buick	2-6	33	+5.50	1-2	50	+2.50	0-2	-	-2.00	1-2	50	+5.00
Pat Cosgrave	1-1	100	+1.75	0-0	-	+0.00	1-1	100	+1.75	0-0	-	+0.00
Ian Mongan	1-2	50	+5.50	1-1	100	+6.50	0-0	-	+0.00	0-1	-	-1.00

By jockey – 2011

	Overall			Two-year-olds			Three-year-olds			Older horses		
	W-R	%	£1	W-R	%	£1	W-R	%	£1	W-R	%	£1
Frankie Dettori	15-116	13	-63.22	4-21	19	-8.69	4-39	10	-29.70	7-56	13	-24.83
Ted Durcan	11-75	15	-20.43	7-24	29	-2.43	1-26	4	-15.00	3-25	12	-3.00
William Buick	9-29	31	+16.55	6-9	67	+18.32	2-7	29	+1.23	1-13	8	-3.00
Kieren Fallon	4-14	29	+4.41	1-4	25	+0.50	0-4	-	-4.00	3-6	50	+7.91
S De Sousa	3-7	43	+15.38	0-1	-	-1.00	2-2	100	+13.38	1-4	25	+3.00
Paul Hanagan	3-10	30	+7.50	2-5	40	+5.50	0-2	-	-2.00	1-3	33	+4.00
Ian Mongan	2-6	33	+14.00	1-2	50	+9.00	1-1	100	+8.00	0-3	-	-3.00
Richard Hills	2-7	29	+0.58	1-3	33	+0.25	1-3	33	+1.33	0-1	-	-1.00
Jimmy Fortune	1-1	100	+2.50	1-1	100	+2.50	0-0	-	+0.00	0-0	-	+0.00

By course – 2010-2013

	Overall			Two-year-olds			Three-year-olds			Older horses		
	W-R	%	£1	W-R	%	£1	W-R	%	£1	W-R	%	£1
Ascot	16-118	14	+30.01	4-16	25	+2.43	7-31	23	+30.83	5-71	7	-3.25
Ayr	2-9	22	-2.25	0-2	-	-2.00	0-1	-	-1.00	2-6	33	+0.75
Bath	5-13	38	+2.50	2-7	29	-1.75	3-6	50	+4.25	0-0	-	+0.00
Beverley	0-3	-	-3.00	0-1	-	-1.00	0-2	-	-2.00	0-0	-	+0.00
Brighton	6-13	46	+25.83	2-5	40	+24.25	4-8	50	+1.58	0-0	-	+0.00
Catterick	0-2	-	-2.00	0-1	-	-1.00	0-1	-	-1.00	0-0	-	+0.00
Chepstow	0-4	-	-4.00	0-1	-	-1.00	0-3	-	-3.00	0-0	-	+0.00
Chester	2-30	7	-24.38	1-6	17	-3.63	1-8	13	-4.75	0-16	-	-16.00
Doncaster	21-109	19	-29.29	8-26	31	-1.05	7-38	18	-7.88	6-45	13	-20.37
Epsom	9-38	24	-4.51	0-4	-	-4.00	2-14	14	-7.75	7-20	35	+7.24
Ffos Las	0-1	-	-1.00	0-0	-	+0.00	0-1	-	-1.00	0-0	-	+0.00
Folkestone	2-13	15	-9.06	1-3	33	-1.56	1-10	10	-7.50	0-0	-	+0.00
Goodwood	9-92	10	-41.40	0-7	-	-7.00	4-31	13	-7.00	5-54	9	-27.40
Hamilton	1-8	13	-5.00	0-0	-	+0.00	1-4	25	-1.00	0-4	-	-4.00
Haydock	10-62	16	-17.98	5-15	33	+1.02	3-13	23	+7.00	2-34	6	-26.00
Kempton (AW)	55-197	28	+33.66	29-67	43	+24.26	17-86	20	+8.78	9-44	20	+0.63
Leicester	8-29	28	-9.28	3-12	25	-1.00	3-15	20	-8.83	2-2	100	+0.55
Lingfield	1-15	7	-12.80	0-6	-	-6.00	1-7	14	-4.80	0-2	-	-2.00
Lingfield (AW)	22-66	33	+2.80	8-20	40	+9.28	10-35	29	-8.67	4-11	36	+2.18
Musselburgh	0-2	-	-2.00	0-0	-	+0.00	0-1	-	-1.00	0-1	-	-1.00
Newbury	18-76	24	+0.83	5-12	42	+6.75	4-24	17	-9.88	9-40	23	+3.96
Newcastle	4-26	15	+4.00	2-8	25	+9.00	1-10	10	-4.00	1-8	13	-1.00
Newmarket	13-134	10	-43.98	2-34	6	-29.33	8-53	15	+14.35	3-47	6	-29.00
Newmarket (J)	28-132	21	-18.40	15-49	31	+10.14	9-43	21	-3.84	4-40	10	-24.70
Nottingham	16-58	28	-0.66	6-18	33	-2.45	8-31	26	+1.29	2-9	22	+0.50
Pontefract	6-29	21	-13.43	1-6	17	-3.75	3-12	25	-3.43	2-11	18	-6.25
Redcar	3-21	14	-8.39	3-10	30	+2.62	0-4	-	-4.00	0-7	-	-7.00
Ripon	2-16	13	-5.25	1-4	25	+3.00	1-9	11	-5.25	0-3	-	-3.00
Salisbury	8-43	19	-4.02	0-9	-	-9.00	5-19	26	-5.52	3-15	20	+10.50
Sandown	8-81	10	-41.40	3-13	23	+1.00	3-31	10	-11.50	2-37	5	-30.90
Southwell (AW)	5-16	31	-2.96	3-6	50	+0.54	2-10	20	-3.50	0-0	-	+0.00
Thirsk	2-16	13	-10.50	0-5	-	-5.00	0-7	-	-7.00	2-4	50	+1.50
Warwick	5-20	25	+3.50	2-8	25	-1.25	0-6	-	-6.00	3-6	50	+10.75
Windsor	11-36	31	+29.30	1-2	50	+5.50	6-19	32	+1.80	4-15	27	+22.00
Wolves (AW)	25-74	34	-4.58	12-32	38	-3.05	12-38	32	-0.53	1-4	25	-1.00
Yarmouth	6-34	18	-4.74	3-17	18	+0.60	3-12	25	-0.34	0-5	-	-5.00
York	10-98	10	-46.35	1-8	13	-3.00	0-20	-	-20.00	9-70	13	-23.35

Ten-year summary

	Wins	Runs	%	Win prize-money	Total prize-money	£1
2013	106	523	20	£1,934,401.24	£2,665,780.91	-54.19
2012	85	436	19	£1,020,127.41	£1,817,649.48	-42.99
2011	58	375	15	£494,862.68	£921,445.34	-100.23
2010	90	400	23	£1,383,089.08	£2,064,698.09	-42.77
2009	148	530	28	£1,743,062.05	£2,765,249.72	+17.66
2008	58	313	19	£758,691.92	£1,268,209.97	-56.42
2007	72	285	25	£1,225,192.68	£1,680,865.13	-20.61
2006	70	247	28	£935,405.65	£1,610,204.02	+13.15
2005	78	407	19	£901,450.30	£1,522,250.25	-52.73
2004	115	455	25	£3,057,921.70	£4,319,646.12	+12.99

AHZEEMAH: a progressive and consistent stayer in the Godolphin blue

Andrew Balding

From lesser beginnings in spite of the family name, Balding's yard is now one of the most respected in Britain known for producing top riding talent. He improved his tally for a sixth year out of seven with 99 winners.

By month – 2013

	Overall			Two-year-olds			Three-year-olds			Older horses		
	W-R	%	£1	W-R	%	£1	W-R	%	£1	W-R	%	£1
January	4-28	14	-4.75	0-0	-	+0.00	1-11	9	-8.25	3-17	18	+3.50
February	2-13	15	+0.50	0-0	-	+0.00	1-4	25	+2.50	1-9	11	-2.00
March	5-21	24	-2.84	0-0	-	+0.00	3-12	25	-4.45	2-9	22	+1.62
April	7-57	12	+5.30	0-0	-	+0.00	6-37	16	+21.30	1-20	5	-16.00
May	9-92	10	-29.97	0-4	-	-4.00	7-46	15	-17.97	2-42	5	-8.00
June	16-101	16	+14.80	1-7	14	-2.50	5-48	10	-6.20	10-46	22	+23.50
July	8-84	10	-43.25	1-10	10	-6.50	5-44	11	-12.00	2-30	7	-24.75
August	14-90	16	-14.63	3-18	17	-3.64	4-38	11	-17.25	7-34	21	+6.25
September	15-96	16	-7.38	4-34	12	-23.53	5-35	14	-7.06	6-27	22	+23.21
October	13-86	15	+39.20	7-38	18	+27.57	2-28	7	-21.25	4-20	20	+32.88
November	3-29	10	+38.00	2-10	20	+31.00	0-7	-	-7.00	1-12	8	+14.00
December	3-16	19	-8.33	2-6	33	-2.08	1-2	50	+1.75	0-8	-	-8.00

By month – 2012

	Overall			Two-year-olds			Three-year-olds			Older horses		
	W-R	%	£1	W-R	%	£1	W-R	%	£1	W-R	%	£1
January	1-13	8	-11.82	0-0	-	+0.00	0-4	-	-4.00	1-9	11	-7.82
February	0-5	-	-5.00	0-0	-	+0.00	0-2	-	-2.00	0-3	-	-3.00
March	2-13	15	-8.55	0-0	-	+0.00	0-7	-	-7.00	2-6	33	-1.55
April	6-54	11	-16.13	0-0	-	+0.00	5-37	14	-1.88	1-17	6	-14.25
May	15-96	16	-0.71	0-7	-	-7.00	9-58	16	-10.21	6-31	19	+16.50
June	10-98	10	-58.60	2-9	22	+2.25	5-58	9	-43.97	3-31	10	-16.88
July	11-89	12	-9.50	1-15	7	-11.25	8-50	16	+10.25	2-24	8	-8.50
August	20-122	16	+49.15	4-39	10	-14.00	8-46	17	+50.40	8-37	22	+12.75
September	13-88	15	-28.53	5-29	17	-6.90	6-33	18	-0.25	2-26	8	-21.39
October	7-70	10	-29.25	1-31	3	-25.50	5-28	18	+3.50	1-11	9	-7.25
November	3-37	8	-29.35	2-18	11	-14.10	0-10	-	-10.00	1-9	11	-5.25
December	5-27	19	-7.25	3-14	21	-2.25	2-10	20	-2.00	0-3	-	-3.00

By month – 2011

	Overall			Two-year-olds			Three-year-olds			Older horses		
	W-R	%	£1	W-R	%	£1	W-R	%	£1	W-R	%	£1
January	0-15	-	-15.00	0-0	-	+0.00	0-8	-	-8.00	0-7	-	-7.00
February	2-7	29	+2.88	0-0	-	+0.00	2-4	50	+5.88	0-3	-	-3.00
March	4-10	40	+4.25	0-0	-	+0.00	3-6	50	+2.25	1-4	25	+2.00
April	3-39	8	-27.54	0-1	-	-1.00	2-19	11	-11.88	1-19	5	-14.67
May	12-71	17	+3.95	1-4	25	+9.00	5-31	16	-7.83	6-36	17	+2.78
June	11-72	15	+28.38	1-10	10	+5.00	6-31	19	+17.38	4-31	13	+6.00
July	14-88	16	+21.88	2-20	10	+12.50	9-35	26	+21.38	3-33	9	-12.00
August	8-69	12	-32.25	2-27	7	-21.25	1-20	5	-17.25	5-22	23	+6.25
September	8-77	10	+8.00	5-34	15	+23.00	2-23	9	-5.00	1-20	5	-10.00
October	3-57	5	-38.00	1-33	3	-28.50	2-15	13	-0.50	0-9	-	-9.00
November	3-24	13	-10.00	3-14	21	+0.00	0-4	-	-4.00	0-6	-	-6.00
December	2-14	14	-5.60	0-8	-	-8.00	1-3	33	-1.60	1-3	33	+4.00

By race type – 2013

	Overall			Two-year-olds			Three-year-olds			Older horses		
	W-R	%	£1	W-R	%	£1	W-R	%	£1	W-R	%	£1
Handicap	58-422	14	-15.58	1-12	8	-10.33	25-190	13	-33.83	32-220	15	+28.58
Group 1,2,3	1-27	4	-1.00	0-2	-	-2.00	0-8	-	-8.00	1-17	6	+9.00
Maiden	28-193	15	+4.37	15-99	15	+31.89	12-89	13	-24.14	1-5	20	-3.39

By race type – 2012

	Overall			Two-year-olds			Three-year-olds			Older horses		
	W-R	%	£1	W-R	%	£1	W-R	%	£1	W-R	%	£1
Handicap	43-375	11	-102.33	1-29	3	-25.00	26-199	13	-36.83	16-147	11	-40.50
Group 1,2,3	4-38	11	-20.25	0-3	-	-3.00	1-10	10	-6.00	3-25	12	-11.25
Maiden	34-215	16	-5.59	16-113	14	-37.25	16-98	16	+33.27	2-4	50	-1.62

By race type – 2011

	Overall			Two-year-olds			Three-year-olds			Older horses		
	W-R	%	£1	W-R	%	£1	W-R	%	£1	W-R	%	£1
Handicap	34-251	14	-4.88	2-16	13	+0.50	18-111	16	+6.00	14-124	11	-11.39
Group 1,2,3	2-28	7	-18.50	0-4	-	-4.00	1-5	20	+1.50	1-19	5	-16.00
Maiden	21-182	12	-38.60	9-111	8	-30.50	11-63	17	-6.10	1-8	13	-2.00

By jockey – 2013

	Overall			Two-year-olds			Three-year-olds			Older horses		
	W-R	%	£1	W-R	%	£1	W-R	%	£1	W-R	%	£1
David Probert	33-227	15	+62.51	10-60	17	+25.06	15-99	15	+2.95	8-68	12	+34.50
Thomas Brown	14-68	21	+24.27	3-13	23	+2.41	6-30	20	+12.50	5-25	20	+9.37
Oisin Murphy	12-41	29	+39.71	0-4	-	-4.00	4-18	22	-1.00	8-19	42	+44.71
Liam Keniry	10-84	12	-39.41	1-16	6	-14.39	5-41	12	-22.15	4-27	15	-2.88
Jimmy Fortune	7-91	8	-40.20	0-9	-	-9.00	1-40	3	-38.20	6-42	14	+7.00
Jamie Spencer	5-24	21	-5.33	2-8	25	-3.33	2-8	25	+2.00	1-8	13	-4.00
Cathy Gannon	4-20	20	+5.50	0-0	-	+0.00	3-14	21	+7.75	1-6	17	-2.25
Ryan Moore	3-11	27	-4.49	2-4	50	+1.07	1-5	20	-3.56	0-2	-	-2.00
Jack Garritty	2-11	18	-2.75	0-0	-	+0.00	0-3	-	-3.00	2-8	25	+0.25
William Buick	2-11	18	-1.67	0-0	-	+0.00	1-4	25	+0.33	1-7	14	-2.00
Harry Bentley	1-2	50	+24.00	1-2	50	+24.00	0-0	-	+0.00	0-0	-	+0.00
J Willetts	1-6	17	-0.50	0-0	-	+0.00	0-0	-	+0.00	1-6	17	-0.50

By jockey – 2012

	Overall			Two-year-olds			Three-year-olds			Older horses		
	W-R	%	£1	W-R	%	£1	W-R	%	£1	W-R	%	£1
David Probert	42-259	16	+28.10	7-51	14	-16.95	24-140	17	+49.42	11-68	16	-4.37
Jimmy Fortune	21-225	9	-119.09	4-58	7	-37.00	8-94	9	-50.70	9-73	12	-31.39
Liam Keniry	8-65	12	-26.90	3-19	16	-6.15	5-37	14	-11.75	0-9	-	-9.00
Franny Norton	4-7	57	+16.25	1-2	50	+3.50	3-5	60	+12.75	0-0	-	+0.00
Thomas Brown	4-18	22	+1.75	1-4	25	+0.00	2-8	25	+4.00	1-6	17	-2.25
Richard Mullen	3-5	60	+15.50	0-0	-	+0.00	2-2	100	+12.00	1-3	33	+3.50
Jamie Spencer	3-16	19	-7.28	2-10	20	-4.15	1-5	20	-2.13	0-1	-	-1.00
Daniel Muscutt	2-27	7	-16.00	0-1	-	-1.00	1-16	6	-10.00	1-10	10	-5.00
Cristian Demuro	1-1	100	+5.50	0-0	-	+0.00	0-0	-	+0.00	1-1	100	+5.50

By jockey – 2011

	Overall			Two-year-olds			Three-year-olds			Older horses		
	W-R	%	£1	W-R	%	£1	W-R	%	£1	W-R	%	£1
David Probert	29-170	17	+11.37	3-45	7	-29.50	18-62	29	+48.75	8-63	13	-7.89
Jimmy Fortune	25-193	13	-15.81	8-63	13	+28.75	9-74	12	-37.81	8-56	14	-6.75
Liam Keniry	8-90	9	-27.38	3-30	10	-10.50	2-33	6	-13.38	3-27	11	-3.50
William Buick	2-6	33	+7.38	0-0	-	+0.00	1-1	100	+1.38	1-5	20	+6.00
Hugh Bowman	1-2	50	+2.50	0-0	-	+0.00	0-1	-	-1.00	1-1	100	+3.50
Steve Drowne	1-2	50	+11.00	0-0	-	+0.00	1-1	100	+12.00	0-1	-	-1.00
Richard Hughes	1-3	33	+2.00	0-0	-	+0.00	1-2	50	+3.00	0-1	-	-1.00
Franny Norton	1-7	14	+8.00	1-2	50	+13.00	0-1	-	-1.00	0-4	-	-4.00
Simon Pearce	1-13	8	-10.13	0-1	-	-1.00	1-8	13	-5.13	0-4	-	-4.00

By course – 2010-2013

	Overall			Two-year-olds			Three-year-olds			Older horses		
	W-R	%	£1	W-R	%	£1	W-R	%	£1	W-R	%	£1
Ascot	11-180	6	-123.42	0-20	-	-20.00	4-70	6	-51.25	7-90	8	-52.17
Ayr	3-8	38	+25.62	0-1	-	-1.00	1-2	50	+9.00	2-5	40	+17.62
Bath	11-75	15	-27.20	2-13	15	-2.75	7-45	16	-13.70	2-17	12	-10.75
Beverley	0-1	-	-1.00	0-1	-	-1.00	0-0	-	+0.00	0-0	-	+0.00
Brighton	5-34	15	-12.26	2-6	33	+2.62	3-17	18	-3.88	0-11	-	-11.00
Carlisle	1-6	17	-3.25	1-1	100	+1.75	0-2	-	-2.00	0-3	-	-3.00
Chepstow	17-65	26	+20.48	1-8	13	+2.00	10-41	24	+8.61	6-16	38	+9.87
Chester	16-83	19	+25.75	1-13	8	+2.00	12-40	30	+26.75	3-30	10	-3.00
Doncaster	8-60	13	+36.63	2-9	22	+24.00	2-19	11	-9.75	4-32	13	+22.38
Epsom	18-98	18	+15.36	8-23	35	+22.61	4-38	11	-4.75	6-37	16	-2.50
Ffos Las	4-20	20	-6.42	1-7	14	-3.00	1-7	14	-5.00	2-6	33	+1.58
Folkestone	4-13	31	+2.10	1-3	33	+0.25	3-7	43	+4.85	0-3	-	-3.00
Goodwood	10-125	8	-42.75	2-30	7	-18.00	4-45	9	-15.25	4-50	8	-9.50
Hamilton	0-4	-	-4.00	0-0	-	+0.00	0-3	-	-3.00	0-1	-	-1.00
Haydock	8-52	15	-10.93	0-6	-	-6.00	4-17	24	+2.44	4-29	14	-7.38
Kempton (AW)	55-364	15	-27.54	8-75	11	-48.03	25-171	15	+12.60	22-118	19	+7.88
Leicester	4-41	10	-7.93	1-13	8	-11.43	2-19	11	-8.50	1-9	11	+12.00
Lingfield	2-19	11	-8.43	0-3	-	-3.00	2-7	29	+3.57	0-9	-	-9.00
Lingfield (AW)	30-189	16	-29.16	9-40	23	+25.22	16-95	17	-29.56	5-54	9	-24.82
Musselburgh	0-3	-	-3.00	0-0	-	+0.00	0-3	-	-3.00	0-0	-	+0.00
Newbury	11-127	9	-38.48	4-50	8	+10.00	7-50	14	-21.48	0-27	-	-27.00
Newcastle	0-4	-	-4.00	0-0	-	+0.00	0-0	-	+0.00	0-4	-	-4.00
Newmarket	17-175	10	+34.88	4-55	7	+20.25	7-58	12	+9.38	6-62	10	+5.25
Newmarket (J)	13-103	13	-10.63	1-21	5	-12.50	3-49	6	-20.25	9-33	27	+22.13
Nottingham	2-32	6	-20.50	1-14	7	-8.00	1-13	8	-7.50	0-5	-	-5.00
Pontefract	2-15	13	+0.50	1-4	25	+0.50	0-7	-	-7.00	1-4	25	+7.00
Redcar	0-2	-	-2.00	0-1	-	-1.00	0-1	-	-1.00	0-0	-	+0.00
Salisbury	17-136	13	-34.20	5-41	12	-8.75	6-56	11	-13.20	6-39	15	-12.25
Sandown	26-135	19	+47.44	4-28	14	+1.44	15-67	22	+29.25	7-40	18	+16.75
Southwell (AW)	0-7	-	-7.00	0-2	-	-2.00	0-3	-	-3.00	0-2	-	-2.00
Thirsk	0-2	-	-2.00	0-1	-	-1.00	0-1	-	-1.00	0-0	-	+0.00
Warwick	6-38	16	-1.75	0-9	-	-9.00	5-22	23	+11.00	1-7	14	-3.75
Windsor	22-98	22	+44.92	5-18	28	+15.00	11-57	19	+23.50	6-23	26	+6.42
Wolves (AW)	12-104	12	-21.14	3-24	13	-14.29	8-58	14	+0.15	1-22	5	-7.00
Yarmouth	1-13	8	-9.25	0-5	-	-5.00	0-4	-	-4.00	1-4	25	-0.25
York	4-48	8	-35.22	1-7	14	-1.50	2-17	12	-11.33	1-24	4	-22.39

Ten-year summary

	Wins	Runs	%	Win prize-money	Total prize-money	£1
2013	99	713	14	£873,940.78	£1,356,742.43	-13.36
2012	93	712	13	£779,847.73	£1,365,377.42	-155.54
2011	70	543	13	£620,393.39	£971,676.62	-59.07
2010	78	511	15	£707,996.22	£1,116,809.38	-11.81
2009	68	498	14	£460,056.19	£783,172.54	-38.44
2008	67	436	15	£510,631.82	£865,416.84	+12.56
2007	39	410	10	£525,039.35	£711,375.94	-114.90
2006	48	467	10	£357,958.81	£563,634.99	-160.67
2005	40	507	8	£212,863.31	£389,047.11	-128.11
2004	48	542	9	£389,774.22	£680,579.32	-164.29

HIGHLAND COLORI: scooting up the stands' rail to win the Ayr Gold Cup

Kevin Ryan

Ryan has been unable to kick on from his 2011 peak of 133 winners, but his record is still incredibly consistent as last year's tally of 94 makes eight in a row when he has topped the 90 mark. However, just 7% of his horses won first time out.

By month – 2013

	Overall			Two-year-olds			Three-year-olds			Older horses		
	W-R	%	£1	W-R	%	£1	W-R	%	£1	W-R	%	£1
January	3-21	14	-0.50	0-0	-	+0.00	1-7	14	-3.50	2-14	14	+3.00
February	1-19	5	-15.50	0-0	-	+0.00	1-10	10	-6.50	0-9	-	-9.00
March	2-26	8	-16.75	0-0	-	+0.00	2-13	15	-3.75	0-13	-	-13.00
April	3-64	5	-41.00	0-3	-	-3.00	2-35	6	-21.50	1-26	4	-16.50
May	14-110	13	-14.25	1-14	7	+1.00	6-51	12	-19.25	7-45	16	+4.00
June	12-106	11	+22.25	3-32	9	-12.75	5-37	14	+4.25	4-37	11	+30.75
July	16-92	17	-25.42	9-35	26	-7.79	2-26	8	-20.88	5-31	16	+3.25
August	21-126	17	-12.28	11-43	26	+3.33	6-38	16	-3.42	4-45	9	-12.20
September	7-96	7	+44.88	3-44	7	+69.50	2-19	11	-10.13	2-33	6	-14.50
October	7-63	11	-16.42	4-37	11	-11.75	0-10	-	-10.00	3-16	19	+5.33
November	3-34	9	-17.63	2-15	13	-1.13	1-10	10	-7.50	0-9	-	-9.00
December	5-24	21	-5.10	3-11	27	-2.35	1-9	11	-2.50	1-4	25	-0.25

By month – 2012

	Overall			Two-year-olds			Three-year-olds			Older horses		
	W-R	%	£1	W-R	%	£1	W-R	%	£1	W-R	%	£1
January	4-18	22	-5.82	0-0	-	+0.00	2-9	22	-4.15	2-9	22	-1.67
February	0-10	-	-10.00	0-0	-	+0.00	0-3	-	-3.00	0-7	-	-7.00
March	2-20	10	-10.00	0-0	-	+0.00	2-10	20	+0.00	0-10	-	-10.00
April	7-64	11	-7.65	2-8	25	+6.00	3-36	8	-25.15	2-20	10	+11.50
May	16-131	12	+26.94	5-29	17	-13.68	6-55	11	+19.00	5-47	11	+21.63
June	19-127	15	+78.75	4-32	13	+47.00	11-49	22	+42.25	4-46	9	-10.50
July	5-90	6	-66.15	3-30	10	-19.65	2-28	7	-14.50	0-32	-	-32.00
August	12-96	13	-6.96	5-36	14	-8.31	5-30	17	+3.25	2-30	7	-1.90
September	12-98	12	+38.58	9-48	19	+57.08	2-18	11	-3.50	1-32	3	-15.00
October	9-75	12	-6.29	4-38	11	+5.88	3-18	17	-3.00	2-19	11	-9.17
November	6-40	15	-12.40	3-16	19	-0.50	1-7	14	-1.50	2-17	12	-10.40
December	3-20	15	-4.00	1-8	13	-1.50	1-4	25	+2.00	1-8	13	-4.50

By month – 2011

	Overall			Two-year-olds			Three-year-olds			Older horses		
	W-R	%	£1	W-R	%	£1	W-R	%	£1	W-R	%	£1
January	9-32	28	-1.77	0-0	-	+0.00	2-8	25	-3.90	7-24	29	+2.13
February	9-35	26	+3.82	0-0	-	+0.00	4-13	31	+2.13	5-22	23	+1.70
March	8-30	27	+15.74	0-1	-	-1.00	4-14	29	+0.99	4-15	27	+15.75
April	7-66	11	-26.32	1-11	9	-6.00	2-21	10	-18.07	4-34	12	-2.25
May	28-104	27	+37.52	9-24	38	+20.94	12-34	35	+18.04	7-46	15	-1.46
June	17-104	16	+57.67	5-32	16	+28.88	8-31	26	+22.79	4-41	10	+6.00
July	21-111	19	+16.71	5-40	13	-23.59	10-34	29	+19.80	6-37	16	+20.50
August	10-87	11	-21.02	3-39	8	+0.50	5-20	25	-1.25	2-28	7	-20.27
September	11-106	10	-11.38	4-45	9	+4.00	3-23	13	-7.38	4-38	11	-8.00
October	6-65	9	-34.20	4-33	12	-13.20	1-15	7	-13.00	1-17	6	-8.00
November	4-31	13	+13.25	1-6	17	+3.00	1-7	14	-3.75	2-18	11	+14.00
December	3-26	12	-17.72	0-6	-	-6.00	2-11	18	-5.09	1-9	11	-6.63

By race type – 2013

	Overall			Two-year-olds			Three-year-olds			Older horses		
	W-R	%	£1	W-R	%	£1	W-R	%	£1	W-R	%	£1
Handicap	46-482	10	-114.41	5-53	9	-23.25	19-193	10	-70.04	22-236	9	-21.12
Group 1,2,3	3-31	10	-10.50	3-14	21	+6.50	0-6	-	-6.00	0-11	-	-11.00
Maiden	25-177	14	-57.79	16-128	13	-43.92	9-44	20	-8.88	0-5	-	-5.00

By race type – 2012

	Overall			Two-year-olds			Three-year-olds			Older horses		
	W-R	%	£1	W-R	%	£1	W-R	%	£1	W-R	%	£1
Handicap	52-493	11	-34.84	9-56	16	+25.13	26-195	13	+9.35	17-242	7	-69.32
Group 1,2,3	2-29	7	+4.00	1-12	8	-5.00	0-10	-	-10.00	1-7	14	+19.00
Maiden	27-189	14	+21.42	21-147	14	+36.20	6-41	15	-13.77	0-1	-	-1.00

By race type – 2011

	Overall			Two-year-olds			Three-year-olds			Older horses		
	W-R	%	£1	W-R	%	£1	W-R	%	£1	W-R	%	£1
Handicap	82-496	17	+36.70	4-50	8	-1.50	39-173	23	+4.33	39-273	14	+33.87
Group 1,2,3	2-24	8	-12.00	1-14	7	-7.00	0-0	-	+0.00	1-10	10	-5.00
Maiden	32-167	19	+23.02	22-132	17	+25.13	10-33	30	-0.11	0-2	-	-2.00

By jockey – 2013

	Overall			Two-year-olds			Three-year-olds			Older horses		
	W-R	%	£1	W-R	%	£1	W-R	%	£1	W-R	%	£1
Neil Callan	19-97	20	+50.08	6-24	25	+19.00	7-28	25	+18.08	6-45	13	+13.00
Jamie Spencer	12-48	25	+23.33	6-15	40	+10.58	2-16	13	-7.00	4-17	24	+19.75
Phillip Makin	12-128	9	-74.67	6-44	14	-25.84	3-44	7	-28.13	3-40	8	-20.70
Kevin Stott	8-54	15	-9.13	4-14	29	+8.50	2-17	12	-11.13	2-23	9	-6.50
Paul Mulrennan	7-20	35	+109.50	4-10	40	+108.50	1-3	33	+2.00	2-7	29	-1.00
Graham Lee	7-57	12	-30.08	4-25	16	-12.58	1-12	8	-10.00	2-20	10	-7.50
Amy Ryan	6-82	7	-34.50	1-9	11	+2.00	3-42	7	-27.00	2-31	6	-9.50
Franny Norton	3-18	17	+17.50	0-2	-	-2.00	2-9	22	+3.50	1-7	14	+16.00
Julie Burke	3-35	9	-15.25	0-2	-	-2.00	2-22	9	-10.25	1-11	9	-3.00
Tom Eaves	3-38	8	-23.50	1-21	5	-16.50	2-13	15	-3.00	0-4	-	-4.00
S De Sousa	2-7	29	+2.25	1-3	33	+2.50	1-3	33	+0.75	0-1	-	-1.00
David Nolan	2-10	20	-5.85	2-4	50	+0.15	0-2	-	-2.00	0-4	-	-4.00

By jockey – 2012

	Overall			Two-year-olds			Three-year-olds			Older horses		
	W-R	%	£1	W-R	%	£1	W-R	%	£1	W-R	%	£1
Phillip Makin	32-250	13	-11.80	16-87	18	+50.86	10-87	11	-30.92	6-76	8	-31.73
Amy Ryan	24-196	12	-22.04	11-71	15	-4.04	8-65	12	-5.25	5-60	8	-12.75
Graham Lee	11-59	19	+50.72	3-15	20	+46.50	6-19	32	+10.13	2-25	8	-5.90
Julie Burke	5-65	8	-17.50	3-13	23	+23.50	1-25	4	-17.50	1-27	4	-23.50
Jamie Spencer	4-41	10	+11.00	1-16	6	-10.50	2-9	22	+11.50	1-16	6	+10.00
Neil Callan	3-12	25	+6.00	1-3	33	+1.50	1-4	25	+1.00	1-5	20	+3.50
Franny Norton	3-16	19	+14.38	1-5	20	-0.50	0-3	-	-3.00	2-8	25	+17.88
G Gibbons	2-3	67	+8.00	0-0	-	+0.00	2-3	67	+8.00	0-0	-	+0.00
Paul Mulrennan	2-30	7	+14.00	0-10	-	-10.00	2-14	14	+30.00	0-6	-	-6.00

By jockey – 2011

	Overall			Two-year-olds			Three-year-olds			Older horses		
	W-R	%	£1	W-R	%	£1	W-R	%	£1	W-R	%	£1
Phillip Makin	68-380	18	-23.91	19-133	14	-46.75	24-103	23	-11.21	25-144	17	+34.05
Amy Ryan	15-90	17	+25.63	3-16	19	+33.50	8-22	36	+19.63	4-52	8	-27.50
Julie Burke	12-60	20	+1.46	0-7	-	-7.00	9-26	35	+13.13	3-27	11	-4.67
Paul Hanagan	5-22	23	-5.38	1-7	14	-2.00	4-10	40	+1.63	0-5	-	-5.00
Jamie Spencer	5-26	19	+12.33	1-3	33	+2.50	3-6	50	+21.83	1-17	6	-12.00
Frederik Tylicki	3-4	75	+34.80	1-2	50	+24.00	2-2	100	+10.80	0-0	-	+0.00
Stephen Craine	3-35	9	+12.00	3-20	15	+27.00	0-4	-	-4.00	0-11	-	-11.00
Brian Toomey	2-3	67	+15.00	1-1	100	+9.00	0-0	-	+0.00	1-2	50	+6.00
Neil Callan	2-11	18	+0.00	0-2	-	-2.00	1-5	20	+0.50	1-4	25	+1.50

By course – 2010-2013

	Overall			Two-year-olds			Three-year-olds			Older horses		
	W-R	%	£1	W-R	%	£1	W-R	%	£1	W-R	%	£1
Ascot	9-84	11	+16.00	3-22	14	+5.50	2-16	13	-5.00	4-46	9	+15.50
Ayr	16-148	11	-23.58	8-52	15	-15.58	2-31	6	-17.50	6-65	9	+9.50
Beverley	24-154	16	+9.21	9-50	18	-3.00	8-51	16	-4.38	7-53	13	+16.58
Carlisle	12-72	17	+77.10	6-32	19	+37.63	1-14	7	+5.00	5-26	19	+34.48
Catterick	14-91	15	-6.51	7-34	21	-1.35	4-31	13	-8.50	3-26	12	+3.33
Chepstow	0-1	-	-1.00	0-0	-	+0.00	0-1	-	-1.00	0-0	-	+0.00
Chester	11-86	13	-10.79	1-13	8	-7.50	5-22	23	+3.38	5-51	10	-6.67
Doncaster	7-185	4	-38.17	1-50	2	+51.00	5-55	9	-13.50	1-80	1	-75.67
Epsom	6-34	18	-4.13	1-3	33	+1.00	4-8	50	+8.88	1-23	4	-14.00
Goodwood	3-63	5	-45.00	0-13	-	-13.00	1-14	7	-5.50	2-36	6	-26.50
Hamilton	33-131	25	+39.48	7-39	18	+9.88	14-41	34	+27.67	12-51	24	+1.92
Haydock	18-146	12	+101.32	4-54	7	+55.11	8-39	21	+50.33	6-53	11	-4.13
Kempton (AW)	17-88	19	+3.87	6-29	21	+10.00	5-24	21	+8.58	6-35	17	-14.72
Leicester	8-58	14	-14.77	5-23	22	+12.25	3-24	13	-16.02	0-11	-	-11.00
Lingfield	0-3	-	-3.00	0-2	-	-2.00	0-1	-	-1.00	0-0	-	+0.00
Lingfield (AW)	21-136	15	-43.68	4-19	21	-2.75	7-44	16	-6.42	10-73	14	-34.51
Musselburgh	14-106	13	-41.92	7-26	27	-3.77	2-30	7	-21.00	5-50	10	-17.15
Newbury	0-34	-	-34.00	0-19	-	-19.00	0-4	-	-4.00	0-11	-	-11.00
Newcastle	18-126	14	-22.26	6-42	14	+3.17	10-43	23	+0.82	2-41	5	-26.25
Newmarket	3-42	7	-20.50	1-10	10	-1.00	0-17	-	-17.00	2-15	13	-2.50
Newmarket (J)	8-53	15	+10.33	1-8	13	-6.17	4-22	18	+16.50	3-23	13	+0.00
Nottingham	8-63	13	-18.02	3-26	12	-4.50	3-29	10	-12.75	2-8	25	-0.77
Pontefract	13-88	15	+41.08	6-36	17	+42.00	6-35	17	+6.58	1-17	6	-7.50
Redcar	12-98	12	-14.17	7-46	15	-9.67	4-37	11	-15.50	1-15	7	+11.00
Ripon	10-132	8	-75.54	3-37	8	-21.50	3-38	8	-27.29	4-57	7	-26.75
Salisbury	0-2	-	-2.00	0-1	-	-1.00	0-0	-	+0.00	0-1	-	-1.00
Sandown	0-9	-	-9.00	0-3	-	-3.00	0-3	-	-3.00	0-3	-	-3.00
Southwell (AW)	46-212	22	-9.90	9-40	23	-5.84	20-83	24	-4.32	17-89	19	+0.26
Thirsk	18-156	12	-19.18	5-44	11	-21.56	5-41	12	-9.13	8-71	11	+11.50
Warwick	4-22	18	+27.00	1-7	14	+6.00	3-11	27	+25.00	0-4	-	-4.00
Windsor	1-10	10	+0.00	0-5	-	-5.00	0-2	-	-2.00	1-3	33	+7.00
Wolves (AW)	49-333	15	-48.03	8-79	10	-13.83	26-124	21	-0.53	15-130	12	-33.67
Yarmouth	4-18	22	-2.22	2-7	29	-2.10	0-6	-	-6.00	2-5	40	+5.88
York	22-196	11	-24.04	15-72	21	+21.46	2-32	6	-7.50	5-92	5	-38.00

Ten-year summary

	Wins	Runs	%	Win prize-money	Total prize-money	£1
2013	94	781	12	£1,067,445.28	£1,588,817.31	-97.72
2012	95	789	12	£853,827.11	£1,228,983.17	+15.01
2011	133	797	17	£984,501.51	£1,326,031.93	+32.30
2010	107	813	13	£510,410.42	£865,913.67	-155.62
2009	96	867	11	£603,355.68	£1,024,522.80	-313.68
2008	108	889	12	£553,275.27	£955,575.07	-244.64
2007	107	932	11	£628,750.47	£1,111,861.68	-218.21
2006	95	827	11	£621,912.82	£1,314,626.82	-195.53
2005	82	643	13	£722,268.12	£1,030,981.10	-35.89
2004	67	489	14	£371,653.22	£640,902.62	+13.03

MORNING POST: 100-1 winner of a hugely valuable sales race at Doncaster

Top trainers by winners (Turf)

Won	Ran	%	Trainer	Won	Ran	%	Won	Ran	%
	All runs				First time out			Horses	
187	1130	17	Richard Hannon Snr	53	309	17	157	309	51
166	1176	14	Mark Johnston	35	253	14	121	253	48
147	1110	13	Richard Fahey	39	240	16	113	240	47
105	701	15	David O'Meara	24	152	16	76	152	50
88	408	22	William Haggas	28	128	22	70	128	55
80	430	19	Saeed bin Suroor	48	200	24	88	200	44
74	611	12	Kevin Ryan	10	140	7	60	140	43
72	511	14	Andrew Balding	15	153	10	71	153	46
69	355	19	John Gosden	26	157	17	78	157	50
68	326	21	Sir Michael Stoute	22	118	19	63	118	53
66	301	22	Roger Varian	22	123	18	64	123	52
60	739	8	Mick Channon	13	136	10	55	136	40
59	794	7	Tim Easterby	6	144	4	41	144	28
55	300	18	David Barron	13	70	19	43	70	61
53	439	12	Charles Hills	15	132	11	57	132	43
52	266	20	Luca Cumani	15	77	19	50	77	65
51	299	17	David Simcock	15	105	14	53	105	50
46	286	16	Ralph Beckett	17	103	17	50	103	49
45	376	12	Keith Dalgleish	6	76	8	33	76	43
43	383	11	Brian Ellison	12	104	12	42	104	40
39	345	11	Michael Dods	10	56	18	25	56	45
38	209	18	Charlie Appleby	22	131	17	46	131	35
38	419	9	David Nicholls	5	68	7	30	68	44
36	190	19	Roger Charlton	9	75	12	36	75	48
36	371	10	Michael Easterby	9	72	13	32	72	44
36	371	10	David Evans	13	94	14	48	94	51
35	256	14	Ed Dunlop	11	89	12	33	89	37
34	350	10	Jim Goldie	3	50	6	23	50	46
34	263	13	Tom Dascombe	10	81	12	34	81	42
33	270	12	Marco Botti	25	149	17	64	149	43
32	349	9	Michael Bell	6	108	6	35	108	32
31	159	19	James Tate	7	63	11	38	63	60
31	373	8	Ruth Carr	2	37	5	23	37	62
30	123	24	Sir Mark Prescott Bt	4	53	8	20	53	38
29	128	23	Lady Cecil	18	72	25	27	72	38
29	205	14	Mrs K Burke	8	66	12	28	66	42
29	258	11	Brian Meehan	6	75	8	25	75	33
29	156	19	Jeremy Noseda	7	63	11	37	63	59
29	195	15	Ian Williams	6	59	10	27	59	46
28	242	12	John Quinn	6	62	10	26	62	42
27	264	10	Clive Cox	9	80	11	27	80	34
27	150	18	Philip Kirby	4	43	9	18	43	42
26	130	20	James Fanshawe	10	54	19	23	54	43
23	181	13	William Muir	4	50	8	21	50	42
23	228	10	Tracy Waggott	2	26	8	15	26	58
22	147	15	Eric Alston	1	22	5	14	22	64
22	180	12	Alan Swinbank	7	56	13	19	56	34

Top trainers by prize-money (Turf)

Total prizemoney	Trainer	Win prizemoney	Wins	Class 1-3 Won	Ran	%	Class 4-6 Won	Ran	%
£4,233,900	**Richard Hannon Snr**	£2,923,741	187	65	481	14	122	649	19
£3,819,986	**A P O'Brien**	£2,700,650	13	13	79	16	0	1	—
£2,492,082	**Saeed bin Suroor**	£1,802,479	80	38	246	15	42	184	23
£2,406,327	**Mark Johnston**	£1,619,887	166	51	487	10	115	689	17
£2,344,899	**Richard Fahey**	£1,527,548	147	49	482	10	98	628	16
£1,817,076	**John Gosden**	£1,133,475	69	35	181	19	34	174	20
£1,775,610	**William Haggas**	£1,045,040	88	28	194	14	60	214	28
£1,612,949	**Sir Michael Stoute**	£1,112,280	68	29	158	18	39	168	23
£1,500,222	**Kevin Ryan**	£1,018,988	74	25	235	11	49	376	13
£1,200,157	**Andrew Balding**	£780,208	72	34	237	14	38	274	14
£1,182,139	**Roger Varian**	£796,347	66	27	128	21	39	173	23
£1,171,545	**Charles Hills**	£532,886	53	19	185	10	34	254	13
£1,073,759	**Roger Charlton**	£782,628	36	11	79	14	25	111	23
£1,032,967	**David O'Meara**	£693,826	105	29	275	11	76	426	18
£995,906	**J S Bolger**	£425,325	2	2	19	11	0	0	—
£982,807	**Ralph Beckett**	£545,621	46	14	98	14	32	188	17
£971,457	**Clive Cox**	£792,554	27	9	82	11	18	182	10
£937,366	**Luca Cumani**	£525,082	52	15	115	13	37	151	25
£836,319	**Charlie Appleby**	£587,527	38	21	99	21	17	110	15
£799,711	**James Fanshawe**	£502,037	26	7	38	18	19	92	21
£781,903	**Lady Cecil**	£581,316	29	11	50	22	18	78	23
£752,219	**Mick Channon**	£325,926	60	10	232	4	50	507	10
£748,955	**Tim Easterby**	£450,285	59	11	194	6	48	600	8
£744,559	**David Simcock**	£404,079	51	19	157	12	32	142	23
£708,819	**Brian Ellison**	£275,783	43	7	114	6	36	269	13
£696,811	**Edward Lynam**	£497,077	4	4	14	29	0	0	—
£656,610	**Marco Botti**	£345,702	33	12	116	10	21	154	14
£644,864	**Mrs K Burke**	£213,960	29	8	66	12	21	139	15
£641,305	**Ed Dunlop**	£325,943	35	14	112	13	21	144	15
£626,037	**David Barron**	£368,919	55	20	149	13	35	151	23
£624,137	**A Wohler**	£603,962	1	1	6	17	0	0	—
£484,296	**Michael Bell**	£191,300	32	6	110	5	26	239	11
£444,211	**Jim Goldie**	£210,353	34	6	77	8	28	273	10
£386,144	**Tom Dascombe**	£245,171	34	8	101	8	26	162	16
£381,614	**Brian Meehan**	£179,247	29	5	87	6	24	171	14
£381,531	**Robert Cowell**	£261,333	7	5	89	6	2	65	3
£370,456	**Clive Brittain**	£186,377	15	8	82	10	7	76	9
£365,465	**Michael Dods**	£208,258	39	7	75	9	32	270	12
£343,410	**David Wachman**	£77,375	1	1	10	10	0	0	—
£336,584	**Mme C Barande-Barbe**	£0	0	0	2	—	0	0	—
£331,009	**David Nicholls**	£168,632	38	4	117	3	34	302	11
£328,855	**Jeremy Noseda**	£197,364	29	7	61	11	22	95	23
£315,142	**Ian Williams**	£180,246	29	8	64	13	21	131	16
£311,256	**Henry Candy**	£133,300	20	5	56	9	15	115	13
£310,380	**Michael Easterby**	£181,165	36	4	85	5	32	286	11
£291,714	**M F De Kock**	£87,900	3	2	16	13	1	2	50
£277,356	**Bryan Smart**	£165,792	20	7	65	11	13	167	8

Top trainers by winners (AW)

	All runs			First time out			Horses		
Won	Ran	%	Trainer	Won	Ran	%	Won	Ran	%
80	509	16	**David Evans**	13	94	14	48	94	51
56	271	21	**Marco Botti**	25	149	17	64	149	43
50	381	13	**Mark Johnston**	35	253	14	121	253	48
48	282	17	**Richard Hannon Snr**	53	309	17	157	309	51
42	250	17	**Michael Appleby**	7	83	8	39	83	47
39	170	23	**John Gosden**	26	157	17	78	157	50
33	191	17	**David Simcock**	15	105	14	53	105	50
32	202	16	**Gary Moore**	9	86	10	36	86	42
31	139	22	**James Tate**	7	63	11	38	63	60
31	204	15	**David O'Meara**	24	152	16	76	152	50
29	188	15	**Jamie Osborne**	4	61	7	25	61	41
27	202	13	**Andrew Balding**	15	153	10	71	153	46
27	132	20	**Ralph Beckett**	17	103	17	50	103	49
27	246	11	**Ronald Harris**	3	61	5	26	61	43
26	93	28	**Saeed bin Suroor**	48	200	24	88	200	44
26	268	10	**Derek Shaw**	2	46	4	18	46	39
26	293	9	**Tony Carroll**	9	81	11	29	81	36
23	101	23	**Roger Varian**	22	123	18	64	123	52
23	220	10	**Alan McCabe**	7	63	11	18	63	29
22	95	23	**Charlie Appleby**	22	131	17	46	131	35
22	115	19	**Tom Dascombe**	10	81	12	34	81	42
22	86	26	**Jeremy Noseda**	7	63	11	37	63	59
21	95	22	**Stuart Williams**	4	51	8	21	51	41
21	183	11	**J R Jenkins**	2	51	4	21	51	41
21	138	15	**Chris Dwyer**	2	26	8	12	26	46
20	128	16	**Dean Ivory**	5	41	12	19	41	46
20	170	12	**Kevin Ryan**	10	140	7	60	140	43
19	95	20	**William Haggas**	28	128	22	70	128	55
19	127	15	**Brian Ellison**	12	104	12	42	104	40
19	72	26	**Sir Michael Stoute**	22	118	19	63	118	53
19	127	15	**Michael Bell**	6	108	6	35	108	32
19	84	23	**Daniel Mark Loughnane**	1	27	4	11	27	41
17	177	10	**Richard Fahey**	39	240	16	113	240	47
17	82	21	**Hans Adielsson**	3	17	18	8	17	47
17	67	25	**Luca Cumani**	15	77	19	50	77	65
17	84	20	**David Nicholls**	5	68	7	30	68	44
16	83	19	**Amanda Perrett**	3	45	7	22	45	49
15	136	11	**Alan Bailey**	0	37	—	16	37	43
15	126	12	**Mick Channon**	13	136	10	55	136	40
15	108	14	**Charles Hills**	15	132	11	57	132	43
15	63	24	**David Lanigan**	6	37	16	16	37	43
15	120	13	**Ian Williams**	6	59	10	27	59	46
15	235	6	**Richard Guest**	3	46	7	19	46	41
15	107	14	**Roy Bowring**	1	15	7	8	15	53
15	79	19	**J W Hills**	3	46	7	17	46	37
14	78	18	**James Fanshawe**	10	54	19	23	54	43
14	129	11	**James Given**	3	42	7	19	42	45

Top trainers by prize-money (AW)

Total prizemoney	Trainer	Win prizemoney	Wins	Class 1-3 Won	Class 1-3 Ran	Class 1-3 %	Class 4-6 Won	Class 4-6 Ran	Class 4-6 %
£420,151	Marco Botti	£296,895	56	11	52	21	45	219	21
£337,255	Mark Johnston	£206,742	50	7	42	17	43	339	13
£330,728	David Evans	£229,878	80	6	31	19	73	474	15
£298,564	Richard Hannon Snr	£213,979	48	6	37	16	42	245	17
£216,002	John Gosden	£130,440	39	1	22	5	38	148	26
£173,699	Saeed bin Suroor	£131,922	26	5	16	31	21	77	27
£158,416	Michael Appleby	£102,640	42	0	10	—	42	235	18
£156,585	Andrew Balding	£93,733	27	3	26	12	24	176	14
£150,158	Roger Varian	£124,893	23	2	10	20	21	91	23
£148,242	David Simcock	£90,711	33	0	26	—	33	165	20
£146,254	James Tate	£104,892	31	2	12	17	29	127	23
£134,965	Ralph Beckett	£99,392	27	3	13	23	24	119	20
£134,015	Charlie Appleby	£105,993	22	5	11	45	17	84	20
£131,423	Tom Dascombe	£91,308	22	3	13	23	19	102	19
£126,419	David O'Meara	£83,834	31	1	18	6	29	183	16
£120,457	William Haggas	£88,325	19	2	9	22	17	86	20
£115,258	Derek Shaw	£79,624	26	2	15	13	23	246	9
£114,883	Jamie Osborne	£79,866	29	1	11	9	27	176	15
£113,734	Alan McCabe	£72,836	23	1	22	5	22	195	11
£110,685	Richard Fahey	£61,279	17	2	32	6	15	145	10
£108,961	Alan Bailey	£81,022	15	3	11	27	12	124	10
£107,819	Jeremy Noseda	£86,930	22	1	4	25	21	82	26
£103,839	Stuart Williams	£79,659	21	4	15	27	16	74	22
£102,315	Gary Moore	£74,572	32	0	5	—	32	192	17
£97,031	William Knight	£67,943	12	2	14	14	10	76	13
£95,798	Dean Ivory	£74,988	20	2	4	50	18	123	15
£95,725	Ronald Harris	£62,558	27	0	11	—	27	229	12
£94,276	Tony Carroll	£54,928	26	0	4	—	21	257	8
£92,933	J R Jenkins	£55,389	21	1	6	17	20	174	11
£90,318	Ed Vaughan	£48,711	12	2	9	22	10	61	16
£88,595	Kevin Ryan	£48,457	20	0	18	—	20	151	13
£82,172	Hans Adielsson	£71,297	17	2	5	40	15	74	20
£81,020	George Baker	£65,676	13	1	2	50	12	87	14
£79,512	Chris Dwyer	£54,872	21	1	14	7	18	118	15
£77,602	Mick Channon	£43,424	15	0	9	—	15	117	13
£77,590	David Barron	£58,255	8	2	10	20	6	32	19
£77,152	Scott Dixon	£35,465	11	1	20	5	10	147	7
£76,179	Brian Ellison	£43,877	19	0	6	—	19	121	16
£75,680	Geoffrey Oldroyd	£68,942	7	5	9	56	2	39	5
£75,654	Amanda Perrett	£53,144	16	1	5	20	15	78	19
£74,878	Sir Michael Stoute	£55,441	19	0	7	—	19	65	29
£73,956	Michael Bell	£52,510	19	1	4	25	18	122	15
£73,403	Charles Hills	£51,358	15	1	6	17	14	102	14
£70,676	Luca Cumani	£55,392	17	0	5	—	17	62	27
£68,198	James Fanshawe	£50,802	14	2	9	22	12	69	17
£68,144	David Nicholls	£43,737	17	1	13	8	16	71	23
£67,897	J S Moore	£31,846	12	1	6	17	11	141	8

Top jockeys (Turf)

Won	Ran	%	Jockey	Best Trainer	Won	Ran
159	768	21	Richard Hughes	Richard Hannon Snr	127	530
136	699	19	Ryan Moore	Sir Michael Stoute	52	215
109	600	18	Silvestre De Sousa	Saeed bin Suroor	45	224
94	635	15	Paul Hanagan	Richard Fahey	20	164
94	718	13	Joe Fanning	Mark Johnston	93	639
85	795	11	Graham Lee	Jim Goldie	18	143
81	515	16	William Buick	John Gosden	54	265
80	463	17	Daniel Tudhope	David O'Meara	74	404
69	455	15	Neil Callan	James Tate	26	112
68	466	15	Andrea Atzeni	Roger Varian	33	158
66	450	15	Graham Gibbons	David Barron	38	183
65	469	14	James Doyle	Roger Charlton	21	130
64	409	16	Franny Norton	Mark Johnston	40	244
63	507	12	Paul Mulrennan	Michael Dods	12	87
61	456	13	Jamie Spencer	Kevin Ryan	12	48
61	537	11	Luke Morris	Sir Mark Prescott Bt	31	144
60	493	12	Tom Queally	Lady Cecil	18	88
60	461	13	Jim Crowley	Ralph Beckett	45	253
60	397	15	Dane O'Neill	Roger Varian	14	41
56	514	11	P J McDonald	Ann Duffield	17	132
55	272	20	Mickael Barzalona	Charlie Appleby	32	140
50	462	11	Martin Harley	Marco Botti	28	138
50	436	11	Robert Winston	Alan Swinbank	14	87
49	437	11	Tony Hamilton	Richard Fahey	49	408
48	429	11	Kieren Fallon	Luca Cumani	18	88
47	678	7	Tom Eaves	Keith Dalgleish	20	186
45	285	16	George Baker	Gary Moore	21	114
44	332	13	Jason Hart	Eric Alston	16	98
43	393	11	Adam Kirby	David Evans	30	140
43	348	12	Pat Dobbs	Richard Hannon Snr	30	198
40	289	14	Richard Kingscote	Tom Dascombe	40	235
37	314	12	David Probert	Andrew Balding	33	227
37	267	14	Seb Sanders	William Haggas	9	19
36	320	11	Frederik Tylicki	James Fanshawe	14	81
35	344	10	Martin Lane	David Simcock	14	115
33	374	9	Barry McHugh	Tracy Waggott	10	73
32	360	9	Liam Keniry	David Elsworth	12	58
32	289	11	Sean Levey	Richard Hannon Snr	23	191
32	358	9	Cathy Gannon	Jo Hughes	7	53
31	192	16	Oisin Murphy	Andrew Balding	12	41
31	347	9	David Allan	Tim Easterby	24	245
31	365	8	Phillip Makin	Kevin Ryan	12	128
30	228	13	Robert Havlin	John Gosden	35	134
29	253	11	Liam Jones	William Haggas	15	70
29	328	9	Steve Drowne	Charles Hills	8	85
29	284	10	Shane Kelly	Daniel Mark Loughnane	19	79
29	274	11	Connor Beasley	Michael Dods	17	120
28	266	11	Pat Cosgrave	George Baker	22	137

Top jockeys (AW)

Won	Ran	%	Jockey	Best Trainer	Won	Ran
125	629	20	**Adam Kirby**	David Evans	30	140
107	869	12	**Luke Morris**	Sir Mark Prescott Bt	31	144
77	449	17	**Jim Crowley**	Ralph Beckett	45	253
64	431	15	**George Baker**	Gary Moore	21	114
62	462	13	**Joe Fanning**	Mark Johnston	93	639
58	200	29	**Ryan Moore**	Sir Michael Stoute	52	215
53	326	16	**Martin Harley**	Marco Botti	28	138
52	349	15	**Andrea Atzeni**	Roger Varian	33	158
51	221	23	**Silvestre De Sousa**	Saeed bin Suroor	45	224
50	371	13	**Shane Kelly**	Daniel Mark Loughnane	19	79
49	242	20	**Richard Hughes**	Richard Hannon Snr	127	530
48	317	15	**Robert Winston**	Alan Swinbank	14	87
46	197	23	**Jamie Spencer**	Kevin Ryan	12	48
45	320	14	**David Probert**	Andrew Balding	33	227
42	303	14	**Graham Lee**	Jim Goldie	18	143
41	321	13	**Robert Tart**	Alan Bailey	8	49
40	258	16	**Seb Sanders**	William Haggas	9	19
39	463	8	**William Carson**	Philip McBride	10	69
37	204	18	**Neil Callan**	James Tate	26	112
37	263	14	**Hayley Turner**	Michael Bell	11	77
36	437	8	**Liam Keniry**	David Elsworth	12	58
35	143	24	**William Buick**	John Gosden	54	265
33	264	13	**Sean Levey**	Richard Hannon Snr	23	191
32	253	13	**Graham Gibbons**	David Barron	38	183
31	321	10	**Robert Havlin**	John Gosden	35	134
31	211	15	**Andrew Mullen**	Michael Appleby	40	295
30	385	8	**Jimmy Quinn**	Dean Ivory	6	27
29	318	9	**Tom Eaves**	Keith Dalgleish	20	186
28	234	12	**William Twiston-Davies**	Michael Bell	8	34
26	218	12	**Frederik Tylicki**	James Fanshawe	14	81
26	304	9	**Fergus Sweeney**	Jamie Osborne	15	150
25	197	13	**Richard Kingscote**	Tom Dascombe	40	235
25	113	22	**Thomas Brown**	Andrew Balding	14	68
22	254	9	**Martin Dwyer**	William Muir	17	130
22	246	9	**Martin Lane**	David Simcock	14	115
22	183	12	**Liam Jones**	William Haggas	15	70
20	146	14	**Ted Durcan**	David Lanigan	24	122
20	166	12	**John Fahy**	Eve Johnson Houghton	17	94
20	112	18	**Daniel Tudhope**	David O'Meara	74	404
19	86	22	**Mickael Barzalona**	Charlie Appleby	32	140
19	204	9	**Tom Queally**	Lady Cecil	18	88
17	133	13	**James Doyle**	Roger Charlton	21	130
17	169	10	**Ryan Tate**	Hans Adielsson	5	19
16	170	9	**Franny Norton**	Mark Johnston	40	244
16	118	14	**Dane O'Neill**	Roger Varian	14	41
16	217	7	**Chris Catlin**	Rae Guest	16	83
16	144	11	**Dale Swift**	Brian Ellison	17	127
15	169	9	**Philip Prince**	Richard Guest	5	84

Est. 1909
RACING & FOOTBALL OUTLOOK

Group 1 records

Year	Winner	Age (if appropriate)	Trainer	Jockey	SP	draw/ran

2,000 Guineas (1m) Newmarket

Year	Winner	Trainer	Jockey	SP	draw/ran
2004	Haafhd	B Hills	R Hills	11-2	11/14
2005	Footstepsinthesand	A O'Brien	K Fallon	13-2	3/19
2006	George Washington	A O'Brien	K Fallon	6-4f	9/14
2007	Cockney Rebel	G Huffer	O Peslier	25-1	8/24
2008	Henrythenavigator	A O'Brien	J Murtagh	11-1	6/15
2009	Sea The Stars	J Oxx	M Kinane	8-1	15/15
2010	Makfi	M Delzangles	C-P Lemaire	33-1	5/19
2011	Frankel	Sir H Cecil	T Queally	1-2f	1/13
2012	Camelot	A O'Brien	J O'Brien	15-8f	12/18
2013	Dawn Approach	J Bolger	K Manning	11-8f	6/13

THIS HAS increasingly become a specialist miler's race rather than a stepping stone to the Derby despite the recent success of Camelot and Sea The Stars – prior to the latter there had been a 20-year wait for a horse to do the double. Most winners had proven themselves at two, with 14 of the last 22 winners having won a Group race, including nine at the highest level. The Dewhurst tends to be a far better guide than the Racing Post Trophy, with Camelot the first to complete that double since High Top in 1973. Favourites had a desperate record until the last three winners hit back for punters. Haafhd, who had landed the Craven in 2004, and Frankel, who warmed up in the Greenham at Newbury, are the only winners to have come via a domestic trial since Mystiko in 1991 and in fact there have been just three British-trained winners in 12 years.

1,000 Guineas (1m) Newmarket

Year	Winner	Trainer	Jockey	SP	draw/ran
2004	Attraction	M Johnston	K Darley	11-2	9/16
2005	Virginia Waters	A O'Brien	K Fallon	12-1	20/20
2006	Speciosa	Mrs P Sly	M Fenton	10-1	11/13
2007	Finsceal Beo	J Bolger	K Manning	5-4f	14/21
2008	Natagora	P Bary	C Lemaire	11-4f	3/15
2009	Ghanaati	B Hills	R Hills	20-1	7/14
2010	Special Duty	C Head-Maarek	S Pasquier	9-2f	18/17
2011	Blue Bunting	M Al Zarooni	L Dettori	16-1	16/18
2012	Homecoming Queen	A O'Brien	R Moore	25-1	16/17
2013	Sky Lantern	R Hannon	R Hughes	9-1	7/15

COURSE FORM is the key factor in this race and is likely to become even more vital with the Fillies' Mile run at Newmarket for the first time in 2011. The Rockfel is the key trial, throwing up five of the last 12 winners with Finsceal Beo, Lahan and Speciosa all doing the double, while Special Duty, Natagora, Attraction and Russian Rhythm had been first or second in the Cheveley Park, Speciosa won the Nell Gwyn, in which Sky Lantern was second, and Blue Bunting won a Listed race over course and distance the previous October. Punters have hit back in recent years with three of the last seven favourites obliging, but still ten of the last 16 winners have been priced in double figures. French fillies have a fair record and all six since 1983 had Group 1 form as a juvenile.

Lockinge Stakes (1m) Newbury

2004	**Russian Rhythm**	4	Sir M Stoute	K Fallon	3-1f	3/15
2005	**Rakti**	6	M Jarvis	P Robinson	7-4f	5/8
2006	**Soviet Song**	6	J Fanshawe	J Spencer	7-2f	10/10
2007	**Red Evie**	4	M Bell	J Spencer	8-1	7/8
2008	**Creachadoir**	4	S bin Suroor	L Dettori	3-1f	7/11
2009	**Virtual**	4	J Gosden	J Fortune	6-1	10/11
2010	**Paco Boy**	5	R Hannon	R Hughes	8-11f	3/9
2011	**Canford Cliffs**	4	R Hannon	R Hughes	4-5f	4/7
2012	**Frankel**	4	Sir H Cecil	T Queally	2-7f	6/6
2013	**Farhh**	5	S bin Suroor	S de Sousa	10-3	5/12

IT'S ESSENTIAL to look for horses who have already shown themselves to be Group 1 milers as 15 of the last 19 winners had won at the top level over the trip and three of the exceptions had been second. Consequently it has been straightforward to identify the winner as eight of the last 11 favourites have obliged and two of the exceptions were second in the market. Four-year-olds have by far the strongest record, accounting for 18 of the last 27 winners, and fillies can also do well with three winners in the last ten years. The Sandown Mile is a popular prep race yet Paco Boy is the only horse to ever do the double with 19 others failing.

Coronation Cup (1m4f) Epsom

2004	**Warrsan**	6	C Brittain	D Holland	7-1	5/11
2005	**Yeats**	4	A O'Brien	K Fallon	5-1	9/7
2006	**Shirocco**	5	A Fabre	C Soumillon	8-11f	5/6
2007	**Scorpion**	5	A O'Brien	M Kinane	8-1	2/7
2008	**Soldier Of Fortune**	4	A O'Brien	J Murtagh	9-4	7/11
2009	**Ask**	6	Sir M Stoute	R Moore	5-1	8/8
2010	**Fame And Glory**	4	A O'Brien	J Murtagh	5-6f	8/9
2011	**St Nicholas Abbey**	4	A O'Brien	R Moore	Evsf	1/5
2012	**St Nicholas Abbey**	5	A O'Brien	J O'Brien	8-11f	4/6
2013	**St Nicholas Abbey**	6	A O'Brien	J O'Brien	3-10f	3/5

AIDAN O'BRIEN has a sensational record in this race with seven of the last nine winners, led by St Nicholas Abbey's hat-trick. That horse was favourite on every occasion, as was 2010 winner Fame And Glory, which bucks the more general trend of fancied horses struggling as there had been just two winning favourites in the previous 12 years, which was a desperate record given the small size of the field. The combination of a false pace and the tricky course could have been responsible for some of the funny results and punters have been too easily seduced by youngsters, with just four of the last 11 runnings being won by four-year-olds.

The Oaks (1m4f) Epsom

2004	**Ouija Board**	E Dunlop	K Fallon	7-2	3/7
2005	**Eswarah**	M Jarvis	R Hills	11-4jf	2/12
2006	**Alexandrova**	A O'Brien	K Fallon	9-4f	1/10
2007	**Light Shift**	H Cecil	T Durcan	13-2	11/14
2008	**Look Here**	R Beckett	S Sanders	33-1	13/16
2009	**Sariska**	M Bell	J Spencer	9-4f	5/10
2010	**Snow Fairy**	E Dunlop	R Moore	9-1	15/15
2011	**Dancing Rain**	W Haggas	J Murtagh	20-1	7/13
2012	**Was**	A O'Brien	S Heffernan	20-1	10/12
2013	**Talent**	R Beckett	R Hughes	20-1	3/11

GUARANTEED STAMINA is more important than proven top-class form for this race, which can make things tricky for punters with four of the last six winners priced at least 20-1. All of the last seven winners had never been tried in a Group 1, yet five of them had triumphed over at least 1m2f and you have to go back to Casual Look in 2003 to find the last winner who hadn't raced beyond a mile. It therefore follows that the 1,000 Guineas has become a weaker guide with none of the four fillies to run in the race having placed at Epsom since Kazzia's 2002 double finishing better than fourth, although none of the

ST NICHOLAS ABBEY: three-time winner of the Coronation Cup at Epsom

DAWN APPROACH: the third 2,000 Guineas hero to win at Ascot in six years

trials stands above any other and too much is often made of the Musidora winner with Sariska the only one to double up since Reams Of Verse in 1997.

The Derby (1m4f) Epsom

2004	**North Light**	Sir M Stoute	K Fallon	7-2jf	6/14
2005	**Motivator**	M Bell	J Murtagh	3-1f	5/13
2006	**Sir Percy**	M Tregoning	M Dwyer	6-1	10/18
2007	**Authorized**	P Chapple-Hyam	L Dettori	5-4f	14/17
2008	**New Approach**	J Bolger	K Manning	5-1	3/16
2009	**Sea The Stars**	J Oxx	M Kinane	11-4	4/12
2010	**Workforce**	Sir M Stoute	R Moore	6-1	8/12
2011	**Pour Moi**	A Fabre	M Barzalona	4-1	7/13
2012	**Camelot**	A O'Brien	J O'Brien	8-13f	5/9
2013	**Ruler Of The World**	A O'Brien	R Moore	7-1	10/12

MANY HIGH-CLASS colts are beaten here due to lack of stamina and it's important to have a top-class staying sire (nine of the last 11 successful sires had a stamina index of at least 1m1f) plus more stamina on the dam's side. Camelot and Sea The Stars followed up 2,000 Guineas victories in the last five years, but that followed a 20-year gap and Dawn Approach's comprehensive defeat last year was a reminder that it's still wiser to follow one of the recognised trials. That was the route taken by 12 of the last 17 winners with four Dante winners (Benny The Dip, North Light, Motivator and Authorized) and a runner-up (Workforce), three Leopardstown winners (Sinndar, Galileo and High Chaparral), three Chester winners (Oath, Kris Kin and Ruler Of The World) and one Lingfield winner (High-Rise). This is a race for fancied runners from the first four in the betting – 20-1 hero High-Rise in 1998 is the biggest-priced winner in 38 years.

Queen Anne Stakes (1m) Royal Ascot

2004	**Refuse To Bend**	4	S bin Suroor	L Dettori	12-1	16/16
2005	**Valixir**	4	A Fabre	C Soumillon	4-1	1/10*
2006	**Ad Valorem**	4	A O'Brien	K Fallon	13-2	6/7
2007	**Ramonti**	5	S bin Suroor	L Dettori	5-1	7/8
2008	**Haradasun**	5	A O'Brien	J Murtagh	5-1	2/11
2009	**Paco Boy**	4	R Hannon	R Hughes	10-3	7/9
2010	**Goldikova**	5	F Head	O Peslier	11-8f	10/10
2011	**Canford Cliffs**	4	R Hannon	R Hughes	11-8	6/7
2012	**Frankel**	4	Sir H Cecil	T Queally	1-10f	8/11
2013	**Declaration Of War**	4	A O'Brien	J O'Brien	15-2	6/13

*Note – all Royal Ascot races were run at York in 2005

FOUR-YEAR-OLDS once considered Classic contenders fit the bill and this age group has taken 20 of the last 25 runnings. No horse older than five has triumphed since 1976 with Goldikova among some top-class ones to fail when defending her crown in 2010, having become the only female winner in 40 years when successful the year before. Six of the last seven winners ran in the Lockinge at Newbury, which is obviously the key trial, though Canford Cliffs and Frankel are the only horses to have won both races since Medicean in 2001.

St James's Palace Stakes (1m) Royal Ascot

2004	**Azamour**	J Oxx	M Kinane	9-2	11/11
2005	**Shamardal**	S bin Suroor	K McEvoy	7-4f	2/8*
2006	**Araafa**	J Noseda	A Munro	2-1f	10/11
2007	**Excellent Art**	A O'Brien	J Spencer	8-1	8/8
2008	**Henrythenavigator**	A O'Brien	J Murtagh	4-7f	3/8
2009	**Mastercraftsman**	A O'Brien	J Murtagh	5-6f	3/10
2010	**Canford Cliffs**	R Hannon	R Hughes	11-4j	4/9
2011	**Frankel**	Sir H Cecil	T Queally	3-10f	5/9
2012	**Most Improved**	B Meehan	K Fallon	9-1	15/16
2013	**Dawn Approach**	J Bolger	K Manning	5-4f	5/9

GUINEAS FORM holds the key to this prize and seven of the last nine winners had come out on top in one of the Classics. The Curragh tends to be the best guide as four Irish 2,000 Guineas winners have followed up in that time compared to three from Newmarket and one from Longchamp (Henrythenavigator had won at Newmarket and the Curragh). One of the excepti ons, Excellent Art, had been the moral winner of the French Guineas so only 2012 victor Most Improved skipped the Classics altogether. Shavian in 1990 was the last winner not to have run previously in a Group 1.

Prince Of Wales's Stakes (1m2f) Royal Ascot

2004	**Rakti**	5	M Jarvis	P Robinson	3-1	1/10
2005	**Azamour**	4	J Oxx	M Kinane	11-8f	3/8*
2006	**Ouija Board**	5	E Dunlop	O Peslier	8-1	3/7
2007	**Manduro**	5	A Fabre	S Pasquier	15-8f	3/6
2008	**Duke Of Marmalade**	4	A O'Brien	J Murtagh	Evsf	1/12

2009	Vision D'Etat	4	E Libaud	O Peslier	4-1	2/8
2010	Byword	4	A Fabre	M Guyon	5-2f	5/12
2011	Rewilding	4	M Al Zarooni	L Dettori	17-2	6/7
2012	So You Think	6	A O'Brien	J O'Brien	4-5f	7/11
2013	Al Kazeem	5	R Charlton	J Doyle	11-4	9/11

A RACE that has altered hugely since gaining Group 1 status in 2000, when Dubai Millennium provided one of the outstanding moments in Royal Ascot history. The race now attracts a field of international quality and nine of the last 14 winners had one of their previous two starts outside Britain whereas traditional trials like the Brigadier Gerard Stakes and the Gordon Richards Stakes tend to lack sufficient quality, although Al Kazeem won the latter last year before becoming the fourth Tattersalls Gold Cup winner to follow up out of the last six to have tried. Thirteen of the last 14 winners had already triumphed at Group 1 level and ten of those over the big-race trip of 1m2f.

Gold Cup (2m4f) Royal Ascot

2004	Papineau	4	S bin Suroor	L Dettori	5-1	10/13
2005	Westerner	6	E Lellouche	O Peslier	7-4f	4/17*
2006	Yeats	5	A O'Brien	K Fallon	7-1	5/12
2007	Yeats	6	A O'Brien	M Kinane	8-13f	13/14
2008	Yeats	7	A O'Brien	J Murtagh	11-8f	7/10
2009	Yeats	8	A O'Brien	J Murtagh	6-4f	4/9
2010	Rite Of Passage	6	D Weld	P Smullen	20-1	1/12
2011	Fame And Glory	5	A O'Brien	J Spencer	11-8f	3/15
2012	Colour Vision	4	S Bin Suroor	L Dettori	6-1	5/9
2013	Estimate	4	Sir M Stoute	R Moore	7-2f	5/14

THREE-QUARTERS of a mile longer than any other British Group 1, this race understandably attracts plenty of real specialists, with Royal Rebel, Kayf Tara, Drum Taps and Sadeem all dual winners since 1988 before Yeats became the first ever four-time winner in 2009. His trainer Aidan O'Brien also won with Fame And Glory in 2011 and their victories underline the fact that any winner older than four has to have proved themselves at the top level already as the last eight had previously won a Group 1. Twelve of the last 14 winners had been successful over at least 2m and the best of the traditional trials is Sandown's Henry II Stakes, the route taken by eight of the 13 winners prior to Yeats's reign, both placed horses in 2009 and the runner-up in 2012.

Coronation Stakes (1m) Royal Ascot

2004	Attraction		M Johnston	K Darley	6-4f	2/11
2005	Maids Causeway		B Hills	M Hills	9-2	9/10*
2006	Nannina		J Gosden	J Fortune	6-1jf	3/15
2007	Indian Ink		R Hannon	R Hughes	8-1	12/13
2008	Lush Lashes		J Bolger	K Manning	5-1	9/11
2009	Ghanaati		B Hills	R Hills	2-1f	5/10
2010	Lillie Langtry		A O'Brien	J Murtagh	7-2f	3/13
2011	Immortal Verse		R Collet	G Mosse	8-1	11/12
2012	Fallen For You		J Gosden	W Buick	12-1	11/10
2013	Sky Lantern		R Hannon	R Hughes	9-2jf	16/17

A CHAMPIONSHIP race for three-year-old fillies. The 1,000 Guineas at Newmarket is much the best guide as four of the last 11 winners – Sky Lantern, Ghanaati, Attraction

YEATS: four Gold Cup wins show the race's propensity for specialists

and Russian Rhythm – had also come out on top on the Rowley Mile and three others achieved a top-six finish there. It's generally best to have been off the track since then, though, as just two of the last 21 winners ran in the Newmarket Classic and the Irish 1,000 Guineas at the Curragh, which often counts against many in the field. Equally any horse who has been stepped up in trip can be opposed as Lush Lashes is the only winner in the last 22 years to have raced over further.

Diamond Jubilee Stakes (6f) Royal Ascot

2004	**Fayr Jag**	4	T Easterby	W Supple	12-1	6/14
2005	**Cape of Good Hope**	7	D Oughton	M Kinane	6-1	2/15*
2006	**Les Arcs**	6	T Pitt	J Egan	33-1	15/18
2007	**Soldier's Tale**	6	J Noseda	J Murtagh	9-1	11/21
2008	**Kingsgate Native**	3	J Best	S Sanders	33-1	15/17
2009	**Art Connoisseur**	3	M Bell	T Queally	20-1	11/14
2010	**Starspangledbanner**	4	A O'Brien	J Murtagh	13-2j	21/24
2011	**Society Rock**	4	J Fanshawe	P Cosgrave	25-1	3/16
2012	**Black Caviar**	5	P Moody	L Nolen	1-6f	15/14
2013	**Lethal Force**	4	C Cox	A Kirby	11-1	15/18

A RACE whose profile has been steadily on the rise and reached fever pitch with its inauguration into the Global Sprint Challenge alongside the King's Stand Stakes, attracting the best sprinters from around the world, most notably the legendary Black Caviar in 2012. Its essence hasn't changed, though, as Black Caviar is the only winner trained outside Britain and Ireland since Cape Of Good Hope in 2005 and in tht time several fancied foreign raiders – Takeover Target (twice), J J The Jet Plane, Sacred Kingdom and Star Witness – have been beaten at 4-1 or shorter whereas course form remains critical with nine of the last 14 winners having a previous top-four finish at Royal Ascot. The race throws up more than its share of shocks, with four winners priced 20-1 or bigger in the last seven years. Two of those are among a host of unfancied three-year-olds to run well from very few representatives including Restiadargent (third at 40-1 last year), Society Rock (second at 50-1 in 2010 prior to his win the following year), Balthazaar's Gift (second at 50-1 in 2006), Baron's Pit (third at 50-1 in 2004) and Indian Country (fourth at 50-1 in 2003).

Coral-Eclipse (1m2f) Sandown

2004	Refuse To Bend	4	S bin Suroor	L Dettori	15-2	4/12
2005	Oratorio	3	A O'Brien	K Fallon	12-1	7/7
2006	David Junior	4	B Meehan	J Spencer	9-4	8/9
2007	Notnowcato	5	Sir M Stoute	R Moore	7-1	8/8
2008	Mount Nelson	4	A O'Brien	J Murtagh	7-2	8/8
2009	Sea The Stars	3	J Oxx	M Kinane	4-7f	6/10
2010	Twice Over	5	H Cecil	T Queally	13-8f	1/5
2011	So You Think	5	A O'Brien	S Heffernan	4-6f	3/5
2012	Nathaniel	4	J Gosden	W Buick	7-2	4/9
2013	Al Kazeem	5	R Charlton	J Doyle	15-8f	2/7

TRADITIONALLY THE first clash of the generations, but in recent times it has suffered from a lack of three-year-old representation. The great Sea The Stars won for the Classic generation in 2009, but the previous four Derby winners to take their chance – Authorized, Motivator, Benny The Dip and Erhaab – were all beaten, which may have put off connections of the top three-year-olds. That said, three-year-old winners tend to be milers stepping up in trip anyway as the last ten had all run in a Guineas. Fillies are to be avoided – Pebbles, in 1985, is the only filly to succeed since the 19th century, since when Bosra Sham and Ouija Board were beaten favourites. Royal Ascot form is the key, particularly the Prince of Wales's Stakes, although Al Kazeem was the first to do the double since Mtoto 26 years earlier with many horses beaten at Ascot, most recently So You Think, Twice Over and David Junior, improving on that form.

July Cup (6f) Newmarket

2004	Frizzante	5	J Fanshawe	J Murtagh	14-1	3/20
2005	Pastoral Pursuits	4	H Morrison	J Egan	22-1	10/19
2006	Les Arcs	6	T Pitt	J Egan	10-1	1/15
2007	Sakhee's Secret	3	H Morrison	S Drowne	9-2	3/18
2008	Marchand d'Or	5	F Head	D Bonilla	5-2f	5/13
2009	Fleeting Spirit	4	J Noseda	T Queally	12-1	5/13
2010	Starspangledbanner	4	A O'Brien	J Murtagh	2-1f	4/14
2011	Dream Ahead	3	D Simcock	H Turner	7-1	2/16
2012	Mayson	4	R Fahey	P Hanagan	20-1	11/12
2013	Lethal Force	4	C Cox	A Kirby	9-2	4/11

THREE OF the last eight winners were following up victories in the Diamond Jubilee Stakes over the same trip at Royal Ascot, but surprisingly it pays to ignore Group 1 form in other races as eight of the last 13 winners were scoring for the first time at the top level. This is a race in which stars are often born with 38 of the 46 winners being aged three or four, including each of the last five. Often that's because horses are dropping into sprints having been tried over further as stamina is an important asset on this stiff uphill finish, as greats like Ajdal and Soviet Song showed many years ago with Dream Ahead the latest to have had his previous run over a mile.

King George VI and Queen Elizabeth Stakes (1m4f) Ascot

2004	**Doyen**	4	S bin Suroor	L Dettori	11-10f	7/11
2005	**Azamour**	4	J Oxx	M Kinane	5-2f	12/12*
2006	**Hurricane Run**	4	A Fabre	C Soumillon	5-6f	3/6
2007	**Dylan Thomas**	4	A O'Brien	J Murtagh	5-4f	3/7
2008	**Duke Of Marmalade**	4	A O'Brien	J Murtagh	4-6f	5/8
2009	**Conduit**	4	Sir M Stoute	R Moore	13-8f	8/9
2010	**Harbinger**	4	Sir M Stoute	O Peslier	4-1	1/6
2011	**Nathaniel**	3	J Gosden	W Buick	11-2	3/5
2012	**Danedream**	4	P Schiergen	A Starke	9-1	4/10
2013	**Novellist**	4	A Wohler	J Murtagh	13-2	3/8

*Run at Newbury

THIS RACE has suffered from a lack of three-year-old representation in recent years, with only Nathaniel, Alamshar and Galileo successful for the Classic generation since the mighty Lammtarra in 1995. However, it still takes a top-class older horse to win, because since Belmez in 1990 just three winners hadn't previously landed a Group 1 and just four hadn't been first or second in a Group 1 at the trip. The Coronation Cup is a poor guide, though, with only Opera House and Daylami doing the double in the last 40 years.

Sussex Stakes (1m) Goodwood

2004	**Soviet Song**	5	J Fanshawe	J Murtagh	3-1	7/11
2005	**Proclamation**	3	J Noseda	M Kinane	3-1	6/12
2006	**Court Masterpiece**	6	E Dunlop	E Dunlop	15-2	3/7
2007	**Ramonti**	5	Sir M Stoute	L Dettori	9-2	1/8
2008	**Henrythenavigator**	3	A O'Brien	J Murtagh	4-11f	4/6
2009	**Rip Van Winkle**	3	A O'Brien	J Murtagh	6-4f	7/8
2010	**Canford Cliffs**	3	R Hannon	R Hughes	4-6f	7/7
2011	**Frankel**	3	Sir H Cecil	T Queally	8-13f	3/4
2012	**Frankel**	4	Sir H Cecil	T Queally	1-20f	3/4
2013	**Toronado**	3	R Hannon	R Hughes	11-4	7/7

THIS IS a great race for glamorous three-year-olds as that age group has provided 27 of the 39 winners since it was opened to all ages in 1975. Seven of the last ten triumphant three-year-olds were favourites and nine of the last 11 had been first or second in the St James's Palace Stakes, which is the key trial. Six of the last eight successful older horses had contested the Queen Anne Stakes, with placed horses doing as well as the winner.

Nassau Stakes (1m1f192yds) Goodwood

2004	**Favourable Terms**	4	Sir M Stoute	K Fallon	11-2	5/6
2005	**Alexander Goldrun**	4	J Bolger	K Manning	13-8f	3/11
2006	**Ouija Board**	5	E Dunlop	L Dettori	Evensf	1/7
2007	**Peeping Fawn**	3	A O'Brien	J Murtagh	2-1f	5/8
2008	**Halfway To Heaven**	3	A O'Brien	J Murtagh	5-1	6/9
2009	**Midday**	3	H Cecil	T Queally	11-2	10/10
2010	**Midday**	4	H Cecil	T Queally	15-8f	6/7
2011	**Midday**	5	Sir H Cecil	T Queally	6-4f	6/6
2012	**The Fugue**	3	J Gosden	R Hughes	11-4	7/8
2013	**Winsili**	3	J Gosden	W Buick	20-1	15/14

DESPITE WINSILI'S 20-1 win last year, this is a fantastic race for punters as the previous 19 winners had all emerged from the top three in the market including 12 favourites. The key is to side with a top-class three-year-old as the Classic generation have provided 30 of the 39 winners since the race was opened to older fillies in 1975, despite Midday's best efforts in racking up a hat-trick. Preferably they should be dropping down in trip rather than stepping up as The Fugue, Midday and Peeping Fawn all followed placed efforts in the Oaks and Winsili had her previous outing in the Ribblesdale, whereas Halfway To Heaven was the last winner to prepare over a mile in 2008.

Juddmonte International Stakes (1m2f85yds) York

Year	Horse	Age	Trainer	Jockey	SP	
2004	**Sulamani**	5	S bin Suroor	L Dettori	3-1	9/9
2005	**Electrocutionist**	4	V Valiani	M Kinane	9-2	5/7
2006	**Notnowcato**	4	Sir M Stoute	R Moore	8-1	5/7
2007	**Authorized**	3	P Chapple-Hyam	L Dettori	6-4f	1/7
2008	**Duke Of Marmalade**	4	A O'Brien	J Murtagh	4-6f	4/9*
2009	**Sea The Stars**	3	J Oxx	M Kinane	1-4f	3/4
2010	**Rip Van Winkle**	4	A O'Brien	J Murtagh	7-4f	7/9
2011	**Twice Over**	6	Sir H Cecil	I Mongan	11-2	4/5
2012	**Frankel**	4	Sir H Cecil	T Queally	1-10f	7/9
2013	**Declaration Of War**	4	A O'Brien	J O'Brien	7-1	2/6

*Note – this race and following two York races all run at Newmarket in 2008

FAMOUS FOR its many upsets since Brigadier Gerard suffered his only defeat to Roberto in 1972, the race has turned in punters' favour in recent times with no winner

JWALA: yet another big-priced Nunthorpe winner when successful at 40-1

returned bigger than 8-1 since Ezzoud in 1993 and five of the last seven favourites winning. Older horses have dominated the three-year-olds with just five younger horses triumphing since 1984, all of whom were recent Group 1 winners. The key trial is the Coral-Eclipse, which has provided nine of the last 17 winners, including six who did the double.

Yorkshire Oaks (1m3f195yds) York

2004	Quiff	3	Sir M Stoute	K Fallon	7-2	3/8
2005	Punctilious	4	S bin Suroor	K McEvoy	13-2	5/11
2006	Alexandrova	3	A O'Brien	M Kinane	4-9f	4/6
2007	Peeping Fawn	3	A O'Brien	J Murtagh	4-9f	8/8
2008	Lush Lashes	3	J Bolger	K Manning	Evsf	2/6*
2009	Dar Re Mi	4	J Gosden	J Fortune	11-2	4/6
2010	Midday	4	H Cecil	T Queally	11-4	6/8
2011	Blue Bunting	3	M Al Zarooni	L Dettori	11-4f	6/8
2012	Shareta	4	A de Royer-Dupre	C Lemaire	2-1	7/6
2013	The Fugue	4	J Gosden	W Buick	2-1f	6/7

ALWAYS A top-class race, this has been won by the Classic generation nine times in the last 15 years, although older horses have a superior strike-rate with fewer representatives. The last three Oaks heroines to run – Was, Snow Fairy and Sariska – were all beaten, the latter pair when favourite, and the last Epsom winner to follow up, Alexandrova, had significantly won the Irish Oaks in between because that has been a better guide. The five-year-old Super Tassa was the ultimate trend-buster in 2001 – the first Italian winner in Britain for 41 years and consequently sent off at 25-1.

Nunthorpe Stakes (5f) York

2004	Bahamian Pirate	9	D Nicholls	S Sanders	16-1	5/12
2005	La Cucaracha	4	B Hills	M Hills	7-1	8/16
2006	Reverence	5	E Ahern	K Darley	5-1	6/14
2007	Kingsgate Native	2	J Best	J Quinn	12-1	13/16
2008	Borderlescott	6	R Bastiman	P Cosgrave	12-1	12/14
2009	Borderlescott	7	R Bastiman	N Callan	9-1	2/16
2010	Sole Power	3	E Lynam	W Lordan	100-1	11/12
2011	Margot Did	3	M Bell	H Turner	20-1	11/15
2012	Ortensia	7	P Messara	W Buick	7-2jf	8/19
2013	Jwala	4	R Cowell	S Drowne	40-1	8/17

THIS HAS become a real race for upsets, none bigger than Sole Power at 100-1 in 2010, and there have also been 20-1 and 40-1 winners in the last three years. The main reason is that the race is rarely won by a proven top-level sprinter, with eight of the last 12 winners never having previously landed a Group race, let alone a Group 1 race. It's therefore little wonder that progressive younger horses hold sway, although all five winners older than five since 1945 have come in the last 17 years.

Sprint Cup (6f) Haydock

2004	Tante Rose	4	R Charlton	R Hughes	10-1	14/19
2005	Goodricke	3	D Loder	J Spencer	14-1	4/17
2006	Reverence	5	E Alston	K Darley	5-1	6/14
2007	Red Clubs	4	B Hills	M Hills	33-1	4/18
2008	African Rose	3	Mme C Head	S Pasquier	7-2f	12/15

2009	**Regal Parade**	5	D Nicholls	A Nicholls	14-1	13/14
2010	**Markab**	7	H Candy	P Cosgrave	12-1	14/13
2011	**Dream Ahead**	3	D Simcock	W Buick	4-1f	9/16
2012	**Society Rock**	5	J Fanshawe	K Fallon	10-1	3/13
2013	**Gordon Lord Byron**	5	T Hogan	J Murtagh	7-2	2/13

THIS CAN often be run on ground with plenty of give, so there have been a string of upsets as midsummer form proves misleading, with eight of the last 12 winners returned in double figures including 33-1 Red Clubs in 2007. Dream Ahead was the first July Cup winner to follow up at Haydock since Ajdal in 1987, with Lethal Force, Starspangledbanner and Fleeting Spirit the latest to be beaten favourites in the last five years, and he was only the second winning jolly since Godolphin hotpot Diktat in 1999.

St Leger (1m6f127yds) Doncaster

2004	**Rule Of Law**	S bin Suroor	K McEvoy	3-1f	9/9
2005	**Scorpion**	A O'Brien	L Dettori	10-11f	2/6
2006	**Sixties Icon**	J Noseda	L Dettori	11-8f	11/11*
2007	**Lucarno**	J Gosden	J Fortune	11-8f	11/11
2008	**Conduit**	Sir M Stoute	L Dettori	8-1	5/14
2009	**Mastery**	S bin Suroor	T Durcan	14-1	7/8
2010	**Arctic Cosmos**	J Gosden	W Buick	12-1	8/10
2011	**Masked Marvel**	J Gosden	W Buick	15-2	3/9
2012	**Encke**	M Al Zarooni	M Barzalona	25-1	1/9
2013	**Leading Light**	A O'Brien	J O'Brien	7-2f	7/11

Run at York

THIS HAS rather suffered in recent years with class horses being kept to shorter trips, and with good reason if Camelot's shock defeat in 2012 is any guide. Only three of the last 17 winners came via the traditional route of stepping up on strong Derby form – Silver Patriarch and Rule Of Law were second at Epsom, and Lucarno was third – although ten of the last 14 winners had run in a European Derby. The key race has been the Great Voltigeur at York, with Encke in 2012 becoming the eighth winner to use that as a prep since 1999. Like several others he was actually beaten there, but Bollin Eric led a repeat of the York 1-2-3 in 2002 and Lucarno and Rule Of Law won both races.

Prix de l'Arc de Triomphe (1m4f) Longchamp

2004	**Bago**	3	J Pease	T Gillet	10-1	5/20
2005	**Hurricane Run**	3	A Fabre	K Fallon	11-4	6/15
2006	**Rail Link**	3	A Fabre	S Pasquier	8-1	4/8
2007	**Dylan Thomas**	4	A O'Brien	K Fallon	11-2	6/12
2008	**Zarkava**	3	A de Royer-Dupre	C Soumillon	13-8f	1/16
2009	**Sea The Stars**	3	J Oxx	M Kinane	4-6f	6/19
2010	**Workforce**	3	Sir M Stoute	R Moore	6-1	8/19
2011	**Danedream**	3	P Schiergen	A Starke	20-1	2/16
2012	**Solemia**	4	C Laffon-Parias	O Peslier	33-1	6/18
2013	**Treve**	3	C Head-Maarek	T Jarnet	9-2	15/17

THIS RACE has restored its status as the premier middle-distance championship of Europe, with top-class 1m4f horses now trained specifically for the race from the summer. They also come from all over the world to run in it, with Japan producing three of the last four runners-up and Danedream winning for Germany. Home-trained horses are still holding their own, though the victories of Solemia and Treve followed a three-year blank, but British-trained horses are really struggling with Workforce their only winner since Marienbard in 2002. Three-year-olds tend to dominate, accounting for 18 of the last 26 winners, during which time the Prix Niel (ten of the last 20 winners) has been the key trial, although the sudden emergence of fillies, who have accounted for three of the last six winners after Zarkava was the first since Urban Sea in 1993, has elevated the Prix Vermeille as all three came via that race.

Queen Elizabeth II Stakes (1m) Ascot

2004	**Rakti**	5	M Jarvis	P Robinson	9-2	1/11
2005	**Starcraft**	3	L Cumani	C Lemaire	7-2	5/6
2006	**George Washington**	3	A O'Brien	K Fallon	13-8f	2/8
2007	**Ramonti**	5	S bin Suroor	L Dettori	5-1	1/7
2008	**Raven's Pass**	3	J Gosden	J Fortune	3-1	7/7
2009	**Rip Van Winkle**	3	A O'Brien	J Murtagh	8-13f	4/4
2010	**Poet's Voice**	3	S Bin Suroor	L Dettori	9-2	7/8
2011	**Frankel**	3	Sir H Cecil	T Queally	4-11f	2/8
2012	**Excelebration**	4	A O'Brien	J O'Brien	10-11f	6/8
2013	**Olympic Glory**	3	R Hannon	R Hughes	11-2	7/12

KNOWN AS the mile championship of Europe, and one in which the Classic generation has held sway with 20 of the last 29 winners. That has made the St James's Palace Stakes the key trial as seven of the last 13 winning three-year-olds ran there, although Frankel was the first to do the double since Bahri in 1995, while Frankel and George Washington followed up 2,000 Guineas victories. Nine of the last 11 winners had already won a Group 1 and the last five older winners all contested a Group 1 at Royal Ascot. Milligram was the last winning filly or mare in 1987.

Champion Stakes (1m2f) Ascot

2004	**Haafhd**	3	B Hills	R Hills	12-1	3/11
2005	**David Junior**	3	B Meehan	J Spencer	25-1	3/15
2006	**Pride**	6	A de Royer-Dupre	C Lemaire	7-2	7/8
2007	**Literato**	3	J-C Rouget	C Lemaire	7-2	8/12
2008	**New Approach**	3	J Bolger	K Manning	6-5f	2/11
2009	**Twice Over**	4	H Cecil	T Queally	14-1	6/14
2010	**Twice Over**	5	H Cecil	T Queally	7-2	4/10
2011	**Cirrus Des Aigles**	5	C Barande-Barbe	C Soumillon	12-1	1/12
2012	**Frankel**	4	Sir H Cecil	T Queally	2-11f	6/8
2013	**Farhh**	5	S Bin Suroor	S de Sousa	11-4	5/10

Run at Newmarket until 2011.

THE SUBJECT of a big-money makeover when switched to Ascot in 2011, before which the quality had been dipping due to its proximity to the Breeders' Cup. Older horses have increasingly come to the fore, accounting for each of the last five winners, although three-year-olds still have the edge overall with 23 of the last 40 winners including 17 since 1980. Twelve of those 17 had won a Classic with Guineas form more influential than the Epsom races – New Approach became the first Classic-winning three-year-old over 1m4f to cope with the drop in trip since Time Charter in 1982, while Frankel's win in 2012 also came a year after his 2,000 Guineas victory. This has been the best British Group 1 for French horses, with three winners in the last eight years extending a long tradition of success.

Big handicap records

Lincoln (1m) Doncaster

Year	Winner	Age	Weight	Trainer	Jockey	SP	Draw/ran
2004	Babodana	4	9-10	M Tompkins	P Robinson	20-1	23/24
2005	Stream Of Gold	4	9-0	Sir M Stoute	R Winston	5-1f	13/22
2006	Blythe Knight	6	8-10	J Quinn	G Gibbons	22-1	9/30*
2007	Very Wise	5	8-11	W Haggas	J Fanning	9-1	16/20
2008	Smokey Oakey	4	8-9	M Tompkins	J Quinn	10-1	12/21
2009	Expresso Star	4	8-12	J Gosden	J Fortune	10-3f	9/20
2010	Penitent	4	9-2	W Haggas	J Murtagh	3-1f	1/21
2011	Sweet Lightning	6	9-4	M Dods	J Murtagh	16-1	16/21
2012	Brae Hill	6	9-1	R Fahey	T Hamilton	25-1	12/22
2013	Levitate	5	8-7	J Quinn	D Egan (3)	20-1	3/22

*Run at Redcar

THIS ALWAYS used to be regarded as something of a lottery and the last three winners, none of whom were bigger than 16-1, suggest a return to those days after a run of success for punters, crowned when Expresso Star and Penitent landed nationwide gambles. The last three winners were also aged five or six, bucking a trend that had seen four-year-olds win six of the previous eight runnings. The ongoing shift at this time has been the rating required to get a run becoming higher and higher, so past trends about siding with a progressive horse on a low weight have been rendered obsolete, although a big weight is still a drawback with no winner carrying more than 9st 4lb since Babodana in 2004. The draw is inevitably a factor with just one of the last ten winners at Doncaster coming from a stall higher than 16. Turf horses having their first run of the year remain far preferable to those fit from the all-weather, although the trial won by Very Wise in 2007 was producing the winner for the fourth time that year. Look for trainers who have won the race recently as John Quinn, William Haggas and Mark Tompkins are all dual winners in the last ten years.

Royal Hunt Cup (1m) Royal Ascot

2004	Mine	6	9-5	J Bethell	T Quinn	16-1	24/31
2005	New Seeker	5	9-0	C Cox	P Robinson	11-1	6/22*
2006	Cesare	5	8-8	J Fanshawe	J Spencer	14-1	28/30
2007	Royal Oath	4	9-0	J Gosden	J Fortune	9-1	13/26
2008	Mr Aviator	4	9-5	R Hannon	R Hughes	25-1	26/29
2009	Forgotten Voice	4	9-1	J Noseda	J Murtagh	4-1f	25/25
2010	Invisible Man	4	8-9	S Bin Suroor	L Dettori	28-1	7/29

2011	**Julienas**	4	8-8	W Swinburn	E Ahern	12-1	24/28
2012	**Prince Of Johanne**	6	9-3	T Tate	J Fahy	16-1	33/30
2013	**Belgian Bill**	5	8-11	G Baker	J Doyle	33-1	6/28

*Royal Hunt Cup and the Wokingham run at York in 2005

A GREAT betting race in which there are few pointers and plots are thick on the ground, so most winners go off at a decent price – Forgotten Voice in 2009 was the first winning favourite since Yeast 13 years earlier. A common mistake is to side with a lightly raced improver because experience is in fact a vital commodity. As with most big handicaps, weight trends have changed markedly with fewer runners getting in below the 9st barrier, but three of the last four winners still carried less than that. A high draw is generally essential, with Belgian Bill the first to defy a single-figure berth at Ascot since Surprise Encounter in 2001.

Wokingham (6f) Royal Ascot

2004	**Lafi**	5	8-13	D Nicholls	E Ahern	6-1f	1/29
2005	**Iffraaj**	4	9-6	M Jarvis	P Robinson	9-4f	12/17
2006	**Baltic King**	6	9-10	H Morrison	J Fortune	10-1	23/28
2007	**Dark Missile**	4	8-6	A Balding	W Buick	22-1	2/26
2008	**Big Timer**	4	9-2	Miss L Perrett	T Eaves	20-1	1/27
2009	**High Standing**	4	8-12	W Haggas	R Moore	6-1	4/26
2010	**Laddies Poker Two**	5	8-11	J Noseda	J Murtagh	9-2f	26/27
2011	**Deacon Blues**	4	8-13	J Fanshawe	J Murtagh	15-2	11/25
2012	**Dandy Boy**	6	9-8	D Marnane	P Dobbs	33-1	15/28
2013	**York Glory**	5	9-2	K Ryan	J Spencer	14-1	22/26

'ORK GLORY: maintains the good record of higher weights in the Wokingham

STEER CLEAR: the Ascot Stakes has proved a hugely overrated Plate trial

THE DRAW bias in the Hunt Cup has often completely changed by this race, with lower numbers having the edge, although the opposite is true in years when the Hunt Cup has been won from a low berth so fresher ground is clearly the key. So too fresh horses as eight of the last 12 winners had raced no more than twice that year, which is remarkable for a sprint handicap. Class horses have been increasingly successful since the turn of the century, with nine of the last 16 winners carrying at least 9st 2lb to victory and four winning favourites in 13 years. Ten of the last 12 winners had won over the big-race trip and the two exceptions had won over further, so stamina is clearly important, and a key trial is the Victoria Cup over an extra furlong at the same track in May. Nine of the last 21 winners ran in that race or the 6f handicap at Newmarket's Guineas meeting.

Northumberland Plate (2m) Newcastle

2004	**Mirjan**	8	8-3	L Lungo	P Hanagan	25-1	5/19
2005	**Sergeant Cecil**	6	8-8	D Millman	A Munro	14-1	7/20
2006	**Toldo**	4	8-2	G Moore	N de Souza	33-1	16/20
2007	**Juniper Girl**	4	8-11	M Bell	L Morris	5-1f	13/20
2008	**Arc Bleu**	7	8-2	A Martin	A Nicholls	14-1	6/18
2009	**Som Tala**	6	8-8	M Channon	T Culhane	16-1	4/17
2010	**Overturn**	6	8-7	D McCain	E Ahern	14-1	21/19
2011	**Tominator**	4	8-8	R Hollinshead	P Pickard (3)	25-1	14/19
2012	**Ile De Re**	6	9-3	D McCain	J Crowley	5-2f	9/16
2013	**Tominator**	6	9-10	J O'Neill	G Lee	8-1	4/18

WITH SO much of the season revolving around Royal Ascot and Newcastle's biggest day of the summer generally coming just a week later, this provides a good opportunity for horses laid out for the race rather than coming here as an afterthought. Just two of the last 11 winners had run at Royal Ascot despite several fancied runners, including four beaten favourites, coming from the royal meeting. Older horses have increasingly come to the fore, with five of the last six winners aged at least six and two eight-year-olds among the previous eight to triumph. The first bend comes shortly after the start, so those drawn high can be disadvantaged, with nine of the last 15 winners drawn seven or lower, and Overturn used controversial tactics to overcome that in 2010. The Chester Cup is traditionally a strong guide and that has been reinforced recently with Ile De Re doing the double and Tominator following up a placed effort at Chester last year.

Bunbury Cup (7f) Newmarket

2004	Material Witness	7	9-3	W Muir	M Dwyer	25-1	14/19
2005	Mine	7	9-9	J Bethell	T Quinn	16-1	13/18
2006	Mine	8	9-10	J Bethell	M Kinane	10-1	6/19
2007	Giganticus	4	8-8	B Hills	P Robinson	16-1	16/18
2008	Little White Lie	4	9-0	J Jenkins	D Holland	14-1	1/18
2009	Plum Pudding	6	9-10	R Hannon	R Moore	12-1	15/19
2010	St Moritz	4	9-1	M Johnston	L Dettori	4-1f	4/19
2011	Brae Hill	5	9-1	R Fahey	B McHugh	11-1	2/20
2012	Bonnie Brae	5	9-9	D Elsworth	R Moore	13-2	12/15
2013	Field Of Dream	6	9-7	J Osborne	A Kirby	14-1	20/19

IT'S REMARKABLE how many times this race is won by a horse carrying a big weight. Mine, a three-time winner between 2002 and 2006, twice defied a burden of at least 9st 9lb and has been emulated by Bonnie Brae and Plum Pudding since then. Despite that only one of the last 21 winners had won more than once that year – 13 hadn't won at all, including each of the last four – so the key is clearly to find a horse slipping down the weights but classy enough to still be near the top of the handicap. This is run over a specialist trip and each of the last 11 winners had previously won over the distance.

John Smith's Cup (1m2f85yds) York

2004	Arcalis	4	9-2	H Johnson	R Winston	20-1	18/21
2005	Mullins Bay	4	9-7	A O'Brien	K Fallon	4-1f	19/20
2006	Fairmile	4	9-1	W Swinburn	A Kirby (3)	6-1j	9/20
2007	Charlie Tokyo	4	8-12	R Fahey	J Moriarty (3)	11-1	4/17
2008	Flying Clarets	5	8-12	R Fahey	F Tylicki (7)	12-1	12/16
2009	Sirvino	4	8-8	T Brown	N Brown (3)	16-1	16/18
2010	Wigmore Hall	3	8-5	M Bell	M Lane (3)	5-1	13/19
2011	Green Destiny	4	8-13	W Haggas	A Beschizza (3)	6-1	17-19
2012	King's Warrior	5	8-9	P Chapple-Hyam	R Havlin	33-1	19/18
2013	Danchai	4	8-11	W Haggas	A Atzeni	10-1	16/19

YOUTH SEEMS to be the key to this race, with only two winners aged five – and none older – since Vintage Premium in 2002 despite three-year-olds struggling desperately to get a run. Indeed, subsequent Grade 1 winner Wigmore Hall was the only runner from that age group when coming out on top in 2010 and none have made the field since. Like the Northumberland Plate, this is another handicap in which missing Royal Ascot is vital, in keeping with eight of the last 11 winners, whereas ten of the last 11 beaten favourites registered a top-four finish at the royal meeting. This is run on one of the best Saturdays of the summer and, with many top jockeys engaged elsewhere, it provides an opportunity for some younger riders as six of the last eight winners were partnered by an apprentice.

Stewards' Cup (6f) Goodwood

2004	**Pivotal Point**	4	8-11	P Makin	S Sanders	7-1cf	28/28
2005	**Gift Horse**	5	9-7	D Nicholls	K Fallon	9-2	9/27
2006	**Borderlescott**	4	9-5	R Bastiman	R Ffrench	10-1	10/27
2007	**Zidane**	5	9-1	J Fanshawe	J Spencer	6-1f	17/27
2008	**Conquest**	4	8-9	W Haggas	D O'Neill	40-1	13/26
2009	**Genki**	5	9-1	R Charlton	S Drowne	14-1	17/26
2010	**Evens And Odds**	6	9-1	D Nicholls	B Cray (5)	20-1	11/28
2011	**Hoof It**	4	10-0	M Easterby	K Fallon	13-2jf	18/27
2012	**Hawkeyethenoo**	6	9-9	J Goldie	G Lee	9-1	4/27
2013	**Rex Imperator**	4	9-4	W Haggas	N Callan	12-1	26/27

THIS IS a major betting heat with a strong ante-post market and the betting has become a good guide as six winners at single-figure odds in 11 years, plus three more not a lot bigger, is a fine record given the size of the field. This is a race for established sprint handicappers with 14 of the last 17 winners coming via the Wokingham, though none of them had won at Royal Ascot. Plenty of top-class sprinters drop into handicap company for this race, but the weight tends to stop them as Crews Hill in 1981 was the last winner to have prepped in a Group race and only Hoof It and Hawkeyethenoo have carried more than 9st 7lb to victory since Petong in 1984.

Ebor (1m6f) York

2004	**Mephisto**	4	9-4	L Cumani	D Holland	6-1	3/19
2005	**Sergeant Cecil**	6	8-12	B Millman	A Munro	11-1	18/20
2006	**Mudawin**	5	8-4	J Chapple-Hyam	J Egan	100-1	13/22
2007	**Purple Moon**	4	9-4	L Cumani	J Spencer	7-2f	14/19
2008	**All The Good**	5	9-0	S bin Suroor	D O'Neill	25-1	7/20
2009	**Sesenta**	5	8-8	W Mullins	G Carroll (5)	25-1	16/19
2010	**Dirar**	5	9-1	G Elliott	J Spencer	14-1	22/20
2011	**Moyenne Corniche**	6	8-13	B Ellison	D Swift (3)	25-1	10/20
2012	**Willing Foe**	5	9-2	S Bin Suroor	L Dettori	12-1	16/19
2013	**Tiger Cliff**	4	9-0	Lady Cecil	T Queally	5-1	18/14

*Run at Newbury as the Newburgh Handicap in 2008

ONE OF the oldest and most famous handicaps, first run in 1847, again has an extremely strong ante-post market and was moved to a Saturday in 2011 to boost its profile further. Sea Pigeon brought the house down when lumping top-weight home in 1979, but low weights are massively favoured and only two winners have carried more than 9st 2lb since 1998 – and none more than 9st 4lb – despite the weights becoming more and more condensed. Watch out for three-year-olds as they had a tremendous record around the turn of the century and have simply found it increasingly tough to get a run since then, with two of the three to run since 2006, Honolulu and Changingoftheguard, finishing honourable seconds. Indeed, progressive horses are always preferred with eight of the last 11 winners having raced no more than nine times on the Flat.

Ayr Gold Cup (6f) Ayr

2004	**Funfair Wane**	5	8-6	D Nicholls	P Doe	33-1	8/24
2005	**Presto Shinko**	4	9-2	R Hannon	S Sanders	12-1	2/27
2006	**Fonthill Road**	6	9-2	R Fahey	P Hanagan	16-1	6/28
2007	**Advanced**	4	9-9	K Ryan	J Spencer	20-1	22/28

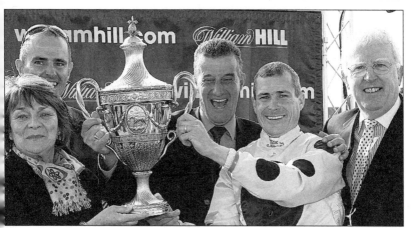

KEVIN RYAN (centre): celebrates one of his three victories in the Ayr Gold Cup

2008	**Regal Parade**	4	8-10	D Nicholls	W Carson (5)	18-1	20/27
2009	**Jimmy Styles**	5	9-2	C Cox	L Dettori	14-1	15/26
2010	**Redford**	5	9-2	D Nicholls	L Dettori	14-1	17/26
2011	**Our Jonathan**	4	9-6	K Ryan	F Norton	11-1	12/26
2012	**Captain Ramius**	6	9-0	K Ryan	P Smullen	16-1	8/26
2013	**Highland Colori**	5	9-4	A Balding	O Murphy (5)	20-1	19/26

A HISTORIC race first run in 1804, but punters are still struggling to get to grips with it – Our Jonathan was the most fancied winner of the last 12 years at 11-1. There seems little clues from the draw in recent runnings, but the effect can be gleaned from the consolation races – the Bronze Cup was run for the first time in 2009 and now precedes the big one, along with the Silver Cup. Be wary of recent winning form as that can mean too much weight, with just two of the last 11 winners having triumphed more than once that year and just three of those 11 having landed any of their previous four outings. Kevin Ryan has won three of the last seven renewals, including two of the last three, to take over from David Nicholls as the trainer to follow.

Cambridgeshire (1m1f) Newmarket

2004	**Spanish Don**	6	8-7	D Elsworth	L Keniry	100-1	30/32
2005	**Blue Monday**	4	9-3	R Charlton	S Drowne	5-1f	3/30
2006	**Formal Decree**	3	8-9	G Swinbank	J Spencer	9-1	17/33
2007	**Pipedreamer**	3	8-12	J Gosden	J Fortune	5-1f	24/34
2008	**Tazeez**	4	9-2	J Gosden	R Hills	25-1	8/28
2009	**Supaseus**	6	9-1	H Morrison	T Block	16-1	7/32
2010	**Credit Swap**	5	8-7	M Wigham	J Crowley	14-1	3/35
2011	**Prince Of Johanne**	5	8-12	T Tate	J Fahy (3)	40-1	31/32
2012	**Bronze Angel**	3	8-8	M Tregoning	W Buick	9-1	21/33
2013	**Educate**	4	9-9	I Mohammed	J Murtagh	8-1f	4/33

THE FIRST leg of the Autumn Double. Because of its unusual distance and its straight course, this has thrown up a number of specialists down the years so consider horses who have run well in the race before. Many of the runners are milers racing over an extra furlong, but proven form over 1m2f is important with ten of the last 12 winners ticking that box. Handicap experience is vital, with nine of the last 11 winners having previously beaten a field of at least 13. The heritage handicap at Newbury in September was the key trial, throwing up four out of seven winners from 2004 to 2010, but the Cambridgeshire's date switch means there's now just a week between them.

Cesarewitch (2m2f) Newmarket

2004	Contact Dancer	5	8-2	M Johnston	R Ffrench	16-1	17/34
2005	Sergeant Cecil	6	9-8	B Millman	A Munro	10-1	7/34
2006	Detroit City	4	9-1	P Hobbs	J Spencer	9-2f	4/32
2007	Leg Spinner	6	8-11	A Martin	J Murtagh	14-1	11/33
2008	Caracciola	11	9-6	N Henderson	E Ahern	50-1	22/32
2009	Darley Sun	3	8-6	D Simcock	A Atzeni (3)	9-2f	8/32
2010	Aaim To Prosper	7	8-2	B Meehan	L-P Beuzelin (3)	16-1	3/32
2011	Never Can Tell	4	8-11	J Osborne	L Dettori	25-1	36/33
2012	Aaim To Prosper	8	9-10	B Meehan	K Fallon	66-1	1/34
2013	Scatter Dice	4	8-8	M Johnston	S de Sousa	66-1	18/33

THE SECOND leg of the Autumn Double. This is another race in which a long sweeping bend makes the draw far more important than you would think from the trip with Caracciola and Never Can Tell the only winners drawn higher than 18 since Turnpole in 1997. Generally punters are too swayed by a young improver as Darley Sun is one of only two winning three-year-olds in 21 years and he was the only favourite to win in the last seven years during a spell that has seen winners returned twice at 66-1 and once at 50-1. One of the big-priced winners, Aaim To Prosper, reinforced the significance of previous form in the race as he followed up his victory two years earlier. There has been a recognised hurdler in the first two in 14 of the last 18 years. The Northumberland Plate is the best trial having thrown up nine of the last 20 winners.

November Handicap (1m4f) Doncaster

2004	Carte Diamond	4	9-6	B Ellison	K Fallon	12-1	3/24
2005	Come On Jonny	3	8-0	R Beckett	N de Souza	14-1	18/21
2006	Group Captain	4	9-5	R Charlton	R Hughes	10-1	20/20
2007	Malt Or Mash	3	8-10	R Hannon	R Moore	5-1	13/21
2008	Tropical Strait	5	8-13	D Arbuthnot	M Dwyer	20-1	22/21
2009	Charm School	4	8-12	J Gosden	J Fortune	17-2	14/23
2010	Times Up	4	8-13	J Dunlop	D O'Neill	14-1	9/22
2011	Zuider Zee	4	8-13	J Gosden	R Havlin	8-1	20/23
2012	Art Scholar	5	8-7	M Appleby	F Norton	20-1	9/23
2013	Conduct	6	9-2	W Haggas	S Sanders	8-1	21/23

THE LAST big betting heat of the season. The last two winners were aged five and six and Malt Or Mash was the last successful three-year-old in 2007, but even so progressive young horses remain the preferred choice. Just seven of the last 34 winners were older than four and, though three-year-olds are finding it increasingly hard to get a run, they are always feared – bear in mind that four of the last eight to come out on top had been unraced as a juvenile and were therefore late developers. A big weight remains a major drawback as six of the last seven winners carried less than 9st. Ten of the last 14 winners were returned at double-figure odds and favourites have a desperate record with the last 18 biting the dust.

Big Race Dates, Fixtures and Track Facts

Fixtures

Key - Flat, **Jumps**

March

29	Saturday	Doncaster, **Stratford**, Kempton, **Uttoxeter**
30	Sunday	Doncaster, **Ascot**
31	Monday	**Hexham**, Kempton, **Plumpton**

April

1	Tuesday	Southwell, Kempton, **Newton Abbot**
2	Wednesday	Southwell, Kempton, Lingfield, **Wincanton**
3	Thursday	**Aintree**, Wolverhampton, Lingfield, **Taunton**
4	Friday	**Aintree**, Leicester, **Sedgefield**, Wolverhampton
5	Saturday	**Aintree**, Wolverhampton, **Chepstow**, Newcastle, Lingfield
6	Sunday	**Market Rasen, Ffos Las**
7	Monday	**Kelso**, Windsor, Redcar
8	Tuesday	**Carlisle**, Southwell, Pontefract
9	Wednesday	Catterick, Nottingham, Kempton, Lingfield
10	Thursday	**Ludlow**, Kempton, **Towcester**, **Taunton**
11	Friday	**Ayr**, Wolverhampton, **Fontwell**, Newbury
12	Saturday	**Ayr, Bangor**, Newbury, Thirsk, Wolverhampton
13	Sunday	**Wetherby, Stratford, Wincanton**
14	Monday	**Hexham**, Windsor, Pontefract
15	Tuesday	Southwell, **Exeter, Kempton**
16	Wednesday	Beverley, **Cheltenham, Sedgefield**, Newmarket, **Southwell**
17	Thursday	Ripon, **Cheltenham**, Newmarket
18	Friday	Musselburgh, Lingfield
19	Saturday	**Carlisle**, Nottingham, Bath, **Haydock**, Kempton, **Newton Abbot**
20	Sunday	Musselburgh, **Towcester, Plumpton**
21	Monday	Redcar, **Fakenham, Chepstow, Huntingdon, Plumpton**, **Market Rasen**, Yarmouth
22	Tuesday	**Kelso, Ludlow, Wetherby**, Wolverhampton, Yarmouth
23	Wednesday	Catterick, **Southwell**, Epsom, **Perth, Taunton**
24	Thursday	Beverley, Warwick, Brighton, Newcastle, **Perth**
25	Friday	Doncaster, **Chepstow, Perth, Newton Abbot**, Sandown
26	Saturday	Doncaster, Leicester, **Sandown**, Haydock, Wolverhampton, Ripon
27	Sunday	Ayr, Kempton
28	Monday	Southwell, Bath, Wolverhampton, Kempton, Windsor
29	Tuesday	Newcastle, Nottingham, Lingfield, Wolverhampton, Yarmouth
30	Wednesday	Pontefract, **Cheltenham**, Ascot, Southwell, Brighton

May

1	Thursday	Redcar, **Towcester, Ffos Las, Sedgefield**, Lingfield
2	Friday	Musselburgh, **Bangor**, Chepstow, **Fontwell**, Lingfield

3 Saturday ....Doncaster, Newmarket, Goodwood, **Hexham**, **Uttoxeter**,
....Thirsk
4 Sunday.. Hamilton, Newmarket, Salisbury
5 Monday.............Beverley, Warwick, Bath, **Ffos Las**, **Kempton**, Windsor
6 Tuesday..........................Catterick, **Fakenham**, Brighton, **Exeter**, Kempton
7 Wednesday......................**Kelso**, Chester, Brighton, **Worcester**, Kempton
8 Thursday...........**Carlisle**, Chester, **Newton Abbot**, Southwell, **Wincanton**
9 Friday...........Ripon, Chester, Ascot, **Market Rasen**, Lingfield, Nottingham
10 Saturday ....**Haydock**, Nottingham, Ascot, **Hexham**, Warwick, Lingfield,
....Thirsk
11 Sunday.. **Ludlow**, **Plumpton**
12 Monday....Doncaster, **Towcester**, Windsor, Musselburgh, Wolverhampton
13 Tuesday...............Beverley, **Southwell**, **Ffos Las**, **Sedgefield**, **Wincanton**
14 Wednesday..........................**Perth**, **Uttoxeter**, Chepstow, York, **Worcester**
15 Thursday.............................. **Perth**, Newmarket, **Fontwell**, York, Salisbury
16 Friday ....**Aintree**, Newmarket, Newbury, Hamilton, York
17 Saturday ......Doncaster, **Bangor**, Newbury, Thirsk, Newmarket, **Uttoxeter**
18 Sunday.. Ripon, **Market Rasen**, **Stratford**
19 Monday......................... Redcar, Leicester, Windsor, Southwell, **Towcester**
20 Tuesday........................ Newcastle, Nottingham, Bath, Warwick, Yarmouth
21 Wednesday...............Ayr, **Worcester**, Kempton, Lingfield, **Newton Abbot**
22 Thursday...........................Ayr, Goodwood, **Wetherby**, Salisbury, Sandown
23 Friday ....Haydock, **Towcester**, Goodwood, Musselburgh, Yarmouth
....Pontefract
24 Saturday ....Beverley, **Ffos Las**, **Cartmel**, Goodwood, Catterick, Haydock
25 Sunday...**Kelso**, **Uttoxeter**, **Fontwell**
26 Monday.................................Carlisle, Leicester, Windsor, **Cartmel**, Redcar
27 Tuesday...................... **Hexham**, **Huntingdon**, Lingfield, Redcar, Leicester
28 Wednesday...................Beverley, Chepstow, **Cartmel**, Kempton, Hamilton
29 Thursday........................Haydock, **Worcester**, Bath, **Wetherby**, Sandown
30 Friday .....Catterick, Newmarket, Brighton, Haydock, **Stratford**, Newcastle
31 Saturday ....Haydock, Chester, Newbury, York, Newmarket, **Stratford**

June

1 Sunday...**Fakenham**, Nottingham
2 Monday.. Carlisle, Leicester, Chepstow, Windsor
3 Tuesday...Ripon, **Southwell**, Brighton, Yarmouth
4 Wednesday..................Ripon, Nottingham, **Fontwell**, Southwell, Kempton
5 Thursday............ Hamilton, Wolverhampton, **Ffos Las**, Kempton, Lingfield
6 Friday .... Catterick, **Market Rasen**, Bath, Epsom, Goodwood
7 Saturday .... Doncaster, **Worcester**, Epsom, **Hexham**, Lingfield
....Musselburgh, Newcastle
8 Sunday... **Perth**, Goodwood
9 Monday..Ayr, **Newton Abbot**, Pontefract, Windsor
10 Tuesday........................**Worcester**, **Fontwell**, Lingfield, Salisbury
11 Wednesday.................. Beverley, Yarmouth, Kempton, Hamilton, Haydock
12 Thursday................ Haydock, Nottingham, Newbury, **Uttoxeter**, Yarmouth
13 Friday ....**Aintree**, Chepstow, Musselburgh, Goodwood, York, Sandown
14 Saturday .... **Hexham**, Chester, Bath, Musselburgh, Leicester, Lingfield
....York, Sandown
15 Sunday.. Doncaster, Salisbury

182

16 Monday...................................Carlisle, Warwick, **Newton Abbot**, Windsor
17 Tuesday............................. Thirsk, Nottingham, Ascot, **Stratford**, Brighton
18 Wednesday........................ Hamilton, **Southwell**, Ascot, Ripon, **Uttoxeter**
19 Thursday...... Ripon, Leicester, Ascot, Wolverhampton, **Ffos Las**, Lingfield
20 Friday.................. Redcar, **Market Rasen**, Ascot, Newmarket, Goodwood
21 Saturday ....Ayr, Newmarket, Ascot, Haydock, Lingfield, Redcar
22 Sunday.. **Hexham**, **Worcester**, Pontefract
23 Monday.............................. Thirsk, Wolverhampton, Chepstow, Windsor
24 Tuesday.............................Beverley, Brighton, Newbury, **Newton Abbot**
25 Wednesday........................Carlisle, **Worcester**, Bath, Kempton, Salisbury
26 Thursday....................Hamilton, Leicester, Newcastle, Warwick, Yarmouth
27 Friday .... Doncaster, Chester, Musselburgh, Newmarket, Newcastle,
.... Yarmouth
28 Saturday ....Doncaster, Chester, Lingfield, Newcastle, Newmarket,
.... Windsor
29 Sunday...**Uttoxeter**, Salisbury, Windsor
30 Monday.............................. Pontefract, Wolverhampton, Ffos Las, Windsor

July

1 Tuesday................................... Hamilton, **Stratford**, Bath, Brighton
2 Wednesday.................... Catterick, **Worcester**, Chepstow, **Perth**, Kempton
3 Thursday............................ Haydock, Yarmouth, Epsom, **Perth**, Newbury
4 Friday ....Beverley, Warwick, Sandown, Doncaster, Haydock
5 Saturday .... Beverley, Leicester, Sandown, Carlisle, Nottingham, Haydock
6 Sunday...Ayr, **Market Rasen**
7 Monday.......................................Ayr, **Newton Abbot**, Ripon, Windsor
8 Tuesday...........................Pontefract, **Uttoxeter**, Brighton, Wolverhampton
9 Wednesday...............Catterick, **Worcester**, Kempton, Yarmouth, Lingfield
10 Thursday...........................Doncaster, Newmarket, Bath, Warwick, Epsom
11 Friday ....York, Chester, Ascot, Newmarket, Chepstow
12 Saturday ....Hamilton, Chester, Ascot, York, Newmarket, Salisbury
13 Sunday.. **Perth**, **Southwell**, **Stratford**
14 Monday..............................Ayr, Wolverhampton, **Newton Abbot**, Windsor
15 Tuesday...................................... Beverley, Yarmouth, Bath, Thirsk
16 Wednesday...............Catterick, **Uttoxeter**, Lingfield, **Worcester**, Sandown
17 Thursday........................Doncaster, Leicester, Brighton, Hamilton, Epsom
18 Friday ....Hamilton, Newmarket, Newbury, Haydock, Nottingham,
.... Pontefract
19 Saturday .... **Cartmel**, **Market Rasen**, Lingfield, Haydock, Newmarket,
....Newbury, Ripon
20 Sunday..Redcar, **Stratford**, **Newton Abbot**
21 Monday...................................... Ayr, Windsor, Beverley, **Cartmel**
22 Tuesday.........................Carlisle, **Bangor**, Musselburgh, **Southwell**
23 Wednesday...............Catterick, Leicester, Lingfield, **Worcester**, Sandown
24 Thursday............. Doncaster, Wolverhampton, Bath, Yarmouth, Sandown
25 Friday ....Thirsk, Newmarket, Ascot, York, **Uttoxeter**, Chepstow
26 Saturday .... Newcastle, Newmarket, Ascot, York, Lingfield, Salisbury
27 Sunday..Carlisle, Ascot, Pontefract
28 Monday...Ayr, **Uttoxeter**, Lingfield, Windsor
29 Tuesday...................... Beverley, **Worcester**, Goodwood, **Perth**, Yarmouth
30 Wednesday....................... **Perth**, Leicester, Goodwood, Redcar, Sandown
31 Thursday.................Nottingham, Epsom, **Stratford**, Ffos Las, Goodwood

August

1	Friday	Musselburgh, **Bangor**, Bath, Thirsk, Newmarket, Goodwood
2	Saturday	Doncaster, Newmarket, Goodwood, Hamilton, Lingfield, Thirsk
3	Sunday	Chester, Newbury, **Market Rasen**
4	Monday	Carlisle, Kempton, Ripon, Windsor
5	Tuesday	Catterick, Ffos Las, Ripon, Kempton
6	Wednesday	Pontefract, Yarmouth, Brighton, Chepstow, Kempton
7	Thursday	Haydock, Southwell, Brighton, Newcastle, Yarmouth, Sandown
8	Friday	Haydock, Newmarket, Brighton, Musselburgh, Lingfield
9	Saturday	Ayr, Newmarket, Ascot, Haydock, Lingfield, Redcar
10	Sunday	Leicester, Windsor
11	Monday	Ayr, Wolverhampton, Windsor, Thirsk
12	Tuesday	Carlisle, Nottingham, Ffos Las, Lingfield
13	Wednesday	Beverley, Yarmouth, Kempton, **Newton Abbot**, Salisbury
14	Thursday	Beverley, Newmarket, Chepstow, **Fontwell**, Salisbury
15	Friday	Catterick, Newmarket, Newbury, Newcastle, Nottingham
16	Saturday	Doncaster, Chester, Lingfield, **Perth**, **Market Rasen**, Newbury, Ripon, Newmarket
17	Sunday	Pontefract, **Southwell**
18	Monday	Thirsk, Wolverhampton, Kempton, Windsor
19	Tuesday	Leicester, Brighton, **Worcester**, Yarmouth
20	Wednesday	Musselburgh, Southwell, Kempton, York, Lingfield
21	Thursday	York, Wolverhampton, Bath, **Ffos Las**, **Newton Abbot**
22	Friday	Hamilton, Newmarket, Ffos Las, Newcastle, Goodwood, York
23	Saturday	**Cartmel**, Newmarket, Goodwood, Redcar, Windsor, York
24	Sunday	Beverley, Yarmouth, Goodwood
25	Monday	**Cartmel**, **Huntingdon**, Chepstow, Newcastle, Warwick, Epsom, Ripon
26	Tuesday	Ripon, Wolverhampton, Epsom, **Sedgefield**
27	Wednesday	Carlisle, **Worcester**, Kempton, Catterick, Lingfield
28	Thursday	Hamilton, **Stratford**, Ffos Las, **Fontwell**, Lingfield
29	Friday	Thirsk, **Bangor**, Salisbury, Wolverhampton, Sandown
30	Saturday	Beverley, Chester, Bath, **Market Rasen**, **Newton Abbot**, Sandown
31	Sunday	**Worcester**, Brighton

September

1	Monday	**Huntingdon**, Brighton, Leicester
2	Tuesday	Hamilton, Warwick, Goodwood, Kempton
3	Wednesday	**Southwell**, Bath, Kempton, Lingfield
4	Thursday	Haydock, Wolverhampton, Salisbury, **Sedgefield**
5	Friday	Haydock, Chepstow, Musselburgh, Kempton, Newcastle
6	Saturday	Haydock, **Stratford**, Ascot, Thirsk, Wolverhampton, Kempton
7	Sunday	York, **Fontwell**
8	Monday	**Perth**, Brighton, **Newton Abbot**
9	Tuesday	**Perth**, Leicester, Redcar, **Worcester**
10	Wednesday	Carlisle, **Uttoxeter**, Kempton, Doncaster
11	Thursday	Doncaster, Wolverhampton, Chepstow, Epsom
12	Friday	Doncaster, Chester, Salisbury, Sandown
13	Saturday	Doncaster, Chester, Bath, Wolverhampton, Lingfield

SUMMER SMASH: York's Ebor Festival, where Tiger Cliff and Tom Queally won the flagship race last year, has become one of the highlights of the calendar

4	Sunday	.... Bath, Ffos Las
5	Monday	....Musselburgh, Wolverhampton, Brighton
6	Tuesday	....................................**Sedgefield**, Yarmouth, Chepstow, Thirsk
7	Wednesday	.... Beverley, Yarmouth, Sandown, **Kelso**
8	Thursday	....Ayr, Yarmouth, Kempton, Pontefract
9	Friday	.... Ayr, **Worcester**, Newbury, **Newton Abbot**
0	Saturday	..................Ayr, Newmarket, Newbury, Catterick, Wolverhampton
1	Sunday	....Hamilton, **Uttoxeter**, **Plumpton**
2	Monday	....Hamilton, Leicester, Kempton
3	Tuesday	.... Beverley, Nottingham, Lingfield, Newcastle
4	Wednesday	....**Perth**, Goodwood, Redcar, Kempton
5	Thursday	......................................**Perth**, Newmarket, Kempton, Pontefract

26 Friday .... Haydock, Newmarket, Wolverhampton, **Worcester**
27 Saturday ....Haydock, Chester, Ripon, **Market Rasen**, Newmarket,
....Wolverhampton
28 Sunday..Musselburgh, Epsom
29 Monday..Hamilton, Bath, **Newton Abbot**
30 Tuesday..Ayr, **Chepstow**, **Sedgefield**

October

1 Wednesday............................Newcastle, Nottingham, Kempton, Salisbury
2 Thursday....................................**Bangor**, Kempton, **Southwell**, **Warwick**
3 Friday ....**Hexham**, Wolverhampton, Ascot, **Fontwell**
4 Saturday .... Redcar, Newmarket, Ascot, Wolverhampton, **Fontwell**
5 Sunday...**Kelso**, **Huntingdon**, **Uttoxeter**
6 Monday.. Pontefract, **Stratford**, Windsor
7 Tuesday..Catterick, Leicester, Brighton
8 Wednesday............................**Ludlow**, Kempton, Nottingham, **Towcester**
9 Thursday.................................... Ayr, Wolverhampton, **Exeter**, **Worcester**
10 Friday ....**Carlisle**, Wolverhampton, **Newton Abbot**, York
11 Saturday ....**Hexham**, Newmarket, **Chepstow**, Musselburgh,
....Wolverhampton, York
12 Sunday ....**Ffos Las**, Goodwood
13 Monday ....**Sedgefield**, Salisbury, Windsor
14 Tuesday...Newcastle, **Huntingdon**, Leicester
15 Wednesday............................**Wetherby**, Nottingham, Kempton, Lingfield
16 Thursday........................**Uttoxeter**, Brighton, Wolverhampton, **Wincanton**
17 Friday ....Haydock, **Cheltenham**, Redcar, Newmarket, Wolverhampton
18 Saturday ....Catterick, **Cheltenham**, Ascot, **Kelso**, Wolverhampton
19 Sunday ....Bath, **Kempton**
20 Monday.......................................Pontefract, **Plumpton**, Windsor
21 Tuesday.. Yarmouth, **Exeter**, Lingfield
22 Wednesday............................ Newmarket, **Fontwell**, **Worcester**, Kempton
23 Thursday....................................**Carlisle**, **Ludlow**, Kempton, **Southwell**
24 Friday .... Doncaster, **Fakenham**, Newbury, Wolverhampton
25 Saturday ....**Aintree**, **Stratford**, **Chepstow**, Doncaster, Wolverhampton,
....Newbury
26 Sunday..**Aintree**, **Wincanton**
27 Monday..**Ayr**, Leicester, Redcar
28 Tuesday..Catterick, Yarmouth, **Ffos Las**
29 Wednesday............................ Nottingham, Kempton, **Worcester**, **Taunton**
30 Thursday................................**Sedgefield**, **Stratford**, Kempton, Lingfield
31 Friday .... **Wetherby**, Newmarket, **Uttoxeter**, Wolverhampton

November

1 Saturday ....**Ayr**, Newmarket, **Ascot**, **Wetherby**
2 Sunday...**Carlisle**, **Huntingdon**
3 Monday...............................Wolverhampton, **Kempton**, **Plumpton**
4 Tuesday.. Redcar, Southwell, **Exeter**
5 Wednesday............................Nottingham, **Chepstow**, **Warwick**, Kempton
6 Thursday..............**Musselburgh**, **Fakenham**, **Towcester**, Wolverhampton
7 Friday ....**Hexham**, Wolverhampton, **Fontwell**, **Musselburgh**
8 Saturday ....Doncaster, **Sandown**, **Kelso**, **Wincanton**
9 Sunday..**Market Rasen**, **Ffos Las**

10 Monday...**Carlisle**, **Southwell**, Kempton
11 Tuesday..**Sedgefield**, **Huntingdon**, **Lingfield**
12 Wednesday...**Ayr**, **Bangor**, **Exeter**, Kempton
13 Thursday...**Ludlow**, Kempton, Southwell, **Taunton**
14 Friday .... **Newcastle**, **Cheltenham**, Lingfield, Wolverhampton
15 Saturday ... **Wetherby**, **Cheltenham**, Lingfield, **Uttoxeter**, Wolverhampton
16 Sunday.. **Cheltenham**, **Fontwell**
17 Monday............................... **Leicester**, **Plumpton**, Wolverhampton
18 Tuesday.......................................**Doncaster**, **Fakenham**, Southwell
19 Wednesday.............................. **Hexham**, **Warwick**, Kempton, Lingfield
20 Thursday...................... **Market Rasen**, **Chepstow**, Kempton, **Wincanton**
21 Friday ....**Haydock**, Wolverhampton, **Ascot**, **Ffos Las**
22 Saturday ....**Haydock**, **Huntingdon**, **Ascot**, Wolverhampton, Lingfield
23 Sunday... **Towcester**, **Exeter**
24 Monday..**Ludlow**, **Kempton**, Wolverhampton
25 Tuesday.................................. **Sedgefield**, Southwell, **Lingfield**
26 Wednesday................................ **Wetherby**, **Fontwell**, Kempton, Lingfield
27 Thursday.............................**Uttoxeter**, Kempton, **Newbury**, **Taunton**
28 Friday .... **Doncaster**, Wolverhampton, **Newbury**, **Musselburgh**
29 Saturday ....**Newcastle**, **Bangor**, **Newbury**, **Towcester**, Wolverhampton
30 Sunday..**Carlisle**, **Leicester**

December

1 Monday...Wolverhampton, Kempton, **Plumpton**
2 Tuesday......................... **Sedgefield**, **Southwell**, Wolverhampton
3 Wednesday............................. **Catterick**, **Ludlow**, Kempton, Lingfield
4 Thursday.......................**Leicester**, Kempton, **Market Rasen**, **Wincanton**
5 Friday .... Wolverhampton, **Exeter**, Lingfield, **Sandown**
6 Saturday ....**Aintree**, Wolverhampton, **Chepstow**, **Wetherby**, **Sandown**
7 Sunday..**Kelso**, **Huntingdon**
8 Monday................................... **Musselburgh**, Kempton, Lingfield
9 Tuesday.................................. Southwell, **Fontwell**, **Uttoxeter**
10 Wednesday.............................**Hexham**, **Leicester**, Kempton, Lingfield
11 Thursday....................................**Newcastle**, **Warwick**, Kempton, **Taunton**
12 Friday ....**Doncaster**, **Bangor**, **Cheltenham**, Wolverhampton
13 Saturday .... **Doncaster**, **Cheltenham**, **Lingfield**, Southwell,
....Wolverhampton
14 Sunday..**Carlisle**, **Southwell**
15 Monday...Wolverhampton, **Ffos Las**, **Plumpton**
16 Tuesday.................................. **Catterick**, Southwell, Kempton
17 Wednesday.................................... **Ludlow**, Kempton, Lingfield, **Newbury**
18 Thursday.................................. Southwell, **Exeter**, **Towcester**, Kempton
19 Friday .... Southwell, **Ascot**, **Uttoxeter**, Wolverhampton
20 Saturday .... **Haydock**, **Ascot**, **Newcastle**, Lingfield
21 Sunday..**Fakenham**, **Lingfield**
22 Monday...**Bangor**, Kempton, Wolverhampton
26 Friday ...... **Sedgefield**, **Huntingdon**, **Fontwell**, **Wetherby**, **Market Rasen**,
...............................**Kempton**, **Towcester**, **Wincanton**, Wolverhampton
27 Saturday .....**Wetherby**, Southwell, **Chepstow**, Wolverhampton, **Kempton**
28 Sunday.................................... **Catterick**, **Leicester**, Lingfield
29 Monday...............................**Doncaster**, Southwell, **Newbury**, **Kelso**
30 Tuesday..**Haydock**, Lingfield, **Taunton**
31 Wednesday..**Uttoxeter**, Lingfield, **Warwick**

Big-race dates

March
29 Mar	Doncaster	Lincoln (Heritage Handicap)

April
12 Apr	Newbury	Fred Darling Stakes (Group 3)
12 Apr	Newbury	Greenham Stakes (Group 3)
12 Apr	Newbury	John Porter Stakes (Group 3)
16 Apr	Newmarket	Nell Gwyn Stakes (Group 3)
17 Apr	Newmarket	Earl of Sefton Stakes (Group 3)
17 Apr	Newmarket	Craven Stakes (Group 3)
25 Apr	Sandown Park	Gordon Richards Stakes (Group 3)
25 Apr	Sandown Park	bet365 Mile (Group 2)
30 Apr	Ascot	Sagaro Stakes (Group 3)

May
3 May	Newmarket	2,000 Guineas (Group 1)
3 May	Newmarket	Dahlia Stakes (Group 3)
4 May	Newmarket	1,000 Guineas (Group 1)
4 May	Newmarket	Jockey Club Stakes (Group 2)
8 May	Chester	Chester Cup (Heritage Handicap)
8 May	Chester	Chester Vase (Group 3)
8 May	Chester	Huxley Stakes (Group 3)
9 May	Chester	Ormonde Stakes (Group 3)
9 May	Chester	Dee Stakes (Group 3)
10 May	Ascot	Victoria Cup (Heritage Handicap)
10 May	Lingfield Park	Derby Trial (Group 3)
14 May	York	Duke of York Stakes (Group 2)
14 May	York	Musidora Stakes (Group 3)
15 May	York	Dante Stakes (Group 2)
15 May	York	Middleton Stakes (Group 3)
16 May	York	Yorkshire Cup (Group 2)
17 May	Newbury	Lockinge Stakes (Group 1)
24 May	Haydock Park	John of Gaunt Stakes (Group 3)
29 May	Sandown Park	Henry II Stakes (Group 2)
29 May	Sandown Park	Brigadier Gerard Stakes (Group 3)
31 May	Haydock Park	Temple Stakes (Group 2)

June
6 Jun	Epsom	Coronation Cup (Group 1)
6 Jun	Epsom	Oaks (Group 1)
7 Jun	Epsom	The Derby (Group 1)
7 Jun	Epsom	Princess Elizabeth Stakes (Group 3)
7 Jun	Haydock Park	John Of Gaunt Stakes (Group 3)
17 Jun	Royal Ascot	King's Stand Stakes (Group 1)
17 Jun	Royal Ascot	Queen Anne Stakes (Group 1)
17 Jun	Royal Ascot	St James's Palace Stakes (Group 1)
17 Jun	Royal Ascot	Coventry Stakes (Group 2)
18 Jun	Royal Ascot	Prince of \Wales's Stakes (Group 1)
18 Jun	Royal Ascot	Queen Mary Stakes (Group 2)
18 Jun	Royal Ascot	Windsor Forest Stakes (Group 2)
18 Jun	Royal Ascot	Jersey Stakes (Group 3)
18 Jun	Royal Ascot	Royal Hunt Cup (Heritage Handicap)

19 Jun	Royal Ascot	Gold Cup (Group 1)
19 Jun	Royal Ascot	Ribblesdale Stakes (Group 2)
19 Jun	Royal Ascot	Norfolk Stakes (Group 2)
20 Jun	Royal Ascot	Coronation Stakes (Group 1)
20 Jun	Royal Ascot	King Edward VII Stakes (Group 2)
20 Jun	Royal Ascot	Albany Stakes (Group 3)
20 Jun	Royal Ascot	Queen's Vase (Group 3)
21 Jun	Royal Ascot	Golden Jubilee Stakes (Group 1)
21 Jun	Royal Ascot	Hardwicke Stakes (Group 2)
21 Jun	Royal Ascot	Wokingham (Heritage Handicap)
28 Jun	Newcastle	Northumberland Plate (Heritage Handicap)
28 Jun	Newmarket	Criterion Stakes (Group 3)

July

5 Jul	Haydock Park	Lancashire Oaks (Group 2)
5 Jul	Sandown Park	Coral-Eclipse Stakes (Group 1)
10 Jul	Newmarket	Falmouth Stakes (Group 1)
10 Jul	Newmarket	Cherry Hinton Stakes (Group 2)
11 Jul	Newmarket	Princess of Wales's Stakes (Group 2)
11 Jul	Newmarket	July Stakes (Group 2)
11 Jul	York	Summer Stakes (Group 3)
12 Jul	Newmarket	July Cup (Group 1)
12 Jul	Newmarket	Superlative Stakes (Group 2)
12 Jul	Newmarket	Bunbury Cup (Heritage Handicap)
12 Jul	York	John Smith's Cup (Heritage Handicap)
12 Jul	Newbury	Weatherbys Super Sprint
26 Jul	Ascot	King George VI and Queen Elizabeth Stakes (Group 1)
26 Jul	Ascot	Summer Mile (Group 2)
26 Jul	York	York Stakes (Group 2)
29 Jul	Goodwood	Lennox Stakes (Group 2)
29 Jul	Goodwood	Gordon Stakes (Group 3)
29 Jul	Goodwood	Molecomb Stakes (Group 3)
30 Jul	Goodwood	Sussex Stakes (Group 1)
30 Jul	Goodwood	Vintage Stakes (Group 2)
31 Jul	Goodwood	Goodwood Cup (Group 2)
31 Jul	Goodwood	King George Stakes (Group 3)

August

1 Aug	Goodwood	Richmond Stakes (Group 2)
1 Aug	Goodwood	Oak Tree Stakes (Group 3)
1 Aug	Goodwood	Mile (Heritage Handicap)
2 Aug	Goodwood	Nassau Stakes (Group 1)
2 Aug	Goodwood	Stewards' Cup (Heritage Handicap)
9 Aug	Ascot	Shergar Cup Day
9 Aug	Haydock Park	Rose of Lancaster Stakes (Group 3)
9 Aug	Newmarket	Sweet Solera Stakes (Group 3)
14 Aug	Salisbury	Sovereign Stakes (Group 3)
16 Aug	Newbury	Hungerford Stakes (Group 2)
16 Aug	Newbury	Geoffrey Freer Stakes (Group 3)
20 Aug	York	Juddmonte International (Group 1)
20 Aug	York	Great Voltigeur Stakes (Group 2)
20 Aug	York	Acomb Stakes (Group 3)
21 Aug	York	Yorkshire Oaks (Group 1)
21 Aug	York	Lowther Stakes (Group 2)
22 Aug	York	Gimcrack Stakes (Group 2)
22 Aug	York	Nunthorpe Stakes (Group 1)

23 Aug	York	Lonsdale Cup (Group 2)
23 Aug	York	Ebor (Heritage Handicap)
23 Aug	Goodwood	Celebration Mile (Group 2)
23 Aug	Goodwood	Prestige Stakes (Group 3)
23 Aug	Windsor	Winter Hill Stakes (Group 3)
24 Aug	Goodwood	Supreme Stakes (Group 3)
30 Aug	Sandown Park	Solario Stakes (Group 3)

September

6 Sep	Haydock Park	Sprint Cup (Group 1)
6 Sep	Kempton Park	Sirenia Stakes (Group 3)
6 Sep	Kempton Park	September Stakes (Group 3)
11 Sep	Doncaster	May Hill Stakes (Group 2)
11 Sep	Doncaster	Park Hill Stakes (Group 2)
12 Sep	Doncaster	Doncaster Cup (Group 2)
12 Sep	Doncaster	Flying Childers Stakes (Group 2)
13 Sep	Doncaster	St Leger (Group 1)
13 Sep	Doncaster	Park Stakes (Group 2)
13 Sep	Doncaster	Champagne Stakes (Group 2)
13 Sep	Doncaster	Portland (Heritage Handicap)
20 Sep	Ayr	Firth Of Clyde Stakes (Group 3)
20 Sep	Ayr	Ayr Gold Cup (Heritage Handicap)
20 Sep	Newbury	Mill Reef Stakes (Group 2)
20 Sep	Newbury	World Trophy (Group 3)
20 Sep	Newbury	Arc Trial (Group 3)
25 Sep	Newmarket	Somerville Tattersall Stakes (Group 3)
26 Sep	Newmarket	Rockfel Stakes (Group 2)
26 Sep	Newmarket	Oh So Sharp Stakes (Group 3)
26 Sep	Newmarket	Joel Stakes (Group 3)
27 Sep	Newmarket	Cheveley Park Stakes (Group 1)
27 Sep	Newmarket	Sun Chariot Stakes (Group 1)
27 Sep	Newmarket	Royal Lodge Stakes (Group 2)
27 Sep	Newmarket	Cambridgeshire (Heritage Handicap)

October

4 Oct	Ascot	Cumberland Lodge Stakes (Group 3)
4 Oct	Ascot	Bengough Stakes (Group 3)
11 Oct	Newmarket	Cesarewitch (Heritage Handicap)
11 Oct	Newmarket	Darley Stakes (Group 3)
17 Oct	Newmarket	Middle Park Stakes (Group 1)
17 Oct	Newmarket	Dewhurst Stakes (Group 1)
17 Oct	Newmarket	Fillies' Mile (Group 1)
17 Oct	Newmarket	Challenge Stakes (Group 2)
17 Oct	Newmarket	Autumn Stakes (Group 3)
17 Oct	Newmarket	Cornwallis Stakes (Group 3)
18 Oct	Ascot	Queen Elizabeth II Stakes (Group 1)
18 Oct	Ascot	Champion Stakes (Group 1)
18 Oct	Ascot	Champions Sprint (Group 2)
18 Oct	Ascot	Champions Filly & Mare Stakes (Group 2)
18 Oct	Ascot	Champions Long Distance Cup (Group 3)
25 Oct	Doncaster	Racing Post Trophy (Group 1)
25 Oct	Newbury	Horris Hill Stakes (Group 3)
25 Oct	Newbury	St Simon Stakes (Group 3)

November

| 8 Nov | Doncaster | November (Heritage Handicap) |

Track Facts

WANT TO size up the layout and undulations of the course where your fancy's about to line up? Over the next 30-odd pages, we bring you three-dimensional maps of all Britain's Flat tracks, allowing you to see at a glance the task facing your selection. The maps come to you courtesy of the *Racing Post*'s website (www.racingpost.com).

We've listed the top dozen trainers and jockeys at each course, ranked by strike-rate, with a breakdown of their relevant statistics over the last five years. The record of favourites is here as well and underline a basic fact of racing – that favourites generally offer very little in the way of value. Market leaders generated a profit to level stakes at only seven tracks during that period and run up colossal losses on the all-weather.

We've included addresses, phone numbers, directions and fixture lists for each track, together with Time Test's standard times for all you clock-watchers.

ASCOT

Ascot, Berkshire SL5 7JX
0870 7227 227

How to get there Road: M4 junction 6 or M3 junction 3 on to A332. Rail: Frequent service from Reading or Waterloo

○ Winning Post
◄ Startpoint
▲ Highest Point
▼ Lowest Point
◢ Open ditch
⬡ Water jump
🏇 Fence

Features RH, stiff climb for final mile on round course

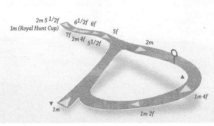

2014 Fixtures April 30, May 9-10, June 17-21, July 11-12, 25-27, August 9, September 6, October 3-4, 18

Time Test standard times

5f	58.85	1m2f	2min3.2
6f	1min12.3	1m4f	2min27.8
6f110yds	1min18.7	2m	3min23.5
7f	1min25.2	2m4f	4min18.7
1m (str)	1min37.9	2m5f195yds	4min41
1m (rnd)	1min38.6		

Trainers	Wins-Runs	%	2yo	3yo+	£1 level stks
Richard Hannon Snr	29-309	9	15-132	14-177	-100.75
Mark Johnston	23-249	9	2-33	21-216	-56.09
John Gosden	20-139	14	3-12	17-127	+14.65
Saeed bin Suroor	16-118	14	4-16	12-102	+30.01
A P O'Brien	15-103	15	3-27	12-76	-9.50
Sir Michael Stoute	13-108	12	1-9	12-99	-44.90
Andrew Balding	11-180	6	0-20	11-160	-123.42
Sir Henry Cecil	11-56	20	1-1	10-55	-2.75
Kevin Ryan	9-84	11	3-22	6-62	+16.00
Mick Channon	8-149	5	6-67	2-82	-82.63
Brian Meehan	8-96	8	3-28	5-68	-21.20
Clive Cox	8-88	9	3-14	5-74	-17.00
Roger Varian	8-58	14	1-7	7-51	+14.13

Jockeys	Wins-Rides	%	£1 level stks	Best Trainer	W-R
Ryan Moore	32-233	14	-59.73	Sir Michael Stoute	10-75
Richard Hughes	23-221	10	-73.60	Richard Hannon Snr	18-125
William Buick	18-153	12	-4.38	John Gosden	14-79
Jamie Spencer	17-155	11	-30.33	Kevin Ryan	4-11
Johnny Murtagh	17-101	17	+34.00	A P O'Brien	3-18
Kieren Fallon	14-159	9	-79.17	Luca Cumani	5-31
Tom Queally	13-127	10	-52.25	Sir Henry Cecil	7-40
James Doyle	12-91	13	-1.63	Roger Charlton	5-20
Frankie Dettori	11-130	8	-42.95	Saeed bin Suroor	7-33
Richard Hills	10-73	14	+18.46	John Gosden	3-7
Jim Crowley	9-111	8	-28.50	William Knight	3-10
Joe Fanning	9-100	9	-5.34	Mark Johnston	9-78
Jimmy Fortune	8-159	5	-101.67	Andrew Balding	4-65

Favourites

2yo	27.3% -24.98	3yo	34.5% +26.24	TOTAL	26.8% -68.40

Whitletts Road Ayr KA8 0JE.
Tel 01292 264 179

AYR

How to get there
Road: south from
Glasgow on A77
or A75, A70, A76.
Rail: Ayr, bus
service from
station on big
race days

Features LH

2014 Fixtures
April 27, May 21-22, June 9, 21, July
6-7, 14, 21, 28, August 9, 11,
September 18-20, 30, October 9

Time Test standard times

5f	57.7	1m2f	2min4.4
6f	1min9.7	1m2f192yds	2min14.3
7f	1min25	1m5f13yds	2min45.4
7f50yds	1min28	1m7f	3min13.2
1m	1min37.7	2m1f105yds	3min46
1m1f20yds	1min50	2m4f90yds	4min25

Trainers	Wins-Runs	%	2yo	3yo+	£1 level stks
Jim Goldie	44-435	10	0-31	44-404	-81.71
Richard Fahey	43-304	14	19-79	24-225	-12.59
Keith Dalgleish	26-173	15	4-38	22-135	+41.05
Linda Perratt	21-249	8	1-8	20-241	-3.50
Michael Dods	20-153	13	3-29	17-124	-17.05
Tim Easterby	19-118	16	6-21	13-97	+14.57
Kevin Ryan	16-148	11	8-52	8-96	-23.58
David Nicholls	12-125	10	0-10	12-115	-23.11
Alistair Whillans	12-80	15	0-1	12-79	-2.27
Alan Swinbank	10-61	16	4-11	6-50	+4.25
Brian Ellison	10-50	20	0-2	10-48	-2.34
David O'Meara	10-49	20	1-4	9-45	+14.63
John Quinn	10-41	24	2-8	8-33	+25.00

Jockeys	Wins-Rides	%	£1 level stks	Best Trainer	W-R
Tom Eaves	28-207	14	+20.05	Keith Dalgleish	9-62
Paul Hanagan	27-133	20	-16.72	Richard Fahey	17-81
P J McDonald	24-166	14	+4.25	Alan Swinbank	8-33
Phillip Makin	20-175	11	-19.95	Michael Dods	5-33
Graham Lee	20-153	13	-2.70	Jim Goldie	14-94
Robert Winston	17-96	18	-3.90	Charles Hills	5-13
Paul Mulrennan	16-114	14	-22.00	Michael Dods	4-22
Joe Fanning	15-131	11	-32.38	Keith Dalgleish	5-30
Tony Hamilton	15-128	12	+17.78	Richard Fahey	10-84
David Allan	14-100	14	-7.08	Tim Easterby	10-61
Daniel Tudhope	13-101	13	-12.98	David O'Meara	4-24
Graham Gibbons	12-106	11	-36.55	David Barron	5-40
Dale Swift	11-67	16	+15.50	Brian Ellison	4-17

Favourites

2yo	39.3% -10.71		3yo	30.5% -4.59	TOTAL	31.2% -47.88

BATH

Lansdown, Bath, Glos BA1 9BU
Tel 01291 622 260

How to get there
Road: M4, Jctn 18, then A46 south.
Rail: Bath Spa, special bus service to course on race days

Features LH uphill 4f straight

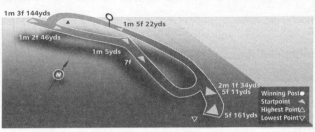

2014 Fixtures April 19, 28, May 5, 20, 29, June 6, 14, 23, July 1, 10, 15, 29, August 1, 21, 30, September 3, 13-14, 29, October 19

Time Test standard times

5f11yds	1min0.5	1m3f144yds	2min26
5f161yds	1min9	1m5f22yds	2min47.3
1m5yds	1min38	2m1f34yds	3min44
1m2f46yds	2min6.2		

Trainers	Wins-Runs	%	2yo	3yo+	£1 level stks
Richard Hannon Snr	31-132	23	19-79	12-53	+24.42
Mick Channon	27-214	13	11-76	16-138	-64.92
Ron Hodges	16-115	14	0-5	16-110	-26.29
Ronald Harris	15-231	6	3-54	12-177	-112.88
Malcolm Saunders	15-117	13	3-21	12-96	+8.75
Clive Cox	15-81	19	3-20	12-61	+17.13
David Evans	11-132	8	3-32	8-100	-67.37
Andrew Balding	11-75	15	2-13	9-62	-27.20
Mark Johnston	11-47	23	2-12	9-35	+19.83
Sir Mark Prescott Bt	11-29	38	3-11	8-18	-5.24
Tony Carroll	10-91	11	1-10	9-81	-11.75
Brian Meehan	10-46	22	5-23	5-23	+5.27
William Muir	9-58	16	0-11	9-47	-11.88

Jockeys	Wins-Rides	%	£1 level stks	Best Trainer	W-R
Richard Hughes	21-73	29	+35.63	Richard Hannon Snr	7-27
Cathy Gannon	20-181	11	-66.27	Eve Johnson Houghton	5-19
Luke Morris	18-195	9	-64.88	Sir Mark Prescott Bt	6-13
Liam Keniry	17-157	11	-53.83	J S Moore	4-20
Chris Catlin	17-149	11	-68.27	Mick Channon	3-23
Dane O'Neill	17-114	15	-29.40	Henry Candy	3-18
Pat Dobbs	17-84	20	+1.28	Richard Hannon Snr	8-39
Tom McLaughlin	13-118	11	-37.25	Malcolm Saunders	6-67
Fergus Sweeney	12-143	8	-41.50	Henry Candy	2-5
David Probert	12-115	10	-31.25	Andrew Balding	5-21
Martin Dwyer	12-56	21	-12.40	Brian Meehan	6-13
Richard Kingscote	11-83	13	-18.42	Tom Dascombe	5-23
Jimmy Fortune	11-52	21	-8.33	Andrew Balding	4-20

Favourites

2yo	39.7%	-7.66	3yo	31.1%	-45.00	TOTAL 34%	-57.84

York Road, Beverley, E Yorkshire
HU17 8QZ. Tel 01482 867 488

BEVERLEY

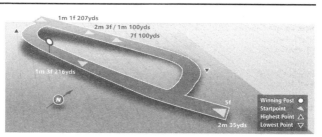

How to get there
Road: Course is
signposted from
the M62. Rail:
Beverley, bus
service to course
on race days

Features RH,
uphill finish

2014 Fixtures
April 16, 24, May 5, 13, 24, 28, June
11, 24, July 4-5, 15, 21, 29, August
13-14, 24, 30, September 17, 23

Time Test standard times

5f	1min0.5	1m3f216yds	2min30.6
7f100yds	1min29.5	1m4f16yds	2min32
1m100yds	1min42.4	2m35yds	3min29.5
1m1f207yds	2min0	2m3f100yds	4min16.7

Trainers	Wins-Runs	%	2yo	3yo+	£1 level stks
Mark Johnston	56-212	26	12-50	44-162	+43.11
Richard Fahey	25-234	11	13-84	12-150	-102.72
Kevin Ryan	24-154	16	9-50	15-104	+9.21
Tim Easterby	22-299	7	2-99	20-200	-172.25
David O'Meara	19-106	18	0-21	19-85	-7.38
Mel Brittain	16-94	17	1-22	15-72	+1.21
Paul Midgley	14-171	8	0-28	14-143	-50.78
Michael Easterby	14-158	9	0-34	14-124	-64.63
David Nicholls	13-112	12	0-17	13-95	+17.00
Bryan Smart	12-98	12	2-30	10-68	+15.90
Tracy Waggott	12-72	17	0-0	12-72	+3.83
Ann Duffield	11-83	13	8-46	3-37	+25.10
Neville Bycroft	11-83	13	0-0	11-83	+10.88

Jockeys	Wins-Rides	%	£1 level stks	Best Trainer	W-R
Silvestre De Sousa	45-178	25	+33.52	Mark Johnston	17-44
Paul Hanagan	24-155	15	-58.28	Richard Fahey	10-70
Robert Winston	23-129	18	+6.08	Mel Brittain	8-27
Graham Gibbons	19-159	12	-20.84	David Barron	4-25
Paul Mulrennan	16-138	12	-47.17	Michael Easterby	3-22
Joe Fanning	16-108	15	-35.89	Mark Johnston	15-71
James Sullivan	15-178	8	-73.13	Ruth Carr	7-55
P J McDonald	14-118	12	+1.21	James Turner	3-4
Franny Norton	14-77	18	+21.00	Mark Johnston	6-21
Tom Eaves	13-168	8	-46.10	Bryan Smart	7-45
Daniel Tudhope	12-77	16	-22.03	David O'Meara	7-41
Frederik Tylicki	11-72	15	+5.75	Richard Fahey	3-8
Amy Ryan	11-60	18	-3.58	Richard Whitaker	5-26

Favourites

2yo	35.5% -14.45	3yo	36.6% -4.91	TOTAL	34.4% -17.44

BRIGHTON

Freshfield Road, Brighton, E Sussex
BN2 2XZ. Tel 01273 603 580

How to get there
Road:
Signposted from
A23 London
Road and A27.
Rail: Brighton,
bus to course on
race days

Features LH,
undulating, sharp

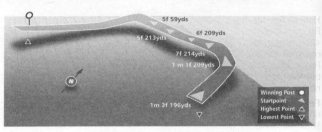

2014 Fixtures April 24, 30, May 6-7,
30, June 3, 17, 24, July 1, 8, 17,
August 6-8, 19, 31, September 1, 8,
15, October 7, 16

Time Test standard times

5f59yds	59.5	7f214yds	1min32
5f213yds	1min7.5	1m1f209yds	1min57.5
6f209yds	1min19.6	1m3f196yds	2min26

Trainers	Wins-Runs	%	2yo	3yo+	£1 level stks
Gary Moore	17-139	12	2-14	15-125	-57.57
David Evans	17-136	13	2-10	15-126	-4.13
David Simcock	17-42	40	7-13	10-29	+25.87
Richard Hannon Snr	16-90	18	11-50	5-40	-14.98
Mick Channon	14-112	13	4-37	10-75	-31.68
John Bridger	11-115	10	0-5	11-110	-47.00
Eve Johnson Houghton	11-59	19	1-9	10-50	+6.00
Mark Johnston	11-56	20	3-16	8-40	-3.48
George Margarson	9-58	16	0-2	9-56	-13.79
George Baker	9-49	18	0-9	9-40	+22.75
Alan Bailey	9-35	26	2-5	7-30	+17.70
Sir Mark Prescott Bt	9-24	38	2-6	7-18	+9.22
Ronald Harris	8-64	13	0-9	8-55	-6.00

Jockeys	Wins-Rides	%	£1 level stks	Best Trainer	W-R
Neil Callan	21-106	20	-30.80	James Tate	4-10
Seb Sanders	21-105	20	-14.08	Sir Mark Prescott Bt	3-11
George Baker	20-132	15	-24.37	Gary Moore	9-49
Chris Catlin	17-114	15	+4.10	Peter Hiatt	5-16
Richard Hughes	17-62	27	-10.79	Richard Hannon Snr	8-21
Liam Keniry	16-129	12	-26.28	Joseph Tuite	3-9
Cathy Gannon	15-140	11	-45.13	Eve Johnson Houghton	3-18
Tom Queally	14-93	15	-30.50	Sir Henry Cecil	3-9
Martin Lane	14-89	16	-14.73	David Simcock	7-17
Darryll Holland	13-48	27	+49.58	John Gallagher	2-4
Fergus Sweeney	11-110	10	-14.75	J R Jenkins	2-9
Jim Crowley	11-79	14	-27.13	Tony Carroll	2-8
Hayley Turner	11-74	15	-17.50	Michael Bell	3-17

Favourites

2yo	46.4%	-8.34	3yo	38.1%	-9.32	TOTAL 37.3% -16.73

Durdar Road, Carlisle, Cumbria,
CA2 4TS. Tel 01228 554 700

CARLISLE

How to get there
Road: M6 Jctn 42, follow signs on Dalston Road. Rail: Carlisle, 66 bus to course on race days

Features RH, undulating, uphill finish

2014 Fixtures May 26, June 2, 16, 25, July 5, 22, 27, August 4, 12, 27, September 10

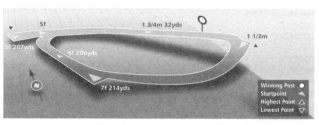

Time Test standard times

5f	59.6	1m3f107yds	2min23
5f193yds	1min11.8	1m6f32yds	2min59.2
6f192yds	1min24.7	2m1f52yds	3min42
7f200yds	1min37.6		
1m1f61yds	1min55		

Trainers	Wins-Runs	%	2yo	3yo+	£1 level stks
Tim Easterby	24-155	15	4-48	20-107	+6.13
Richard Fahey	18-144	13	8-49	10-95	-28.13
Brian Ellison	14-64	22	1-1	13-63	+21.08
Kevin Ryan	12-72	17	6-32	6-40	+77.10
Michael Easterby	10-75	13	2-14	8-61	+26.50
Mark Johnston	10-69	14	3-21	7-48	-0.75
Keith Dalgleish	9-73	12	1-17	8-56	+16.25
David O'Meara	9-53	17	2-9	7-44	-2.13
David Nicholls	8-50	16	0-5	8-45	-9.75
Ann Duffield	7-50	14	3-23	4-27	+25.25
Declan Carroll	7-36	19	1-9	6-27	+1.91
Mrs K Burke	7-36	19	2-4	5-32	+15.48
Michael Dods	6-83	7	1-24	5-59	-18.75

Jockeys	Wins-Rides	%	£1 level stks	Best Trainer	W-R
Paul Hanagan	18-94	19	-8.98	Richard Fahey	9-51
David Allan	15-83	18	-9.55	Tim Easterby	12-65
Joe Fanning	14-75	19	+38.25	Mark Johnston	7-39
P J McDonald	12-96	13	-22.72	Ann Duffield	4-11
Tom Eaves	9-124	7	-11.50	Bryan Smart	3-29
Tony Hamilton	8-90	9	-8.63	Richard Fahey	4-38
Duran Fentiman	8-71	11	+10.88	Tim Easterby	7-38
Graham Gibbons	8-54	15	+36.33	Michael Easterby	3-17
Dale Swift	8-44	18	+34.75	Brian Ellison	4-16
James Sullivan	7-97	7	+1.08	Ruth Carr	2-21
Phillip Makin	7-80	9	-5.76	Kevin Ryan	2-16
Andrew Elliott	7-67	10	+5.98	Mrs K Burke	3-13
Daniel Tudhope	7-44	16	-0.88	David O'Meara	5-20

Favourites
2yo 32.7% -10.22   3yo 35.2% -4.33   TOTAL 30.8% -26.06

CATTERICK

Catterick Bridge, Richmond, N Yorks
DL10 7PE. Tel 01748 811 478

How to get there
Road: A1, exit 5m
south of Scotch
Corner. Rail:
Darlington or
Northallerton and
bus

Features LH,
undulating, tight

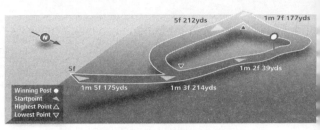

2014 Fixtures
April 9, 23, May 6, 24, 30, June 6,
July 2, 9, 16, 23, August 5, 15, 27,
September 20, October 7, 18, 28

Time Test standard times

5f	57.5	1m3f214yds	2min31
5f212yds	1min10.5	1m5f175yds	2min55.3
7f	1min23.2	1m7f177yds	3min21.2

Trainers	Wins-Runs	%	2yo	3yo+	£1 level stks
Tim Easterby	27-217	12	10-72	17-145	-30.94
David Nicholls	24-173	14	6-25	18-148	-69.97
David O'Meara	24-150	16	3-23	21-127	-28.70
Richard Fahey	20-118	17	12-49	8-69	-17.92
Mark Johnston	20-118	17	5-39	15-79	-21.36
Ruth Carr	16-111	14	0-1	16-110	+21.00
Kevin Ryan	14-91	15	7-34	7-57	-6.52
Geoffrey Harker	12-74	16	1-3	11-71	-15.13
Brian Ellison	12-63	19	0-1	12-62	+55.50
John Quinn	11-112	10	2-34	9-78	-32.25
Paul Midgley	10-144	7	0-21	10-123	-40.38
Michael Easterby	10-120	8	0-28	10-92	-4.50
Ann Duffield	10-99	10	3-50	7-49	-28.04

Jockeys	Wins-Rides	%	£1 level stks	Best Trainer	W-R
Silvestre De Sousa	34-142	24	+29.73	Mark Johnston	7-17
P J McDonald	22-199	11	+3.25	Ruth Carr	6-32
Daniel Tudhope	22-121	18	+12.36	David O'Meara	12-61
Paul Mulrennan	17-111	15	+4.00	James Tate	2-5
David Allan	16-127	13	-51.31	Tim Easterby	13-99
Paul Hanagan	14-108	13	-50.42	Richard Fahey	4-20
James Sullivan	13-170	8	-67.92	Ruth Carr	7-46
Duran Fentiman	13-141	9	+32.38	Tim Easterby	7-55
Adrian Nicholls	13-99	13	-55.60	David Nicholls	11-82
Michael O'Connell	13-93	14	-28.50	David Nicholls	3-14
Graham Gibbons	12-104	12	+113.67	David Barron	2-16
Barry McHugh	12-94	13	+40.75	Tracy Waggott	4-10
Graham Lee	12-79	15	-5.65	Conor Dore	1-1

Favourites

2yo	38.8% -4.81	3yo	31.1% -27.56	TOTAL	31.2% -45.89

Chepstow, Monmouthshire,
NP16 6BE. Tel 01291 622 260

CHEPSTOW

How to get there
Road: M4 Jct 22
on west side of
Severn Bridge,
A48 north, A446.
Rail: Chepstow,
bus to course on
race days

Features LH,
undulating

2014 Fixtures May 2, 14, 28, June 2,
13, 23, July 2, 11, 25, August 6, 14,
25, September 5, 11, 16

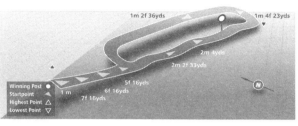

Time Test standard times

5f16yds	57	1m4f23yds	2min31.3
6f16yds	1min8.8	2m49yds	3min28
7f16yds	1min20.5	2m1f40yds	3min41
1m14yds	1min32.6	2m2f	3min52
1m2f36yds	2min4.2		

Trainers	Wins-Runs	%	2yo	3yo+	£1 level stks
Richard Hannon Snr	17-101	17	11-47	6-54	-31.60
Andrew Balding	17-65	26	1-8	16-57	+20.48
Bernard Llewellyn	16-101	16	0-0	16-101	+13.33
Ronald Harris	14-159	9	6-34	8-125	-40.50
Malcolm Saunders	13-65	20	1-12	12-53	+22.00
Ralph Beckett	13-46	28	2-14	11-32	+29.38
John Spearing	11-35	31	0-2	11-33	+9.13
Mick Channon	10-80	13	5-32	5-48	-40.29
John O'Shea	9-45	20	0-0	9-45	+67.00
Mark Johnston	9-37	24	0-7	9-30	+5.88
David Evans	8-131	6	1-31	7-100	-73.50
Tony Carroll	8-93	9	1-6	7-87	-47.13
Dai Burchell	8-45	18	0-1	8-44	+61.13

Jockeys	Wins-Rides	%	£1 level stks	Best Trainer	W-R
Cathy Gannon	20-133	15	+4.13	John Spearing	6-14
David Probert	19-110	17	-12.27	Andrew Balding	13-32
Richard Hughes	18-84	21	-10.31	Richard Hannon Snr	5-22
Jim Crowley	14-80	18	+4.22	Ralph Beckett	8-28
Tom McLaughlin	12-67	18	+36.63	Malcolm Saunders	6-21
Martin Lane	10-77	13	+35.38	Bernard Llewellyn	4-28
Luke Morris	8-107	7	-50.39	Sir Mark Prescott Bt	2-3
Chris Catlin	8-94	9	-49.15	David Simcock	1-1
James Doyle	8-41	20	+25.75	John Spearing	3-3
Pat Dobbs	8-36	22	-6.26	Richard Hannon Snr	8-25
William Carson	7-68	10	-11.50	Anthony Carson	2-5
Dane O'Neill	7-67	10	-36.75	Henry Candy	3-11
Liam Keniry	6-81	7	-42.75	Alan Coogan	1-1

Favourites

2yo	30.5%	-18.84		3yo	33.3%	-26.99		TOTAL	30.5%	-64.18

CHESTER

Steam Mill Street, Chester, CH1 2LY
Tel 01244 304 600

How to get there
Road: Inner Ring
Road and A458
Queensferry
Road.
Rail: Chester
General, bus to
city centre

Features LH, flat,
very sharp

2014 Fixtures May 7-9, 31, June 14,
27-28, July 11-12, August 3, 16, 30,
September 12-13, 27

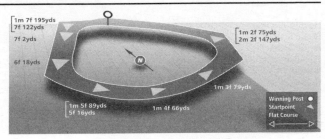

Time Test standard times

5f16yds	59.8	1m3f79yds	2min22.7
6f18yds	1min13	1m4f66yds	2min35
7f2yds	1min24.7	1m5f89yds	2min48.6
7f122yds	1min31.2	1m7f195yds	3min22
1m1f70yds	1min55	2m2f147yds	4min1
1m2f75yds	2min8		

Trainers	Wins-Runs	%	2yo	3yo+	£1 level stks
Mark Johnston	33-201	16	6-35	27-166	+68.24
Richard Fahey	32-252	13	10-50	22-202	-54.38
Andrew Balding	16-83	19	1-13	15-70	+25.75
Mick Channon	14-93	15	5-31	9-62	+12.00
Tom Dascombe	11-127	9	6-49	5-78	-35.63
Kevin Ryan	11-86	13	1-13	10-73	-10.79
Paul Green	11-77	14	1-9	10-68	+6.25
John Gosden	11-41	27	1-4	10-37	+8.71
A P O'Brien	9-18	50	0-0	9-18	+4.94
David Evans	8-158	5	2-58	6-100	-96.50
Ian Williams	8-61	13	0-0	8-61	+40.50
Sir Michael Stoute	8-38	21	0-4	8-34	-9.19
William Haggas	8-35	23	5-9	3-26	-9.39

Jockeys	Wins-Rides	%	£1 level stks	Best Trainer	W-R
Franny Norton	37-221	17	+78.57	Mark Johnston	12-53
Joe Fanning	19-125	15	-1.00	Mark Johnston	12-77
Ryan Moore	16-60	27	-8.68	A P O'Brien	6-9
Tony Hamilton	12-85	14	+23.50	Richard Fahey	8-56
Paul Hanagan	12-62	19	+7.88	Richard Fahey	7-34
Robert Winston	10-65	15	+1.32	B W Hills	3-9
Richard Kingscote	9-83	11	-24.63	Tom Dascombe	8-67
Silvestre De Sousa	9-55	16	+7.41	Mark Johnston	5-16
Graham Lee	9-35	26	+4.54	James Tate	2-2
Jamie Spencer	8-56	14	+3.38	David Barron	1-1
Richard Mullen	8-45	18	+12.83	Andrew Balding	3-6
William Buick	8-30	27	+15.50	John Gosden	5-16
David Probert	7-52	13	-16.00	Andrew Balding	7-38

Favourites

2yo	43.9%	+2.70	3yo	35.8% +4.93	TOTAL	31.7% -29.79

Leger Way, Doncaster
DN2 6BB. Tel 01302 320066/7

DONCASTER

How to get there
Road: M18 Jct 3,
A638, A18 to Hull.
Rail: Doncaster
Central

Features LH, flat

2014 Fixtures
March 29-30,
April 25-26, May
3, 12, 17, June 7,
15, 27-28, July 4, 10, 17, 24, August 2,
16, September 10-13, October 24-25,
November 8

Course diagram labels: 1m 6f 132yds, 2m 110yds, 2 1/4m, 5f, 5f 140yds, 6f 110yds, 6f, 7f, 1m, 1 1/2m, 1m 2f 60yds, 1m

Winning Post ●
Startpoint ◄
Highest Point △
Lowest Point ▽

Time Test standard times

5f	58.7	1m (Rnd)	1min 37.2
5f140yds	1min7.4	1m2f60yds	2min6
6f	1min11.5	1m4f	2min30
6f110yds	1min18	1m6f132yds	3min3
7f	1min24.3	2m110yds	3min32
1m (Str)	1min36.8	2m2f	3min53

Trainers	Wins-Runs	%	2yo	3yo+	£1 level stks
Richard Fahey	36-339	11	11-84	25-255	-69.77
John Gosden	28-127	22	5-32	23-95	+25.31
Richard Hannon Snr	27-154	18	20-96	7-58	-3.62
Saeed bin Suroor	21-109	19	8-26	13-83	-29.29
Mark Johnston	16-198	8	2-53	14-145	-104.40
Tim Easterby	15-264	6	2-56	13-208	-123.75
Charles Hills	14-90	16	5-32	9-58	+37.63
Michael Bell	14-87	16	5-22	9-65	-20.50
Roger Varian	14-55	25	3-14	11-41	+35.41
David Barron	13-99	13	2-9	11-90	+17.11
Luca Cumani	13-72	18	0-9	13-63	-13.13
David O'Meara	11-141	8	0-11	11-130	-29.00
William Haggas	11-75	15	1-21	10-54	-28.13

Jockeys	Wins-Rides	%	£1 level stks	Best Trainer	W-R
Paul Hanagan	36-231	16	+6.00	Richard Fahey	18-119
William Buick	31-127	24	+33.23	John Gosden	15-58
Jamie Spencer	20-137	15	+0.07	Michael Bell	8-27
Silvestre De Sousa	19-164	12	-44.47	Saeed bin Suroor	7-21
Richard Hughes	17-102	17	-23.96	Richard Hannon Snr	13-55
Robert Winston	15-133	11	-1.63	Alan Swinbank	4-11
Kieren Fallon	14-139	10	-59.50	Luca Cumani	5-27
Ryan Moore	14-97	14	-48.66	Jeremy Noseda	3-10
Dane O'Neill	14-55	25	+62.25	Richard Hannon Snr	3-6
Neil Callan	13-110	12	+1.75	Michael Jarvis	2-7
Frankie Dettori	13-79	16	-14.65	Saeed bin Suroor	7-27
Tom Queally	12-100	12	-4.92	Sir Henry Cecil	6-19
Ted Durcan	12-91	13	+29.95	David Lanigan	4-12

Favourites

2yo	39.4%	-3.07	3yo	31.1%	-38.75	TOTAL	30.9%	-76.39

EPSOM

Epsom Downs, Surrey, KT18 5LQ
Tel 01372 726 311

How to get there
Road: M25 Jct 8
(A217) or 9 (A24),
2m south of
Epsom on B290.
Rail: Epsom
and bus, Epsom
Downs or
Tattenham
Corner

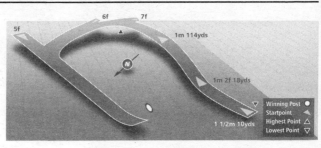

Features LH,
undulating

2014 Fixtures April 23, June 6-7,
July 3, 10, 17, 31, August 25-26,
September 11, 28

Time Test standard times

5f	53.8	1m114yds	1min41.6
6f	1min8	1m2f18yds	2min3.5
7f	1min20.2	1m4f10yds	2min33.6

Trainers	Wins-Runs	%	2yo	3yo+	£1 level stks
Richard Hannon Snr	24-121	20	16-49	8-72	-28.47
Andrew Balding	18-98	18	8-23	10-75	+15.36
Mark Johnston	16-131	12	4-26	12-105	-51.05
Sir Mark Prescott Bt	11-25	44	3-9	8-16	+17.52
Mick Channon	10-99	10	5-42	5-57	-19.05
David Simcock	10-37	27	1-4	9-33	+22.92
Saeed bin Suroor	9-38	24	0-4	9-34	-4.51
Richard Fahey	8-58	14	2-6	6-52	+10.50
Stuart Kittow	8-28	29	0-1	8-27	+22.00
Ralph Beckett	7-41	17	2-7	5-34	+2.13
A P O'Brien	7-36	19	0-0	7-36	+1.48
Stuart Williams	6-39	15	0-1	6-38	+22.04
John Bridger	6-35	17	0-0	6-35	+22.00

Jockeys	Wins-Rides	%	£1 level stks	Best Trainer	W-R
Richard Hughes	22-95	23	+6.97	Richard Hannon Snr	12-58
Neil Callan	14-90	16	-9.50	James Tate	3-8
Ryan Moore	14-72	19	+4.82	A P O'Brien	2-3
David Probert	12-56	21	+30.50	Andrew Balding	9-38
Kieren Fallon	12-54	22	+36.91	Mark Johnston	6-14
Seb Sanders	11-57	19	+28.65	Sir Mark Prescott Bt	7-11
Jamie Spencer	9-69	13	-4.25	Michael Bell	2-10
Ian Mongan	9-62	15	-8.05	Sir Henry Cecil	2-6
Jim Crowley	8-50	16	+9.13	Ralph Beckett	4-21
Jimmy Fortune	7-60	12	-20.93	Andrew Balding	4-29
Silvestre De Sousa	7-53	13	-19.25	Mark Johnston	4-29
Tom Queally	7-46	15	-4.56	Sir Henry Cecil	3-15
Luke Morris	7-27	26	+56.75	John Best	2-2

Favourites

2yo	34.5% -17.40	3yo	27.5% -37.55	TOTAL	29.5% -72.41

CLINICAL: a big winner for Sir Mark Prescott on Derby day in 2012 at Epsom, where the trainer has a staggering 44% strike-rate in the last four seasons

FFOS LAS

Trimsaran, Carmarthenshire, SA17 4DE
Tel: 01554 811092

How to get there
Road: M4 Jctn
48 and follow the
A4138 to Llanelli.
Rail: Llanelli,
Kidwelly or
Carmarthen

Features LH, flat,
galloping

2014 Fixtures
June 30, July 31, August 5, 12, 22, 28,
September 14

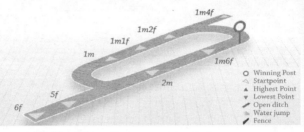

1m4f
1m2f
1m1f
1m
1m6f
2m
5f
6f

O Winning Post
◁ Startpoint
▲ Highest Point
▼ Lowest Point
✐ Open ditch
≋ Water jump
✐ Fence

Time Test standard times

5f	56.1	1m2f	2min1.7
6f	1min7.4	1m4f	2min29
1m	1min38	1m6f	2min54
1m1f	1min49.7	2m	3min23

Trainers	Wins-Runs	%	2yo	3yo+	£1 level stks
David Evans	16-105	15	4-28	12-77	+5.82
David Simcock	11-39	28	2-9	9-30	+14.66
Ronald Harris	8-67	12	5-20	3-47	-22.50
Mark Johnston	8-42	19	2-8	6-34	-7.38
Brian Meehan	8-27	30	3-11	5-16	+4.48
Mick Channon	7-55	13	3-27	4-28	-20.17
Bernard Llewellyn	7-54	13	0-0	7-54	-13.00
Ralph Beckett	7-20	35	2-7	5-13	+17.58
Rod Millman	6-61	10	2-14	4-47	-28.00
Roger Charlton	6-26	23	4-11	2-15	-12.66
Daniel Mark Loughnane	5-31	16	0-3	5-28	-4.75
Richard Hannon Snr	5-24	21	2-11	3-13	-3.89
Peter Makin	5-19	26	1-3	4-16	+16.00

Jockeys	Wins-Rides	%	£1 level stks	Best Trainer	W-R
Steve Drowne	13-57	23	+51.71	Peter Makin	4-7
Cathy Gannon	10-67	15	-5.01	David Evans	5-31
Martin Lane	10-62	16	+20.79	David Simcock	3-15
Martin Dwyer	10-37	27	+7.23	Brian Meehan	4-7
Martin Harley	9-28	32	+14.38	Mick Channon	4-10
Richard Hughes	8-34	24	-4.05	Patrick Morris	1-1
Joe Fanning	8-24	33	+16.63	Mark Johnston	5-15
Chris Catlin	7-30	23	+15.88	David Simcock	1-1
Shane Kelly	6-27	22	-1.84	William Knight	2-6
Declan Bates	6-23	26	+20.88	David Evans	5-16
Tadhg O'Shea	6-16	38	+126.00	John Gallagher	2-4
David Probert	5-54	9	-40.64	Gay Kelleway	1-1
James Doyle	5-34	15	-16.75	David Evans	2-9

Favourites

2yo	39.6%	-7.21	3yo	45.1% +8.56	TOTAL 33.8%	-36.82

Chichester, W Sussex,
PO18 0PS. Tel 01243 755 022

GOODWOOD

How to get there
Road: signposted
from A27 south
and A285 north.
Rail: Chichester,
bus to course on
race days

Features RH,
undulating

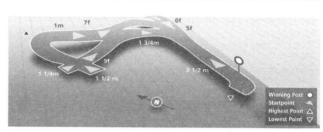

2014 Fixtures
May 3, 22-24, June 6, 8, 13, 20, July
29-31, August 1-2, 22-24, September
2, 24, October 12

Time Test standard times

5f	56.4	1m3f	2min20
6f	1min10	1m4f	2min32.7
7f	1min24.4	1m6f	2min59
1m	1min36.8	2m	3min22
1m1f	1min52	2m4f	4min13
1m1f192yds	2min2.2	2m5f	4min27.3

Trainers	Wins-Runs	%	2yo	3yo+	£1 level stks
Richard Hannon Snr	71-417	17	36-195	35-222	+33.63
Mark Johnston	24-194	12	8-45	16-149	-1.88
Amanda Perrett	20-159	13	2-29	18-130	+20.75
Sir Michael Stoute	19-93	20	1-9	18-84	-6.23
Jeremy Noseda	16-64	25	3-10	13-54	+23.25
John Gosden	15-102	15	3-28	12-74	-5.96
Brian Meehan	14-76	18	7-30	7-46	+16.13
Sir Henry Cecil	14-60	23	0-2	14-58	-9.53
John Dunlop	13-91	14	4-19	9-72	-23.25
Mick Channon	12-215	6	4-94	8-121	-74.09
Roger Charlton	12-54	22	2-6	10-48	+14.63
Luca Cumani	11-55	20	1-1	10-54	-12.08
Mahmood Al Zarooni	11-54	20	6-28	5-26	-5.25

Jockeys	Wins-Rides	%	£1 level stks	Best Trainer	W-R
Richard Hughes	65-302	22	+37.73	Richard Hannon Snr	48-207
Ryan Moore	28-181	15	-41.08	Sir Michael Stoute	12-57
Kieren Fallon	27-147	18	+0.07	Luca Cumani	7-33
William Buick	25-159	16	+7.78	John Gosden	10-61
Pat Dobbs	22-140	16	+46.75	Amanda Perrett	10-33
Tom Queally	19-141	13	-42.75	Sir Henry Cecil	12-47
George Baker	19-123	15	+30.25	Patrick Chamings	3-9
Frankie Dettori	19-118	16	-36.65	Mahmood Al Zarooni	6-20
Ted Durcan	10-79	13	-20.50	John Dunlop	6-20
Dane O'Neill	9-100	9	-15.68	Derek Haydn Jones	2-2
Jim Crowley	8-168	5	-74.00	Amanda Perrett	2-24
Adam Kirby	8-85	9	-15.63	Walter Swinburn	2-16
Hayley Turner	8-75	11	-16.50	James Fanshawe	3-4

Favourites

2yo	42.5%	+18.26	3yo	33%	-3.99	TOTAL 33.5% +12.01

HAMILTON

Bothwell Road, Hamilton, Lanarkshire
ML3 0DW. Tel 01698 283 806

How to get there
Road: M74 Jct 5,
off the A74. Rail:
Hamilton West

Features RH,
undulating, dip
can become
testing in wet
weather

2014 Fixtures
May 4, 16, 28, June 5, 11, 18, 26,
July 1, 12, 17-18, August 2, 22, 28,
September 2, 21-22, 29

Time Test standard times

5f4yds	58.2	1m1f36yds	1min54.3
5f200yds	1min9.2	1m3f16yds	2min19.2
6f5yds	1min10	1m4f17yds	2min32.2
1m65yds	1min43.5	1m5f9yds	2min45.4

Trainers	Wins-Runs	%	2yo	3yo+	£1 level stks
Mark Johnston	46-203	23	6-42	40-161	+15.24
Kevin Ryan	33-131	25	7-39	26-92	+39.48
Richard Fahey	27-171	16	6-42	21-129	-64.38
Keith Dalgleish	22-152	14	4-22	18-130	-15.93
Alan Swinbank	18-102	18	1-4	17-98	+37.40
Bryan Smart	17-83	20	7-20	10-63	+18.97
David Nicholls	17-74	23	0-3	17-71	+40.88
Linda Perratt	16-280	6	0-7	16-273	-101.25
Jim Goldie	16-182	9	0-4	16-178	-85.00
Ann Duffield	14-76	18	4-15	10-61	+13.08
Richard Guest	13-93	14	1-4	12-89	+31.25
Tim Easterby	13-90	14	1-14	12-76	+9.58
David Barron	13-55	24	3-10	10-45	+22.91

Jockeys	Wins-Rides	%	£1 level stks	Best Trainer	W-R
Joe Fanning	41-162	25	+38.81	Mark Johnston	31-104
Paul Hanagan	24-101	24	-16.48	Richard Fahey	16-52
P J McDonald	20-143	14	-17.24	Alan Swinbank	6-35
Tom Eaves	19-225	8	-81.80	Bryan Smart	8-49
Silvestre De Sousa	16-62	26	+10.39	Mark Johnston	7-14
Julie Burke	15-83	18	+3.05	Kevin Ryan	9-26
Paul Mulrennan	12-115	10	-74.65	Kevin Ryan	2-4
David Allan	12-65	18	-10.69	Tim Easterby	6-34
Jason Hart	12-65	18	+6.95	Eric Alston	8-36
Phillip Makin	11-125	9	-80.10	Kevin Ryan	6-35
Daniel Tudhope	11-68	16	+23.25	David O'Meara	4-22
Graham Lee	10-86	12	-29.23	Jim Goldie	3-31
Andrew Elliott	9-61	15	+10.13	Alan Swinbank	3-8

Favourites

2yo	45.2%	-3.35		3yo	37.7%	-13.51	TOTAL 36.1% -28.85

Newton-Le-Willows, Merseyside
WA12 0HQ. Tel 01942 725 963

HAYDOCK

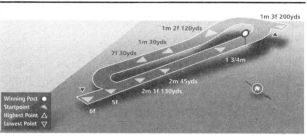

How to get there
Road: M6 Jct 23,
A49 to Wigan.
Rail: Wigan & 320
bus or Newton-le-
Willows

Features LH, flat,
easy turns, suits
the galloping type

2014 Fixtures
April 26, May 23-24, 29-31, June
11-12, 21, July 3-5, 18-19, August 7-9,
September 4-6, 26-27

Time Test standard times

5f4yds	58.2	1m1f36yds	1min54.3
5f200yds	1min9.2	1m3f16yds	2min19.2
6f5yds	1min10	1m4f17yds	2min32.2
1m65yds	1min43.5	1m5f9yds	2min45.4

Trainers	Wins-Runs	%	2yo	3yo+	£1 level stks
Tom Dascombe	34-163	21	14-69	20-94	+43.28
Richard Fahey	26-265	10	7-65	19-200	-76.75
Mark Johnston	22-227	10	2-47	20-180	-78.01
Roger Varian	20-64	31	5-12	15-52	+34.37
John Gosden	19-70	27	3-15	16-55	+9.44
Kevin Ryan	18-146	12	4-54	14-92	+101.32
William Haggas	18-57	32	5-11	13-46	+34.85
B W Hills	17-57	30	8-18	9-39	+25.24
Mrs K Burke	16-87	18	4-20	12-67	+21.52
Richard Hannon Snr	15-122	12	12-65	3-57	-60.68
David O'Meara	12-82	15	0-7	12-75	-21.88
Mick Channon	11-101	11	6-46	5-55	-20.06
Ian Williams	11-75	15	0-1	11-74	+15.50

Jockeys	Wins-Rides	%	£1 level stks	Best Trainer	W-R
Richard Kingscote	31-148	21	+48.13	Tom Dascombe	27-113
Paul Hanagan	24-181	13	-71.10	Richard Fahey	7-65
Jamie Spencer	22-136	16	-18.17	Michael Bell	4-16
Neil Callan	16-107	15	+2.51	Roger Varian	7-20
Graham Gibbons	15-133	11	-28.45	Ed McMahon	5-21
Silvestre De Sousa	15-119	13	-34.59	Mark Johnston	4-34
Kieren Fallon	15-84	18	+11.67	Brian Meehan	2-9
Tom Queally	14-84	17	-12.42	Sir Henry Cecil	4-17
Daniel Tudhope	13-73	18	-12.63	David O'Meara	8-37
William Buick	13-73	18	-10.26	John Gosden	9-35
Joe Fanning	12-136	9	-42.29	Mark Johnston	11-91
Phillip Makin	12-116	10	+13.28	Kevin Ryan	5-48
Franny Norton	12-97	12	-29.38	Mark Johnston	3-13

Favourites

2yo	36.5%	-26.06		3yo	39.6%	+7.41		TOTAL	34.7%	-23.34

KEMPTON

Staines Rd East, Sunbury-On-Thames
TW16 5AQ. Tel 01932 782 292

How to get there
Road: M3 Jct 1,
A308 to Kingston-
on-Thames. Rail:
Kempton Park
from Waterloo

Features RH,
all-weather, sharp

2014 Fixtures
March 29, 31,
April 1-2, 9-10, 19,
27-28, May 6-7, 21, 28, June 4-5, 11,
23, July 2, 9, August 4-6, 13, 18, 20,
27, September 2-3, 5-6, 10, 18, 22, 24-
25, October 1-2, 8, 15, 22-23, 29-30,
November 5, 10, 12-13, 19-20, 26-27,
December 1, 3-4, 8, 10-11, 16-18, 22

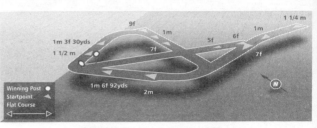

Time Test standard times

5f	59.5	1m2f	2min3.7
6f	1min11.5	1m3f	2min17.8
7f	1min24.2	1m4f	2min30.5
1m	1min37.6	2m	3min27
1m1f	1min50.5		

Trainers	Wins-Runs	%	2yo	3yo+	£1 level stks
Richard Hannon Snr	113-707	16	58-356	55-351	-50.56
Ralph Beckett	56-253	22	24-98	32-155	+33.13
Andrew Balding	55-364	15	8-75	47-289	-27.54
Saeed bin Suroor	55-197	28	29-67	26-130	+33.66
John Gosden	53-282	19	16-96	37-186	-52.40
Mark Johnston	48-378	13	8-86	40-292	-118.13
Tony Carroll	47-474	10	0-17	47-457	-122.59
Marco Botti	47-280	17	14-87	33-193	-68.76
James Fanshawe	47-195	24	1-22	46-173	+83.42
Gary Moore	43-331	13	8-42	35-289	-114.38
Ronald Harris	35-278	13	3-45	32-233	+74.58
Dean Ivory	34-314	11	2-30	32-284	+31.00
David Evans	34-314	11	7-69	27-245	-124.59

Jockeys	Wins-Rides	%	£1 level stks	Best Trainer	W-R
Jim Crowley	131-832	16	+27.08	Ralph Beckett	44-185
Adam Kirby	114-724	16	-3.40	Marco Botti	18-89
Luke Morris	110-965	11	-132.87	Ronald Harris	22-140
Richard Hughes	104-566	18	-91.76	Richard Hannon Snr	59-254
George Baker	67-566	12	-127.47	Gary Moore	15-125
Neil Callan	62-376	16	+71.76	Tony Carroll	8-47
William Buick	61-316	19	-11.11	John Gosden	29-150
David Probert	60-465	13	+18.38	Andrew Balding	24-148
Ryan Moore	59-276	21	+1.61	Sir Michael Stoute	14-53
Silvestre De Sousa	52-292	18	+32.65	Saeed bin Suroor	12-48
Dane O'Neill	51-541	9	-226.48	David Elsworth	7-45
Liam Keniry	49-656	7	-283.70	Sylvester Kirk	9-80
Kieren Fallon	48-346	14	-73.69	Luca Cumani	14-67

Favourites

2yo	36.7%	-45.42	3yo	34.7%	-114.27

TOTAL 33.4% -197.24

LEICESTER

London Road, Oadby, Leicester,
LE2 4QH. Tel 0116 271 6515

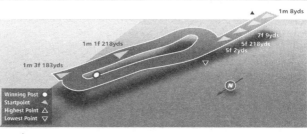

How to get there
Road: M1 Jct 21,
A6, 2m south of
city. Rail:
Leicester, bus

Features RH,
straight mile is
downhill for first
4f, then uphill to
finish

2014 Fixtures April 4, 26, May 19, 26-
27, June 2, 14, 19, 26, July 5, 17, 23,
30, August 10, 19, September 1, 19,
22, October 7, 14, 27

Time Test standard times

5f2yds	58.3	1m60yds	1min41.9
5f218yds	1min10.2	1m1f218yds	2min2.7
7f9yds	1min22.3	1m3f183yds	2min28.6

Trainers	Wins-Runs	%	2yo	3yo+	£1 level stks
Richard Hannon Snr	29-148	20	19-80	10-68	-18.80
Mark Johnston	17-121	14	9-47	8-74	-18.30
Mick Channon	14-88	16	11-50	3-38	-9.49
Luca Cumani	12-44	27	2-16	10-28	+6.23
Richard Fahey	11-61	18	2-18	9-43	+93.00
Sir Michael Stoute	11-46	24	5-22	6-24	-10.64
Ralph Beckett	9-45	20	3-19	6-26	+37.83
John Gosden	9-37	24	3-18	6-19	+3.70
David Evans	8-111	7	3-46	5-65	-45.43
Rod Millman	8-68	12	4-17	4-51	-27.50
Brian Meehan	8-59	14	4-33	4-26	-25.75
Kevin Ryan	8-58	14	5-23	3-35	-14.78
Saeed bin Suroor	8-29	28	3-12	5-17	-9.28

Jockeys	Wins-Rides	%	£1 level stks	Best Trainer	W-R
Ryan Moore	29-77	38	+21.53	Sir Michael Stoute	8-21
Richard Hughes	22-81	27	-6.37	Richard Hannon Snr	12-42
Kieren Fallon	19-78	24	+2.31	Luca Cumani	6-18
Silvestre De Sousa	15-66	23	+9.19	Mark Johnston	5-22
Paul Hanagan	14-83	17	-22.87	William Haggas	2-4
James Doyle	12-75	16	-4.57	Roger Charlton	3-7
Tom Queally	11-94	12	-37.43	Sir Henry Cecil	3-20
Chris Catlin	11-85	13	+23.13	Rae Guest	4-9
Andrea Atzeni	11-74	15	+27.85	Roger Varian	3-8
Adam Kirby	10-65	15	-12.72	Clive Cox	5-24
Shane Kelly	10-60	17	+38.63	Brian Meehan	4-9
Jamie Spencer	10-50	20	-19.50	Paul Cole	2-4
Jack Mitchell	10-33	30	+29.25	Ralph Beckett	3-7

Favourites

2yo	36.4%	-18.09	3yo	46.1%	+33.68	TOTAL	37.9%	-1.11

LINGFIELD turf

Racecourse Road, Lingfield
RH7 6PQ. Tel 01342 834 800

How to get there
Road: M25 Jctn 6, south on A22, then B2029. Rail: Lingfield from London Bridge or Victoria

Features LH, undulating

2014 Fixtures
May 9-10, 21, June 5, 7, 10, 14, 21, 28, July 9, 16, 19, 26, 28, August 2, 9, 16, 20, 28, September 3, 13

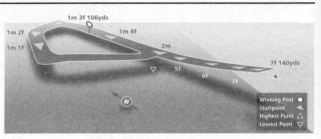

Time Test standard times

5f	56.3	1m2f	2min5.4
6f	1min9	1m3f106yds	2min24.4
7f	1min20.7	1m6f	2min58.6
7f140yds	1min28.2	2m	3min24.6
1m1f	1min52.5		

Trainers	Wins-Runs	%	2yo	3yo+	£1 level stks
Richard Hannon Snr	13-87	15	11-48	2-39	-33.70
Mick Channon	13-70	19	3-29	10-41	+30.50
Gary Moore	8-60	13	3-10	5-50	-19.25
J R Jenkins	8-35	23	1-7	7-28	+5.21
Tony Carroll	8-33	24	0-1	8-32	+1.25
Roger Charlton	8-17	47	3-5	5-12	+9.23
Sir Michael Stoute	7-34	21	1-6	6-28	-3.57
Ralph Beckett	7-30	23	1-8	6-22	-5.56
Sir Henry Cecil	7-21	33	1-2	6-19	+5.39
Mahmood Al Zarooni	7-17	41	5-10	2-7	+13.98
David Evans	6-50	12	0-7	6-43	-12.00
William Haggas	6-26	23	2-9	4-17	-6.03
Alan Jarvis	6-22	27	1-10	5-12	+29.83

Jockeys	Wins-Rides	%	£1 level stks	Best Trainer	W-R
Richard Hughes	14-68	21	+12.09	Richard Hannon Snr	6-24
Jim Crowley	9-44	20	-5.35	Ralph Beckett	4-15
Ryan Moore	9-44	20	-10.21	Gary Moore	2-7
Harry Bentley	9-43	21	+26.60	Alan Jarvis	2-4
Dane O'Neill	8-55	15	-17.70	Roger Varian	2-2
Ian Mongan	8-50	16	-13.79	Sir Henry Cecil	2-2
Adam Kirby	8-41	20	-1.96	David Evans	2-4
Luke Morris	7-77	9	-45.70	Ed Walker	1-1
Liam Keniry	7-62	11	-33.84	Conor Dore	1-1
Tom Queally	7-53	13	-33.36	Sir Henry Cecil	5-16
Andrea Atzeni	7-45	16	+17.25	Derek Haydn Jones	2-3
James Doyle	7-37	19	+3.29	Roger Charlton	3-6
William Buick	7-33	21	+4.00	Jeremy Noseda	2-3

Favourites

2yo	59.7% +28.16	3yo	43.5% +9.54		TOTAL	42.6% +30.61

LINGFIELD sand

Features LH, all-weather, tight

2014 Fixtures
March 28, April 2-3, 5, 9, 18, 29, May 1-2, 27, June 19, July 23, August 8, 12, 27, September 23, October 15, 21, 30, November 14-15, 19, 22, 26, December 3, 5, 8, 10, 13, 17, 28, 30-31

Time Test standard times

5f	58	1m2f	2min3
6f	1min11	1m4f	2min29.6
7f	1min23.2	1m5f	2min43
1m	1min36.6	2m	3min21.5

Trainers	Wins-Runs	%	2yo	3yo+	£1 level stks
David Evans	65-493	13	2-35	63-458	-142.49
Mark Johnston	59-335	18	4-39	55-296	-102.01
Richard Hannon Snr	58-324	18	18-117	40-207	-88.67
Gary Moore	42-347	12	4-34	38-313	-131.06
John Gosden	42-181	23	9-49	33-132	+23.69
Jeremy Noseda	40-123	33	9-27	31-96	+10.91
Ronald Harris	35-299	12	4-22	31-277	-80.08
J S Moore	35-270	13	12-84	23-186	-60.33
Andrew Balding	30-189	16	9-40	21-149	-29.16
Stuart Williams	30-149	20	0-10	30-139	+17.54
Jim Boyle	29-309	9	0-25	29-284	-149.43
David Simcock	29-160	18	3-12	26-148	-40.61
Conor Dore	25-226	11	0-1	25-225	-103.75

Jockeys	Wins-Rides	%	£1 level stks	Best Trainer	W-R
Jim Crowley	101-578	17	+10.64	Ralph Beckett	18-79
Adam Kirby	94-481	20	+73.56	David Evans	16-56
Luke Morris	87-768	11	-175.47	Ronald Harris	21-139
George Baker	87-518	17	-74.06	Gary Moore	21-123
Joe Fanning	65-407	16	-27.73	Mark Johnston	36-209
Ryan Moore	59-213	28	+8.11	Sir Michael Stoute	14-36
Hayley Turner	54-397	14	-110.01	Conor Dore	16-89
Liam Keniry	53-501	11	-152.78	J S Moore	15-82
Shane Kelly	49-376	13	-65.38	Daniel Mark Loughnane	7-23
David Probert	46-349	13	-32.20	Andrew Balding	15-83
Jamie Spencer	44-228	19	+2.27	Ian Williams	6-16
William Carson	40-378	11	-143.43	Stuart Williams	8-40
Andrea Atzeni	40-258	16	+45.87	Stuart Williams	5-19

Favourites

2yo	37.8%	-33.16		3yo	42.4%	-32.93		TOTAL	37.8%	-107.06

MUSSELBURGH

Linkfield Road EH21 7RG
Tel 0131 665 2859

How to get there
Road: M8 Jct 2,
A8 east, follow
Ring Road, A1
east. Rail:
Musselburgh
from Edinburgh
Waverley

Features RH, flat,
tight

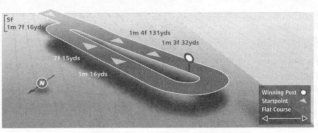

2014 Fixtures April 18, 20, May 2,
12, 23, June 7, 13-14, 27, July 22,
August 1, 8, 20, September 5, 15, 28,
October 11

Time Test standard times

5f	57.6	1m4f100yds	2min38.7
7f15yds	1min26.3	1m6f	2min58.4
1m	1min38.3	1m7f16yds	3min11.3
1m1f	1min50.7	2m	3min25
1m3f32yds	2min20		

Trainers	Wins-Runs	%	2yo	3yo+	£1 level stks
Richard Fahey	44-185	24	10-46	34-139	+50.56
Mark Johnston	33-192	17	8-45	25-147	-28.11
Jim Goldie	24-316	8	0-17	24-299	-103.25
Tim Easterby	18-139	13	4-27	14-112	-45.58
Bryan Smart	16-89	18	9-28	7-61	-10.83
Keith Dalgleish	14-137	10	5-35	9-102	-26.90
Kevin Ryan	14-106	13	7-26	7-80	-41.92
Paul Midgley	13-110	12	0-15	13-95	-28.25
David O'Meara	13-75	17	0-14	13-61	-7.92
Philip Kirby	13-46	28	0-2	13-44	+46.81
Linda Perratt	12-272	4	0-8	12-264	-101.50
David Nicholls	11-122	9	1-8	10-114	-62.39
Noel Wilson	11-96	11	0-9	11-87	+12.75

Jockeys	Wins-Rides	%	£1 level stks	Best Trainer	W-R
Paul Hanagan	42-133	32	+31.67	Richard Fahey	21-57
Joe Fanning	34-180	19	-0.98	Mark Johnston	27-102
Tom Eaves	24-209	11	+1.78	Bryan Smart	10-49
Frederik Tylicki	16-80	20	+50.63	Tracy Waggott	2-3
Graham Lee	15-128	12	+5.97	Jim Goldie	7-72
Robert Winston	14-72	19	+15.25	Alan Swinbank	5-22
Silvestre De Sousa	13-72	18	-13.35	Geoffrey Harker	3-12
Paul Mulrennan	12-102	12	-8.30	Linda Perratt	2-14
David Allan	12-102	12	-34.03	Tim Easterby	8-64
Phillip Makin	11-123	9	-80.90	Kevin Ryan	6-38
Daniel Tudhope	11-89	12	-25.13	David O'Meara	6-34
Barry McHugh	11-81	14	+8.25	Richard Fahey	4-14
Neil Farley	11-77	14	+2.67	Declan Carroll	6-23

Favourites

2yo	47.5%	+8.48		3yo	37%	+8.40		TOTAL	36.1%	+2.28

Newbury, Berkshire, RG14 7NZ
Tel: 01635 400 15 or 01635 550 354

NEWBURY

How to get there
Road: M4 Jct 13
and A34 south.
Rail: Newbury
Racecourse

Features LH,
wide, flat

2014 Fixtures
April 11-12, May
16-17, 31, June
12, 24, July 3, 18-19, August 3, 15-16,
September 19-20, October 24-25

Time Test standard times

5f34yds	1min0	1m1f	1min49.7
6f110yds	1min16.6	1m2f6yds	2min2
7f	1min23	1m3f5yds	2min15.8
7f64yds (rd)	1min26.4	1m4f4yds	2min29.3
1m (str)	1min36	1m5f61yds	2min45.8
1m7yds (rd)	1min35.3	2m	3min23

Trainers	Wins-Runs	%	2yo	3yo+	£1 level stks
Richard Hannon Snr	63-519	12	45-292	18-227	-130.36
John Gosden	25-128	20	6-30	19-98	+24.71
Roger Charlton	19-114	17	8-52	11-62	+67.38
William Haggas	18-88	20	3-34	15-54	+7.93
Saeed bin Suroor	18-76	24	5-12	13-64	+0.83
Clive Cox	16-148	11	6-44	10-104	-38.70
Sir Michael Stoute	14-90	16	3-21	11-69	-25.47
Ralph Beckett	14-87	16	1-24	13-63	+16.38
Luca Cumani	12-61	20	1-5	11-56	-15.92
Mick Channon	11-227	5	5-119	6-108	-124.00
Andrew Balding	11-127	9	4-50	7-77	-38.48
Mark Johnston	10-75	13	5-22	5-53	-22.00
Sir Henry Cecil	9-62	15	0-1	9-61	-27.38

Jockeys	Wins-Rides	%	£1 level stks	Best Trainer	W-R
Richard Hughes	49-305	16	-36.29	Richard Hannon Snr	40-228
Ryan Moore	29-196	15	-63.34	Sir Michael Stoute	11-68
William Buick	23-175	13	-62.22	John Gosden	14-73
Jim Crowley	23-174	13	+25.69	Ralph Beckett	13-66
Kieren Fallon	20-166	12	-45.38	Luca Cumani	7-37
Frankie Dettori	18-79	23	+39.08	Saeed bin Suroor	6-20
Silvestre De Sousa	17-71	24	+59.42	Saeed bin Suroor	8-20
Dane O'Neill	14-133	11	+32.63	Henry Candy	4-29
Tom Queally	14-130	11	-15.88	Sir Henry Cecil	8-46
Hayley Turner	14-76	18	+140.50	Michael Bell	5-27
James Doyle	13-111	12	-10.33	Roger Charlton	7-40
Adam Kirby	12-125	10	-25.25	Clive Cox	7-64
Jamie Spencer	11-112	10	-25.38	Paul Cole	2-18

Favourites

2yo	33.8% -14.40	3yo	26.9% -36.86		TOTAL	28.7% -80.55

NEWCASTLE

High Gosforth Park NE3 5HP
Tel: 0191 236 2020 or 236 5508

How to get there
Road: Signpost-
ed from A1. Rail:
Newcastle
Central, metro to
Regent Centre or
Four Lane End
and bus

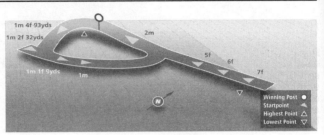

Features: LH,
galloping, 4f
uphill straight

2014 Fixtures April 5, 24, 29, May 20,
30, June 7, 26-28, July 26, August 7,
15, 22, 25, September 5, 23, October
1, 14

Time Test standard times

5f	59	1m1f9yds	1min52.5
6f	1min11.8	1m2f32yds	2min6.7
7f	1min24.2	1m4f93yds	2min37
1m (rnd)	1min39.7	1m6f97yds	3min2
1m3yds (str)	1min37.2	2m19yds	3min23.7

Trainers	Wins-Runs	%	2yo	3yo+	£1 level stks
Richard Fahey	28-208	13	15-58	13-150	-67.32
Michael Dods	24-161	15	4-30	20-131	+21.04
Kevin Ryan	18-126	14	6-42	12-84	-22.26
Brian Ellison	17-142	12	1-12	16-130	-64.64
Mark Johnston	17-126	13	6-37	11-89	-37.17
Tim Easterby	15-193	8	1-52	14-141	-107.75
Tracy Waggott	14-122	11	0-2	14-120	-16.25
Richard Guest	14-95	15	1-8	13-87	+49.17
David O'Meara	12-107	11	4-15	8-92	-26.44
Alan Swinbank	11-97	11	1-15	10-82	-10.00
Michael Easterby	11-96	11	2-14	9-82	-8.50
Jim Goldie	10-86	12	0-3	10-83	-15.45
David Barron	10-58	17	1-9	9-49	-4.65

Jockeys	Wins-Rides	%	£1 level stks	Best Trainer	W-R
P J McDonald	24-200	12	-9.29	Alan Swinbank	5-48
Paul Hanagan	22-150	15	-60.98	Richard Fahey	7-59
Paul Mulrennan	20-156	13	-26.88	Michael Dods	7-22
Barry McHugh	19-155	12	+48.50	Tony Coyle	5-17
Tony Hamilton	19-138	14	-19.34	Richard Fahey	11-57
Tom Eaves	16-255	6	-88.43	Michael Dods	4-42
Graham Lee	16-102	16	-15.25	Kevin Ryan	3-9
David Allan	15-129	12	-14.00	Tim Easterby	8-75
Dale Swift	15-124	12	-49.30	Brian Ellison	9-53
Graham Gibbons	15-117	13	-38.03	David Barron	7-25
Silvestre De Sousa	15-111	14	-9.00	Mark Johnston	5-20
Jamie Spencer	14-54	26	+6.02	Michael Bell	3-6
Phillip Makin	13-148	9	-10.05	Michael Dods	3-27

Favourites

2yo	33%	-19.77	3yo	37.3% -11.20	TOTAL	32.1% -45.90

Westfield House, The Links,
Newmarket, Suffolk. CB8 0TG

NEWMARKET

Rowley Mile

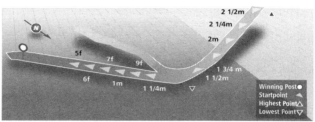

How to get there
Road: from
south M11 Jct
9, then A11,
otherwise A14
and A11. Rail:
Newmarket

Features RH, wide, galloping,
uphill finish

2014 Fixtures April 16-17, May 3-4,
15-17, September 20, 25-27, October
4, 11, 17, 22, 31, November 1

Time Test standard times

5f	57.5	1m2f	2min1.4
6f	1min10.5	1m4f	2min27.7
7f	1min22.7	1m6f	2min54.4
1m	1min35.7	2m	3min20.3
1m1f	1min48.6	2m2f	3min48

Trainers	Wins-Runs	%	2yo	3yo+	£1 level stks
Richard Hannon Snr	40-325	12	20-168	20-157	+7.49
Mark Johnston	29-221	13	5-55	24-166	+34.33
Mahmood Al Zarooni	27-113	24	13-52	14-61	+69.38
John Gosden	25-199	13	9-66	16-133	-8.93
Andrew Balding	17-175	10	4-55	13-120	+34.88
William Haggas	15-139	11	8-63	7-76	-35.56
Sir Henry Cecil	15-89	17	1-11	14-78	-19.26
Saeed bin Suroor	13-134	10	2-34	11-100	-43.98
Mick Channon	12-115	10	6-41	6-74	-23.42
Roger Varian	12-59	20	4-28	8-31	+20.67
Roger Charlton	12-59	20	3-10	9-49	+39.75
Brian Meehan	11-153	7	3-72	8-81	-9.99
Sir Michael Stoute	11-117	9	3-33	8-84	-70.76

Jockeys	Wins-Rides	%	£1 level stks	Best Trainer	W-R
Richard Hughes	31-210	15	-0.29	Richard Hannon Snr	20-134
Ryan Moore	30-232	13	-34.73	Sir Michael Stoute	9-74
Frankie Dettori	27-177	15	-0.55	Mahmood Al Zarooni	9-37
William Buick	24-239	10	-75.67	John Gosden	13-120
Kieren Fallon	23-181	13	+9.71	Luca Cumani	7-51
Tom Queally	20-189	11	-40.01	Sir Henry Cecil	11-61
Michael Hills	18-114	16	+20.50	B W Hills	9-45
Mickael Barzalona	17-85	20	+19.14	Mahmood Al Zarooni	10-37
Paul Hanagan	16-141	11	-50.02	Richard Fahey	5-32
Silvestre De Sousa	16-87	18	+98.01	Mark Johnston	6-22
Joe Fanning	14-130	11	-7.03	Mark Johnston	12-98
Jimmy Fortune	12-148	8	-22.25	Andrew Balding	7-70
Jim Crowley	12-120	10	-6.63	Ralph Beckett	6-52

Favourites

2yo	37.4%	-3.93	3yo	36.8%	+29.40	TOTAL	34.5%	+16.88

NEWMARKET
Westfield House, The Links,
Newmarket, Suffolk. CB8 0TG

July Course

How to get there
See previous
page

Features RH,
wide, galloping,
uphill finish

2014 Fixtures
May 30-31, June
20-21, 27-28, July
10-12, 18-19, 25-
26, August 1-2,
8-9, 14-16, 22-23

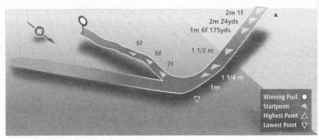

Time Test standard times

5f	57.7	1m110yds	1min42	1m6f175yds	3min3
6f	1min10	1m2f	2min1	2m24yds	3min21.2
7f	1min22.8	1m4f	2min26.7	2m1f65yds	3min36
1m	1min35.7	1m5f	2min39		

Trainers	Wins-Runs	%	2yo	3yo+	£1 level stks
Richard Hannon Snr	48-338	14	30-174	18-164	-16.31
John Gosden	34-180	19	10-65	24-115	+24.24
Saeed bin Suroor	28-132	21	15-49	13-83	-18.40
Mark Johnston	26-178	15	1-33	25-145	+8.38
Mahmood Al Zarooni	26-133	20	18-100	8-33	+74.00
Brian Meehan	16-147	11	9-76	7-71	-68.15
David Elsworth	16-103	16	3-28	13-75	+61.38
Jeremy Noseda	15-74	20	5-26	10-48	-3.56
Luca Cumani	13-106	12	3-31	10-75	-45.99
Andrew Balding	13-103	13	1-21	12-82	-10.63
Sir Michael Stoute	13-99	13	2-33	11-66	-44.15
Richard Fahey	12-91	13	4-26	8-65	-5.63
Mick Channon	10-108	9	5-53	5-55	+12.50

Jockeys	Wins-Rides	%	£1 level stks	Best Trainer	W-R
William Buick	39-183	21	+30.53	John Gosden	21-77
Mickael Barzalona	38-142	27	+61.37	Saeed bin Suroor	13-40
Ryan Moore	34-182	19	+8.64	Richard Hannon Snr	9-39
Richard Hughes	31-149	21	+4.32	Richard Hannon Snr	19-97
Kieren Fallon	25-188	13	-43.62	Luca Cumani	9-55
Paul Hanagan	24-121	20	+26.69	Richard Fahey	4-21
Jamie Spencer	21-138	15	-40.98	Michael Bell	4-29
Tom Queally	20-155	13	+66.75	Sir Henry Cecil	6-32
Neil Callan	18-144	13	-35.80	Mark Johnston	5-17
Frankie Dettori	16-154	10	-78.00	Saeed bin Suroor	4-26
Ted Durcan	13-134	10	-61.54	Saeed bin Suroor	5-21
Dane O'Neill	11-96	11	+69.13	David Elsworth	3-13
Eddie Ahern	11-48	23	+14.63	Sir Henry Cecil	2-3

Favourites

| 2yo | 36.5% -16.16 | 3yo 32.9% -22.34 | TOTAL 31.5% -72.19 |

CERTIFY: made a winning debut on the July Course in 2012 for Saeed bin Suroor, who does much better there in midsummer than on the Rowley Mile

NOTTINGHAM

Colwick Park, Nottingham,
NG2 4BE. Tel 0115 958 0620

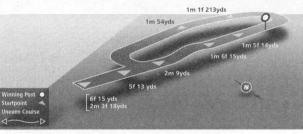

How to get there
Road: M1 Jct 25,
A52 east to B686,
signs for Trent
Bridge, then
Colwick Park.
Rail:
Nottingham

Features LH, flat,
easy turns

2014 Fixtures April 9, 19, 29, May
9-10, 20, June 1, 4, 12, 17, July 5,
18, 31, August 12, 15, September 23,
October 1, 8, 15, 29, November 5

Time Test standard times

5f13yds	58.7	1m6f15yds	2min58.5
6f15yds	1min11.3	2m9yds	3min24.3
1m75yds	1min41.5	2m2f18yds	3min52.3
1m2f50yds	2min5.6		

Trainers	Wins-Runs	%	2yo	3yo+	£1 level stks
Richard Hannon Snr	18-101	18	10-56	8-45	+21.32
Saeed bin Suroor	16-58	28	6-18	10-40	-0.66
David Evans	12-81	15	6-34	6-47	+56.33
Luca Cumani	12-47	26	1-14	11-33	+13.93
Roy Bowring	11-83	13	0-3	11-80	+29.75
Michael Appleby	10-51	20	1-4	9-47	+46.00
Richard Fahey	9-71	13	3-12	6-59	+3.38
Ralph Beckett	9-53	17	2-21	7-32	-5.72
Mrs K Burke	9-26	35	2-10	7-16	+14.81
Mick Channon	8-76	11	4-37	4-39	-29.08
Michael Bell	8-73	11	2-22	6-51	-32.97
Kevin Ryan	8-63	13	3-26	5-37	-18.02
Roger Charlton	8-33	24	2-10	6-23	+9.03

Jockeys	Wins-Rides	%	£1 level stks	Best Trainer	W-R
Silvestre De Sousa	16-95	17	-1.60	Saeed bin Suroor	6-18
Tom Queally	15-92	16	+65.86	Sir Henry Cecil	5-22
Paul Hanagan	13-106	12	+0.80	David Evans	2-3
James Doyle	12-85	14	-23.37	Roy Brotherton	2-2
Jim Crowley	11-47	23	+14.12	Ralph Beckett	8-27
Dane O'Neill	10-69	14	+6.13	Henry Candy	4-16
Pat Dobbs	9-59	15	+0.50	Richard Hannon Snr	9-41
Hayley Turner	9-58	16	+25.63	Michael Bell	3-27
William Buick	9-43	21	+12.87	John Gosden	3-20
Frankie Dettori	9-33	27	-4.85	Saeed bin Suroor	4-11
Luke Morris	8-87	9	-27.00	Michael Appleby	2-3
Kieren Fallon	8-73	11	-37.20	Luca Cumani	2-13
Andrea Atzeni	8-73	11	-17.25	Marco Botti	3-12

Favourites

2yo	32.2%	-23.17	3yo	29.9%	-44.19	TOTAL 29.9%	-90.21

33 Ropergate, Pontefract,
WF8 1LE. Tel 01977 703 224

PONTEFRACT

How to get there
Road: M62 Jct
32, then A539.
Rail: Pontefract
Monkhill or
Pontefract Baghill
from Leeds

Features LH,
undulating, sharp
home turn, last
half-mile all uphill

2014 Fixtures April 8, 14, 30, May 23,
June 9, 22, 30, July 8, 18, 27, August
6, 17, September 18, 25, October 6,
20

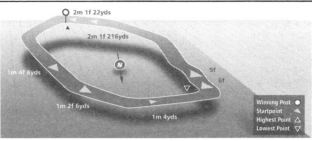

Time Test standard times

5f	1min1.3	1m4f8yds	2min34.5
6f	1min14.2	2m1f22yds	3min42.2
1m4yds	1min41.8	2m1f216yds	3min52
1m2f6yds	2min7.2	2m5f122yds	4min48

Trainers	Wins-Runs	%	2yo	3yo+	£1 level stks
Richard Fahey	31-181	17	10-45	21-136	+2.83
Mark Johnston	26-174	15	2-36	24-138	-32.60
Kevin Ryan	13-88	15	6-36	7-52	+41.08
David Barron	12-57	21	3-11	9-46	+20.21
Tim Easterby	11-144	8	2-37	9-107	-59.17
Micky Hammond	11-115	10	0-11	11-104	+23.50
Paul Midgley	10-105	10	0-13	10-92	+1.50
Alan McCabe	10-71	14	1-21	9-50	+31.90
William Haggas	10-34	29	3-7	7-27	-12.13
David O'Meara	8-79	10	0-9	8-70	-23.75
Alan Swinbank	8-60	13	2-8	6-52	-5.50
John Quinn	7-82	9	1-17	6-65	+0.50
Tom Dascombe	7-39	18	2-18	5-21	+7.83

Jockeys	Wins-Rides	%	£1 level stks	Best Trainer	W-R
Silvestre De Sousa	38-158	24	+73.11	Mark Johnston	12-49
Paul Hanagan	28-178	16	-26.31	Richard Fahey	17-76
Franny Norton	14-72	19	+66.13	Mark Johnston	3-11
Robert Winston	13-104	13	-17.65	Alan Swinbank	3-12
Paul Mulrennan	13-95	14	+67.00	James Given	4-12
Kieren Fallon	12-75	16	-5.25	Luca Cumani	3-9
Joe Fanning	10-77	13	-16.22	Mark Johnston	5-52
Tom Eaves	9-112	8	-38.50	Bryan Smart	3-26
Phillip Makin	9-99	9	-47.18	Kevin Ryan	3-31
Graham Gibbons	9-68	13	-14.88	David Barron	6-17
Tony Hamilton	8-76	11	-14.65	Richard Fahey	6-35
Dale Swift	8-61	13	-7.50	Nigel Tinkler	2-2
P J McDonald	7-93	8	-43.50	Alan Swinbank	3-21

Favourites

2yo	32.1% -16.53	3yo	39.2% +3.35	TOTAL	32.5% -18.55

REDCAR

Redcar, Teesside,
TS10 2BY. Tel 01642 484 068

How to get there
Road: A1, A168,
A19, then A174.
Rail: Redcar
Central from
Darlington

Features LH, flat,
galloping

2014 Fixtures
April 7, 21, May 1,
19, 26-27, June 20-21, July 20, 30, August 9, 23, September 9, 24, October 4, 17, 27, November 4

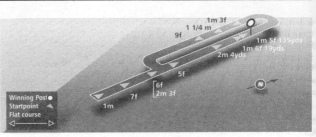

Time Test standard times

5f	56.7	1m3f	2min17
6f	1min9.4	1m4f	2min30
7f	1min22	1m5f135yds	2min54.7
1m	1min34.7	1m6f19yds	3min0
1m1f	1min49.3	2m4yds	3min25
1m2f	2min2.6	2m3f	4min5.3

Trainers	Wins-Runs	%	2yo	3yo+	£1 level stks
David O'Meara	25-154	16	5-32	20-122	+3.04
Tim Easterby	23-297	8	7-105	16-192	-128.42
Richard Fahey	23-153	15	12-66	11-87	-45.36
David Nicholls	18-131	14	4-24	14-107	-49.08
Bryan Smart	17-113	15	3-35	14-78	+65.18
Michael Dods	14-106	13	2-21	12-85	-28.95
John Quinn	14-82	17	2-22	12-60	-20.33
Kevin Ryan	12-98	12	7-46	5-52	-14.17
Mark Johnston	11-87	13	3-33	8-54	-38.06
Paul Midgley	10-145	7	0-29	10-116	-75.75
David Barron	10-56	18	2-11	8-45	-21.13
Tracy Waggott	9-108	8	0-0	9-108	-14.00
Ruth Carr	9-88	10	0-0	9-88	-9.63

Jockeys	Wins-Rides	%	£1 level stks	Best Trainer	W-R
Paul Hanagan	25-108	23	-3.01	Richard Fahey	10-38
Daniel Tudhope	23-105	22	+52.71	David O'Meara	16-53
Tom Eaves	19-240	8	-124.50	Bryan Smart	7-62
James Sullivan	18-140	13	+56.13	Ruth Carr	5-42
Graham Gibbons	18-107	17	-26.01	David Barron	7-25
Silvestre De Sousa	17-111	15	-18.47	Geoffrey Oldroyd	3-4
P J McDonald	16-161	10	-4.40	Alan Swinbank	3-31
David Allan	16-158	10	-45.67	Tim Easterby	11-98
Paul Mulrennan	15-117	13	+21.85	Howard Johnson	2-5
Adrian Nicholls	15-85	18	-25.70	David Nicholls	14-61
Michael O'Connell	14-86	16	+11.17	John Quinn	5-22
Barry McHugh	12-173	7	-97.68	Richard Fahey	3-17
Phillip Makin	12-102	12	-9.67	Kevin Ryan	4-20

Favourites

2yo	49.5% +28.13	3yo	33.1% -8.76		TOTAL	36.3% +20.33

7 North Street, Ripon, N Yorkshire
HG4 1DS. Tel 01765 602 156 or 01765 603 696

RIPON

How to get there
Road: A1, then
36265. Rail:
Harrogate, bus to
Ripon centre, 1m
walk

Features RH,
sharp

2014 Fixtures
April 17, 26, May
?, 18, June 3-4, 18-19, July 7, 19,
August 4-5, 16, 25-26, September 27

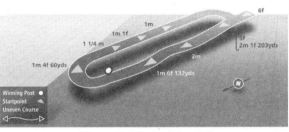

Time Test standard times

5f	57.8	1m2f	2min3.3
6f	1min10.6	1m4f10yds	2min31
1m	1min37.8	2m	3min27
1m1f170yds	2min0.4	2m1f203yds	3min52

Trainers	Wins-Runs	%	2yo	3yo+	£1 level stks
Tim Easterby	35-333	11	16-109	19-224	-6.04
Richard Fahey	29-202	14	12-57	17-145	-39.45
David O'Meara	26-142	18	4-25	22-117	+26.58
Mark Johnston	18-150	12	1-26	17-124	-65.65
David Nicholls	15-155	10	2-18	13-137	-30.88
David Barron	15-83	18	0-15	15-68	-1.50
Ruth Carr	12-95	13	0-0	12-95	-3.38
Kevin Ryan	10-132	8	3-37	7-95	-75.54
Michael Dods	10-58	17	2-10	8-48	+47.50
Paul Midgley	9-99	9	1-21	8-78	-35.29
Alan Swinbank	9-79	11	0-4	9-75	-17.00
Tom Tate	8-45	18	3-10	5-35	-4.50
William Haggas	8-28	29	2-7	6-21	-6.23

Jockeys	Wins-Rides	%	£1 level stks	Best Trainer	W-R
P J McDonald	19-155	12	+32.13	Alan Swinbank	9-42
Silvestre De Sousa	19-116	16	+18.56	David O'Meara	5-26
Graham Gibbons	17-113	15	-16.13	David Barron	7-32
Tony Hamilton	17-92	18	-19.57	Richard Fahey	16-63
David Allan	16-164	10	-41.79	Tim Easterby	15-143
Paul Hanagan	16-127	13	-40.73	Richard Fahey	8-62
Adrian Nicholls	14-88	16	-5.67	David Nicholls	10-68
Daniel Tudhope	14-86	16	+11.25	David O'Meara	11-61
Phillip Makin	12-114	11	-21.38	Kevin Ryan	3-41
James Sullivan	11-117	9	-30.00	Ruth Carr	6-45
Duran Fentiman	10-146	7	-19.25	Tim Easterby	8-97
Tom Eaves	10-112	9	-17.67	John Spearing	1-1
Robert Winston	10-80	13	+10.75	Ruth Carr	2-3

Favourites

2yo	41.6% +9.94	3yo	38.1% -0.29		TOTAL 36.4%	+3.08

SALISBURY

Netherhampton, Salisbury, Wilts
SP2 8PN. Tel 01722 326 461

How to get there
Road: 2m west
of Salisbury on
A3094. Rail:
Salisbury, bus

Features RH,
uphill finish

2014 Fixtures
May 4, 15, 22,
June 10, 15, 25,
29, July 12, 26, August 13-14, 29,
September 4, 12, October 1, 13

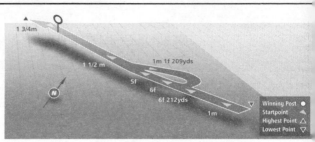

Time Test standard times

5f	59.6	1m1f209yds	2min5
6f	1min12	1m4f	2min32
6f212yds	1min25.2	1m6f21yds	2min58.6
1m	1min39.2		

Trainers	Wins-Runs	%	2yo	3yo+	£1 level stks
Richard Hannon Snr	72-361	20	45-190	27-171	-42.59
Andrew Balding	17-136	13	5-41	12-95	-34.20
David Evans	17-106	16	5-36	12-70	+116.66
Ralph Beckett	14-116	12	5-47	9-69	-33.42
Mick Channon	12-105	11	5-49	7-56	-23.81
Rod Millman	10-111	9	1-25	9-86	-16.50
Hughie Morrison	9-76	12	0-18	9-58	-36.38
Clive Cox	8-86	9	5-36	3-50	-22.29
Sir Michael Stoute	8-57	14	1-16	7-41	-11.68
Saeed bin Suroor	8-43	19	0-9	8-34	-4.02
Luca Cumani	8-38	21	1-3	7-35	-7.07
John Dunlop	7-68	10	4-27	3-41	+5.00
Henry Candy	7-67	10	2-23	5-44	-34.15

Jockeys	Wins-Rides	%	£1 level stks	Best Trainer	W-R
Richard Hughes	56-223	25	-1.73	Richard Hannon Snr	44-155
Pat Dobbs	15-125	12	-32.12	Richard Hannon Snr	13-76
Kieren Fallon	15-49	31	+28.97	Luca Cumani	4-15
Jim Crowley	14-118	12	-29.86	Ralph Beckett	10-64
James Doyle	14-68	21	+80.50	Ian Williams	2-3
Dane O'Neill	13-120	11	-54.65	Henry Candy	7-33
Jimmy Fortune	11-103	11	-45.45	Andrew Balding	6-45
William Buick	10-50	20	+5.19	John Gosden	5-20
Martin Dwyer	10-46	22	+52.83	Brian Meehan	4-13
Steve Drowne	9-80	11	-17.63	Hughie Morrison	3-17
Tom Queally	9-40	23	+26.94	Lady Cecil	4-4
Ian Mongan	9-40	23	+29.38	Sir Henry Cecil	5-12
Frankie Dettori	8-34	24	-13.77	Saeed bin Suroor	4-12

Favourites

2yo	44.3%	+1.91		3yo	35.5%	-18.81	TOTAL 35.4%	-44.09

Esher, Surrey, KT10 9AJ.
Tel 01372 463 072 or 01372 464 348

SANDOWN

How to get there
Road: M25 Jct 10
then A3. Rail:
Esher from
Waterloo

Features RH, last
7f uphill

2014 Fixtures
April 25, May 22,
29, June 13-14,
July 4-5, 16, 23-24, 30, August 7, 29-
30, September 12, 17

Time Test standard times

5f6yds	59.2	1m2f7yds	2min5
7f16yds	1min27	1m3f91yds	2min21.7
1m14yds	1min40	1m6f	2min57
1m1f	1min52	2m78yds	3min30.4

Trainers	Wins-Runs	%	2yo	3yo+	£1 level stks
Richard Hannon Snr	44-301	15	25-113	19-188	-14.59
Andrew Balding	26-135	19	4-28	22-107	+47.44
John Gosden	25-134	19	6-31	19-103	-28.39
Sir Michael Stoute	23-134	17	1-25	22-109	-12.75
William Haggas	11-52	21	0-9	11-43	-1.88
Jeremy Noseda	9-43	21	5-10	4-33	-4.52
Henry Candy	9-40	23	1-5	8-35	+15.50
Mark Johnston	8-108	7	1-19	7-89	-65.25
Brian Meehan	8-81	10	3-32	5-49	-23.00
Saeed bin Suroor	8-81	10	3-13	5-68	-41.40
Mahmood Al Zarooni	8-47	17	2-21	6-26	+14.50
Michael Bell	8-41	20	2-7	6-34	+25.10
Luca Cumani	7-55	13	0-1	7-54	-28.76

Jockeys	Wins-Rides	%	£1 level stks	Best Trainer	W-R
Ryan Moore	40-213	19	-49.45	Sir Michael Stoute	13-82
Richard Hughes	34-212	16	-53.14	Richard Hannon Snr	26-139
William Buick	28-167	17	-41.41	John Gosden	18-82
Tom Queally	14-93	15	+12.75	Sir Henry Cecil	5-26
Jamie Spencer	14-58	24	+14.80	Michael Bell	3-11
Jimmy Fortune	13-131	10	-3.75	Andrew Balding	10-55
Kieren Fallon	13-107	12	-29.85	Luca Cumani	5-31
James Doyle	13-84	15	-8.26	Roger Charlton	5-22
Dane O'Neill	12-119	10	-46.75	Henry Candy	6-27
Jim Crowley	12-113	11	+4.50	Ralph Beckett	4-31
Adam Kirby	12-109	11	+12.50	Walter Swinburn	4-23
Pat Dobbs	12-73	16	+23.93	Richard Hannon Snr	9-50
Frankie Dettori	11-111	10	-59.27	Saeed bin Suroor	3-30

Favourites

2yo	39.6% -9.28		3yo	29.6% -48.88	TOTAL 33.2%	-39.22

SOUTHWELL

Rolleston, Newark, Notts
NG25 0TS. Tel 01636 814 481

How to get there Road: A1 to Newark, then A617 or M1 to Nottingham, then A612. Rail: Rolleston

Features LH, all-weather, sharp

Please note there are no turf fixtures scheduled for 2014 Stats relate to sll-weather only

2014 Fixtures April 1-2, 8, 15, 28, 30, May 8, 19, June 4, August 7, 20, November 4, 13, 18, 25, December 9, 13, 16, 18-19, 27, 29

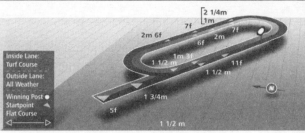

Time Test standard times

5f	57.7	1m4f	2min34
6f	1min13.5	1m5f	2min47.4
7f	1min27	1m6f	3min1.7
1m	1min40	2m	3min30
1m3f	2min21.6	2m2f	3min58

Trainers	Wins-Runs	%	2yo	3yo+	£1 level stks
Brian Ellison	63-287	22	2-13	61-274	-2.47
Mark Johnston	60-253	24	9-54	51-199	-14.77
David Nicholls	52-265	20	6-36	46-229	+35.49
Alan McCabe	47-417	11	8-62	39-355	-84.04
Kevin Ryan	46-212	22	9-40	37-172	-9.90
Bryan Smart	42-245	17	4-32	38-213	+66.68
J R Jenkins	34-208	16	3-15	31-193	-12.68
Michael Appleby	33-180	18	1-13	32-167	+14.99
Richard Fahey	32-199	16	9-45	23-154	-26.05
David Barron	31-119	26	5-12	26-107	+18.61
Alan Swinbank	29-121	24	1-1	28-120	+9.29
Hughie Morrison	29-119	24	3-10	26-109	+18.46
Richard Guest	25-379	7	0-20	25-359	-169.18

Jockeys	Wins-Rides	%	£1 level stks	Best Trainer	W-R
Joe Fanning	78-355	22	-17.75	Mark Johnston	41-137
Phillip Makin	46-204	23	+5.30	Kevin Ryan	27-71
Tom Eaves	42-398	11	-48.42	Bryan Smart	19-134
Luke Morris	41-342	12	-33.11	Ronald Harris	7-57
Barry McHugh	40-233	17	-19.33	Brian Ellison	24-79
Graham Gibbons	34-209	16	+9.09	David Barron	8-31
Andrew Mullen	33-196	17	-30.47	Michael Appleby	17-73
Robert Winston	31-230	13	-48.88	Alan Swinbank	6-26
Hayley Turner	31-175	18	-14.25	Conor Dore	14-76
Frederik Tylicki	26-145	18	-0.97	J R Jenkins	14-59
Silvestre De Sousa	24-126	19	-29.64	Mark Johnston	8-29
Adrian Nicholls	22-109	20	+13.88	David Nicholls	20-76
William Carson	21-166	13	-15.17	Peter Hiatt	6-25

Favourites

2yo	47.4%	+6.88		3yo	39.5%	-48.68		TOTAL	38.4%	-66.15

Station Road, Thirsk, N Yorkshire,
YO7 1QL. Tel 01845 522 276

THIRSK

How to get there
Road: A61 from A1 in the west or A19 in the east. Rail: Thirsk, 10min walk

Features LH, sharp, tight turns

2014 Fixtures
April 12, May 3, 10, 17, June 17, 23, July 15, 25, August 1-2, 11, 18, 29, September 6, 16

Time Test standard times

5f	57.4	1m	1min35.8
6f	1min9.5	1m4f	2min30
7f	1min23	2m	3min22.6

Trainers	Wins-Runs	%	2yo	3yo+	£1 level stks
Tim Easterby	22-280	8	8-78	14-202	-112.54
Richard Fahey	21-161	13	11-52	10-109	-33.59
David Nicholls	20-206	10	3-31	17-175	-69.83
Kevin Ryan	18-156	12	5-44	13-112	-19.18
David O'Meara	17-129	13	2-16	15-113	-12.30
David Barron	15-99	15	3-24	12-75	-17.75
Michael Dods	14-126	11	1-26	13-100	-1.00
Ruth Carr	13-124	10	0-1	13-123	-8.88
Mark Johnston	12-110	11	3-23	9-87	-23.79
Jim Goldie	10-54	19	0-0	10-54	-1.30
Declan Carroll	8-99	8	0-8	8-91	-6.38
Richard Guest	8-84	10	0-12	8-72	+35.00
Alan Swinbank	8-69	12	1-7	7-62	-18.10

Jockeys	Wins-Rides	%	£1 level stks	Best Trainer	W-R
P J McDonald	21-190	11	-20.63	Ruth Carr	7-34
Graham Gibbons	20-115	17	+65.80	David Barron	7-29
Robert Winston	19-133	14	+8.30	B W Hills	3-6
Daniel Tudhope	19-103	18	+56.15	David O'Meara	10-40
Adrian Nicholls	14-115	12	-24.83	David Nicholls	11-94
Paul Mulrennan	13-169	8	-95.80	David Nicholls	2-5
Phillip Makin	13-141	9	-31.93	Kevin Ryan	6-41
Paul Hanagan	13-90	14	-32.00	Richard Fahey	7-32
Tom Eaves	11-178	6	-61.38	Bryan Smart	3-44
Barry McHugh	11-101	11	+35.00	Kevin Ryan	2-3
Silvestre De Sousa	11-81	14	-38.00	David O'Meara	3-12
Frederik Tylicki	11-72	15	+15.50	James Given	2-7
David Allan	10-120	8	-64.04	Tim Easterby	8-90

Favourites

| 2yo | 35.4% | -10.76 | | 3yo | 33.1% | -6.62 | | TOTAL | 31% | -26.70 |

WARWICK

6 Hampton Street, Warwick
CV34 6HN. Tel 01926 491 553

How to get there
Road: M40 Jct
14, A429. Rail:
Warwick

Features LH,
sharp turns

2014 Fixtures
April 24, May
5, 10, 20, June
16, 26, July 4,
10, August 25,
September 2

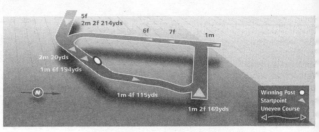

Time Test standard times

5f	58	1m4f134yds	2min34.6
5f110yds	1min4	1m6f213yds	3min6
6f	1min10.6	2m39yds	3min24
7f26yds	1min22.2	2m2f214yds	3min58
1m22yds	1min35.3	2m3f13yds	4min0
1m2f 188yds	2min12		

Trainers	Wins-Runs	%	2yo	3yo+	£1 level stks
Richard Hannon Snr	9-70	13	3-33	6-37	-38.17
David Evans	8-61	13	3-17	5-44	-29.06
Mark Johnston	8-47	17	3-13	5-34	-17.50
Tony Carroll	7-72	10	0-4	7-68	+2.00
Andrew Balding	6-38	16	0-9	6-29	-1.75
Ralph Beckett	6-28	21	1-9	5-19	-0.50
William Haggas	6-27	22	3-14	3-13	+12.67
Ed McMahon	6-20	30	2-7	4-13	+12.03
Rod Millman	5-37	14	0-11	5-26	+25.50
Declan Carroll	5-26	19	0-3	5-23	+12.50
Charles Hills	5-24	21	3-17	2-7	-1.58
Hughie Morrison	5-21	24	0-3	5-18	+8.50
Saeed bin Suroor	5-20	25	2-8	3-12	+3.50

Jockeys	Wins-Rides	%	£1 level stks	Best Trainer	W-R
Neil Callan	10-58	17	-4.33	Kevin Ryan	2-2
Tom Queally	10-30	33	+25.25	Sir Henry Cecil	4-5
Cathy Gannon	7-71	10	-14.89	David Evans	4-18
Richard Kingscote	7-37	19	-1.42	Tom Dascombe	3-13
Kieren Fallon	7-37	19	-7.09	Luca Cumani	4-9
Richard Mullen	7-24	29	+14.50	Ed McMahon	5-11
Joe Fanning	7-20	35	+21.04	Mark Johnston	4-13
Andrea Atzeni	6-33	18	+14.75	Rod Millman	3-5
Dane O'Neill	5-52	10	-21.17	Henry Candy	2-8
Liam Jones	5-40	13	-9.00	J S Moore	2-3
George Baker	5-36	14	-5.27	Sir Michael Stoute	1-1
Steve Drowne	5-35	14	-15.42	Roger Charlton	2-10
Jim Crowley	5-31	16	-13.67	Ralph Beckett	4-14

Favourites

2yo	35.9%	-10.70		3yo	38.5%	+6.46		TOTAL	36.2%	-6.42

Maidenhead Road, Windsor, Berks
SL4 5JJ. Tel 01753 498 400

WINDSOR

How to get there
Road: M4 Jctn 6,
A355, A308. Rail:
Paddington to
Windsor Central/
Waterloo to Wind-
sor Riverside

Features Figure
of eight, flat, long
straight

2014 Fixtures April 7, 14, 28, May 5,
12, 19, 26, June 2, 9, 16, 23, July 7,
14, 21, 28, August 4, 10-11, 18, 23,
October 6, 13, 20

Time Test standard times

5f10yds	58	1m2f7yds	2min3.6
5f217yds	1min10.2	1m3f135yds	2min22.6
1m67yds	1min41.6		

Trainers	Wins-Runs	%	2yo	3yo+	£1 level stks
Richard Hannon Snr	73-423	17	43-187	30-236	-103.55
Andrew Balding	22-98	22	5-18	17-80	+44.92
Sir Michael Stoute	20-90	22	1-7	19-83	+6.08
Jeremy Noseda	18-66	27	1-8	17-58	+4.64
David Evans	15-166	9	4-51	11-115	-40.25
Ralph Beckett	15-100	15	5-40	10-60	-14.99
Roger Charlton	12-70	17	3-23	9-47	+11.63
William Haggas	12-47	26	2-11	10-36	+0.39
Hughie Morrison	11-100	11	1-13	10-87	-37.35
John Gosden	11-58	19	1-10	10-48	-11.35
Saeed bin Suroor	11-36	31	1-2	10-34	+29.30
Brian Meehan	10-74	14	4-27	6-47	+18.67
Walter Swinburn	10-71	14	2-14	8-57	-7.75

Jockeys	Wins-Rides	%	£1 level stks	Best Trainer	W-R
Richard Hughes	71-312	23	-57.87	Richard Hannon Snr	48-199
Ryan Moore	44-216	20	-47.10	Sir Michael Stoute	12-56
Jimmy Fortune	28-157	18	-28.06	Andrew Balding	12-40
Jim Crowley	25-202	12	-1.37	Ralph Beckett	9-66
Adam Kirby	18-125	14	-34.00	Walter Swinburn	5-25
James Doyle	18-120	15	+29.25	Roger Charlton	6-27
William Buick	14-91	15	-19.45	Jeremy Noseda	5-9
Ian Mongan	14-89	16	+11.47	Sir Henry Cecil	3-8
Andrea Atzeni	14-68	21	+15.50	Robert Eddery	4-13
George Baker	13-100	13	+10.63	Hugo Palmer	2-2
Dane O'Neill	12-172	7	-74.54	Henry Candy	3-38
Kieren Fallon	12-101	12	-41.38	Luca Cumani	4-21
Pat Dobbs	11-109	10	-27.79	Richard Hannon Snr	7-70

Favourites

2yo 46%	+15.48	3yo 38.6%	+16.47	TOTAL 36.8%	+18.19

WOLVES

Dunstall Park, Gorsebrook Road, Wolverhampton
West Midlands. WV6 0PE. Tel 08702 202 44:

How to get there
Road: A449,
close to M6, M42
and M54. Rail:
Wolverhampton

Features LH, all-
weather, sharp

2014 Fixtures
March 28, April
3-5, 11-12, 22, 26,
28-29, May 12, June 5, 19, 23, 30, July
8, 14, 24, August 11, 18, 21, 26, 29,
September 4, 6, 11, 13, 15, 20, 26-27,
October 3-4, 9-11, 16-18, 24-25, 31,
November 3, 6-7, 14-15, 17, 21-22, 24,
28-29, December 1-2, 5-6, 12-13, 15,
19, 22, 26-27

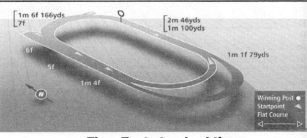

Time Test standard times

5f20yds	1min0.2	1m1f103yds	1min57.5
5f216yds	1min13.1	1m4f50yds	2min35.2
7f32yds	1min26.9	1m5f194yds	3min
1m141yds	1min46.7	2m119yds	3min36.6

Trainers	Wins-Runs	%	2yo	3yo+	£1 level stks
David Evans	93-794	12	21-157	72-637	-159.14
Mark Johnston	81-458	18	8-97	73-361	-96.52
Marco Botti	68-320	21	22-108	46-212	-19.66
Tom Dascombe	57-305	19	22-122	35-183	-35.37
Richard Fahey	53-456	12	14-106	39-350	-114.78
Michael Easterby	49-402	12	3-47	46-355	-23.95
Kevin Ryan	49-333	15	8-79	41-254	-48.03
Derek Shaw	42-452	9	2-54	40-398	-176.46
Richard Guest	40-429	9	1-29	39-400	-163.00
Jamie Osborne	40-233	17	18-80	22-153	+22.28
Ronald Harris	39-494	8	0-74	39-420	-143.07
Reg Hollinshead	39-446	9	2-59	37-387	-115.03
Ian Williams	38-270	14	0-15	38-255	-11.01

Jockeys	Wins-Rides	%	£1 level stks	Best Trainer	W-F
Luke Morris	125-1271	10	-375.89	Ronald Harris	18-231
Adam Kirby	114-607	19	-102.94	Marco Botti	26-69
Joe Fanning	108-668	16	-61.87	Mark Johnston	40-245
Graham Gibbons	88-669	13	-108.66	Michael Easterby	21-112
Shane Kelly	73-582	13	-157.16	Daniel Mark Loughnane	11-60
Richard Kingscote	71-445	16	-28.19	Tom Dascombe	52-220
Silvestre De Sousa	65-353	18	-30.40	Saeed bin Suroor	13-26
Jamie Spencer	62-331	19	-66.01	Ian Williams	9-4
George Baker	61-309	20	+96.98	Gary Moore	6-3
Paul Hanagan	58-350	17	-51.84	Richard Fahey	11-76
Robert Winston	57-388	15	-24.47	Charles Hills	7-2
Tom Eaves	54-657	8	-258.86	Bryan Smart	15-12
Jimmy Quinn	52-493	11	-69.24	Richard Guest	4-11

Favourites

2yo	38.3%	-62.69	3yo	38%	-72.87	TOTAL 35.2% -296.7

North Denes, Great Yarmouth, Norfolk
NR30 4AU. Tel 01493 842 527

YARMOUTH

How to get there
Road: A47 to
end, A1064. Rail:
Great Yarmouth,
bus

Features LH, flat

2014 Fixtures
April 21-22, 29,
May 20, 23, June
3, 11-12, 26-27,
July 3, 9, 15, 24, 29, August 6-7, 13,
19, 24, September 16-18, October
21, 28

Time Test standard times

5f43yds	1min0.4	1m3f101yds	2min23
6f3yds	1min10.7	1m6f17yds	2min58
7f3yds	1min23	2m	3min25
1m3yds	1min35.5	2m1f170yds	3min48
1m1f	1min48.4	2m2f51yds	3min54
1m2f21yds	2min3.3		

Trainers	Wins-Runs	%	2yo	3yo+	£1 level stks
William Haggas	26-97	27	10-42	16-55	+8.91
Michael Bell	23-131	18	9-37	14-94	-3.68
Chris Wall	22-111	20	0-13	22-98	+9.53
Mark H Tompkins	19-193	10	1-41	18-152	-54.38
Luca Cumani	17-65	26	4-21	13-44	+9.32
John Gosden	16-78	21	7-33	9-45	-36.97
Mick Channon	14-107	13	6-26	8-81	+11.09
Julia Feilden	13-106	12	0-10	13-96	-13.38
Clive Brittain	13-98	13	6-28	7-70	+133.00
James Fanshawe	13-79	16	1-14	12-65	+10.42
Sir Michael Stoute	13-75	17	5-29	8-46	-35.31
J R Jenkins	12-131	9	0-13	12-118	-11.75
Mark Johnston	12-102	12	5-33	7-69	-34.46

Jockeys	Wins-Rides	%	£1 level stks	Best Trainer	W-R
Kieren Fallon	27-163	17	-2.59	Luca Cumani	4-24
Jamie Spencer	27-154	18	-31.46	Peter Chapple-Hyam	3-11
Ryan Moore	26-115	23	-17.24	Sir Michael Stoute	8-34
Hayley Turner	24-140	17	-0.39	Michael Bell	15-54
Paul Hanagan	23-96	24	+16.59	William Haggas	4-12
Ted Durcan	21-157	13	-42.12	Chris Wall	9-42
William Buick	21-112	19	-42.08	John Gosden	6-38
Frederik Tylicki	20-101	20	+164.48	J R Jenkins	5-30
Seb Sanders	20-101	20	+13.49	Sir Mark Prescott Bt	5-15
Tom Queally	19-167	11	-40.24	Sir Henry Cecil	5-21
Adam Beschizza	18-155	12	-24.68	William Haggas	3-7
Luke Morris	17-126	13	-6.48	Sir Mark Prescott Bt	4-14
Martin Lane	16-150	11	-38.06	David Simcock	4-28

Favourites

2yo	46.9% +7.49	3yo	34.8% -39.66	TOTAL	34.6% -91.54

YORK

Knavesmire Road, York, YO23 1EX
Tel 01904 620 911

How to get there
Road: Course
is south of city.
From north, A1,
A59 to York,
northern bypass
from A19 to A64.
Otherwise, A64.
Rail: York, bus

Features LH, flat

2014 Fixtures May 14-16, 31, June
13-14, July 11-12, 25-26, August
20-23, September 7, October 10-11

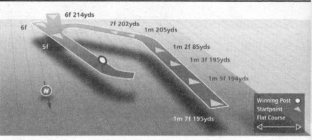

Time Test standard times

5f	56.6	1m2f88yds	2min7.2
5f89yds	1min1.2	1m4f	2min27.7
6f	1min9.2	1m6f	2min54.5
7f	1min22	2m88yds	3min26.5
1m	1min36.4	2m2f	3min49.7
1m208yds	1min48.2		

Trainers	Wins-Runs	%	2yo	3yo+	£1 level stks
Richard Fahey	42-529	8	17-142	25-387	-178.20
Tim Easterby	22-301	7	6-82	16-219	-77.13
Kevin Ryan	22-196	11	15-72	7-124	-24.04
William Haggas	22-88	25	5-20	17-68	+32.85
David O'Meara	20-177	11	1-18	19-159	-25.00
Sir Michael Stoute	13-67	19	0-2	13-65	-8.92
Michael Easterby	12-200	6	3-52	9-148	-78.50
David Barron	11-115	10	3-17	8-98	-8.67
Richard Hannon Snr	11-94	12	8-55	3-39	-32.75
Sir Henry Cecil	11-49	22	0-1	11-48	-8.68
Saeed bin Suroor	10-98	10	1-8	9-90	-46.35
Mick Channon	10-89	11	7-40	3-49	-38.58
John Gosden	10-59	17	0-4	10-55	-2.88

Jockeys	Wins-Rides	%	£1 level stks	Best Trainer	W-R
Paul Hanagan	33-251	13	-4.67	Richard Fahey	24-184
Ryan Moore	27-119	23	+24.83	Sir Michael Stoute	11-31
Kieren Fallon	25-162	15	+55.25	Luca Cumani	6-36
Jamie Spencer	19-138	14	+21.99	Kevin Ryan	4-21
Silvestre De Sousa	18-160	11	-40.40	Saeed bin Suroor	3-19
Frankie Dettori	17-106	16	-16.70	Mahmood Al Zarooni	5-20
David Allan	15-168	9	-20.63	Tim Easterby	13-134
Phillip Makin	14-135	10	-29.17	Kevin Ryan	9-60
William Buick	14-99	14	+18.63	John Gosden	7-40
Graham Gibbons	12-160	8	-41.13	David Barron	5-46
Tom Queally	12-92	13	-43.18	Sir Henry Cecil	8-34
Daniel Tudhope	11-120	9	-40.25	David O'Meara	11-87
Robert Winston	11-114	10	+19.50	Dean Ivory	3-3

Favourites

2yo	33.3%	-7.00	3yo	29.3%	-0.30	TOTAL	27.5%	-45.39

GRAPHIC: *winning at York in October to extend the fine course record of William Haggas, who has a far better strike-rate than any other top trainer there*

Win - free form!

THIS YEAR'S QUIZ could hardly be more simple, and the prize should prove invaluable to our lucky winner. We're offering a free subscription to The Flat Form Book, the BHA's official form book – every week from May to November, you could be getting the previous week's results in full, together with Notebook comments highlighting future winners, adjusted Official Ratings and Racing Post ratings. The winner will also get a copy of last year's complete form book.

All you have to do is this: identify the three horses pictured on the following pages. And the clue is they all helped Richard Hannon to the trainers' title last year when winning Group 1 races in Britain. If you think you know the answer write their names in the box below in the order in which they appear.

Send your answers along with your details on the entry form below, to:

**2014 Flat Annual Competition, Racing & Football Outlook,
Floor 23, 1 Canada Square, London, E14 5AP.**

Entries must reach us no later than first post on April 25. The winner's name and the right answers will be printed in the RFO's April 29 edition.

Six runners-up will each receive a copy of last year's form book.

Name

Address

Town

Postcode

In the event of more than one correct entry, the winner will be drawn at random from the correct entries. The Editor's decision is final and no correspondence will be entered into.

BETTING CHART

ON	ODDS	AGAINST
50	Evens	50
52.4	11-10	47.6
54.5	6-5	45.5
55.6	5-4	44.4
58	11-8	42
60	6-4	40
62	13-8	38
63.6	7-4	36.4
65.3	15-8	34.7
66.7	2-1	33.3
68	85-40	32
69.2	9-4	30.8
71.4	5-2	28.6
73.4	11-4	26.6
75	3-1	25
76.9	100-30	23.1
77.8	7-2	22.2
80	4-1	20
82	9-2	18
83.3	5-1	16.7
84.6	11-2	15.4
85.7	6-1	14.3
86.7	13-2	13.3
87.5	7-1	12.5
88.2	15-2	11.8
89	8-1	11
89.35	100-12	10.65
89.4	17-2	10.6
90	9-1	10
91	10-1	9
91.8	11-1	8.2
92.6	12-1	7.4
93.5	14-1	6.5
94.4	16-1	5.6
94.7	18-1	5.3
95.2	20-1	4.8
95.7	22-1	4.3
96.2	25-1	3.8
97.2	33-1	2.8
97.6	40-1	2.4
98.1	50-1	1.9
98.5	66-1	1.3
99.0	100-1	0.99

The table above (often known as the 'Field Money Table') shows both bookmakers' margins and how much a backer needs to invest to win £100. To calculate a bookmaker's margin, simply add up the percentages of all the odds on offer. The sum by which the total exceeds 100% gives the 'over-round' on the book. To determine what stake is required to win £100 (includes returned stake) at a particular price, just look at the relevant row, either odds-against or odds-on.

RULE 4 DEDUCTIONS

When a horse is withdrawn before coming under starter's orders, but after a market has been formed, bookmakers are entitled to make the following deductions from win and place returns (excluding stakes) in accordance with Tattersalls' Rule 4(c).

	Odds of withdrawn horse	*Deduction from winnings*
(1)	3-10 or shorter	75p in the £
(2)	2-5 to 1-3	70p in the £
(3)	8-15 to 4-9	65p in the £
(4)	8-13 to 4-7	60p in the £
(5)	4-5 to 4-6	55p in the £
(6)	20-21 to 5-6	50p in the £
(7)	Evens to 6-5	45p in the £
(8)	5-4 to 6-4	40p in the £
(9)	13-8 to 7-4	35p in the £
(10)	15-8 to 9-4	30p in the £
(11)	5-2 to 3-1	25p in the £
(12)	100-30 to 4-1	20p in the £
(13)	9-2 to 11-2	15p in the £
(14)	6-1 to 9-1	10p in the £
(15)	10-1 to 14-1	5p in the £
(16)	longer than 14-1	no deductions

(17) .... When more than one horse is withdrawn without coming under starter's orders, total deductions shall not exceed 75p in the £.

Starting-price bets are affected only when there was insufficient time to form a new market.

Feedback!

If you have any comments or criticism about this book, or suggestions for future editions, please tell us.

Write

Nick Watts/Dylan Hill
2014 Flat Annual
Racing & Football Outlook
Floor 23
1 Canada Square
London E14 5AP

email

rfo@rfoutlook.com

Horse index

All horses discussed, with page numbers, except for references in the Group 1 and two-year-old form sections (pages 81-111), which have their own indexes